BACKSPIN

120 YEARS OF GOLF *in* BRITISH COLUMBIA

ARV OLSON

HERITAGE

VICTORIA | VANCOUVER | CALGARY

Heritage House Publishing Company Ltd.
heritagehouse.ca

Library and Archives Canada Cataloguing in Publication

Olson, Arv, 1935–
    Backspin: 120 years of golf in British Columbia / Arv Olson.

Includes bibliographical references and index.
Issued also in electronic format.
ISBN 978-1-927051-41-2

    1. Golf—British Columbia—History. 2. Golfers—British Columbia—Biography. I. Title.

GV985.C35O47 2012   796.352'09711   C2012-901439-7

Edited by Lesley Cameron
Proofread by Renate Preuss
Cover design by Jacqui Thomas
Interior design by Pete Kohut

Front cover: Green and tee by molka/iStockphoto.com; Joyce Wethered by Stuart Thomson, City of Vancouver Archives CVA99-1836; (left to right) John Johnston, Alvie Thompson, Lyle Crawford and John Russell by Bill Cunningham
Back cover: Ken Black courtesy of BC Golf House 007.128.196; David Jones at Sheep Pasture by Steve Bosch

This book was produced using FSC®-certified, acid-free paper, processed chlorine free and printed with vegetable-based inks.

Heritage House acknowledges the financial support for its publishing program from the Government of Canada through the Canada Book Fund (CBF), Canada Council for the Arts and the province of British Columbia through the British Columbia Arts Council and the Book Publishing Tax Credit.

16 15 14 13 12   1 2 3 4 5

Printed in Canada

CONTENTS

FOREWORD

For me, golf was a vehicle for my father and me to spend some quality time together. I will always have fond memories of the early mornings at Burnaby Golf Course or Fraserview, walking side by side to the sound of a squeaky cart wheel. At that time there were very few dreams, if any, of aspiring to be a professional golfer but flash ahead 15 years and the aspirations grew.

Once the competitive juices started to flow I vowed that I would play Augusta—during the Masters. I envisioned the PGA tour. I even saw myself conducting witty and charming press conferences, leaving the writers drooling with profound sound bites.

My very first encounter with a "real" reporter was with Arv Olson. I thought it was a prank at first. Would I meet Arv Olson at the Marine Drive Golf Club . . . to do interviews . . . have some pictures taken? Yeah, right! Who is this again?

Well, the meeting happened and Arv made me feel like a golf star. Asking what my plans were . . . my dreams . . . my golfing goals. The picture was taken—a low angle shot of me standing on the tee. It was Arv Olson who first called me the Gentle Giant. When you are 22 and wanting to be feared by all golfers, this hardly seems the best moniker and at the time I resented it. With reflection and the benefit of time, I now take it as the compliment that he intended and I also thank Arv for taking the time to notice a 6-foot-7 underdog.

I had some successes as my journey in golf continued. And Arv was there many times to discuss my round—hole by hole if I was in contention, just the score if I wasn't. But he was always interested.

Golf took me many places around the world. I never did make it to Augusta but I did travel in Europe, Asia and Australia. I golfed with Rick Gibson, Dave Barr, Ray Stewart, Jim Rutledge and even Bill Wakeham. I won in Florida and almost won in Ontario. I won in BC, too—with partners and without them. In later years Arv Olson seemed able to recall them all. He was still interested.

And as time ticked on and the dreams faded, I ended up in paradise. Vancouver Island, the perfect place to raise and be a family. I have been a golf professional at Nanoose Bay's Fairwinds Golf Club for almost 20 years, ensconced in a career that may not share the glamour of the Professional Golf Tour but is, in many ways, very gratifying.

And guess who moved here too? Arv Olson. Retired from his long career with the *Vancouver Sun* newspaper, Arv called me when he was writing for the *Comox Valley Echo* and working on one of his books. And you know what? He was still interested.

Golf in BC is rich in history and it is very fortunate to have Arv Olson, a man still committed to "mining" that richness. Building on his earlier books, *Backspin: 120 Years of Golf in British Columbia* delivers a bounty that I think every golfer should share in.

On the course, golf is a game where it is best "to stay in the present." And yet I know that my performance is largely based on my experiences of the past. And it is learning from the past that will help me contribute to the future.

The new *Backspin* will sit on my shelf as a reminder of my many connections to people and places throughout BC. And also of how professional golfers and golf professionals contribute to the game of golf. It shows how the people in the business of golf help to keep the game itself alive. Golf is a game that has survived tough times politically and economically and it continues to face challenges. In fact, it is really more than a game; it is a healthy pastime for men and women, young and old, a lifestyle that, from tee to green, teaches life skills.

Backspin also reminds me of the great golfers whom I have met and who began their golf in BC: Ben Colk, Dave Barr, Rick Gibson, Ray Stewart, Bob Cox . . . I could go on, but why not read the book and discover for yourself why British Columbia plays such a large part in the history of golf.

Finally, this book reminds me most of how proud I am of my involvement in golf. I am very honoured and privileged to know Arv Olson.

Congratulations on another great book, Arv.

Ward Stouffer
PGA BC Professsional,
Director of Golf Operations, Fairwinds Golf Course

PREFACE

In 30 years' time, BC golf will mark its 150th anniversary. But don't expect the celebrations to spill over a surplus of wide-open fairways. By then, our golf landscape will be shrinking at a frightening pace, with too few courses available to accommodate the demands of a growing golf population.

Not only is land for new courses becoming especially scarce in densely populated urban areas, the costs, including construction and taxes, are soaring. Today, with a sluggish economy and many new projects relying on real estate sales to justify their costs, too many of BC's estimated 300 courses are struggling to break even. In some areas they have chosen to increase green fees, membership initiation fees and annual dues to survive—only to find that they have alienated some of their golfers. Elsewhere, oversupply has resulted in more competition leading to lower fees in a buyers' market. Creative solutions to cut operating costs and modify the game to suit changing time demands will be mandatory if we want to preserve this sport for future generations of weekend golfers. Let the tour pros deal with the hardships and obstacles of shooting pars on courses lengthened solely to counteract the capacities of modern equipment. The successful architects will be those who downsize courses to make them more enjoyable to amateur players. The solution is straightforward: ease the degree of difficulty, lower admission rates and increase the pace of play.

There have been various attempts to overcome slow play problems. To accelerate play on greens, for example, Marine Drive taped all members' putter shafts about 12 inches from the blades; all putts left inside the tape were gimmes. On weekends and holidays, some courses staged double shotgun starts at 7:00 AM and noon. The courses filled instantly with as many as 24 to 28 foursomes, two on each par five and the longest par fours. Stragglers were easily identified by course marshals who could insist that the tortoises pick up the pace or even miss a hole to get back on schedule.

However, there are less annoying methods of speeding up play and addressing rising costs, that also keep the enjoyment in golf. Better creative maintenance practices can cut labour costs. Using less water, fuel and chemicals restricts the growth of the grass, so mowing isn't required as frequently. Trimmer fairways and rough make for faster-paced, improved golf. Smart superintendents have adopted more ecologically sound policies, in many cases creating environmentally sensitive areas where golfers cannot go to retrieve or hunt for balls, thus speeding up play. Some solutions lie in going back to traditional ways. For example, maintenance costs would go down and land would be conserved by creating classic double-greens and double-tees. Difficult topography doesn't always permit compact design but extended road trips between holes need to be abbreviated. In Scotland, with out-going and in-coming nines, you almost fall off some greens to the following tees.

BC's population since golf's centenary in 1992 has increased from 3.3 million to 4.5 million. An estimated 800,000 rounds were played on 18-hole courses in BC last year. The demographic projections for BC in 2020 are 5.2 million—which could translate into well over 1 million rounds in golf terms. Over half the population inhabits the province's southwestern extremities, where some courses can get as congested as highways at rush hour. Congestion is less of a problem in regions like the Kootenays, Kamloops or Vancouver Island where many courses rely on tourism or seasonal residents to support the limited local user base. More courses have been developing in the vast outer reaches of Metro Vancouver and Victoria—and many are crying out for customers.

There's no hard evidence—least of all from the golf industry—to support the notion that recent golf converts are so disillusioned with the time and cost factors that they're turning their backs on the game. Having said that, though, golf needs to work harder at being both user friendly and environmentally friendly. And certainly, in recent years many courses have made substantial progress in the latter category. For example, there are currently five golf courses on Vancouver Island that have been certified through the Audubon Cooperative Sanctuary Program. To achieve certification, a course must demonstrate environmentally friendly practices in six categories: environmental planning, wildlife and habitat management, outreach and education, chemical use reduction and safety, water conservation and water quality management.

Be it in course design, ecological concerns, professional management, social issues (like the elimination of prejudice) or junior golf programs, golf in BC has come a long way since its beginnings. In these pages, I've endeavoured to acquaint you with its history in the province with accounts of some of the people, places and events that have shaped that history over the past 120 years.

CHAPTER I

OUR GOLFING LORE

This chapter provides an overview of where and how golf
gained a foothold in British Columbia and the role that
many Scottish immigrants played in the process.

THE ORIGINS OF GOLF

The origins of the game of golf are lost in the mists of time. Many
historians trace the game as far back as the Roman Empire when the
game of *paganica,* in which men used sticks to pummel a leather ball,
gained popularity as the empire gradually consumed most of modern-
day Europe. Others believe that the first golfers were Chinese, and that
the Chinese played *chiuwan*—"the ball-hitting game"—as early as AD
943. Another theory is that a Dutch boy invented *het kolfen* in the 14th
century by swatting pebbles with a stick. Or perhaps the Royal and
Ancient game as we know it today was born in the heather and gorse and
rock of the windswept Scottish seashores?

Whatever its origins are, it is fair to assume that the game had
gained enough popularity by 1457 that both *gawlf* and football had
to be banned by the Scottish Parliament to appease King James II who
saw these games as a distraction from military training in preparation
for war against England. Less than five decades later, the ban was lifted
by James IV who made the first recorded purchase of clubs from a
Perthshire bow maker.

The Scots transformed the game into a pastime for kings and queens
and commoners alike and its popularity gradually spread across England.

However, it was 1754 before the first documented rules of the game were published by the St Andrews Golfers (later known as the Royal and Ancient Golf Club) who made it clear that the game was never meant to be an indulgence for the affluent or a dalliance for dawdlers. Even today, no dyed-in-tweed Scot will ever let you forget that St Andrews is the Home of Golf, the Mecca of the game.

The first golf club in North America, originally called the Montreal Golf Club, was a nine-hole layout on a part of Mount Royal Park known as Fletcher's Field. It was founded in 1873 and 11 years later, Queen Victoria granted permission to add the Royal prefix.

Golf's arrival in British Columbia is more of a mystery.

As far as we can tell, British Columbia's first golfers seem to have been immigrants from the British Isles who arrived in Victoria by ship or by rail through the Rockies. In the 1890s there were reports of hardy golfers flailing away near the shores of Juan de Fuca Strait on Vancouver Island and beside English Bay driftwood near Vancouver. Farmers were spotted wielding golf implements, rather than scythes, in virgin fields off the roads near Duncan and Kelowna. More than that, we don't know. A romantic would like to believe that the initial divot deliberately taken in soil was the handiwork of a prudent pioneer with the foresight to replace it, thereby inadvertently covering over the first traces of golf in BC.

Scottish settlers presumably played golf, albeit with harsh form on equally rudimentary grounds, at various locations before then but there is no authenticated evidence of organized golf on formal grounds prior to the founding of the short-lived original Vancouver Golf Club near the sandy shores of Jericho and the opening of links on rented farmland beside Oak Bay at Victoria the following year. Many source documents relating to golf's beginnings in BC suffered the fate of wispy cobwebs that have been carelessly brushed away, leaving us with no reliable historical information about its beginnings.

For the sheer sake of affirming the game's starting place and date in this province, 1993 was designated as the centennial of golf in British Columbia.

EARLY COURSES

A handful of gentlemen reportedly first golfed at Beacon Hill Park on a seven-hole "course" laid out in 1889. One year earlier, the first club in the United States was founded in Yonkers, New York; that course was named Saint Andrew's—with an apostrophe, unlike its namesake.

Beacon Hill's architects were an Englishman named Wastie Green and Harry Pooley, a Victoria lawyer who later became BC's attorney general. Wastie Green had come to Victoria via Asia, where it is said he had tutored the Prince of Siam in the art of golf. His golf clubs were reportedly the first to arrive on these shores.

In addition to golf, Beacon Hill, originally designated parkland by Governor James Douglas in 1858 and officially made a 75-hectare municipal park in 1882, was used primarily for hiking and picnicking. By 1893 a second parkland, the more remote Macaulay Plains, provided an area barely large enough to accommodate four fairways. The plains sat behind the jagged coastline of Macaulay Point, where today the remnants of strategically positioned artillery guns sit idle, a reminder of a time when they protected naval installations and ships at Esquimalt Harbour. The Royal Navy had moved its Pacific Fleet headquarters from Valparaíso, Chile, to Esquimalt in 1865 and eventually built a naval base on the land mass between the Esquimalt and Victoria harbours.

Golf at Macaulay was informal. No records were kept of the activity there. Some holes were allegedly laid out by 1891; other unsupported claims put golfers on the site in 1887 and 1889—but the site was a veritable cow pasture until the Royal Marines Artillery Detachment at Esquimalt arrived in 1893 and two lieutenants, George Barnes and Frederick Templer, informally founded the United Service Club.

The golfers of Victoria required more suitable golfing terrain and found it a few kilometres east of Beacon Hill beside the craggy coast of Oak Bay. This time there was a more formal approach to the founding of a club and the Victoria Golf Club was thus established at a time when there were only 16 courses in the United States and 6 in Canada.

The Victoria Golf Club's 14 founding members created a primary layout of 14 holes—one for each member it seemed—with an annual

These three golfers and a caddy pose on Ladies' Day at the short-lived United Service course at Macaulay Point. ESQUIMALT MUNICIPAL ARCHIVES V992.3416 NEG.#52N6

five-dollar fee. The location, on land owned by retired BC surveyor-general Joseph Despard Pemberton in south Oak Bay, was chosen by local sportsman Harvey Combe. Within three months of the club's opening, the membership had reached its maximum limit of 50 and the dues were doubled. The addition of four more holes standardized the links in 1895, a year after Chicago Golf Club became North America's first 18-hole course.

While golf quickly established its home base on Vancouver Island, things took a little longer in the young city of Vancouver.

The Vancouver Golf Club's adventurous club members opened their first season in 1893 on a semblance of a course laid out on English Bay's southern shoreline, at what is now known as Jericho Park. They would later locate to Brockton Point, and then Moodyville on the North Shore. The Moodyville course lasted only one season, as a majority of the members resided in Vancouver and found the ferry service across the inlet inadequate and inconvenient.

However, as golf was dying on the North Shore, its popularity across the continent was accelerating. Three-time British Open champion Harry Vardon made a barnstorming tour of America in 1900, winning the US

Open while he was at it. Vardon used a newly invented wound ball, made with rubber windings around a rubber core. On average it travelled some 20 yards farther than the traditional "guttie," gutta percha latex balls that had dominated the sport for the last half of the 19th century.

In the meantime, both New Westminster and Kelowna residents welcomed golf into their communities before the end of the century. The first tournament on the mainland of BC, for example, is believed to have been hosted by the City Flats course in Kelowna in 1899. The New Westminster Golf Club was active at Moody Square, now Moody Park, from 1894 through 1907. Seven gentlemen convened at the Bank of British Columbia on April 28, 1894, to form their club after city council granted permission to golf on the grounds. Club membership never exceeded more than 25, perhaps because of a rather unique course hazard—council gave the New Westminster Gun Club equal rights on the grounds. The golfers eventually gave way to deadlier shooters who sprayed ammunition across the second and third fairways.

Save Moody Square, mainland golf virtually ceased to exist until 1907 when Captain Maciver Campbell led the reorganization of the Vancouver Golf Club and they returned to the links site at Jericho.

During those interim years, Vancouver's starved golfers had learned of Combe's accomplishments in Victoria and of the famed Ontario golfer George S. Lyon's win at the 1904 Olympics after a run of Canadian Amateur victories that had started in 1898. With roadways and railways gradually connecting remote areas of the province, golfers were also starting to flail about in fields near Nanaimo, Vernon and Hedley.

Once re-established in Vancouver, the Jericho Golf and Country Club, the only golf facility in the young boomtown of 70,000, was soon overcrowded and a second group of Vancouver businessmen assembled for the purpose of launching a country club in the suburbs. By then Jericho had abandoned its original name, Vancouver Golf Club, which would eventually end up in the suburban region known as Burquitlam. Originally known as the British Columbia Golf Club, and built on a parcel of Coquitlam farmland in 1910, today's Vancouver Golf Club remains one of the most popular courses in the Lower Mainland.

On Vancouver Golf Club's heels came Shaughnessy Heights, a luxurious course created by the Canadian Pacific Railway in 1912 to enhance the property values of the city's first authentic subdivision. Later, courses were developed in Colwood, Vernon, Kamloops, Qualicum Beach, Penticton and Nelson.

POSTWAR PROGRESS

The postwar years were a time of prosperity and innovations in the game. Across North America, jobs were plentiful, wages soared and the demand for recreational facilities increased. Demand for accessible golf courses grew rapidly.

Shoes were first fitted with special spikes for golf in 1920, and F.W. Woolworth, the dime-store chain, flooded the market with wooden "Reddy Tees," invented by a New Jersey dentist who disliked dirtying his hands while forming tee mounds of sand. On the club design front, steel and aluminum were taking over from hickory shafts and persimmon head drivers. In many cases the 1920s were a time of refinement, most of which was occurring in the United States. Hand-forged aluminum club heads dated back to the turn of the century and grooved club faces had actually been used since 1902, when E. Burr designed them to induce backspin. Blacksmiths, the original craftsmen of club making, had experimented with shaft weight distribution for more than three decades before metal clubs were legalized by the Royal and Ancient at St Andrews, Scotland, after the Prince of Wales played the course with a set. In North America, the first effective metal shafts came into play and colourful names like mashie and niblick were replaced with a numbering system based on the incline of the club face. Irons were sloped and numbered two through nine. They gained real popularity after Billy Burke used a set to succeed Bobby Jones as US Open champion in 1931. That was also the year the first sand wedge was custom designed to help get balls out of bunkers.

These were the beginnings of a quest, which would only grow over time, for the ultimate golf clubs. Many advances have been based on science and engineering but just as many have been cosmetic. These started with some manufacturers painting the steel to simulate wood to appease golfers who didn't want to abandon hickory.

After the war Vancouver welcomed two new private courses: Marine Drive in 1922 and Point Grey in 1923, both located on the Fraser delta flatlands. Throughout the province the game spread: to Rossland–Trail, Powell River, Courtenay, Salt Spring Island, Princeton, Kaslo, Revelstoke, Kimberley, Sidney and Oliver. In some cases courses proved to be a temporary measure to preserve tracts of land for a grander scheme. The old Hastings Park course on the PNE grounds, for example, existed from 1925 through 1953, when it was expropriated for a stadium for the coming British Empire Games.

Precious few courses blossomed during the economic turmoil of the Great Depression but there were exceptions. In Vancouver the University course opened in 1930 and Fraserview followed in 1934, the same year the legendary Bobby Jones visited and played a round at Shaughnessy Heights. Gleneagles had been constructed on the Larson Ranch fruit orchard near Horseshoe Bay in 1927 and almost a decade later the spectacular Capilano course was incorporated in conjunction with the British Properties development and pending construction of the Lions Gate Bridge. By the early 1930s several exceptional players had come to the fore (as it were), including the troika of Ken Black, Stan Leonard and Fred Wood on the men's side and Vera Hutchings on the women's side.

Golf, like many other organized sports, again came to a virtual standstill during the Second World War. Equipment was as scarce as money, fuel and rubber. Several courses were threatened with bankruptcy, greens crews and clubhouse employees worked part-time and pro shop staff repainted old balls to resell. Even after the soldiers returned home, in some communities where the war had taken its toll courses were desperate for golfers. There were bargain basement green fees and advertisements for cut-rate memberships. Between 1946 and 1954, only a handful of new BC courses were established: in Prince George, Dawson Creek, Castlegar, Chemainus, Cowichan and Terrace.

The postwar revival period for the game was aided by the gritty heroics of Bantam Ben Hogan, the fluid swing of Slammin' Sammy

Snead and the emergence of the legendary Arnold Palmer. The great Babe Didrikson Zaharias, the 1932 Olympics star, made golf her game and won 17 straight amateur titles in 1946 and 1947 before turning pro.

Television brought the game into people's living rooms. People dreamed about playing Augusta and fantasized about playing like Hogan, Snead, Palmer and a college kid named Nicklaus who had earned the moniker Golden Bear.

Prime players on the local amateur scene were Percy Clogg, Bill Mawhinney, Kay Farrell, Walter McElroy, and then Bob Kidd, Lyle Crawford, Doug Bajus, Margaret Todd and Babs Davies.

Skeena Valley, in Terrace, and Seymour, on Vancouver's North Shore, were carved out of dense forests; new courses popped up in Creston, Radium and Chilliwack; two opened in Richmond and the Vancouver Park Board added McCleery.

In 1954 at Point Grey, Victoria product Pat Fletcher became the first Canadian in 40 years to win the Canadian Open. It's now almost 60 years since Fletcher's victory and at time of writing no other Canadian has yet matched his feat. When Point Grey hosted the 1958 BC centennial tournament, the Vancouver Open Invitational, a little-known PGA tour player named Jim Ferree fashioned a memorable second-round 61 and held on for his sole PGA Tour victory, besting the other big-name tourists and collecting $6,400.

By 1964 Arnold Palmer had won his fourth Masters green jacket and seventh major tournament. He had also triggered a tsunami of new golfers that created a suddenly serious shortage of courses across North America. During the upswing of the 1960s, 27 new courses were added to the BC landscape, more than double the number added the decade before. And more capable contenders for provincial honours began to emerge, such as Billy Wakeham, John Johnston, Bert Ticehurst, John Russell, Doug Roxburgh, Gayle Hitchens, Barb Renwick and Marilyn Palmer. In a rare western Canadian appearance, Texan Don Massengale won the Canadian Open at the newly located Shaughnessy course in 1966.

During the 1970s, when 24 courses were built in BC, Roxburgh won his first two of four national amateurs and Jim Nelford reigned in

1975 and 1976. Sophisticated, often colourful, equipment became the norm: graphite, boron, titanium, metal woods, technicolour clothes and yellow and orange golf balls. Dave Barr, the bearish Kelowna pro with the 10-finger grip and whippy wrists, twice took the BC Open before joining the PGA Tour. Precocious, promising Jim Rutledge became a factor, and Lisa Young Walters of Prince Rupert won successive provincial championships.

More than 30 courses were built during the 1980s. In that decade Roxburgh still topped the tournament lists, Rick Gibson came of age, Brent Franklin went on a binge of national championships for six successive years, Barr made his first million and Dawn Coe started to make her mark. In 1992, Disco Dick Zokol won his first and only PGA victory at the Milwaukee Open.

As golf approached its centennial in the early 1990s, some 40 new projects were in various stages of construction with many more courses on drawing boards throughout the province. It was in this environment that the original edition of *Backspin* was released in 1992. Based on the state of the industry, I wrote,

> The game hasn't been without serious growing pains. Though studies reveal supply isn't meeting demand, least of all with public courses in the province's most densely populated mainland-valley areas, golf has been stifled with a plethora of developmental problems.
>
> Golf will remain an affordable, enjoyable pursuit only if grave environmental concerns are addressed by organized representatives of the golf industry and golfing community. The complacent industry has neglected the area of public relations and golf's functionaries, professional and amateur alike, have treated participants outside their spheres, the general public, with indifference. Too many of their concerns are virtually restricted to management and members of their own clubs and to their own associations. (*Backspin*, p. 8)

From my perspective there were some serious challenges. "Far too many juniors, pensioners and public course players are being dissuaded because courses are too expensive or too crowded. The starkly frightening consequences for a game still bursting with growth: prohibitive costs are driving the price of enjoying it far beyond the average person's means."

As I saw it, environmental concerns, the economy, participatory costs and course accessibility would dictate the game's growth. Two decades later those factors remain as relevant now as they were then.

CHAPTER 2

VICTORIA: THE CAPITAL OF GOLF

The evolution of golf on southern Vancouver Island was quite independent of the mainland story and has its own heroes, yarns and legacy. It also brought BC's greatest golf architect, A.V. Macan, to the fore.

VICTORIA GOLF CLUB

Based on the origins of the Victoria Golf Club, the long-established natural setting of Royal Colwood and the architectural mastery of one of Victoria's early citizens, it is fitting to declare BC's oldest community as the capital of golf.

During the first summers at Pemberton meadows overlooking Oak Bay, the links were closed to golfers. Labour costs were too high to permit proper maintenance, the machinery couldn't cope with the uncontrollable grass of early spring and the resident cattle couldn't chew fast enough to be considered efficient greenskeepers.

Nowhere in the minutes of the Victoria Golf Club's first years does it stipulate that landowners J.D. and R.B. Pemberton banned golfers from the seaside lea while their sheep and cows were grazing, but the pioneer golfers apparently respected the Pemberton property and livestock. They refrained from playing on the land for three months each summer, leaving the fairways undisturbed for the animals. The putting greens were fenced to protect against hoof prints. The members learned to adapt to their environment and tolerated the hazards dropped by the voracious stock.

Although patriarch J.D. Pemberton had died in late 1893, it seems that at least some of his three sons and three daughters must have been keen golfers. The first reference to rental payment for use of the land for golf was in June 1905, more than a decade after golfers first played at Oak Bay. However, there must have been some form of nominal remuneration before the members agreed to pay the family business, Pemberton & Sons, the princely annual rental sum of $100.

Sir Richard Musgrave, later premier of BC, chaired the club's first meeting in 1893, when the first labour costs were entered in the books. The expenditure for two Chinese gardeners who worked 11 days for $1.25 a day each was $27.50. In addition to Musgrave, Harvey Combe, the club's first secretary, influenced club policy from the beginning. Referring to the course closure after late spring championships, he commented that

> I consider golf essentially a pastime for early spring or fall. I do not think it can be classed a summer game. Still there are many who like to play golf, off and on, during the warm weather. One reason to allow them to continue is the increasing influx of visitors who desire to play the course. The consensus of opinion is that it would be a pity to deprive them of playing when it's such a small matter to keep it in proper slope.

Combe initiated the enthusiasm for the development of a course; he scouted for and chose the site. Therefore, it can only be assumed that he was one of the first golf pioneers to arrive at the Temple Building on the evening of November 7, 1893. Yet the man widely considered as the father of golf in British Columbia, the man who captured the provincial championship on nine occasions over a 13-year span, implausibly wasn't listed as present at the club's historic first meeting. However, this didn't preclude his selection to the first executive board. The impressible English sportsman had discovered golf the summer before on an excursion from Victoria to his homeland, and had set out almost immediately upon his return to explore the city for a prospective course site.

The original eighth tee on the front-nine par three was positioned atop the shoreline rocks.
VICTORIA GOLF CLUB 990.7.4A

Combe and son Brian quickly favoured the sea-splashed, rocky shoreline of Oak Bay, going as far as forming an experimental hole before permission to use the land was even granted. He didn't hesitate to enthuse about the merits of the game and a course to his friends and associates. It was he who approached owner F.B. Pemberton for permission to use the grazing land that was called the Pemberton meadow for a course.

Combe and Musgrave were the prime movers; Lionel Webber and Hewitt Bostock, the Victoria police chief and later senator, were named the provisional committee. The appointed directors—Musgrave, W.A. Ward, Bostock, the Honourable Forbes G. Vernon, W. Ridgway Wilson and Combe—diplomatically named the Honourable E. Dewdney, BC's lieutenant-governor, as the club's first president.

In the ensuing years it would be Combe who gave the club and the game their long-lasting high profiles. In 1894, at age 32, Combe shot 113 in the very first BC championships, also his tournament debut. It tied him for third among 15 contestants.

As crude as the original course was the first "clubhouse," a piano box six feet long, three feet wide and six feet high that was used to store clubs. (The containers in which cumbersome 1,250-pound upright pianos were transported from eastern factories were usually converted into tool boxes.) It was discarded after only one season as too small even for club storage. By 1894 a three-room building with a verandah and small stove was in place at a cost of fifty-five dollars, excluding eleven dollars for painting. That year's expenditures of $485.60 included $15 to make 100 keys to the clubhouse. The club roster was 75-strong, with 45 playing members, 12 women, 11 privileges members and 7 country members, presumably out-of-town players. Total receipts of $536.05 in 1894 included $13.55 from 16 entrance fees to the first BC championships.

The Oak Bay links weren't extended to 18 holes until the fall of 1895, when the course measured 4,898 yards and E.H. Maitland-Dougal of Duncan established 85 as the course record. William Edgar Oliver matched this the following year in winning his third straight provincial championship, but it is Harvey Combe who ranks as the era's premier golfer. Until a teenager named Doug Roxburgh came along six decades later, it seemed inconceivable that Combe's mark of nine BC championships would ever be threatened. Combe had excelled in several other sports, including rugby, cricket and tennis in England. As an adventurous teenager, he opted to seek opportunity abroad rather than fulfilling his family's wishes that he pursue a military career.

A common option at the time for men in his position was farm life in Ontario. However, this didn't attract the erudite young Englishman. He ventured west instead. By 1886, four years after settling in Victoria, Combe had earned a prominent appointment as registrar of the Supreme Court and collector of voters. He was 24. His rise in golf was equally meteoric. In 1897, four years after taking up the game, he ended Oliver's three-year championship run—although it should be noted that Oliver

William Edgar Oliver won the first three provincial championships
from 1894 through 1896. BC ARCHIVES HP99680

had won the inaugural event with 102, a score 11 better than that of
the self-taught Combe. Harvey Combe would be almost unbeatable for
more than a decade. By the time he won his last BC championship at
age 47, he had established several scoring precedents in the northwest.
He was the first to break 90, then 80 and, in November 1907, he posted
a record 72 that stood for several years. Two years later, in a 72-hole
challenge match against Seattle's Charles Newton, rated the best player
on the Pacific Coast, Combe won the home-and-home match 3 and 2.

By that time the Victoria Club had also groomed one of the finest
women golfers in the province's history, Violet Pooley Sweeny. Her skill
was probably a major factor in the club directors' decision to permit
women to play on Saturdays as well as other days by becoming honorary
members for a three-dollar annual fee.

Harry Pooley took quick steps to counter a real estate development proposal in 1906 and saved the Oak Bay course for future generations. BC ARCHIVES HP6882

American golfers were also starting to discover Victoria's two courses at Oak Bay and Macaulay Plains. A.H. Finlay, a noted player from Boston, visited in 1904 and expressed delight with the Oak Bay links after several games with Harvey Combe and a Captain Davidson. One day Finlay lowered Combe's course record of 75 by a stroke.

The condition of the course improved with each season, probably because it was kept fallow in summer. And with the intrusion of man, the numbers of animals roaming the property decreased.

Certain members were allowed to erect a shelter on the grounds for their horses at their own expense. The club owned a horse and once, for some unknown reason, borrowed a cow from member E.S. Barnard. In 1908 the same Mr. Barnard received permission to build a garage to house his car, a novelty owned by very few at the time.

In 1906 landowner Frederick B. Pemberton received a $50,000 offer for his 100 acres, an inflated price in a time before any real estate boom. The club was given 24 hours to match the terms of $10,000 down and a similar sum annually for each of four years at the going rate of interest.

Harry Pooley immediately set out to save the course for the 540 members, beginning by rousing coal baron James Dunsmuir from his bed one morning with a telephone call. Dunsmuir, who owned mines at Extension and Cumberland, was Victoria's wealthiest citizen. He agreed to loan the club $10,000 and promised a $40,000 advance with first security to the property. The members had only $897.06 on hand from receipts of $3,721.35 that year, but they were able to purchase the Pemberton property, remaining forever indebted to Dunsmuir's patronage and Pooley's initiative.

In 1907 the club's first municipal taxes were $252, earthquakes were rumbling throughout the Americas, balloon racing was all the rage and Rudyard Kipling, winner of the year's Nobel Prize, appeared as a guest of honour during the Pacific Northwest tournament at Oak Bay. The *Daily Colonist* described Victoria as the core of a great golf boom.

> Victorians have come to realize the attractions of the pastime. As a result, it has become popular even among those who until recently spoke of the game as a tame recreation, and scarcely worth the trouble of becoming familiar with. It has been stated by some that there is nothing to golf that is not as simple as ABC, requiring only the ability of hitting the ball straight and strong, and an inclination for long walks. Such people should visit the links any fine afternoon and their ideals about this would vanish. The performances of some of the students are amusing to everyone but themselves, and especially do the caddies delight in witnessing crude exhibitions of the beginners.

Jack Moffat, a transplanted Scottish pro who discovered Victoria while on a trip from Portland, had been retained in 1905 as the club pro for forty dollars a month.

Harry Pooley's sister, Violet, also arrived, so to speak, in 1905 when she won her first of five Pacific Northwest titles and her first of nine BC championships.

SUNG WAI

Any recollection of the early days of Victoria Golf Club would be incomplete without mention of Sung Wai, likely the province's first Chinese golfer. Many early members would say that he ran the club for three decades after 1903, providing an impeccable service to members.

In his 1993 commissioned club history to celebrate the club's centennial, Peter Corley-Smith wrote of Sung Wai,

> He had been employed as Harvey Combe's personal house-boy [and] was engaged as a "steward" in the club . . . Most contemporary members conceded that he ran the club. He collected dues from the members, green fees from guests and payments . . . for refreshments. One of his most unusual accomplishments for a Chinese-Canadian at that time was to learn to play golf. On a return trip to China, when anxiety about smallpox still prevailed, he was placed in quarantine at William Head and, while he was there, laid out a three-hole golf course . . . As a result, and in due course, he became a competent golfer . . . Members were genuinely distressed by his passing in 1933 and as a memorial his portrait has graced the walls of the 19th hole ever since.

THE LEGACY OF HARVEY COMBE

It is fair to say that Harvey Combe not only dominated on the links but by having Sung Wai administer all clubhouse matters, he also brought order to the whole establishment.

The finest BC player of his day and a driving force behind the formation of the Victoria Golf Club, Harvey Combe was a nine-time champion in both golf and tennis.
BC GOLF HOUSE 007.131.026B

Combe's wife and their daughter, Nora, were his successful protégés. Neither of his two sons, Brian nor Boyce, mastered golf. Edith Combe preceded her husband as the family champion by capturing three of the first four provincial women's championships that started in 1895, while Nora defeated her mother in the 1907 final and won the PNGA title in both 1910 and 1911.

Eminently respected in the community, Harvey Combe was appointed the club secretary at $150 annually in 1904 and held this title until he was superannuated by the government in 1919. Three years later he died of heart failure at age 60. Not until Ken Black in the 1930s and Bob Kidd in the 1960s did any man manage to win more than two BC amateur championships.

Born Leonora Combe to Harvey and Edith, both provincial champions, Nora Combe Paterson won the Pacific Northwest Golf Association's premier event in 1910 and 1911. BC GOLF HOUSE 007.131.024A

EARLY VICTORIA TOURNAMENTS

The CPR chose February for the Empress tournament to attract guests during the hotel's slack month. It became an annual Victoria event that became a fixture on the social and golf calendars. Golfers from across western Canada and the Pacific Northwest, many escaping their frigid climes, gathered at the Empress for the popular handicap event, which was advertised as Victoria's leading winter sports event. One year, with the links under several inches of snow, officials improvised by staging a competition on a novel "course" set up on the hotel's carpeted hallways.

In February 1929, Nora Combe Paterson and T.L. Swan were winners of the first recorded Empress Hotel tournament. Paterson was an active golfer until 1965, when arthritis forced her to give up the game she had enjoyed for more than 50 years. The inaugural tournament included an exhibition match that attracted more than 1,000 spectators. Oak Bay pro Phil Taylor and Seattle amateur Bon Stein combined to defeat Davey Black of Shaughnessy Heights and Chuck Hunter of Tacoma one up. Lieutenant-Governor Randolph Bruce, accompanied by his niece, Helen MacKenzie, presented the tournament prizes in the brilliant sunshine on the final day.

Snow and ice prevented Royal Colwood from taking the event in 1930 but thereafter the popular event was alternated with Oak Bay when officials decided that February weather would be more favourable near the coast than inland. The event was eventually moved ahead to March and then April to take advantage of the milder weather. In 1955 Oak Bay was designated as the site for the men's division, Uplands for the women. Seattle newspapers enthusiastically endorsed the Empress as the new northern Del Monte (California) tournament of the west coast. Golfers from the Pacific Northwest and the Prairies became annual visitors Golfers from the Pacific Northwest and the Prairies became annual visitors for the social event that didn't always escape the wrath of winter.

Apparently nothing could keep the competitors from the Empress. Herb Fritz, Vancouver Golf Club's champion, solved the problem of playing matches at Oak Bay and Fraserview in Vancouver on the same Sunday in 1968 by travelling to Vancouver by helicopter. "I'm glad I salvaged something today," sighed Fritz after beating Al Greenstreet one up in the second round of the City Match Play Open. The chopper had set down on the first fairway at Fraserview a few minutes before his scheduled tee-off time. Fritz had been flown directly from an area near Victoria Golf Club's 15th fairway after losing the Empress semifinal on the 18th green.

A.V. Macan was an able golfer and an outstanding architect, one of his crown jewels being the Royal Colwood course. BC GOLF HOUSE 007.141.073A

A.V. MACAN

Oak Bay's next player of prominence, Arthur Vernon Macan, arrived from Dublin in 1910 to practise law in Victoria. He was one of Ireland's leading amateurs. After winning his second successive BC championship in 1913 as well as the Pacific Northwest title, Macan left law and began his long, illustrious career as a golf course architect.

Macan's architectural prowess grabbed the attention of lumber baron Joseph Sayward, who enlisted the audacious Irishman to design his first complete course.

Macan completed the Colwood course before he was summoned to war. The volatile, outspoken Irishman returned home from France with his left leg shattered and requiring amputation below the knee. But such a minor detail failed to daunt the obstinate Macan, a charmer who became an authority on every endeavour he pursued.

He never won another BC championship, though he reached the final in 1919, having returned from Europe two days before the tournament, and again in 1921, while maintaining a four-handicap with his wooden leg. Macan was a superb ball striker and technician. At age 56 he captured his third Victoria Golf Club championship on the links he was instrumental in remodelling over the years.

Macan's credits as a prolific golf architect are impressive. His reputation from Colwood earned him assignments to design Marine Drive and Langara in Vancouver, followed later by McCleery and the new Shaughnessy and Richmond. South of the border there was Seattle Inglewood, Seattle Golf Club, Tacoma Fircrest, Columbia Edgewater, Colwood National in Portland, and the California Club of San Francisco. On Vancouver Island there was Nanaimo and Cowichan. In all he created or redesigned 55 courses.

When he could no longer golf, Macan taught bridge. He also claimed expertise in the quality of whiskey. In August 1964 he suffered a fatal heart attack while on site redesigning the Sunland course in Sequim, Washington, on the Olympic Peninsula. He couldn't have chosen a more appropriate place to die.

FRANCIS M. RATTENBURY

Rising taxes created the Oak Bay club's next crisis in 1913. Luckily, Francis M. Rattenbury, who rocketed to prominence as an architect in 1893 with the winning design for the province's Parliament buildings, came to the rescue. The arrogant young Englishman designed many major buildings of the day, including the Empress Hotel, Government House and courthouses in Vancouver, New Westminster and Nanaimo.

A co-founder of the PGA BC and three-time BC Open champion, Phil Taylor thrived on exhibition golf and was the Victoria Club pro for 37 years. BC GOLF HOUSE 007.131.060

Rattenbury took it upon himself to save the links from rising municipal taxation by running for the reeveship of Oak Bay. Some council members were of the opinion that the course should be assessed at the same rate as residential property. If the assessment went beyond the lease payments of $3,000, the Gonzales Point Land Co. could reclaim and subdivide the property. Rattenbury decided to run to prevent the destruction of the area, which he said would be a calamity for

Victoria and Oak Bay. With support from the outgoing reeve, first BC champion William Oliver, Rattenbury won by 24 votes. Meanwhile, Dunsmuir and fellow members Joseph Sayward, Frank Barnard and A.C. Flumerfelt, fearing the Victoria club might be taxed out of existence, prepared for such an eventuality by organizing a new club in faraway Colwood.

OAK BAY PROS

A string of pros including the Moffat brothers, Jack and Bill, Tom Gallop and Harry Eve presided in the Oak Bay pro shop before Phil Taylor arrived in 1921 and stayed for 37 years.

Taylor came from Great Yarmouth, on the east coast of England, in 1921. A stocky, quiet man, Taylor was an accomplished player and fine teacher. He competed in every British Open from 1909 through 1920. In 1913 his leading qualifying round of 71 was a Hoylake course record and he tied for eighth in the Open proper. The BC Open was initiated in 1928 when Taylor was almost 40 years old. Still, he captured the title on three occasions, the last of which was 1933. Taylor and Shaughnessy's Davey Black alternated winning the first four Opens. Taylor's forte was medal competition. His typically flat, old-country swing was starkly simple and consistently kept him in play. His tournament success, a special gift for teaching the game and his uncanny recall of names endeared him to the membership. When Taylor wasn't practising, he was in great demand for lessons.

"Golf became such a social game in the 1930s there weren't enough hours in the day for Dad to accommodate the requests for instruction," says his son Allan. "One of his pupils was Premier Pattullo."

The golf genes of both Taylor and Black were passed on to the next generation. Allan Taylor played for BC's 1933 Willingdon Cup team and won the club title four times, the last in 1949. But he wasn't raised on the Oak Bay links and he wasn't his father's protégé. Only the offspring of members were allowed to play the course as juniors, so Allan Taylor ventured to the United Service course at Macaulay Plains for his early golf. At 18, he became one of the club's first intermediate members.

Host pro Phil Taylor waits to play while Joyce Wethered, the best woman player in the world, lines up a putt in a 1935 exhibition match played at the Victoria Golf Club. Taylor, paired that day with Marjorie Todd, achieved a rare two-up win over Wethered and her partner, Colwood pro Joe Pryke. ARV OLSON COLLECTION

The Taylors resided on Newport, a street behind Oak Bay's 15th hole, and young Allan spent many hours scouring the course's gorse and bramble for lost balls. He repainted the balls and sold them to his father for ten cents a dozen. Phil Taylor did much of his club making and repairs in the basement of the house after the almost completed new clubhouse burned to the ground in August 1927.

Phil retired in 1958 but remained on the club payroll for several years as a course consultant. He and Davey Black, his friendly adversary, both died in 1973. Taylor was 83, Black was 90.

Laurie Carroll, Taylor's assistant for six years, became head pro in 1959, but resigned in 1963 to develop and operate a driving range. On a mission to find a new pro in England, the club's Bert Osborough interviewed five applicants before hiring Paul Trapp of Churston, Devon. The veteran second-generation pro brought an assistant with him, his son Vaughn.

Three-time BC Open winner, Phil Taylor helped found the PGA BC and remained highly regarded throughout his career. Dressed to impress, his pals check out the fabric. From left, Fred Wood, Jock McKinnon, Billy Thompson, Dunc Sutherland and Ben Colk. BC SPORTS HALL OF FAME 1501.23

Margaret and Jack Todd, seen here August 6, 1948, were fixtures on the post-war Victoria golf scene. Margaret was reigning BC Women's champion at the time. Four generations of the Todd family have made a huge contribution to the Victoria golf community for over a century. VANCOUVER PUBLIC LIBRARY 84182

Although he actually putted his ball out of bounds on the slippery seventh green at Victoria Golf Club, a little bit of BC fishing could put a smile back on Ben Hogan's face.
BC GOLF HOUSE 007.85.42A

Ever since Oak Bay's inception, weather has been a factor when playing the course—the capricious winds at Gonzales Point make the links unpredictable. Its unique challenge is intriguing, however. When the seventh hole was originally played as a 200-yard par-three from an exposed tee box atop the rocks to a staircase green that tilted sharply toward the sea, club selection ranged from a pitching wedge to a driver, depending on the wind's direction. During a 1937 exhibition, it is said that Ben Hogan—then an unknown young touring pro—putted from the top right edge off the green, his ball cascading to the beach below.

Given its longevity, the course has hosted relatively few significant events. Lanky Steve Berry captured the last BC Amateur at Oak Bay in 1981. The only Victoria Golf Club members who have worn the provincial crown since the First World War were Jimmy Squires in 1950 at his home course and Carl Schwantje in 1970. New Zealand and Britain tied for first at the quadrennial Commonwealth Team matches of 1967 at Oak Bay. Dawn Coe, from the tiny logging base of Honeymoon Bay north of Victoria, became the 1983 Canadian women's champion, a win that launched a successful professional career.

Proving that golf makes lifetime friends, (L to R) J.M. Wood, J.N. Findlay, H.P. Hodges and G.Y. Simpson reunited at the Victoria Golf Club on February 21, 1949, 30 years after they originally posed on the tee box. ARV OLSON COLLECTION

Golfer Ede Thomas addresses the ball on one of Royal Colwood's early raised tees.
ESQUIMALT MUNICIPAL ARCHIVES V992.34.U

COLWOOD: THE ROYAL COURSE

The world was preoccupied with a war when Colwood quietly opened in November 1914 as the eighth active course in BC. The regal prefix was applied 17 years later by permission of King George V and today Colwood is one of only six Canadian courses to have earned the "Royal" designation from a reigning monarch.

The king's son, the Prince of Wales, later King Edward VIII, had played the course several times and consented to become a patron of the club. While here, the prince was a guest at Hatley Castle, now Royal Roads University, on the immense estate of James Dunsmuir, the retired former premier and later eighth lieutenant-governor of the province. Dunsmuir and lumber baron Joseph Austin Sayward collaborated to develop a course on 240 acres of the original Esquimalt Farm managed by Captain Edward E. Langford. The 73rd Regiment captain had named his house, opposite the 17th green, Colwood after the family estate in England.

Dunsmuir and Sayward paid $183,722 for the land on which a steeplechase course existed at the turn of the century. Sayward, a gruff man by nature, hired A.V. Macan to create the course. St Andrews inspired the irascible Irishman's work, though the Langford site wasn't a seaside locale on which he could shape a tribute course to the Scottish links. However, the idyllic setting afforded him the necessities for a course: gentle sloping terrain, towering evergreens and gnarled oaks. Royal Colwood rates as one of his finest creations, and is arguably his best in BC. Macan was especially proud of the 11th, 12th and 13th holes, frequently referring to them as his "masterpieces." Macan's trademarks are demanding par-four holes that require two well-played shots and undulating, crowned greens "to defy backspin players."

An explosion in golf interest coupled with predictions that Victoria's population would exceed 100,000 prompted Dunsmuir and Sayward to develop a course directly across the road to Sooke from Dunsmuir's stately estate. They feared the Victoria Club's tax assessments would become prohibitive with increased housing in the Oak Bay area and that members would be forced to vacate the links.

On November 20, 1913, the Colwood Land Co. was registered, with Biggerstaff Wilson, Thomas W. Paterson, Frederick B. Pemberton, C.E. Todd and Francis M. Rattenbury holding one share each. The course opened for play almost a year to the day later, but with war spreading like wildfire throughout Europe hardly anyone noticed. Despite this, unlike some courses that deteriorated through neglect during the war, Colwood thrived in its early years. It certainly never lacked moisture. When Sayward sold the Esquimalt Water Works he inserted a clause in the transaction that guaranteed the club unlimited water for 30 years at a fixed annual rate of $400.

The club prospered following the war and by 1922 a new luxurious clubhouse stood on the rock bluff behind the ninth green. But the building, valued at $50,000 and insured for $30,000, burned to the ground in February 1929. Everything in the clubhouse—records, trophies and clubs—was destroyed in the spectacular blaze that attracted spectators from as far away as the city. The replacement clubhouse was a $75,000 Elizabethan-style structure with an exterior of California stucco supplemented by half-timber work and weather-boarded gables.

A twosome tee off at Royal Colwood's fourth on a tranquil morning, *circa* 1920s.
ROYAL COLWOOD GOLF CLUB

With its reputation as a championship course, Royal Colwood was the choice location for many leading tournaments. The prestigious Pacific Northwest Golf Association's event came to Colwood in 1922 and 1927, as did the BC Amateur championships of 1925, 1929 and 1935, the 1934 BC Open and the 1935 Canadian Ladies' Closed.

Davey Black came over from his new position at Shaughnessy Heights and took the Open division of the 1922 PNGA. Much to the dismay of the members, Colwood pro Willie Black had lost a big early lead as brother Davey equalled his course record 71. A closing 73 gave Davey 300, three better than Willie.

Colwood pro Joe Pryke and Phil Taylor of Victoria pose with Marjorie Todd, a fine golfer in her own right but who played in the shadows of her sister-in-law, Margaret.
BC GOLF HOUSE 007.131.022A

George Von Elm of Salt Lake City successfully defended his PNGA Amateur title in 1922 at Colwood by defeating Seattle's Bon Stein at the 36th hole. Four years later Von Elm became 1926 US Amateur champion by beating the great Bobby Jones, to whom he had lost in the 1924 final.

Walter Pursey, pro at Seattle Inglewood, was the 1927 PNGA Open winner with 297 on a lengthened Colwood layout. Frank Dolp won the all-Portland amateur final over Rudi Wilhelm, the first man ever to break par 70 on the course with a 68 in the morning round. Violet Pooley Sweeny kept the women's trophy in Victoria, making Colwood's Nan Hutchinson her sixth victim in the final.

The first BC Open staged at Colwood was Don Sutherland's only triumph in the provincial championship. The Silent Scot from Vancouver Golf Club was runner-up for three of four years before winning in 1934 with 291 over young amateur Ken Lawson's 297. Toronto's great Ada MacKenzie arrived at Colwood in September 1935, heavily favoured to capture her sixth Canadian Closed title. She had won the National Open the previous week at Vancouver's Jericho course. But at Colwood she fell in an early-round match to Marjorie Todd of Oak Bay. Todd eliminated

MacKenzie with a 10-foot putt on the first extra hole after being two down with three holes to play, but she lost in the next round to eventual champion Mrs. Roy Horne of Calgary.

COLWOOD PROS

Colwood's first professional, the colourful Jimmy Huish, had arrived in Victoria from Musselburgh with Bill Moffat in 1910. After working under Moffat at Oak Bay, Huish went first to Macaulay Point and then to Colwood in 1914. Upon Huish's departure for Vancouver Golf Club in 1917, Colwood brought in Willie Black via Troon and New Brunswick.

Black's replacement in 1923 was Englishman Edward McInnes of Surrey, who gave way to yet another Scottish pro, Alex Marling. The popular Marling, former Scottish and Glasgow pro champion, rarely played competitive golf after he lost an eye during the First World War. He died in October 1934.

Joe Pryke of Edmonton succeeded Marling before Fred Burns took over Colwood's pro shop in 1944. Burns's seven-year stint through 1951 was without question the course's most difficult time. Wartime caused the federal government to requisition Colwood's clubhouse for use as a military hospital and the members were moved to an auxiliary facility.

When Burns retired, fewer than 50 members were active and the club had accumulated debts of nearly $115,000. The course was saved by selling the exquisite clubhouse to the Catholic Sisterhood for $125,000. A new facility was eventually constructed.

The man whom Burns recommended as his replacement, Bill Court, returned to Victoria after three years as Nanaimo's pro. Court was courage personified. In 1945, at the age of 25, he had been left completely paralyzed from the waist down after undergoing spinal surgery and the removal of a chest tumour. Driven by a love for golf and the outdoors, Court literally dragged himself around the Uplands course near his home to hunt for golf balls and enjoy the wildlife. This form of therapy eventually enabled him to regain mobility in his legs. When he joined Burns at Colwood as an assistant in 1946, Court still relied on a cane to walk. He soon discarded his canes, however, and his limp never stopped him from golfing.

Joe Louis, the Brown Bomber, is welcomed to Victoria by Royal Colwood's Ted Colgate as they loosen up on the practice range before heading to the first tee. BC GOLF HOUSE 007.131.023A

Colwood hasn't been without fine players, including Byrnie Schwengers, Ted Colgate, Bill McColl, Vic Painter and Dave Mick. Schwengers was more noted for his tennis prowess while Painter won his first of five club titles in 1947 and his last 32 years later. Pat Derry was unbeatable as women's club champion for 10 straight years through 1986. Yet the course that prides itself in developing shot makers hasn't turned out a BC amateur champion since 1962 when Lawrie Kerr stopped teenager Dick Munn at Uplands. It was Kerr's most memorable golfing day since being chosen to caddy for a US Army recruit named Joe Louis, known as the Brown Bomber, who came to Victoria for a 1945 exhibition bout at the Bay Street Armories. Louis played only nine holes and paid Kerr US$20, almost 50 times the going nine-hole rate.

Kerr, who was BC Amateur medallist in 1960, beat Fred Painter, Bill Wakeham and defending champion Ron Willey before running into a husky carpenter, Bud Bird of Langara, who wielded his driver like a hammer. His swing was short and choppy, his putting stroke as deadly as his glare. Kerr consistently hit approach shots inside his opponent during the semifinal, but Bird kept draining putts. After Bird squared the match with a long birdie putt on 17, Kerr popped his drive at the 18th and flushed a career four-wood to the stick for a winning birdie-three. He won the title 4 and 3 over Dick Munn. In 2005 the course's Lawrie Kerr pond was dedicated to him for his accomplishments.

One of Canada's great female golfers, Marlene Stewart Streit of Ontario, graced Colwood's fairways in 1955. She trounced Mary Gay, also of Ontario, 11-9 in the 36-hole Open final and finished 15 strokes ahead of runner-up Gay in the Closed. Streit's 71 on the third day for 223 remains the best women's score at Colwood.

Rounds under 70 weren't commonplace over the years, although Stan Leonard, Bob Fleming and Doug Roxburgh are among the superlative shot makers who also have captured BC Amateur titles at Colwood.

The Canadian Amateur has been held at Colwood twice, with battlers named Stuart Jones and Jim Nelford the triumphant survivors. Jones, a former rugby scrum half, took the measure of compatriot Ross Murray in an all–New Zealand final the week after the 1967 Commonwealth Team matches at Oak Bay. Nelford, the Fraserview-reared future pro, repeated as national amateur champion in 1976 by beating Mexican Rafael Alarcón on the second hole of a sudden-death playoff. They had tied at 287.

Bill Court cheered on Jim Nelford as a spectator at the 1976 final, having retired the year before when the club promoted assistant Bob Hogarth as head pro. Hogarth had also apprenticed under both Court and former Victorian Pat Fletcher at Royal Montreal.

Regrettably, Colwood's picturesque clubhouse-hospital-nunnery was demolished in 1987. A spacious new clubhouse opened in 1993, two years before the club hosted the RCGA Canadian Seniors Championships in an event where Bob Wylie of Calgary set a record by claiming his seventh and last John Rankin Memorial Trophy to set a Canadian record that still stands.

In 2010, Prince Andrew, Duke of York became a Royal Colwood patron. Royal Colwood was well established when the members of the United Service Club voted in 1920 to vacate Macaulay Point in favour of a larger, more practical location about four miles to the northeast in Oak Bay.

While a heritage landmark is lost forever, Macan's Royal Colwood course is a lasting legacy for golfers in British Columbia.

CEDAR HILL

Cedar Hill, founded by Harry Eve, catered to Victoria's public players as early as 1917, well before Uplands opened. It took the overflow of people who couldn't access the United Service course at Macaulay Point or membership to Victoria or Royal Colwood. Short and rudimentary, it was originally known as the Cow Pasture because Eve, who had been the Victoria pro for two years following the war, couldn't obtain mowing rights from the property owner who insisted the golfers share the land with his 400 cattle. The original green fee was ten cents.

When bigger, better Gorge Vale opened in 1930, play dwindled at Cedar Hill. Attempts to revive the course were unsuccessful until 1936 when H.W. Young obtained a lease with both grazing and cutting rights. Golf at last had precedence over cows.

Many fine players—including future pros Dick Munn, Bill Wakeham, Jim Rutledge, Rick Gibson and Don Billsborough—learned on this course that barely stretches 5,000 yards. At age 20, Munn became the country's youngest head pro when he accepted proprietor Lyle Barnes's offer of $400 a month plus lodging. Cedar Hill's pro shop was the basement of a house on the premises. Wakeham, Rutledge and Gibson each went on to win national and provincial championships while Billsborough eventually took the pro job at Uplands.

UPLANDS

The Uplands Golf Club course blossomed on 120 acres that two farmers had been leasing from the Hudson's Bay Company for grazing and harvesting hay. The members rented the property for 15 years at $3,000 annually. Uplands was officially opened in 1922 and has survived several

July 1, 1922, saw a large crowd on hand for the opening of Uplands in Victoria.
ESQUIMALT MUNICIPAL ARCHIVES V992.34.99

setbacks, including a fire that destroyed the clubhouse in 1925 and years of financial difficulties.

With the postwar boom, the club's solvency permitted the members to purchase the property in 1948 from the Hudson's Bay Company for $60,000. Noted for its immaculate fairways and superlative greens, Uplands has been a regular venue for top tournaments, including the Canadian Seniors.

Members Harold Brynjolfson and Ken Lawson and Colwood's Lawrie Kerr have captured BC Amateurs at Uplands, while Victoria pros Phil Taylor and Bill Wakeham were BC Open champions there. Victor Price, a lefthander, was Uplands's first noteworthy amateur while Joan Lawson won her first club championship in 1942 and her 20th in 1978. She continued her fine play in Seniors' competitions, twice winning the BC title and twice coming second. Uplands has had only three professionals, including the venerable Walter Gravlin who came with Macaulay Point members in 1922 and retired in 1963. Gravlin's loyal assistant, Johnny Wren, was head pro through 1973—he left just two years before the death of Uplands legend Charles Arthur Thompson. Wren's successor, now with almost four decades at the helm, is Don Billsborough.

CHAPTER 3
THE LOWER MAINLAND: IN THE BEGINNING

While golf's popularity grew in parallel to Vancouver's emergence as the economic hub of British Columbia there were successes and setbacks, good decisions and bad. This chapter looks at some of the key early courses in the Lower Mainland and the people who established them.

JERICHO

The original nine holes at Vancouver's Jericho golf course were scratched out haphazardly in the sands and seaweed on the south shore of English Bay. Scattered with barnacled driftwood and reed beds that never went away, Jericho was the first organized golf club in British Columbia, and the first playable course on the mainland.

The organizational meeting for the formation of the club was called in the offices of Wulffsohn, Bewicke & Co., at 524 West Cordova Street, in November 1892, by Dr. Duncan Bell-Irving, a Scot who had arrived in 1883 and became Vancouver's first medical doctor. Bell-Irving was appointed secretary.

As the man in charge of the club's meager funds, the resourceful Dr. Bell-Irving set about building a clubhouse by expending only ten dollars to purchase logs from a fisherman. He elicited a twenty-five-dollar donation from a visitor to the city named Robert Austin, who obviously was a keen golfer. With no wooden floor in the shack that was the clubhouse, the members stashed their possessions in the bare ground and sand. Private cellars, or caches, were also hidden outside under driftwood for safekeeping.

Dr. Duncan Bell-Irving arrived from Scotland in 1883 and was Vancouver's first doctor. A founding member of the Vancouver Golf Club at Jericho, in November 1892, he was the club's first secretary. BC GOLF HOUSE 007.128.176

John Moody Dalgleish owned property that included a house built in 1870 by Jeremiah Rogers, one of the area's early settlers. The name Jericho was derived from Jerry's Cove, home of Rogers's Hastings Sawmill Company. Dalgleish had also acquired a lease on part of the adjoining Admiralty Reserve, including flats and marshland, for $100 a year. Dalgleish was especially enthusiastic about the golf course project, having spent his boyhood days at St Andrews. Wearing a red coat, the old man wandered the course on weekends, watching the play. The flow of language on the links reminded him of home, often bringing tears to his eyes.

The course was accessible from town only by boat or by hiking through the bushy telegraph trail that followed the shoreline, and the destination did not always justify the journey. Driftwood deposited by tides on fairways of sand, rock and seaweed constantly had to be hauled aside. Errant shots often found sloughs or alit under logs, though a local rule permitted removal of any loose impediments without penalty. Equipment was extremely scarce in golf's first days on the mainland shores. Most members possessed only a cleek and regularly had to replace shattered shafts by purchasing a hickory bull-punch and whittling new ones. Gutty balls were remoulded in a homemade press which one enterprising member, W.M. Hayes, had made out of Babbitt metal and a used letterpress. Later that first year, C.E. Tisdal stocked his store on Cordova Street with golfing apparatus.

The Jericho golfers were forced to abandon the site in the winter of 1894 after a fierce gale and extraordinarily high tides ruined the primitive links beyond repair. Undaunted, the pioneer members reorganized the following year and relocated to Brockton Point in Stanley Park. The Bell-Irvings were on the greens committee and honorary presidents were Cameron Sweeny and Colonel Alfred St. George Hamersley, a name that was inextricably connected to the founding of Vancouver and North Vancouver and to the introduction of hop-farming in Agassiz. The wives and female relatives of the club's first officers were honorary members.

The nine-hole course at Brockton Point was laid out to follow the line fences save two holes, which boldly crossed the cricket and lacrosse grounds. By the end of 1897, the club's golfers had grown weary of clamouring for space at busy Brockton and they missed playing on Sundays. City bylaws prohibited all games on the Sabbath, a restriction that the Scots members had grown up with but one that sat badly with other members. Encouraged by a persuasive Hamersley, they relinquished the Stanley Park course and ventured across the inlet to the foot of the North Shore's cloud-cloaked mountains.

Moodyville was the site of the most extensive lumber mill north of Puget Sound and the chief townsite on Burrard Inlet until the railway linked Vancouver to the east. Land was plentiful on the Moodyville flats east of Lonsdale Avenue, the ribbon that rose out of the water as North Vancouver's first major roadway. An open area between the mouths of Lynn Creek and Seymour River had been used occasionally as a rifle range. At a meeting on the night of December 22, 1897, Bell-Irving, in his capacity as golf club secretary, reported that he had interviewed about 30 players who were willing to continue their membership at the proposed new locale on the north shore of the inlet. E.M. Chaldecott and R. Byron-Johnson were duly appointed to negotiate a three-year lease for about 30 acres of the rifle range for $100 per annum. The annual membership subscription was fixed at five dollars.

Before the spring of 1898, the members were playing a nine-hole Moodyville course that measured approximately 1,700 yards. The fourth hole was the longest at 310 yards, and required two wooden shots and an iron. The distance of the shortest, the ninth, was appropriately listed as "short." Construction of the impromptu links cost thirty-five dollars. The work was undertaken by Tom Wilson, a district fruit inspector, and two labourers under the supervision of L.B. Keyser, Dr. Jack Carruthers and Chaldecott. They created a bridge to cross Lynn Creek by felling a tree and cutting footways, at an added cost of ten dollars. Dr. Bell-Irving donated a garden roller for the greens and Captain Marshall provided a steam launch to deliver the implement from Vancouver. The S.S. *Senator* provided a regular triangular ferry schedule between Vancouver, Moodyville and Lonsdale, transporting golfers to the course. The club was headquartered at Moodyville Hotel, then under the management of A.J. "Sandy" MacPherson who had reputedly been a pupil of Old Tom Morris, the famed St Andrews pro, from whom he had certainly acquired a croucher's stance if nothing else.

The S.S. *Senator* had been built at Moodyville in 1880 for the Moodyville Ferry Co., which later that decade consolidated with Burrard Inlet Towing to form Union Steamships Co. Men commuted daily on the vessel to their workplaces in Vancouver, regularly taking the 7:45 or 9:15 AM sailings, armed with empty half-gallon cans. When they returned on the 5:15 PM sailing their cans were filled with fresh milk.

On the shores of English Bay, the Jericho course, seen here *circa* 1937, eventually gave way to the training needs of the Canadian military. CITY OF VANCOUVER ARCHIVES CVA-1042

However, the travel time and inconvenience discouraged the Vancouver golfers, and the Moodyville club was dissolved in June 1899. Hamersley, never one to miss a business opportunity, formed a company to take over the existing ferry service. By the middle of 1904 he had launched a double-ended boat that accommodated 1,000 passengers and 12 teams of horses with wagons. The ferry was named *St. George* after the company president.

From 1899 through 1905 there was no golf in Vancouver until the original club reorganized once again and returned to English Bay. The CPR had made an abortive attempt to revive the game in 1902 on property between 33rd and 37th, west of Granville and opposite the future site of the Shaughnessy Heights course. But after the land had been cleared and prepared for seeding at an expenditure of $3,600, the golf scheme was scrapped in favour of a housing project. The game was played at an improvised course named New Westminster Golf Club in New Westminster's Moody Square from about 1894 through 1907 and was the only course in play until 1905 when the original course in Vancouver at Jericho was resurrected.

Hamersley returned to his native England in 1906 to retire. But he couldn't sit still. He subsequently served eight years as a member of parliament and at the age of 67 saw action in the First World War. He died at his Oxfordshire birthplace in 1929.

In 1905 a 123-member Vancouver group intent on establishing a permanent home for local golf and other sporting grounds purchased eight acres of the old Rogers homestead, including numerous outbuildings, from John Moody Dalgleish, and also negotiated to lease 69 acres of the Admiralty Reserve, sufficient land for a course. Construction commenced in late 1905, and intent on avoiding a repeat of their original problems, they first built substantial dikes and installed a drainage system. Funds were allocated to road making and restoration of the original residence for a clubhouse under the supervision of architect W.H. Archer.

The club aimed to cater to a broad sporting audience. Soon tennis, bowling and croquet lawns were seeded and fences and jumps erected for Hunt Club members. Moorings for yachts and a landing float were installed, an 80-foot tower was erected for clay pigeon practice, and badminton and squash courts were added for winter indoor sport. Jericho was a true country club set to appeal to the city's population, which was rapidly mushrooming toward 85,000.

BC'S FIRST CLUB PROS AT JERICHO

In November 1908 Albert Kam was hired as the Vancouver area's first golf professional and his wife took charge as Jericho's housekeeper. However it was the June 1910 arrival of Kam's successor, Alex Duthie, that would define the early years of the Jericho course. Duthie was a transplanted mason, originally from Carnoustie, who arrived at Jericho after learning the trade in South Africa, Australia, New Zealand, California and Portland, Oregon.

Duthie's first pro appointment in 1902 was at Transvaal near a military base. Most members were officers and one of Duthie's regular opponents was Major MacPherson, the chaplain. "Early in my career," he often said of his formative years in South Africa, "I learned to speak gently to the ball." After surviving San Francisco's 1907 earthquake, Duthie finally

Jericho pro Alex Duthie aided the design of many early courses around Vancouver.
BC SPORTS HALL OF FAME

made his way north in the fall of 1909. He spent his first Canadian winter at Esquimalt's Macaulay Point course before landing at Jericho.

Duthie almost immediately rearranged Jericho's original nine in 1910. He subsequently assisted in the design of what was initially called the British Columbia Golf Club at Coquitlam in 1911 and soon started Jericho's expansion to 18 holes, an extended undertaking finally completed in 1924. Duthie remained a fixture at Jericho until the property was requisitioned by the government as a Second World War military headquarters and training base; he then worked at the Capilano course in West Vancouver during the war. He died in 1947 at the age of 70.

BC GOLF CLUB (VANCOUVER GOLF CLUB)

In 1910, the year Thomas Edison introduced talking pictures to the world, a group of hardy Scots assembled in downtown Vancouver on November 22 to establish the Fraser Valley Golf Club. Obviously P.R. Brooke, J.R. Brown, F.J. Furnivall, J.R. Duncan and H.E.A. Robertson had gathered previously to plan the new club, as a club seal was presented for approval and the club name changed to BC Golf Club.

By December 5 the first 150 members had been admitted for $100 with "$10 payable on application, $15 on allotment and the balance when called upon, but no greater amount than $25 to be asked for at any one time and 15 days' notice to be given for each call." It was agreed that the first 50 women could join for ten dollars. As secretary-treasurer, Furnivall accepted the share applications.

The provisional directors agreed to put $500 down toward the $60,000 price of the 200-acre Austin farm "near New Westminster." The January 31, 1911, sale agreement called for $3,000 cash immediately, $8,000 by February 28 and the balance in six equal annual installments at 7.5 percent interest. An order was placed with William Gibsons & Co. Ltd. of Kinghorn, Fife, for 50 six-piece sets of the finest hickories, a half gross of extra drivers and brassies, one gross of new balls and a half gross of remade balls.

The start-up expenditures were onerous. A team of horses from Mainland Transfer Co. cost $500—$200 up front with the balance paid at $50 per month at 7 percent interest—and a horse-drawn roller was found in Seattle for $36, excluding freight, duty and brokerage. Charles Locke, from Tacoma Country Club, got a four-month contract as pro. It paid $100 per month with a tent on site for living quarters.

An area known as tent alley housed club employees and course labourers for several years, and bushes between tents were the only washroom facilities. The encampment was just beyond the present back parking

Teams of horses were used to uproot trees and clear the planned
fairways at Vancouver Golf Club in 1912. COQUITLAM 100 YEARS

and 10th tee. The original Austin farmhouse, which was situated almost
directly east of the fifth green, served as a clubhouse until 1915 when a
larger, more appropriate building was completed. It was converted into
a caddy shack and pro shop while a small house near the current first tee
was provided for Tom Gallop, who remained as the club's second pro
through 1919.

Several months before the course was ready for play, 100 people had
signed up for membership to the course in the hinterland. By opening
day it boasted 180 male members and 20 women. The club's original
concept was as a golfing retreat from the city for Vancouver businessmen; Jericho was the only other mainland alternative and the links off
English Bay were overflowing with golfers. In heralding the club's formation, the *Saturday Sunset* newspaper ran an extensive feature story with
two photographs.

Traffic to the VGC clubhouse was via the Sapperton tram and this two-horse democrat. The BCGC on the side stands for the short-lived original name, BC Golf Club. COQUITLAM 100 YEARS

To make a golf course is usually a matter of years. One notable exception to this rule, however, is the British Columbia Golf Club Limited, which has probably established a new golf history in having a nine-hole course ready in something like two months.

When workers on the playing field received their cheques at the end of last month (May) it was the second month's salary expended in creating what in a short time should become one the finest courses on the continent. What it has taken other clubs years to accomplish has been done by the B.C. Golf Club in months.

The original course opened on June 24, 1911, with about 100 people present. The leaders were Furnivall, club president Phil Brooks, A.P. Foster and James Yellowlees, who became first club champion. Next came pro Charles Locke and Jericho's Alex Duthie, who received ten dollars for

The old Austin farmhouse served as VGC's original clubhouse and
was a popular Sunday afternoon meeting place. COQUITLAM 100 YEARS

his appearance. The Saturday proceedings didn't go entirely smoothly.
The automobile tallyho hired for sixty dollars to convey golfers from
the Sapperton Station on the B.C. Electric Railway line broke down,
forcing them to hike more than a mile to the course. Later, a light
horse-and-buckboard and three-seat democrat were purchased to haul
supplies from New Westminster and to meet the Sapperton tram.

Before the land had been purchased, about 70 acres of the 190-acre
parcel had been cleared. The original nine consisted of the present 1st,
4th, 5th, 6th, 9th, 17th and 18th and two practice fairways. Mike
Gardner, a charter member and civil engineer, designed the second
nine in concert with Duthie. A Russian work crew started clearing
the 10th fairway in 1914 but they were discharged because of the
language barrier and labour difficulties. They were replaced by workers from India.

With completion of the second nine in 1916, the men from tent
alley could play the full 18 before dinner. Their wives met them with
gasoline lanterns to guide them through the final holes and back home.

VGC's post-war pro, Jimmy Huish, ever-present pipe in place, tees off from a wooden tee box.
ARV OLSON COLLECTION

Construction of the clubhouse started in 1914. The U-shaped building stood in the parking lot immediately north of the current 18th green and had a 150-foot frontage facing the final green. The men's dormitory above the west wing remained unfinished due to financial constraints, but any member who paid to finish an upstairs room could use it free of charge for a specified period. And it seems that while there, a member could set his own house rules. H.A. Stewart, historian of the club's early years, recalls a framed motto on the wall of Mr. McAdam's room: "Swearing in this room is forbidden, not that we give a damn. But it sounds like hell to strangers."

In 1917 the club bought a McLaughlin Buick to use as a bus from Sapperton and Mr. Cowan of Skelmorlie, Scotland, accepted seventy-five dollars per month as greenskeeper. Jimmy Huish came from the United Service Club at Esquimalt via Royal Colwood to be the new pro in 1920. He had accompanied Billy Moffat to Victoria Golf Club in 1910 from Mussleburgh, Scotland, and moved to United Service during the war.

From 1914 through 1945, the club faced one problem after another. A 1921 fire destroyed timber left of the 11th fairway. Debts mounted and, as they showed no sign of diminishing, entrance fees were waived to attract potential members, clubhouse staff were dismissed November through February and pro Don Sutherland's salary was discontinued until further notice. On November 15, 1937, the night before Premier Thomas Duff Pattullo opened the new $4 million Pattullo Bridge spanning the Fraser River, the clubhouse burned to the ground. Many regulars were forced to relinquish their memberships and weekend visits by members who resided and worked in Vancouver dropped, partly because of the remoteness of the course. During the war years when the club couldn't afford a pro, Sutherland and his brother Hamish, who had been his assistant, were forced to earn their living at Fraser Mills. Although they weren't retained during or after the Second World War, the Sutherlands devoted themselves to the club. They gave lessons, repaired clubs and acted as starters. Manager Bill Kirby operated the pro shop until 1950.

Following the First World War, the club's debts had been gradually erased through various financial manipulations such as deferred shares, convertible debentures and ordinary shares. The directors converted a lawn bowling green to a putting-chipping area, scrapped plans for tennis courts and dropped the "country" from the club name, which had been Vancouver Golf and Country Club.

During the Depression, the Vancouver Golf Club (VGC) remained viable by operating illegal slot machines. The police always telephoned in advance to announce their pending arrival for the purpose of checking the premises. The local constabulary obviously was not without avid golfers.

In 1932, associate and shareholder members were accepted without entrance fees. The following spring, pro Sutherland's salary resumed but at only fifty dollars a month and with a provision that he provide a starter on weekends. In the fall of 1933 the clubhouse was closed, except for the locker rooms and the men's bar. From November through February the only staff members retained were the club secretary and a steward.

Frank Cotton, a New Westminster native who joined the club in 1931 for $100, won the club championship five times and played until the age of 88, recalls that some expenses were offset by a green-fee surcharge of twenty-five cents per round.

The fire of 1937 was a huge setback. The clubhouse, only partly covered by insurance, was valued at about $45,000 while personal effects lost in 100 lockers were estimated at $10,000. Member Charlie Smith, a well-known insurance and financial businessman, spearheaded the drive to raise funds through debentures for a new clubhouse.

The club has survived by selling parcels of property in times of crisis. Cotton, a former sheriff of New Westminster, lives in a house he had built on 2.5 acres off Austin Road that he purchased from the club in 1945.

The upper level of the original clubhouse included a dormitory and six bedrooms that were rented to bachelors on weekend visits and for private parties during club dances. Cotton remembers that two golfers lived permanently upstairs for a time before joining Shaughnessy Heights.

The layout of the VGC course has undergone many alterations over the years, outdating course records. The most recent changes, with new greens at the 10th and 15th holes, have lengthened the course considerably as the course prepares to host the CN Canadian Women's Open in August 2012.

DON SUTHERLAND

Twenty-nine-year-old Don Sutherland arrived at VGC in 1929 directly from Inverness, Scotland, where he worked as greenskeeper for three years. Sutherland grew up with golf on his front doorstep. He and his twin brother, Andrew, were born in a house no more than 25 paces from the turf of the Royal Dornoch course.

Sutherland's prowess as a player and his quiet disposition didn't go unnoticed very long at Burquitlam. He had won county and district championships and the North of Scotland Amateur several times. The "Silent Scot" quickly established himself at VGC, where his 64 stood as a record until the course changed. He was three times BC Open runner-up before winning in his fifth start, in 1934 at Royal Colwood. An exceptional shot maker, he rarely counted more than 80 strokes even after his 80th birthday.

The staunchly traditional Sutherland passed through the clubhouse doors only for special occasions and only when he was invited—even in retirement after he was made a life member. After golfing with members, he never joined them for post-game refreshments. He never forgot that in his culture the men's lounge was out of bounds to professionals; it wasn't the pro's place to socialize with members.

In retirement the Sutherland brothers played together frequently during midweek, teeing off at dawn's earliest light. As they were putting out on 18, the day's first foursomes of members were gathering at the first tee. With his golf bag strapped over his shoulder, the unobtrusive old pro slipped down the practice fairway to his Walker Street house, less than half a block from the club's Austin Road entrance. Sutherland removed his spikes before crossing Austin, retrieving the street shoes he had strung over an evergreen's branch upon arrival at the course.

When his brother Hamish dropped dead of a heart attack on the practice fairway in 1978 before Don's eyes, he was devastated. He had already seen his twin brother killed while both were in France with the Blackwatch during the war. After Hamish's death, Sutherland had to ask pro Al Nelson to lead him to the locker room to gather his brother's belongings; he didn't know the way.

Sutherland didn't keep track of the times he broke his age. Deadly accurate with driver and putter, he had learned at Dornoch the art of deftly playing pitch-and-run and mashie shots off close lies to firm fast greens. In May 1980 his par 32-40-72 was nine strokes under his age. In 1983, after the death of his wife, Sutherland returned to the land he loved so dearly. The remarkable octogenarian enjoyed many rounds on Dornoch's links before passing away in 1990 after reaching his 91st birthday.

ERNIE TATE

In 1950, Ernie Tate became professional to Jericho, where he had once caddied with brothers Alf, John and George. Ernie was the best player in the family. After winning the 1935 City caddy championship at Jericho, he chose golf for a career and served eight different courses.

In his formative pro years playing out of Marine Drive, Tate fared well in tournaments. In the 1931 Open he tied Davey Black for fourth and placed seventh in 1936 and fifth in 1937 after moving to Powell River. He later joined the army but upon discharge he inherited Fraserview's pro post, which had been vacated by Hal Rhodes in 1946. At the southeast Vancouver public course he encountered Alvin Nelson. Nelson couldn't get enough golf. When he wasn't caddying, he was playing or hitting balls after school. He hung around so much that Tate put him to work in the back shop.

Tate preferred playing and teaching over tending to pro shop business, which might explain why he served so many clubs. He tutored Nelson, who won the 1948 City Junior championship before turning pro under Tate's guardianship. Tate also operated clinics at the Grandview Acres driving range, hiring Nelson and Malcolm Tapp as his teaching assistants.

ALVIN NELSON

When Tate went to Vancouver Golf Club in 1950, Alvin Nelson found his way to Revelstoke after one season at Winnipeg St. Charles. Revelstoke hired the engaging 19-year-old in March 1951 as pro and greenskeeper charged with cutting the greens and changing the hole locations and pin placements. Nelson—later known as Smilin' Al Nelson—received $150 monthly from May 15 through September 15, plus the concessions to balls, clubs, equipment and rental carts and a place to display the items, if he so wished. Nelson's special rate for six lessons was ten dollars.

After a second season at Revelstoke, Nelson returned to the Lower Mainland and West Vancouver where he spent two years at Gleneagles. There he posted a record 27 with a hole-in-one, before the nine-hole course near Horseshoe Bay was remodelled.

Nelson next went to VGC in Burquitlam, replacing his mentor Tate in

1954. Smilin' Al lit up that pro shop for the next 35 years before retiring in 1989. "When I took over, the club was advertising for members," says Nelson. "It cost $175 to join, a $75 initiation fee and a $100 refundable share. At that time the public was welcome to play when the members weren't booked; the club needed the $7.50 green fees." Nelson played within his limitations and recognized that his career was in the pro shop and not on the course. He epitomized the ideal club pro, serving members with an ever-ready smile. Nelson made four City Match Play finals but lacked tournament toughness and couldn't put away the likes of Lyle Crawford or Bob Cox.

The course, which has been called Johnston's Alley, underwent dramatic changes during Nelson's tenure. With an exquisite short game, Johnny Johnston thrived on VGC's treacherously slippery greens and dominated the annual New Westminster Amateur.

Few original greens remain and hundreds of trees have disappeared. Nelson estimates that 4,500 trees on the property were uprooted by the infamous Typhoon Freda in October 1962. Towering evergreens were strewn like matchsticks throughout the property, leaving only seven holes playable. The two-week cleanup costs were offset by selling fallen timber to a local mill. Freda toppled trees at most Lower Mainland courses. On the North Shore Seymour lost 500 while New Shaughnessy and Fraserview lost 100 each, and Old Shaughnessy, Langara and University all lost 50. Lesser-hit courses included Capilano and Gleneagles in West Vancouver; Point Grey, Marine Drive and McCleery in the city lost a total of about 100 trees.

VGC became exclusive to members and their guests in 1965 following a decision by the board of directors that included the sale of two acres on the southwest corner of the course for $250,000. The lost land did not greatly affect the layout of the course, and required alterations only to the sixth and seventh holes. The 620-yard sixth didn't actually play as long until modern irrigation was in place. Only two flushed woods would leave occasional eagle putts on the old and new sixth green. The funds from the land sale were used to install an automatic sprinkling system. Until then a 40,000-gallon water tank off the 11th fairway, the highest elevation on the course, had maintained only the tees and greens. Without water the fairways were parched brown and hard as concrete by early spring.

For reasons members can't explain, VGC probably produces more winning pro-amateur teams than all the other city courses combined. The members, among the area's most enthusiastic gamblers, scoff at sandbagging accusations. The names of Ken Matheson and Barney Denomy readily come to mind as frequent pro-am winners, and Bill Hill stooped pretty low when he drew George Knudson in the pro-am of the 1966 Canadian Open at Shaughnessy.

After the Knudson foursome walked off with the blue-ribbon prizes, thanks to Hill's contributions, the car dealership owner attributed his exceptional play to a zombie-like state. Hill had been hypnotized the night before. Appropriately, he was president of Fogg Motors.

SHAUGHNESSY

While Alex Duthie was lending his expertise to help create the British Columbia course on the old Austin farm in Coquitlam, a third regional course to be known as Shaughnessy Heights was taking shape on CPR-owned property that had been logged and then abandoned in 1903. Land between modern-day 33rd and 37th streets east of Granville had been evacuated pending the railway's development of a suitable residential project. Richard Marpole, CPR president and a man of vision, revived the scheme and announced the plan for a golf course. Within 18 months, by November 1912, a nine-hole course stood on what had been a tangle of stumps, rock and swamp.

Marpole was joined on the club's first board of directors by B.M. Humble, W.E. Burns, H.E. Ridley, W. Fordham-Johnson, John Hope, W. McMullen, J.H. Poff and E.A.C. Studd. They had a 20-year lease with the CPR.

In September 1912, Willard Bowden was appointed Shaughnessy's first pro for a stipend of seventy-five dollars per month with an additional fifteen dollars if his wife attended to the clubhouse. The initial roster boasted 178 members who paid a fifty-dollar entry fee, and despite fluctuations on the rolls there was soon a waiting list. By August 1913 membership ceilings were established at 325 men and 225 women. A full 18 holes became playable after two additional parcels of adjoining land were leased from the CPR to bring the total to 103 acres.

Shaughnessy wasn't in prime condition in 1928 when Davey Black won the inaugural BC Open with 292 on his home course, 13 strokes over runner-up Dunc Sutherland of Point Grey. In what proved the club's most colossal blunder, short-sighted members voted to accept a CPR property lease extension through 1940 over an attractive alternative offer from the government, who had put forward a proposal for collaboration on the development of a new course on 130 acres at the University Endowment Lands. The government planned to expend $130,000 to clear the property and install a sprinkling system if the private club agreed to spend $150,000 for course and clubhouse construction within three years of execution of a 40-year lease. The government proceeded on its own and built the Macan-designed University course in time for a 1930 opening.

When the CPR informed Shaughnessy in 1947 that their lease wouldn't be extended beyond 1960, club directors procrastinated for six years. A special committee was finally appointed to study the feasibility of buying the CPR property or relocating. The railway was willing to sell at fair market value, between $1.5 million and $2 million, but club directors considered the proposition unsound. They wanted a new clubhouse and service buildings thrown in.

The Endowment Lands were again considered as a new locale along with several other properties before the club decided to lease 160 acres on the Musqueam Indian Reserve off Southwest Marine Drive. A.V. Macan of Victoria was commissioned to design the new course in the late 1950s. The club directors permitted Macan to build a course that he swore would

Three fires have destroyed Shaughnessy clubhouses, the first two at the old course in 1916 and 1930 and the third at its new location on New Year's Day 1982. The third fire destroyed club records and extensive memorabilia.

challenge the leading pros. In the fall of 1966 Don Massengale won the Canadian Open at New Shaughnessy with four rounds of 70. Less than three years later, architect Norman Woods and agronomist Dr. Roy Coss reduced the course's length and severity by rebuilding the greens and tees. Old Quilchena, born in 1925, didn't live to be 30. Macan designed the original par-74, 6,630-yard layout on which two BC Amateur and four BC Open championships were conducted.

QUILCHENA AND THE NEW QUILCHENA

Old Quilchena, born in 1925, didn't live to be 30. A.V. Macan designed the original par-74, 6,630-yard layout on which two BC Amateur and four BC Open championships were conducted. The CPR spent $150,000 in 1925 to build the private club on 140 acres bounded by 25th and 33rd avenues, near the old B.C. Electric interurban tracks and Arbutus Street. *Quilchena* means "running or sweet water," and is taken from the First Nations name of the salmon-rearing creek that meandered through the course. The Arbutus area was also known as Asthma Flats or Consumption Hollow because of the heavy fogs in fall.

Dr. G.F. Strong and A. J. Cowan headed a 15-man group that quickly enlisted more than 200 members who were playing 9 holes by late 1925 and the full 18 the following July.

Bill Mawhinney, Dick Moore, Jimmy Robertson, Dorothy Silcock Chandler and Jim Burgess were among the notable early members. The first pro was Art Sheppard, followed by Billy Barr, Dave McLeod, Fred Wood, Ernie Brown through 1954 and, for its final gasp, Bill Mawhinney in 1957–58.

In Quilchena's first major event, the 1935 Amateur championship, Dick Moore sank his second shot at the 34th hole to overtake Stan Leonard. Leonard took the most memorable BC Open and last major tournament there 19 years later, a marathon playoff over Johnny Langford in 1954. When the CPR started to get out of the golf business, it announced that Quilchena would be the first course to go. Shaughnessy Heights was warned that it was also on the chopping list. The Quilchena lease expired in 1954 and Vancouver's city council dismissed a preserve-the-course lobby, knowing that subdivision of the prime land would increase the city's tax revenue more than tenfold to $230,000.

The club members, headed by president Ernie Farmer, provisionally purchased 80 acres of what is now the McCleery course for a new site. But they failed to obtain an additional 22 acres required to construct 18 holes and went instead to the northwest corner of Richmond. Many members were disenchanted with the more remote location and chose to join other clubs. Known in its early days for washboard fairways, grainy greens and hazardous Fraser delta swamplands, the course survived its notoriety as a "goat ranch." However, New Quilchena improved dramatically over three decades after it opened in 1957. An extensive, ongoing remodelling program has converted it into a course worthy of championship events.

With former pro Cecil "Cec" Ferguson at the helm, the 1990 Transamerica Canadian PGA championships were an unqualified success at Quilchena, with Victoria touring pro Rick Gibson coming home the winner. Jim Burgess, a founding member of both Quilchenas, was there to see the championship. Burgess, a lifelong golfer, was a sight to behold, continuing to play despite serious health problems. He finally succumbed in early 1992 to the recurring poliomyelitis he had so courageously endured for almost all of his 75 years. In his last years, Burgess frequently fell flat on his face when his crutches gave way in soft turf as he played shots. He always picked himself up and tried again.

CHAPTER 4

GOLF ON VANCOUVER ISLAND AND THE GULF ISLANDS

Golf fever spread throughout British Columbia with the emergence of company towns tied to mining and forestry and the initiatives of pioneer settlers with an affinity for the game. As golf evolved, the PGA BC and BC Golf emerged as the main organizing forces for the province's golfing community and divided the province into five golfing regions: The Interior, The North, The Kootenays, The Lower Mainland and Vancouver Island.

COWICHAN VALLEY

The seeds of golf were sown on Vancouver Island beyond Victoria on farm fields in the Cowichan Valley, probably in the late 1890s, by Fred Maitland-Dougal, a gentleman farmer who had arrived in the valley from England in 1886. By that time tennis had already taken hold. The South Cowichan Tennis Club, established in 1887, today remains the only lawn tennis club in Canada, a fate dictated in part because use of the land was bequeathed in perpetuity on the condition that tennis be played there on grass courts.

The first golf club, named Koksilah, was established on polo grounds at Colonel Pridham's farm about a mile south of Duncan in 1909. Selwyn E. Hatfield won the first WW Bundock Bogey Competition Cup there in 1910. Maitland-Dougal died in 1916, and Koksilah died around the same time as many of its members went off to fight in the First World War. When the troops returned, Captain J. Gell supervised the development of a new course at the Cowichan Station townsite on either side of the railway tracks (a present-day Safeway site). H.W. May's apple orchard off Bench Road served as a makeshift golf course for more than a decade and E.W. Carr-Hilton, a local bank manager who had organized Duncan's first cricket club in 1911, was instrumental in starting golf on Cowichan reserve lands off Trunk Road in 1920.

The valley provided the largest enlistment per capita in the country for the Second World War, leaving the club a major casualty again. The remaining members couldn't meet the $600-per-annum lease with the tribal council and after 23 years it expired in October 1943.

The course on the present Cowichan Golf & Country Club site, about four kilometres south of Duncan adjacent to the Island Highway, was designed in 1947 by A.V. Macan. Premier John Hart drove the first ball at the official opening on August 21, 1949. The opening celebrations included an exhibition match in which Duncan's own Ben Colk and Dave Crane, shooting 70 and 74, defeated Phil Taylor and Ron McLeod 4 and 3.

Jack Egger captured the inaugural Cowichan Open in 1953. One of the Island's most popular annual events, it has had many multiple winners, including Art Donaldson, Vaughn Trapp, Bob Fleming, Jim Rutledge, Dick Munn, Bill McColl and Bill Wakeham.

Expansion to 18 holes finally came in 1984, followed by a new clubhouse in 1989. The modern facilities attracted the E.C. Amateur in 1990 and the 1991 Payless-Pepsi Open. Ontario pro Rick Todd won the Canadian Tour's opening event with a 262 total, closing with 63 that he started bogey-bogey. It fell one stroke short of Nanaimo golfer Jamie Harper's course record. Cowichan has been managed by Bob Kidd's protégé, the irrepressible Stormin' Norm Jackson who joined the club in 1990 and was head pro at time of writing. Often recognized for his club-fitting skills, Jackson was recognized in 1993 as the PGA BC's best pro.

MID-ISLAND

The game also germinated mid-Island, first at Qualicum in 1913, then in Nanaimo, Comox and Courtenay. With a promised railway under construction, Qualicum Beach basically formed around a hotel and the golf course. In 1912 the Merchants Trust and Trading Company had constructed a stately hotel overlooking the sandy shores and the site for the proposed 18-hole course. The first nine opened the following year, but because of the war the second nine was never completed. Despite its auspicious beginning, Merchants Trust had moved into bankruptcy protection by 1915.

In his book *Qualicum Beach: Vancouver Island's Best Kept Secret*, Brad Wylie calls the bankruptcy of Merchants Trust one of the town's great mysteries. General Noel Money resigned as project manager to rejoin his old English regiment and the federal government converted the hotel into a convalescent hospital for wounded officers, some of whom played the neglected course. The enterprising General Money returned in 1920 and revived the course—originally it had no bunkers and thick links-type broom surrounded the fairways and greens—and hotel, turning them into first-class facilities. During the Depression Money couldn't pay Frank Topliffe, who followed Captain Ned Kennedy as greenskeeper, and instead gave him three building lots for his services.

Tourists flocked to the friendly shoreline and some families, unable to afford the hotel, camped on the beaches and fished for salmon out of rowboats available for five dollars a week. Their boys gravitated to the course to caddy, and were joined by others who came on their own from Nanaimo and Victoria. Pros Phil Taylor, Alex Marling and Art Sheppard took advantage of slow summer weeks at their Victoria courses to teach the visitors to Qualicum.

In 1938 Vancouver businessmen Frank Oliver White, Fred Sweet and Leonard Boultbee purchased the course and hotel from Money for a reported $50,000. The course changed hands again in 1950 when Calgarian R.A. Brown bought it. His widow, Mrs. Genevieve Brown, sold the course to the township of Qualicum in 1981 for a reported $1 million. Today the course, the fourth-oldest in the province, is known for its year-round play and lovely new clubhouse.

Nanaimo's original course on rocky acreage on Wakesiah Avenue was leased from the Western Fuel Company in 1920. A narrow bridge over the Millstream River joined the course to the first clubhouse, today known as the Quarterway Hotel, located on Bowen Road. The barren 86 acres served the members well, but in 1948, the New Course Committee, headed by Stan Dyde, was formed in anticipation of finding property that would be suitable for an 18-hole course.

The purchase of 123 acres from Lynburn Estates for $10,000 in 1951 came complete with several problems. At the time, residential lots ranged from $1,200 to $1,800; with confirmation of the course sale, they rose to $3,600–$5,500. The club had no money, the property no visible water. The members got a $1,000 loan from George Siborne, a golfer who managed Nanaimo's Royal Bank, for the down payment on the property, with the balance to be paid at $75 monthly at 4 percent interest. Water was discovered in an old coal mine shaft 100 yards from the course property and 400 feet below the surface. The mine shaft was quickly purchased from owner Mr. Inch when more than 500 gallons of water per minute discharged from three pumps over a 48-hour period.

The founding members—Larry Harris, Elmer Bradshaw, Don Cunliffe, Don Allis, Ken Alexander and Bert Pichard—were patient. Macan designed the course but resources from the issuance of 1,000 common shares at $250 permitted the completion of only 14 holes by 1962; the remaining holes opened in 1968. Mike Rivers served the club for 40 years as professional, manager and superintendent through 1990.

Jim Nelford captured the 1975 BC Amateur at Nanaimo after a sudden-death playoff with Doug Roxburgh. They had tied at 289, one over par. The course's degree of difficulty is emphasized by the modest competitive records—67s by Roxburgh and Jamie Harper and a 73 by Vernon's Jackie Little. In co-hosting the 1990 BC Amateur with Cowichan, Nanaimo yielded only one sub-par round, veteran Dave Mick's 70. Only champion Rob Anderson, with a pair of 73s, and Mick broke 150 over the final two days. Winds that reached 40 kilometres per hour buffeted the course during the final round.

By the time of the 1931 census, Courtenay and the nearby coal mining community of Cumberland were home to only 3,500 residents, yet the

Comox Valley had two golf courses. The first club, on the Upper Road about four kilometres from Courtenay, was spearheaded by A.B. Dundas in the fall of 1922. The retired Coldstream Guards colonel convinced potential members to abandon earlier plans to build a course on the huge Robb Estate. Instead they leased 89 acres of the Westwood Estate from Whittcome & Co. of Nanaimo for $160 a year, and exercised an option to purchase the land for $8,500 in July 1923. The property had been used previously for practice and some locals had been permitted to hit shots on two improvised holes. Memberships for what was called the Sandwick course included 30 women whose five-dollar annual fee entitled them to play Mondays and Thursdays.

As there was no clubhouse until 1926, club secretary John Aitken called meetings at City Hall for the 62 members. A 1928 match between teams of married men and bachelors culminated in a victory for the married men, among them Aitken, Herbert Cooke, Tom Graham, Robert Filberg, George Tarbell and Hugh Cliffe. The next day's headline in the local paper proclaimed: "Get married and improve your game."

While Sandwick was being organized, the nearby Elk Hotel in Comox retained A.M. Fairbairn of Victoria to create a private course of 2,500 yards. By 1934 lumber tycoon Bob Filberg had gained control of the hotel's course. He concluded that the valley could support only one facility—his new Comox acquisition. The clubs amalgamated, with Graham, Aitken and Mrs. S.H. Cliffe elected chief executive officers. Sandwick pro-greenskeeper Johnnie Stevenson went to the Comox course, taking all the club trophies with him.

Sandwick, however, wasn't forgotten. Joe Idiens, a local businessman, purchased and renamed the course Sunnydale. It opened for play two weeks after the Comox–Sandwick merger. Sunnydale underwent four more ownership changes between 1943 and 1976.

The second of these owners, Elsie, operated the course from 1945 to 1951 and after he obtained a liquor licence in 1947 the club became a real social centre in the community. Elsie was famed for his advertisement in local newspapers: "Why follow the birds to Victoria when you can get a chicken dinner at Sunnydale for a $1.25." Elsie sold

Sunnydale to Fred Richardson of Victoria and he in turn was bought out in 1966 by four pilots in the 442 Squadron stationed at Comox: Doug and Frank Metcalfe, Earle Neil and Ed Riley. After a decade of ups and downs they decided to sell and considered parcelling out the land. In an effort to save the course, members formed the Sunnydale Golf Society and appealed to the provincial government who agreed to preserve the course for the community by buying it from the partnership for $525,000. The course property was brought into the city of Courtenay which provided both water and sewer services. Relying largely on volunteers and goodwill and material discounts from local suppliers, additional land was cleared and an irrigation reservoir completed. When the expanded 18-hole course opened in June 1983, Phil Bickle, Bill Finlayson and Doug Newson received special recognition for their efforts during six years of planning and construction of the second nine. In 2013 Sunnydale will celebrate its 90th year as a vibrant part of the Courtenay recreational scene.

In 1939 Bob Filberg had built a new Comox clubhouse. Slot machines in the lounge helped with club expenses until the one-arm bandits were outlawed. In 1966 philanthropist Filberg, whose home estate today remains the site of the annual Filberg Festival, bestowed ownership of the course on the township of Comox, stipulating that the central property remain a golf course for at least 99 years. Among the dominant Comox players were Owen Ellis, club champion 20 times from 1941 through 1975, and the pro's wife, Margaret Stevenson, who counted her last of seven titles in 1970.

Probably the most isolated course on Vancouver Island is the charming little nine-holer at Port Alice. Encouraged and aided by BC Pulp and Paper Co., an enthusiastic band of Scottish millworkers developed the course, with the original membership including 34 men and 17 women. The course was advertised as being open to men anytime except on Thursday afternoons and Sundays during divine services. Four hours of Thursday tee-times were reserved for distaff golfers and on Sunday mornings the church bells of St. Paul's, the small whitewashed Anglican church that looked over the first fairway, told the men when to cease playing, and then signalled permission to return to their game. "Absolutely no one played golf during Sunday service, as I remember," said Vi Gilmour, whose husband, Jim, was a founding member. "If the service started after the men had teed off, they were bound to retire to the clubhouse until church was over or they took off their cleated shoes and joined the congregation."

In 1929 there were five holes playable in a stumpy field of potatoes and cabbage. The expansion of the course to seven holes in 1931 and to nine in 1934 meant that the course literally revolved around St. Paul's. Ripley's Believe-It-Or-Not once listed Port Alice as the only course in the world with a church in the middle of it. It was a two-stroke penalty for encroaching on the church grounds and window replacement was seventy-five dollars. Play was very cautious around the church, to be sure. The course was also peculiar because of the protective barbed-wire fences around the greens that played havoc with approach shots. The fences kept farm animals from damaging the greens with hooves and droppings, explained long-time Vancouver Club member Bill McGhee, who grew up in Port Alice and was married at St. Paul's in 1945.

Golfers entered the greens through turnstile-type gates that discouraged animals. The mountainside course itself is known for its tree-lined fairways and small greens.

McGhee recalls that members had to initial their golf balls for identification purposes and there was a severe penalty for using someone else's marked ball. Part of the course was expropriated for victory gardens during the Second World War and the townsite was relocated at Ramble Beach, some four miles from the course. The church was abandoned and eventually demolished. One of the club's original, and classic, do's and don'ts could be carved above the door of any golf pro shop: "Don't allow enthusiasm to get the better of your arithmetic."

In 1982 a second north island course, Seven Hills Golf and Country Club, opened equidistant from the three main communities of the region, Port Hardy, Port McNeil and Port Alice. With RV sites on location it is an ideal stopover for the nomadic golfer who is exploring Vancouver Island.

The Port Alice course eventually encircled St Paul's Anglican Church. VI GILMOUR

OTHER VANCOUVER ISLAND COURSES

While it is impossible to document development histories of all the courses it is fair to say that golf has become an integral part of Vancouver Island life.

On the Saanich Peninsula, Cedar Hill Golf Course dates back to 1924; the first pro was former Victoria club pro Harry Eve. Other resident pros over the years were Dick Munn in the mid-1960s and the ever-confident Lyle Crawford, whose long residence at Cedar Hill started in 1984.

In Victoria the challenging Gorge Vale layout was designed by A.V. Macan in 1927. The course's first pro, William Wills, was in place by 1930. The championship layout was further enhanced when Les Furber oversaw a significant renovation in 2001. Recently a new clubhouse made the facility more compatible with the quality of the course. One unique aspect of the course is the par-four 12th hole setting where a functioning fenced naval cemetery, complete with a quaint historic chapel on the right side, encourages all slicers to start their tee shots well left.

Up-island, Port Alberni's Alberni Golf Club enjoys a proud history dating back to the 1920s. The course in salmon country landed its own big Scottish fish in the form of Nat Cornfoot, who emigrated from St Andrews and settled in at Alberni for the long term. Today the amiable Bruce MacDonald—who at time of writing has been Alberni's pro for 18 years—is in the process of matching Cornfoot's long stint as pro, which only ended with the economic challenges of the mid-1940s.

Island golf enjoyed its biggest development boom from 1988 through 1993 and architect Les Furber was at the centre of it all. Three of his courses opened almost simultaneously in Nanoose Bay, Parksville and Campbell River. At Nanoose, where former touring pro Ward Stouffer has run the show for over a decade, Fairwinds sits as a memorable jewel at the centre of a well-established golf community. Nestled near Schooner Cove with its popular marina, the course has steadily upgraded its drainage and irrigation and benefits from a climate that makes it a year-round destination. Morningstar in Parksville has tees challenging enough to make it suitable for hosting the annual Canadian tour qualifying tournament. And Storey Creek, 14 kilometres south of Campbell River, is blessed with a setting amid old-growth and second-growth forest that's so natural it's a sin to take a cellphone anywhere near it.

Other courses from this era include two Victoria-area courses: Cordova Bay on the Saanich Peninsula and Olympic View in Metchosin. Both Olympic View and Arbutus Ridge, near Duncan, opened to rave reviews between 1988 and 1990 and are now part of Caleb Chan's GolfBC holding which, at last count, owns and operates 13 courses in BC and Hawaii. These courses have continued to age well, as has the Courtenay gem Crown Isle, which opened in 1992 with one of the most impressive clubhouses in BC.

Eaglecrest at Qualicum Beach, March Meadows in Honeymoon Bay near Lake Cowichan, Duncan Lakes (now Duncan Meadows Golf and Country Club) and Long Beach in Tofino all emerged in this era as well.

THE GULF ISLANDS

Also within the Vancouver Island region are courses on four of the Gulf Islands. Far too few of the province's golf clubs have expended the time and energy to document their histories, as the Salt Spring Golf and Country Club discovered when it decided to published a 60th-anniversary memento of its rise from humble beginnings to one of the island's social meccas.

One bright, clear afternoon in the late 1920s, on the largest of the five southern Gulf Islands, Bob Lawson glanced out a window of his home and ruefully chided himself for not having talked G.C. Mouat and T.E. Speed into going to Victoria to golf. Instead, he took his clubs to Norm Wilson's farm at the Barnsbury Estate and hit practice balls that scattered the bleating sheep. Within days three more golfers appeared, and then eight, all firing balls into the Barnsbury pasture.

In March 1928, 33 residents of the sparsely populated island attended an organizational meeting at Mahon Hall in Ganges. A committee of Mouat, Speed, Lawson, W.E. Scott, E.C. Turner and K. Butterfield was struck and endorsed Barnsbury as their preferred course site. After collecting founders' dues, they allocated $123.16 for grass seed and labour, and enlisted G.E. Donaldson of the CPR to assist in laying out nine holes. His first bill was twenty dollars. Owner Wilson helped in the construction and was paid thirty dollars for cutting greens and fairways from June until the end of the growing season. Without water, sand greens were built during the next two seasons.

After 25 years of helping with course upkeep, Wilson sold his share to island logger Jack Brooks and took his family to property at the end of Old Scott Road. After a few years, Brooks sold to Jack Hayes, Wilson's grandson. Less than a year after Hayes purchased the course in November 1958, disaster struck when the main Barnsbury house burned to the ground. At the time Hayes had been negotiating a sale to Vancouver businessmen who were planning to subdivide the course into half-acre residential lots. However, Chuck Harrison, an island newcomer, fortunately recognized the course's importance to the community and stepped in as interim owner while Frank Trethewey packaged a takeover proposal which he presented to members in 1961. The Founders Group, a holding company incorporated to promote financial contributions in the community, exercised an option of purchase for $27,500, with

Harrison agreeing to carry a $12,500 mortgage. Shares in the company were issued—1,000 with a par value of fifty dollars—and plans for a new clubhouse and irrigation system to allow for grass greens were initiated.

By 1964 Malcolm "Mac" Mouat's clubhouse committee had a $16,000 building in place and Hart Bradley's crew had installed the irrigation system. Bob Foulis was the club's first pro and architect Ernie Brown eventually modified the 3,147-yard course. Bud Keetch, Don Atkinson and Nick Birks were subsequent course superintendents.

A small group of enthusiasts led by Sandy Crawford started a Pender Island course in 1938 on 52 acres of farmland acquired from George Grimmer, the son of island pioneer Washington Grimmer. But five holes weren't playable until after the Second World War when young returning servicemen pitched in to help develop the course east of Otter Bay Road.

Pender's golfers persevered through difficult years. By 1968 the 59 members were enjoying nine holes and grass greens by pumping water from a pond below the third tee. The sale of 10 acres provided $95,000 for a clubhouse in 1981. Course improvements and automated sprinkling came with an increasing island population and club membership.

The records indicate 1935 plans for a Galiano course on property at Ellis fields owned by Ivan Denroche of Gossip Island. VGC pro Don Sutherland provided a blueprint for nine holes. Galiano's short, quaint course on leased provincial recreational land off Porlier Pass Road measures a shade under 2,000 yards.

On Gabriola Island, a nine-hole course founded in 1979 skirts the northwest banks of Hoggan Lake where 50 acres was leased from Clyde Coats. The lake played a key role in the mythology of the club one extremely warm summer afternoon in the late 1990s when a group of casual mainland golfers gathered for a pre-wedding weekend of athletics

Early Salt Spring club records were destroyed in the fire of 1959 but it is said that Dermott Crofton fashioned a record 60 for 18 holes in 1935. Prominent members were Mrs. Charlesworth, during the first years, and Mac Mouat, who was made an honorary life member in 1989 for 60 years' service.

and revelry. While many of the party had already finished their round and were sipping cold beer in the clubhouse, one trio of sweaty laggards stopped at the lake late in their round, stripped down for a quick skinny-dip and then proceeded to play the final hole buck-naked. Lifetime bans were said to have been issued *in abstentia* and the event enriched local lore.

Gabriola is yet another course that would not have existed without the vision of tireless volunteers and the use of donated heavy equipment. Dan Kitsul, the ubiquitous architect, designed and constructed the greens for the idyllic layout that stretches almost 3,600 yards. With a two-storey clubhouse made of local logs, the course was officially opened in 1981 by Nanaimo mayor Frank Ney, who sliced a shot off the first tee, and MLA Dave Stupich, who sliced the ceremonial ribbon. The club is still going strong and is an essential part of Gabriola's community.

CHAPTER 5

THE VANCOUVER BOOM AND THE PUBLIC COURSES

Point Grey and Marine Drive were two of 35 courses developed in the Lower Mainland during the 1920s' golf construction boom in North America. In a decade that began with Prohibition and ended with a stock market crash, more than 4,000 courses were built in North America, a staggering four times the number that had previously existed. By 1923 golf availability in the district had doubled, thanks to the openings of Marine, Point Grey and the first nine at Exhibition Park.

MARINE DRIVE

Built on flat, rich farmland on the dike shoreline of the Fraser River's north arm, Marine Drive has flourished as a course of champions. In the early 1920s families came by horse and buggy and small boats from lower Fraser Valley settlements to attend the Kerrisdale Presbyterian Church's summer Sunday school near Marine Drive's present 10th tee. And the prayers of many golfers have since been uttered at the clubhouse turn.

A.E. Philp and Dr. Brett Anderson purchased the historic 93-acre dairy farm from William Murdoch McKenzie in 1921 and the site was a playable course two years later. Under the direction of A.V. Macan and greenskeeper Bob Wood, the owners helped clear the land and shape the course. A milking shed became Sid McCullough's pro shop and the spacious, refurbished barn served for many years as the clubhouse.

During its first 30 years, Marine was fraught with problems. Insufficient memberships and stretched finances often stymied projects, and drainage difficulties persisted. Desperate for members, the club waived entrance fees at one point. It faced foreclosure proceedings in 1948, but was saved by George Norgan, whose company, Bay Finance Corp., picked up outstanding debentures and mortgages totalling about $51,000. It was 1952 before members were finally able to clear the debts, partly through the sale of three lots fronting the main thoroughfare where the original 14th tee was located.

Through the energetic, progressive leadership of Norgan, Bob Samson, Percy White and Jack F. Ellis, among others, the club overcame its problems and ultimately became the lauded site of endless championships. It was also the spawning ground of many fine players. Quite probably, no other Canadian course has turned out as many national champions as Marine did.

Stan Leonard was Marine's resident pro when he won five of his Canadian PGA titles and Doug Roxburgh, reared at Marine, captured four Canadian Amateur championships and a national Junior title in addition to his truckload of provincial honours. Johnny Johnston took the 1959 Canadian Amateur on his home turf, Jim Nelford earned consecutive titles while playing out of Marine in 1975–76 and Dick Zokol became 1981 champion. Laurie Roland was the first of several Marine Drivers to claim the national Junior title. Babs Davies brought the Canadian Closed title to Marine, Val White was a two-time national Junior winner and Marilyn Palmer O'Connor represented the club during 4 of her 10 provincial titles. Barb Renwick and Paula Phillips were also BC champions.

Curiously, however, a Marine member didn't win the BC Amateur until 1947 when Hugh Morrison stopped clubmate Monty Hill at Uplands. It would be another decade before the next Marine Driver won, when Bob Kidd took his first of three BC crowns by beating veteran clubmate Dick Moore. Three of four other Amateurs at Marine were won by Seattle players: Tom "Babe" McHugh in 1928, Harry Givan in 1940 and Fred Couples in 1979.

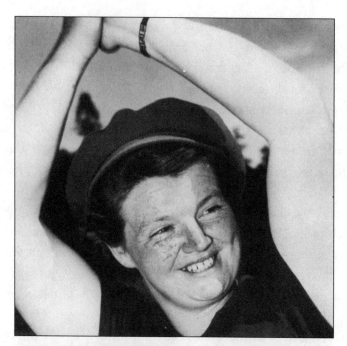

Babs Davies was the pride of Marine Drive in 1949 when she won the Canadian National Closed tournament, while Val White (bottom) was National Junior champ in 1972 and 1973. BC GOLF HOUSE 007.85.17 AND 007.85.21

Marine members have always played well on their own course. Member Russ Case held off Stan Leonard's 1936 charge in the BC Open. Leonard closed with 66 for 278 to beat Chuck Congdon by two. Portland pro Bob Duden's record 268 lapped the 1960 Open field at Marine, then Johnston triumphed at home again in 1967.

There were some strong scoring performances during the course's first 15 years. Jimmy Huish, the club's third pro, established a course record of 67 in 1928. Four years later, member Monty Hill fashioned a nine-under 62, only to be outdone by Brian Hopkins in 1937. In shooting 61, Hopkins made the turn nine-under with two eagles, five birdies and two pars. It read 333-233-334-27.

The popular Huish, known as Jimmy the Hush, was Marine's longest-serving pro. He came by way of Victoria and Vancouver Golf Club in 1926 and retired in 1942. Born and raised in Musselburgh, Scotland, Huish played soccer in fast company, hobnobbing with famed Scottish international Hobby Walker, and taught golf to families of aristocrats. He came to Canada in 1910 after distinguishing himself during the South African war. A tall, slender man who stood straight as a flagstick, Huish's eyes shone with tears of joy during a memorable testimonial dinner in his honour at the old Pacific Athletic Club. "After tonight," Huish said, "I don't care when I die."

Today Marine Drive's compact course places a premium on accuracy that ultimately earns the golfer's respect. Its selection as the host of the 1992 World Amateur men's and women's championships confirmed its status as a most worthy tournament course.

POINT GREY

Major league golf finally arrived at Point Grey in the last week of August 1958. The tournament was the BC Centennial Open and thereafter, the old Mole farm off Southwest Marine Drive and Blenheim Street was known as Ferreeland.

Jim Ferree wouldn't recognize the course today. The majority of Point Grey's tree-lined fairways still run north and south, but the delta course has been extensively remodelled for both aesthetics and playability in various stages over recent decades. Two clubhouses on the dry, top end of the property have also been replaced since Ferree's astounding 11-under-par 61 the year the province celebrated its centennial.

The handiwork of the club's first two pros, Dave Ayton and Duncan Sutherland, remains evident in the basic design of Point Grey. Synonymous with Point Grey are on-site replicas of a water wheel symbolic of the land's heritage and the mounted, bronzed straw hat Ferree wore during his winning streak. Farmer Henry Mole used a water wheel in the stream that gushed down Blenheim Street from Marine Drive to the delta, creating power for his threshing machine. Ferree wore the famed fedora while shooting his memorable round and winning the Centennial. Point Grey was the 1954 site of Fletcher's celebrated Canadian Open victory. At time of writing, no Canadian has since managed to capture the National Open.

Thirty years before, in May 1924, a full course was first playable in the municipality of Point Grey, replacing a temporary nine-holer that had been hastily created by enthusiasts including a number of war veterans. Mole had been enticed from England by the Cariboo gold rush in 1862. A year later he followed the Fraser River to the coast and settled on the present course site, where he built a huge stately house. Only when the full course was established did the pioneer members proceed with alterations and additions to the homestead which would serve as the clubhouse until 1960. In August 1991 construction of a third clubhouse was completed.

The water wheel that Mole's son John erected in 1904 vanished during the Second World War but a replica adorns the pond guarding the 18th green. The wheel is incorporated in the club crest which was unveiled by club president Ernie Palmer in 1954. The old wheel, some 16 feet in diameter, held a dark secret. In 1907, 12-year-old Cecil Craig was peering into the mysteries of the contraption while it was sluggishly rotating. With a sudden jerk the wheel turned over and crushed the boy's neck between the spokes, killing him instantly.

The creek was diverted several years later, rendering the wheel useless. The rich pasture on which the Moles developed their dairy farm was inundated every spring runoff when tidal action led to numerous Fraser River freshets, a problem ultimately corrected by diking. With receding

The stately original Mole farmhouse at Point Grey served from 1924 through the late 1950s as the clubhouse. POINT GREY GOLF & COUNTRY CLUB

tides in the delta lands, it wasn't uncommon to see stranded salmon thrashing in disappearing pools on fairways. "I remember my dad bringing home a good-sized fish he found floundering on the course," recalled Clare Martin Cruise, whose parents were founding club members and who was the first junior member to win the club championship.

Pro Dave Ayton, from a prominent family of St Andrews golfers, was instrumental in designing the course after Mike Gardner and two-time BC champion Robert Bone laid out the original nine. The full course was officially opened on Victoria Day 1924, with Ayton and Huish losing an exhibition match to Davey Black and Alex Duthie. The graceful, unassuming Ayton left Point Grey in 1928, homesick for his Scottish links. One of his two daughters, Florrie, won three successive club titles and came second in the 1927 city championships before the family left Vancouver.

Point Grey's two early pros, Dave Ayton and Dunc Sutherland were prominent in the Lower Mainland for many years. BILL CUNNINGHAM

Ayton's successor, another Scot, was the mischievous, irrepressible Duncan (Dunc) Sutherland. Sutherland's legacy was his spirit and the hundreds of trees that he and Roscoe Brown, a club member with links to UBC's faculty of forestry, planted during the original remodelling of the course.

Sutherland came from Scotland's oldest royal burgh, Tain in Ross-Shire, home of the famed Glenmorangie Distillery. He arrived in Vancouver via Edmonton, knowing that at Point Grey he would be wearing three hats. He was hired as the club's pro, manager and greens superintendent. While not a brilliant player, he was a competent, colourful inclusion in exhibitions against barnstorming pros from the PGA circuit. Prior to arriving in BC to live, Sutherland twice won the Saskatchewan Open, in 1922 and 1923. He finished second in the BC Opens of 1928 and 1935. But his most famous match involved the great Walter Hagen, who quickly recognized that Sutherland had his own brand of showmanship and charisma.

He loved to annoy fellow Scot Jock McKinnon, the Capilano pro. Once, as McKinnon lined up a match-winning stroke on Point Grey's 18th green, the smirking Sutherland pointed his famed shotgun skyward out the pro shop door. He pulled the trigger the instant McKinnon started his stroke; the infuriated McKinnon never caught up to his nemesis. The shotgun blast echoed in the neighbourhood every Armistice Day to signal the club's annual competition between First and Second World War veterans organized by Sutherland, twice wounded while serving with the Seaforth Highlanders.

In another incident, McKinnon was presiding over the PGA BC's annual meeting when the doors of the Georgia Hotel ballroom suddenly burst open. The kilted Sutherland marched in, bagpipes blaring. "You're out of order!" shouted McKinnon, with his arms raised and the delegates roaring in delight. "No, I'm not," replied Sutherland, "or I couldn't have drunk a whole bottle of Scotch and made love to two women earlier this evening."

Sutherland, the first secretary and founding member of the PGA BC, resigned his Point Grey position in 1951 after purchasing the Meadowlands course in Chilliwack. He sold Meadowlands and retired to Delta with his beloved Kay in 1967. Sutherland, who died in 1990 aged 94, once said, "When I go I'll be taking my clubs. That's all I'll need. Old Davey [Black] will have a few old balls in the bottom of his bag."

Point Grey's first celebrated amateur, Don Gowan, defeated Frank Willey of Langara for the 1938 BC championship after having lost the final six years earlier to a precocious Stan Leonard. It was almost 30 years before Point Grey produced another amateur champion. Big Doug Bajus's temperament apparently prevented his winning the title during his best years, and a war cut short Ted Charlton's promising future. But John Russell wasn't to be denied.

Russell suffered a devastating loss at his home course in the 1965 final to Wayne Vollmer, the strapping youngster destined for the Point Grey pro shop. But Russell triumphed in 1967 and 1968, and was second on two other occasions. The six-time club champion represented BC in 13 interprovincial Willingdon Cup team matches.

Long-time regional favourite, Point Grey's Dunc Sutherland knew
how to bang his way out of trouble. BC SPORTS HALL OF FAME 1501.22

Ted Charlton's adversary was the imposing Stan Leonard. Born
10 days apart in 1915, they had two epic matches as teenagers in the
Amateur, with Leonard winning both. In 1932 at Point Grey, where
Charlton played as a junior, Leonard took their semifinal on the first
extra hole. "He almost reached the green with the longest two-wood shot
I'd ever seen in my life," recalled Ted, the son of W.S. "Bill" Charlton, the
first BC man elected president of the Royal Canadian Golf Association.

Three years later at Royal Colwood, in the title match, Charlton, a
third-year UBC commerce student, went up against Leonard amid blustery
rain. Charlton jumped to a quick four-hole lead. Still three holes up with
nine to play, he drove a ball out of bounds, three-putted twice to lose two
more holes and had no answer for Leonard's birdie that closed the match

John Russell, one of the game's steadiest players and
future Hall of Famer, seems to have found a bit of
trouble along the way. BC GOLF HOUSE 007.85.41

on the 35th. "I didn't watch Stan when I played him," said the candid
Charlton, who retired from competitions at 21. "When Stan was getting
ready to shoot, I'd look away because I knew I'd be even more awestruck."

Fred Thompson, Ross Ellison, Don Griffiths, Norm Wilkinson,
Jack Moryson, Clem Watson and Ken Gurney have been among Point
Grey's other fine players, as have Winnifred Evans, Ruth Wilson, Marion
Garnet, Joyce Fairweather, Betty Mcintosh, Helen Cleat and Colleen
McCullogh.

Though he won four straight club championships after joining
The Point in 1923, Fred Thompson isn't best remembered as a player.
In retirement the esteemed Irishman from County Down acted as a
volunteer marshal at tournaments, educating galleries throughout the

city. Shillelagh in hand, he stalked the fairways with the demeanour of a drill sergeant.

Fred Thompson and Billy Thompson, the long-time PGA BC secretary-treasurer, weren't related but they shared an enthusiasm for altruistic authority. They regularly manned tournament course entrances and took silver collections for junior golf. Few spectators got by them without contributing to their slotted tin cans. Both Thompsons lived beyond 90 years. One member known as Old Daddy Ellis played, carrying his own bag, until he was 92.

Sutherland's pro shop replacement, the amiable Leroy Goldsworthy, was best known as a hockey player. He played for the 1934 Stanley Cup champions, the Chicago Blackhawks. He remained at Point Grey for 15 years through 1967. Ron Fitch, one of his faithful assistants, went on to become head pro at Gleneagles in West Vancouver and another aide, Dick Munn, succeeded Goldsworthy.

After turning pro at 17 under Malcolm Tapp in Banff, Munn followed the US tour as a rabbit in a Monday qualifier with little success. He turned club pro at Victoria's Cedar Hill in 1963. Chosen Canadian Club Pro of the Year in 1975, he left Point Grey in 1979 to become managing partner of the Gallagher's Canyon Resort project in Kelowna. The Gallagher's course and Munn hosted the Canadian club championships and the 1988 Canadian Amateur—testimony to the respect that Munn commanded. He also served as managing director for Burrard International's proposed Green Lakes course in Whistler. Burrard eventually purchased Gallagher's from Angus Mackenzie, Munn and associates.

Wayne Vollmer was the fourth Point Grey pro to stay in the job for more than a decade. The former touring pro took over from Chuck Olver in 1981 and was eventually lured to Quail Ridge in Kelowna before returning to the Lower Mainland as director of golf at Morgan Creek.

Point Grey has played host to more major tournaments than any course in the province. Before it disappeared in 1993, 18 BC Open championships were decided at Point Grey.

After Hastings Park opened in 1925, it was common to see a dozen hatted, neatly clad boys waiting in front of the caddy shack for the opportunity to tote a bag.
STUART THOMSON, CITY OF VANCOUVER ARCHIVES CVA99-1617

VANCOUVER'S PUBLIC COURSES

Although many private courses attracted and trained aspiring young golfers, it was the emergence of public venues that really accelerated the popularity of golf across Canada. In BC, public courses first opened in Vancouver. Ultimately, most courses across the province were owned by local governments, took on a semi-private nature or were key attractions at tourist resorts and recreational communities.

The giddy golden years after the First World War were golf's Soaring Twenties. Fuelled by their passion for Bobby Jones, new fans of the game who had previously perceived golf as a rich man's pastime clamoured for more courses. For restless veterans home from the war and hungry for recreational distraction, however, it would take too many years before Mayor L.D. Taylor swatted the opening drive at Hastings Park on May 2, 1925.

HASTINGS PARK

The province's first municipal course, a modest 2,427 yards featuring nine holes on the Exhibition Park grounds, cost the city $18,000 to complete. By that time Canada had about 30 municipal courses, the first of which was built in Edmonton in 1906.

From its opening day, the lineups were long at Hastings Park, Vancouver's first public course.
STUART THOMSON, CITY OF VANCOUVER ARCHIVES CVA99-1616

Hastings Park was a boon for the working man. It provided an opportunity for aspirants who couldn't afford private memberships and a place
for beginners curious to try the game. Golf was generally viewed as an
amusement for those becoming too aged for more active recreations.

Hastings was extended to 18 holes for the 1930 season, when 55,000
green fees produced revenues of $20,000. Rates on the new 4,450-yard
par-65 course were thirty-five cents for nine holes, fifty cents for 18,
seventy-five cents for all day and three dollars a month.

Bobby Jones inspired the youth of America to take hickories in
hand rather than carrying them for someone else. He captured his 13
major titles between the age of 21 and 28, starting in 1923. Some of the
Vancouver youngsters who first came to the fore in that era were Harry
Jones, Bob Gelletly, Jack Fraser and Cec Coville.

Three years before the christening of Hastings Park, Point Grey
and Marine Drive had opened to compete for new members with the
mainland's original private clubs, Jericho, Vancouver and Shaughnessy
Heights. Victoria had the Oak Bay links, Royal Colwood, the United
Service Club and Cedar Hill, and courses were popping up in other
towns throughout the province. But until Hastings, none was considered

public, open to all comers for the price of a green fee. Cedar Hill, which was established around 1917, existed for 20 years before it was taken over by the municipality of Saanich.

The Hastings Park course, on the northeastern portion of the 167-acre Exhibition Grounds, was ploughed under and topped by asphalt to build a stadium for the 1954 British Empire Games. The city's primary stadium for football and soccer, Empire Stadium was deserted by the BC Lions with the 1983 opening of the domed BC Place Stadium. Empire Field was used temporarily while a retractable roof was installed at BC Place. With east-end residents demanding park development on the controversial PNE property, it seems that the area is heading full cycle from a golf course to a grassy playland.

GLENOAKS AT LANGARA

When Hastings was well into its second season, the CPR decided to open up Langara for use by the general public. The railway also leased property in the western part of the city popularly known as Asthma Flats and Consumption Hollow for private development of the original Quilchena course by late 1925. Opening up Langara on the southeast side gave Vancouver a second public course before Seattle had its first. By 1930 two other public facilities were available to mainlanders: Peace Portal and the University course at the entrance to UBC.

Public courses turned out many leading players in an era of membership restrictions on people under the age of 21 at private clubs. Hastings Park and Langara, with the area's first irrigation system, attracted the plebeians, eager youth and Japanese and Jewish citizens—people who couldn't afford or were denied memberships to private clubs. Langara regulars formed a club within the course: Glenoaks. The three-dollar annual dues gave members entry to special competitions and social functions.

Among the original 40 Glenoaks members were Cec Coville, a Jimmy Huish protégé at Vancouver Golf Club, and Monty Hill. Burquitlam veteran Jimmy Yellowlees followed Coville to Langara. Russ Case and Brian Hopkins started there and later joined Hill at Marine Drive. In 1927 Charlie McCadden became the first City Amateur champion from

Glenoaks. His father, Ernie McCadden, managed the course and the family lived upstairs in the clubhouse.

William Leonard joined in 1929, later bringing with him sons Bill and Stan. Before turning pro, Bill Leonard played in a regular Langara foursome with baker Joe Francis, Walter Gaugin of the racetrack and Percy Hicks, who ran the downtown ticket bureau.

With a bank balance of $21.74 to start the 1932 season, Glenoaks picked up the one-dollar City Amateur entry for 18 members and splurged fifteen dollars for a party to celebrate teenager Leonard's BC Amateur triumph. When Noel Daniel, one of the club's steadiest players, won the 1944 City championship, the members presented him with a fifteen-dollar green-fee pass good for six months. The club also paid tournament entry fees and caddy fees for players such as Frank Willey and Jack Fraser. They welcomed Percy Williams, Walter McElroy and Andy Bathgate as members.

When Lyle Hurschman upset Ken Black in the 1941 BC Amateur, club members voted to spend thirty dollars on beer and a victory banquet. Coincidentally, the club first increased its dues a year later to four dollars. By the mid-1950s it was six dollars for the 80 members and two dollars for juniors at Glenoaks. Membership was free for promising youngsters like Colin Riley, Al Galway, Don Elford, Ian Daniel, Bob Cox Jr., Al Kennedy, Irv Taylor and Joe Jeroski—the latter four would eventually become pros. Langara was Hank Mitchell's home course but the future National Seniors champion didn't join Glenoaks until 1957 when dues were fifteen dollars.

Most Langara youngsters caddied at Shaughnessy Heights to earn pocket money but not the enterprising Ted Johnston. He hunted balls at Langara. "I started trampling for balls buried in the deep rough when I was six," said the long-time Glenoaks executive. "I'd get up before the sun. Most days I'd find 30 to 50 balls and make $40 a week selling them on the course. I had more money in my pocket than all the caddies. Even more than Jimmy Pattison, who went to John Oliver High with me. The police threatened to chase us off the course but they could never catch us. I don't think they tried too hard."

Ball hawks were plentiful at Langara, where sprinklers kept the rough lush and high. One of Johnston's ball-hunting competitors, Jimmy Murray, lived in a tent year-round at various locations in the bush across Cambie Street. Johnston speculated that he hid there to avoid the draft.

Wilf Fink, the ill-fated Frank Pitsch, Bill Featherson, Charlie Munro, a course ranger whose dog sniffed out golf balls, and Don Elford were other ball hawks. "It was more profitable and easier than caddying though I guess there was only room for so many of us," Johnston said. "You couldn't make near as much with a paper route or by delivering magazines."

A.V. Macan directed the construction of Langara in concert with former Burquitlam greenskeeper Alex Muirhead and Ed Hassell, the course's future greenskeeper. The CPR spent in excess of $160,000 on Langara, almost 10 times the City's expenditure for Hastings Park. Macan's original layout stretched 6,630 yards over 175 acres. The par-74 course featured novel grass tees of 3,000 square feet and greens that averaged 10,000 square feet. Newspapers lauded Macan's ingenuity as "the last word in golf architecture" and course manager Frank Soutar stated that Langara "opened up the game to the masses." Soutar spent 40 years as Langara secretary-manager.

South Vancouver reeve J.W. Cornett struck the first ball to christen Langara on June 26, 1926. His drive found the fairway. Eight professionals played before what was described as the largest gathering to attend such a function in the province. Dave Ayton, the Point Grey pro, established the course record at 73.

The great Walter Hagen twice visited Langara for exhibitions, the first in 1927 with resident pro Nat Cornfoot, Hastings Park pro Roy Herne and teenager McCadden. The following November, before 3,000 drenched spectators, Hagen and Monty Hill combined for a 2 and 1 best-ball win over 1928 US Open champions Johnny Farrell and Fred Wood.

Early Langara players were the backbone of local competition. They benefitted from the support of Glenoaks, the working man's club, and Langara's first pros, Cornfoot and Colk, both ardent instructors. Langara poker games were apparently tame compared to those at Fraserview but shenanigans were nevertheless rampant at the CPR course. Cornfoot, Fraser, Coley Hall and, according to former caddy and member Dick Blaker, "other rounders" participated in merry diversions that bordered on the zany. The tomfoolery focused on course starter Dave Larg and his ample girth. Properly inebriated, Larg was eased onto the first tee flat on his back. On his mid-section they placed his pocket watch, on the face of which a golf ball was balanced. It's said that Cornfoot, who had a withered right arm from First World War injuries, never broke a watch or bruised Larg with his swing.

City ratepayers in 1965 saved Langara as a course, albeit in a down-sized version. They approved the purchase of 95 acres from the CPR with $2.3 million that the city received as part of an airport sale to the federal government, plus $700,000 from the school board. The board received 20 acres for its Langara College site. Two years later voters rejected a $3 million proposal to buy Langara's remaining 66 acres from the CPR, which reported operating losses of $40,000 after a property tax assessment tilted the railway's ledgers. As city-owned land without the heavy tax burden that the CPR had borne, Langara and the park board's other two courses, Fraserview and McCleery, were profitable. In 1967 they each handled more than 70,000 rounds, clearing almost one dollar per round.

UNIVERSITY GOLF COURSE AND WEST POINT

Road builder John Boyd turned to golf course construction in 1928. He obtained a 40-year government lease on 120 acres of the University Endowment Lands and opened a public course on May 24, 1930. Boyd, whose company had built many Interior highways and upgraded the Fraser Canyon highway, developed the first nine holes under the supervision of Shaughnessy pro Davey Black. Harry Winder, Black's brother-in-law, apprenticed under Black and became University's pro for the life of the lease. Winder twice shot 65 on the original course before Horton Smith fired 64 the first and only time he played it in 1938.

Harry Winder was an avid instructor during his 40-year reign as the head man at the University course. BC GOLF HOUSE 007.85.119A

Among those who started at West Point, University's club within a course, were Johnston and Norm Wilkinson, the 1939 winner of the city's first public championship. Both became country clubbers: Johnston moved to Marine and Wilkinson to Point Grey. Initial West Point membership dues were ten dollars annually. Members paid fifty cents for 18 holes, thirty-five cents for a second round and twenty-five cents for a twilight round.

The province operated University from 1970 through 1985 when a group of Vancouver businessmen headed by Robin Lecky and Jack McLaughlin was awarded a lease that will expire in 2015. They built a lavish clubhouse and driving range, which involved relocating the headquarters behind the old second green, and modernized the rearranged course.

In 2003 the provincial government sold the 59-hectare course to the University of British Columbia but that sale was challenged by the Musqueam Indian Band who ruled against the government. Forced to repurchase the land, the course was then transferred to the Musqueam in 2007 with a restrictive covenant that assured that the lands will be used as a golf course until 2083.

The original clubhouse by the University Boulevard gates at 10th and Blanca was saved from the bulldozers and completely renovated and restored to become the home of the BC Golf Hall of Fame and the BC Golf House museum.

FRASERVIEW

Fraserview, reputedly Canada's busiest course, was almost turfed into deadly grounds. After 1934 operations finished in the red, several non-golfing city officials advocated converting the southeast course into a cemetery. The first nine opened that June with an 18-hole green fee of twenty-five cents. Alderman Fred Crone, himself a golf enthusiast, championed the cause to retain the course on which more than 70,000 rounds have frequently been played annually.

The first phase of Fraser, the original name until lengthened to Fraserview in 1943, was constructed for $150,000 by relief labour, a Depression-era euphemism for unemployed single men. The full 18 wasn't completed until 1938. The historic 211 acres that became the course were part of the only British military land grant ever awarded in today's Vancouver. William Henry Rowling returned from England in 1866 to settle on the grant, and started a grape farm he called Truro. The land later came under the jurisdiction of South Vancouver, the municipality which, before amalgamating with Vancouver in 1929, called the estate Willingdon Park in honour of Canada's Governor-General.

Major H.L. McPherson, a local civil engineer, consulted Shaughnessy's Black to design the original Fraser. The director of construction was the noted D.J. Clark, whose credits were University, Beach Grove and several Pacific Coast courses, including Pebble Beach. Fraser overcame both opposition and setbacks. A.S. Wootton, the former Vancouver Park Board superintendent, deemed the dense bush "fit for nothing else . . . there's a great ravine in it. It was originally set aside (for a park) by the old South Vancouver council."

Among the original members were lefthander Les William, who served five years as president, Jim Maitland, Candy Wallace, Reg Rice and Ken Campbell. Leading Fraserview players were Clogg, Nelford, Ticehurst, Crawford, Jack Ellis, Tommy Molyneaux, Bert Daykin, Bud Bird, Rena O'Callaghan Edward, Norm Nixon, Len Morgan, Gerry Croft and Tommy Ross. In the mid-1990s, as part of a major investment in the game, the Vancouver Parks Board retained renowned architect Thomas McBroom to redesign and rebuild both Fraserview and Langara golf courses. Both courses were rededicated in 1996.

MCLEERY

In 1862 the farming McCleery brothers, Samuel and Fitzgerald, came from Ireland and became the first family of settlers in the area. They selected the site on which a public course was also subsequently built and named after them. The brothers came from County Down, Ireland, to join the Gold Rush but decided instead to farm. In 1873 they built and lived in what was considered Vancouver's first house. It later also became the city's first "hospital" and the scene of innumerable births and deaths as well as a community centre for settlers.

The dairy farm operated until 1950 when Samuel's daughter, Theodora Logan, was forced to sell the 70-acre property because of the tax burden and her son, Gerald, moved their herd and equipment to Princeton. Thanks to the foresight of Park Board chairman Stuart Lefeaux and his colleague Bill Livingston, the city began obtaining the land in 1954 for a course to replace Hastings Park. The city purchased and developed the 110 acres at the foot of Macdonald Street for approximately $500,000.

The former farm normally flooded during the winter months and Woodward's Stores donated about 20,000 yards of topsoil from its Oakridge Shopping Centre site to shore the dike. Against much local opposition, the original farmhouse, which stood near the golf course's original 11th tee, was razed.

McCleery officially opened the A.V. Macan–designed course on July 3, 1959, on the western Fraser River flats adjacent to the private Marine Drive course. Theodora's granddaughter, Katherine Logan of Princeton, cut the ceremonial ribbon close to where her grandmother, Theodora Logan, had been born more than 80 years before.

When first opened, McCleery sparked a minor exodus of Fraserview members. Roy Heisler left Fraserview's pro shop in favour of the new course and was joined by greens superintendent Croft. The revered Bert Ticehurst, who refused to compromise his loyalty to public courses, was the most noted player to switch home courses. Alvie Thompson, the 1962 Canadian PGA champion, returned from Toronto to replace Heisler, who retired in 1976 due to ill health.

As part of its grand scheme, the Parks Board retained Ted Baker and completely rebuilt the course. Katherine Shave, née Logan, returned to where she had helped unveil the original course in 1959 and participated in the rededication of a site with special historical significance to Vancouver.

CHAPTER 6

THE LOWER MAINLAND
AND SUNSHINE COAST

After the false start for golfing on the northern shore of Burrard Inlet, the game was a non-starter there until well after the end of the First World War, and it took the construction of a railway and a bridge to help it develop. A fickle, albeit steadily growing population either embraced or disdained the game. As late as the early 1990s West Vancouver's populace voted down an attempt to build a new course in their midst on the slopes of Cypress Mountain. The District of North Vancouver, however, has been more proactive.

WEST VANCOUVER

GLENEAGLES

Gleneagles, which became the North Shore's first public course, was built on acreage of one of the original West Vancouver waterfront estates. In the late 1800s the entire waterfront running from the Capilano River to Whytecliff near Horseshoe Bay was owned by only 16 different landholders. The records indicate that the current site of the course was part of District Lot 771, 223 acres purchased by a Swedish settler named Peter Larson for $319 in 1900. The Larson family ranch included orchards, hayfields and a large vegetable garden under the care of a man known to all as Dutch Bill. For over a decade the remote ranch was only accessible by boat.

In 1913, with the Pacific Great Eastern Railway knocking at his door in search of an easement to run tracks across his land, Larson negotiated the sale of 11 acres on the condition that the railway would create a stopping point for the ranch. The depot became known as Larson Station and was situated right across from the driveway entrance of today's golf course. As a tribute to this heritage, the current course restaurant is known as Larson Station. Peter Larson later became an hotelier, owning both the original North Vancouver Hotel on Lonsdale Street and the old Canyon View Hotel that sat above the present Cleveland Dam.

In the late 1920s, with real estate development rampant throughout the Lower Mainland, General Robert P. Clark and Vancouver realtor Frank Merrick formed the Gleneagles subdivision after purchasing the 204-acre Larson Ranch for a reported $100,000 in early 1927. A brochure outlined the Gleneagles project as a new concept in seaside living with over a mile of waterfront property. Links in Perthshire, Scotland, inspired architect A.V. Macan's nine-hole design on 46 acres. Jock Glen from St Andrews was hired to run the club's pro shop.

The course opened in July and within eight months local golfer A.J. Finnie had scored the first hole-in-one on the original seventh hole. In November 1928 the course suffered a setback when the provincial government curtailed accessibility by discontinuing train service on the Pacific Great Eastern tracks from the North Van terminal to nearby Whytecliff. The aftermath of the stock market crash and Depression also seriously affected Gleneagles Limited's real estate development. Mortgages were foreclosed and properties repossessed. In late 1931 there were only eight permanent residences near the course.

Despite continuing financial woes and depressed property sales, the course was maintained and, in 1933, General James Duff-Stuart paid $35,000 for Larson's equity in 71 unsold lots and the course. Seventy acres of the land were purchased by local government in a tax sale and then resold in 1943 to A.T. Taylor, who had spearheaded the British Pacific Properties project. In the immediate aftermath of the war, Vancouver's local private courses—like so many others—would not admit non-Christian members. In 1951 Esmond Lando and David Sears took the opportunity to acquire the property on behalf of their fellow golfers in the Jewish community.

The original Gleneagles clubhouse, seen here in 1929, a month before the stock market crash, was the only course on the North Shore at that time. VANCOUVER PUBLIC LIBRARY 22979

In 1958 West Vancouver ratepayers authorized the acquisition of Gleneagles by a vote of 2,435 to 248, believed to be the most overwhelming majority ever given to a financial bylaw in the municipality. Retired judge Harvey Sedgwick, then municipal solicitor and long-time Gleneagles golfer and resident, negotiated the $350,000 transaction.

Slim McArthur presided over the first directorate that included Fred Hutchinson, Roland Wild, Lucy Markham and Phil Eldridge. The Parks and Recreation Commission hired Ron Fitch as pro in 1960 and he stayed almost 30 years. Fitch, a diminutive Londoner who became a war evacuee at age 14, went to Gleneagles after 10 years as Leroy Goldsworthy's aide at Point Grey. One of Fitch's first assistants, Denny McArthur, Slim's son, left in 1974 for the Castlegar pro shop. Fitch, who has presided over both the Canadian and PGA BCs during his career, retired in 1989. He was succeeded by Tryg Wenn who became the 1992 provincial PGA president.

In West Vancouver, the Parks and Community Services had operated the course for more than 50 years when Gleneagles hit a low point with the closing of the clubhouse in 2002. City government, however, came to their senses in 2007 and approved funds to restore the clubhouse, which was opened in May 2010.

BOWEN ISLAND

Across Howe Sound, due west of Gleneagles, a neighborhood nine-hole course is nestled in heavily forested evergreens above Cowan's Point at the southeast end of Bowen Island. Passengers catch glimpses of the verdant ninth fairway in the hills as the Horseshoe Bay–Nanaimo ferry passes by the point.

It's a short, 20-minute ferry trip from Horseshoe Bay to Snug Cove on Bowen Island, and then another 15 minutes by vehicle down-island to the delightful gem of a course.

Opened in 2006, this course was a long time in coming, and well worth the wait. Current club president Brian Russell was the driving force behind development of the course and the modest clubhouse, which was officially opened in 2012. Some islanders say plans for the facility were first discussed as long as 75 years ago. The property for the 3,003-yard layout was donated by Bowen Island Developments. Funding for the project, totaling more than $2 million, was raised locally. Like so many other courses in the province, Bowen Island wouldn't exist today without volunteer labour.

CAPILANO

Lions Gate Bridge was the gateway to Highlands Golf Course, the original name of Capilano Golf and Country Club. Designed by the celebrated Stanley Thompson in rugged wilderness above a burgeoning metropolis, the course opened in July 1936, almost two years before the bridge, and after pioneer member Ken Black had beaten Stan Leonard at Shaughnessy Heights for the Amateur title. Later that summer Black, who had ventured from Shaughnessy to become one of the first residents of the exclusive British Properties, also wore the crown as the province's first National Amateur champion.

The first tee at Capilano has players driving their ball toward the Vancouver skyline across the Burrard Inlet. ARV OLSON COLLECTION

Vancouver photographer Leonard Frank took this 1939 photo of the Capilano clubhouse in West Vancouver. VANCOUVER PUBLIC LIBRARY 15428A

Alfred James Towle Taylor, a dynamic investor and developer from Victoria—and the namesake of Taylor Way—endured considerable financial wrangling before engineering the massive West Vancouver project in concert with the Guinness Brewing Company of Ireland and England and with London financier W.S. Eyre.

Huge stumps amid a forest of second-growth trees and rugged rock outcropping knotted the hills designated for golf in 1933. It was a formidable challenge for architect Thompson, his young associate Robert Trent Jones and Steve Conway, a Vancouver civil engineer engaged to supervise construction. The first fairway and green, the present 12th, were completed by September 1935. Ten months later all 18 holes were playable.

The Capilano Golf and Country Club wasn't actually organized into a private club until late 1938 under the direction of Major P.A. Curry of the British Pacific Properties. Among the officials and guests at the May 17, 1939 opening were club president W.C. "Billy" Woodward, a future lieutenant-governor of BC, Percy Williams and Jock McKinnon, the beloved Scottish pro famed for his eclectic score. Capilano was a refuge for Jericho members during the war when the popular city course was reclaimed for Western Command Headquarters. Even the suddenly unemployed veteran pro Alex Duthie moved from Jericho to mind the Capilano pro shop while McKinnon was overseas with the BC Dragoons tank unit.

McKinnon, the tailor's son from Forfar, Scotland, had served his five-year apprenticeship in three years at Monifieth, and originally took the Capilano position for $150 a month. A county schoolboy champion at age 15, he was Scottish assistant pro champion by age 17 in 1935. His trademark was his dapper attire. He seldom appeared on the first tee without a clipped dark tie, long-sleeved white shirt and cardigan. He often played as well as he looked, though he was imported to attract members to a new course that was difficult to access during times of worry and war.

Four days before the armistice, a jeep in which he was travelling in the Netherlands hit a mine. He escaped the wreckage but was left with injured wrists that bothered him throughout his career. McKinnon, whose career spanned 42 years at Capilano, established what is still believed to be a world record eclectic score, the compilation of best lifetime scores on all 18 holes of a single course. In his Capilano debut he sank a seven-iron to eagle the second hole. In one dazzling stretch he broke par in 22 consecutive outings.

Before retiring in April 1979 he had posted a remarkable eclectic score of 16-17 for a total of 33 on the par 37-35-72 course. The total includes four double-eagles and four holes-in-one. The only holes on which he could have improved were the 245-yard 16th and the uphill par-five 18th. Only exceptionally long hitters could reach those. McKinnon never had a chance for a two at 18; he never reached the green with his second shot. But he came excruciatingly close to acing 16 with a one-iron, his ball coming to rest inches away after clipping the flagstick.

A man who endeared himself to the members and colleagues alike, McKinnon walked the fairways with an unmistakable gait and marched after abusers of the game's ethics and rules, especially admonishing laggards. Slow play was one of his pet peeves. He served two years as the first western president of the Canadian PGA and 20 years as West Vancouver's police commissioner. He was the second man accorded honorary membership in the American PGA. The first was Dwight D. Eisenhower.

The area west of the Capilano River and above the present Upper Levels Highway had been purchased before the turn of the century by a wealthy English textile merchant named Harvey Hadden. He had also acquired city properties, including the northeast corner of Granville and Hastings streets.

During 1903–04, Hadden Hall was built on the present site of Capilano's clubhouse. Abandoned after the First World War, the palatial log residence remained derelict for years and vandals eventually burned it down. The stately new clubhouse opened in May 1939 with a membership of 233 men, 151 women and 7 juniors. The entrance fee was $150, with annual dues of $90 for men and $55 for women. During the war Capilano encountered and survived operational difficulties. A club committee chaired by Gordon "Pappy" Bowers negotiated to purchase the 165-acre property and clubhouse, an agreement with British Pacific Properties that the membership ratified in March 1955.

SEYMOUR

Mel White spent 35 years at Seymour, then the North Shore's only other course. White had caddied at Shaughnessy and worked in pro Fred Wood's back shop. He turned pro under Capilano's Jock McKinnon. Seymour was three years young when White succeeded Ernie Brown, who had aided Eric Negus in the design and construction of the course above Dollarton. The Negus brothers, who both caddied at Jericho, the Kent brothers and Bert Lee were majority shareholders of a private company that leased 165 acres of primeval forest from the District of North Vancouver and purchased an additional four acres for a club-house and parking.

Reeve C.E. Scanlon and president A.W. Dean officially opened the course in September 1954, but Seymour wasn't ready for golfers. The rough was heaped with stumps, logs and dense underbrush, and poor drainage left the fairways waterlogged and barren of grass. People demanded improvements before paying their $175 initiation fees. Needing members to meet the developmental costs, Seymour took several years to erase its notoriety for jungle rough, swampy fairways and abnormally high counts of lost balls.

After almost a decade of negotiating, in 1968 Seymour members finally acquired the assets of Seymour Golf Co. Dave Nicol, a realtor who was 1966 president, concluded negotiations and the club has never looked back. Reconstruction of the back nine commenced in 1969 and major clubhouse alterations accommodated a growing membership. In 1985 course renovations were charged to architect Bill Robinson and a new clubhouse opened in 1989. Under the long-time lease agreement with the district, the course is open to the public every Monday and Friday.

Seymour has never played host to a major men's events but does lay claim to hosting an event won by one of the game's greats. In 1978 a supple, free-swinging youngster from Seattle won the BC Junior by shooting 286. Club lore will always include the story of Fred Couples flying the 18th green with a five-iron second shot at the 500-yard hole.

NORTHLANDS

With only one nine-hole public facility on the entire North Shore, the opening of Northlands on the slopes of Mount Seymour in 1997 was a most welcome event. In its wisdom, the District of North Vancouver retained Les Furber to create yet another masterpiece on the challenging terrain and the resulting 18-hole public play facility was awarded the Best New Course designation by *Golf Digest* in 1998. Although subject to more natural moisture than other public courses in the Lower Mainland, with 15 years of maturity and its attractive clubhouse Northlands is considered by many to be the premier public layout in the Lower Mainland. With its proximity to both the ski slopes of Mount Seymour Provincial Park and tranquil waters of nearby Deep Cove, much of the spring season makes it the perfect West Coast trifecta venue for a morning of skiing, an afternoon of golf and an early evening sail or kayak paddle to end the day.

FARTHER NORTH

SQUAMISH

For almost 40 years Gleneagles was the last golf outpost on the North Shore leading to the Squamish-Whistler-Pemberton corridor. Then Lloyd Ingraham, a member of the Squamish Chamber of Commerce, took it upon himself in 1965 to do something about ending the arduous, dangerous drive to Horseshoe Bay and back for golf. He advertised to start a club.

Eleven people showed up at an organizational meeting, each contributing ten dollars for incidental expenses. City council promised land for a course if Ingraham could find 100 people willing to pledge $240 each. Ingraham, Ray Bryant and Bill Gosling cornered Squamish mayor Pat Brennan and two councillors as their first shareholders. Many of them pledged ten dollars a month over two years. About 80 of the shareholders had never even been on a course, but by July 1967 they were playing the first nine holes on 150 acres that council had leased from the provincial government. It was ready in 1972.

John Drenka, Betty Bryant and Bill Galley were other major contributors to the club's development. The original building on the premises, an army hut purchased in Edmonton, was used as a pro shop and maintenance shed; the first clubhouse was a roundhouse from FMC Chemicals.

Bert Ticehurst won the first Squamish Open in 1970, shooting a course record 69. Three years later Jim Nolan broke the record with 68—but only for an hour. Dave Donaldson quickly followed with 67.

Since then the Squamish course has evolved as an integral part of the community and a fine example of how a collective approach to community recreation can be successful. The property is now home to not only the Squamish Valley Golf Club but also the Howe Sound Curling Club and Squamish Squash Club. Operating as not-for-profit organizations, the clubs have brought almost $20 million into the community. Over two-thirds of golf course revenue comes from green-fee customers.

For the past 12 years the course has hosted the Squamish Health Care Foundation's largest fundraising event, The Annual Charity Golf Classic, and helped raise over $500,000. Like many BC golf courses, Squamish sponsors numerous charity events throughout the golf season.

FURRY CREEK

No overview of area golf courses would be complete without some comment on the controversial Furry Creek course, situated beside the picturesque Sea to Sky Highway north of Lions Bay and south of Squamish. Opened in 1993 and designed by Robert Muir Graves, the course claims to be BC's "most scenic course." Stunning views and challenging terrain support this assertion but the course has also earned its share of criticism due to a few sloping fairways and demanding approach shots. Certainly its signature 14th hole, a 200-yard par-three that juts out into Howe Sound, is as memorable as a golf hole gets.

Now part of Caleb Chan's GolfBC group, it was originally driven by real estate development that, like much of the surrounding landscape, got off to a rocky start. Currently the seasonal course opens as spring weather allows and operates through late fall. Playing 18 at Furry Creek earns one the right to relax with a cold refreshment in the idyllic setting of the 19th hole.

Powell River, the isolated coastal paper mill town, gave golf a home in an old graveyard in 1922. Coffins were exhumed from the town's precipitous foreshore and relocated at a new cemetery in the Cranberry area.

Contortionists excelled on Powell River's frightfully slanted fairways of hardpan and weeds and on terraced greens of cement. Club members were known as side-hill gougers; they had to manipulate shots from lies so severe their clubs or arms were either too short or too long. Visitors faced so many uniquely difficult shots that Powell River lost few inter-club matches. However, these friendly competitions gradually became scarcer as opponents opted not to return.

The scary roller-coaster course, staffed by employees of the Powell River Paper Company, produced excellent players. Foremost were Percy Clogg, who became a two-time BC Amateur champion, Tom Hunter, Blake Cramb, Malcolm Tapp, John and Frank McDonald and Ed Peacock. Sid McCullough and George Pook were the first pros, followed in 1928 by Morris Boxall and then by Ernie Tate, the itinerant Sapperton pro who left after seven years to join the army in 1941. Tate's top juniors were Hunter and Tapp, a future pro. Peacock was a marvellous shot maker who worked wonders with old hickory-shafted clubs on the topsy-turvy turf. Hunter recalled that the hickories were misshapen, like dog's legs, but that Peacock knew exactly how to use them. In the transition to steel shafts, Tate persuaded Peacock to switch. He was never the same player.

Leased for one dollar a year from MacMillan Bloedel, the old course and Sally Scanlon Lodge, which had been converted to a clubhouse, were abandoned in July 1991. Looking to the future and more friendly fairways, the members had purchased the old 175-acre Ward orchard south of town for $350,000. Development got under way on the new course after membership subscription sales raised $250,000, MacBlo provided an interest-free $350,000 loan and the provincial government furnished a $1 million GO BC grant. The first nine of the comparatively flat Myrtle Point course opened in June 1991 and the second nine were completed the following summer.

Today the Les Furber–designed 6,900-yard course remains a vital part of the Powell River community.

FRASER VALLEY
CHILLIWACK AND MATSQUI

The first course in the Fraser Valley, the Chilliwack Golf and Country Club popularly known as the Fairfield Island course, had 90 members when it opened in 1924. Adjacent to the Fraser River and surrounded by a moat, the ill-fated Fairfield's construction presented a challenge to designer Major R.A. Meakin who had also helped to construct Victoria Uplands and Marine Drive's second nine. The course floundered throughout the Depression and was abandoned during the Second World War.

Meadowlands, a second nine-holer east of town off the original highway leading to the Fraser Canyon, became a labour of love for Englishman R.C. Philipson and later Dunc Sutherland. The Philipsons spent two years converting their dairy farmland and had a playable golf course by 1933. The wealthy one-time Vancouver Golf Club member's herd of Jersey cattle hadn't been yielding a fair return on his investment. "Farming was too philanthropic so I made it into a course," said the retired Philipson. Philipson's homemade design included innovative double-tees that presented different holes to those who played a second nine.

In 1951 Sutherland left Point Grey's pro shop after 23 years and, armed with a bank loan and tool kit, purchased Meadowlands. For 16 years he was a one-man work gang; his faithful wife, Kay, handled the clubhouse chores. "I never did a better thing in my life," he said. "Every pro would like to own his own course. When you are your own master, you don't get thumped." He sold the course to Bill Mawhinney and Johnny Johnston in 1967. The former Canadian champions turned their talents to greenskeeping, eventually redesigning the 90 acres into 18 holes of some 5,600 yards.

A decade before, Sutherland had turned down offers from enthusiasts in the Chilliwack–Abbotsford area headed by Roy Gleig and Art Holden. The group formed a club in 1957 and searched for land to build their own course. The first directors of the revived Chilliwack Golf and

There was usually laughter in the air when Dunc Sutherland was in the foursome. Here, (L to R) Powell River product Malcolm Tapp, Dunc, Marine Drive's Jack Ellis and Bill Mawhinney all seem happy with the day's scores. BC GOLF HOUSE 007.121.014

Country Club were facetiously called "The Simple Seven" because, said Holden, "everyone thought we were crazy." They purchased the 109-acre Franz Zink farm for $50,000, added another 10-acre plot and went to work. Most labour for the course and clubhouse was volunteered by the 150 members and heavy equipment was "donated." The price tag for the facility was about $200,000. One volunteer, an energetic logger named Gordie McKay, worked so diligently that he was hired full-time to shape the layout of the course. Once the contouring was complete, 18 teams of volunteers were each assigned a hole to plant trees and rake land tees in preparation for seeding. Roy Gleig, who ran a family sporting goods store, was the club pro and manager until 1978. After he died in 1991, a memorial bursary fund for deserving juniors was established in his name.

While still in its infancy, the 6,155-yard course with the tiny greens received considerable attention by staging the 1961 BC Open. After finishing in a 54-hole tie with Chuck Congdon, Portland pro Bob Duden described the course as "a Tom Thumb course with tricked-up greens." After winning a memorable playoff, Duden changed his tune. "It's a very challenging course and a credit to the community." Gordie McKay's layout had passed the test. McKay, a former Shaughnessy and Langara caddy from east Vancouver, later built courses at Hope and Squamish, where he turned pro in 1964.

When the Open returned to Chilliwack in 1981, Jim Rutledge left no doubt about the outcome, winning by seven strokes. Sandy Harper and Andrew Smeeth—the first notable young player from Ledgeview, the municipal course on the Abbotsford–Matsqui border—have captured BC Junior titles at Chilliwack, Jennifer Wyatt carded an unofficial 67 in defeating Kathy Gooch 10 and 9 for the 1986 BC women's crown and Rob Anderson's chip-in birdie at 18th beat Smeeth in the 1992 Amateur.

Wally Shemenski, an electrician, built and then operated the original Ledgeview course for 15 years after 1958, selling for a reported $850,000 and retiring to Penticton. About 125 area golfers each put up $1,000 for the down payment on the property. In 1974 the municipality of Matsqui took the financial burden off the club members and leased it back to them to operate. Ledgeview steadily progressed and co-operative financing enabled Les Furber and Jim Eremko of GolfDesign to revamp the course, a project completed in 1986. At just over 6,100 yards from the back tees, Ledgeview is a friendly, reasonably priced course with good practice facilities that has gained notoriety in recent years as the home course of some of the province's best young golfers.

NORTH OF THE FRASER RIVER

The first valley course north of the Fraser River was Maple Ridge, a nine-hole 2,557-yard, par-33 layout dating back to 1926. In 1960 the Maple Ridge directors realized that the property could not be expanded and purchased the 130-acre Greybrook Farm off Harris Road in Pitt Meadows with the intent of building a new 18-hole facility. After a committee of chairman Jack Walters, Dr. Laurie Alexander, Art Botham and Herb

Henri walked the site, the sale was completed with a down payment of $5,000 and an agreement to pay $550 an acre. Harold Sutton, the mayor of Pitt Meadows, was contracted to carry out the bulldozing and shaping of the Pitt Meadows course. Financial problems soon developed. The sale of debentures bogged down and a year before the June 1963 opening only 165 had been sold with another 53 pledged.

Jack Kingston volunteered as manager, the women's section donated $250 toward clubhouse furnishings and Walters, who held a position at the UBC experimental farm in Maple Ridge, procured almost all the 2,500 trees planted to frame the fairways. Set against a backdrop of the Golden Ears mountains, Pitt Meadows survived its early financial challenges and was steadily upgraded through extensive renovation of greens and fairways and installation of a sprinkling system.

In the first major tournament at Pitt Meadows, Carl Schwantje of Victoria defeated John Russell in the 1970 BC Amateur. The 1988 Amateur, split between Pitt Meadows and Ledgeview, was captured by Doug Roxburgh. Holly Botham Horwood won both the Canadian and BC junior women's championships while representing Pitt Meadows in 1970. Scott Keenlyside won the 1973 BC men's title at Pitt Meadows and Jim Nelford was a club member when he took the 1973 junior. Kim Cowburn of neighbouring Carnoustie captured the 1988 BC women's title at Pitt Meadows.

PUBLIC COURSES: PEACE PORTAL AND BEACH GROVE

Peace Portal and Beach Grove, products of the Depression years, were the first courses to accommodate BC golfers who resided south of the Fraser River. Beach Grove never succeeded as a public course after opening just prior to the 1929 stock market crash and Peace Portal was something of an afterthought.

Peace Portal's original owner and founder, a Seattle lawyer named Sam Hill, primarily developed the border course as an adjunct to a planned restaurant-hotel. In 1919, after Congress passed the Volstead Act to overrule President Woodrow Wilson's veto, the 14-year era known as Prohibition hit the United States. The enterprising Hill set out to provide dry Americans with an easily accessible watering hole. His company, Ye Olde English Restaurants Ltd., already had Surrey's only liquor permit but a planned second facility took longer than expected to complete. The planned golf course, now known as Peace Portal, took three years to complete, by which point Hill had died. Without his leadership, the bar in the company's second building took even longer to materialize than the golf course. Worse, no sooner had it opened in 1933 than Prohibition was repealed.

Howard Merrill and Chuck Wadey were Peace Portal's primary developers. Merrill, a crafty entrepreneur who had previously worked as a customs broker, railway agent and mailman, managed Peace Portal in exchange for a half interest in the complex. Wadey was course superintendent from 1929 until his 1966 retirement, when his son-in-law Ralph Charlton took over.

Hill had purchased 161 acres from various owners, paying no more than thirty-five dollars an acre. The course was designed by Seattle's Harry James. Fairways no more than 35 yards wide were hacked out of the dense forest and underbrush. Early players lost countless balls in jungle rough almost touching the greens. Some of the land was subsequently expropriated to widen King George Highway and construct the Immigration Building.

Merrill, a skilled trap-skeet shooter, encouraged caddies and his staff to play and founded the BC Lefthanders championship in the late 1930s. He was a fine player, uniquely ambidextrous, hitting woods left-handed and irons right-handed. He switched sides putting. In his 1978 review of the club's first 50 years, member Ed Hanna wrote that Merrill referred to the caddies as "my boys." When he first saw towheaded Bill Watson, Merrill asked, "What's under all that hair? Here's a quarter, get a haircut and you can have a job caddying." Watson was club champion three times and club pro for 25 years through 1975.

Watson once toured the hilly terrain in 61 while it was "playing short." The competitive record of 63 is held jointly by Doug Roxburgh and his son, Rob, an assistant under pro-manager Wendyl Arnold. A former provincial diving champion, Arnold also won three club titles before turning pro.

Andy Morgan, a crafty shot maker and Seniors contender, and Wally Mayers reigned as four- and three-time club champions respectively. Mayers was better known as a BC Hall of Fame basketball player.

Howard and Maude Merrill owned half the course and willed their shares to Bill Watson, Chuck Wadey and Ron McNally. Merrill's wishes that Peace Portal remain public have been shared by subsequent operators.

Beach Grove opened just prior to the 1929 stock market crash. It didn't survive as a public course but it became a seniors' haven, situated on flat land where they claim the sun shines more than anywhere else in the province. In 1971, when Bert Mitchell retired after 17 years in the pro shop, Beach Grove boasted more players over the age of 70 than any other club in BC. Mitchell, an accomplished clarinet and saxophone player with the bands of Dal Richards, Mart Kenney and Barney Potts, was followed in the pro shop by Bill Greatrex, Dave Roach and Sid Dahl. Brent Derrheim is the current pro.

Members converted an old 10-by-l0 gas station into their first clubhouse. The Old Green Shack stood near the present 10th tee until the 1965 opening of a second clubhouse which later became the maintenance shed. A second nine completed in 1964 has accommodated a membership that swelled from 150 after the 1959 opening of the Deas Tunnel under the Fraser River. Membership eventually surged to almost 1,000.

CHAPTER 7

THE NORTH, THE INTERIOR AND THE KOOTENAYS

Early golf in BC was not by any means confined to the coast; courses in Kelowna and Trail date back to the beginning of the 20th century. And it is this part of the province that has yielded the majority of the exciting new courses designed to attract visitors from across North America.

THE NORTH

The earliest signs of the game north of Kamloops were reported in 1925 at Prince George with 16 holes roughed along the Fraser River by George Ternan, one of Vancouver Shaughnessy's original caddies. Within two years there were plans to lease railway land and develop nine holes near the old government offices and Aboriginal graveyard. A ninth hole was finally completed in 1934, on adjoining Hudson's Bay property, and club president Bob Carter organized the Cariboo Open that September. A field of 32 men and 4 women competed. Bill Bexon broke southpaw Harry Gray's course record with a 33 (par was 32) while Carter's 72 was the best 18 holes. The trophy winners were Dr. C. Ewart, J.C. Gowan of Quesnel and a Williams Lake entrant named Alice Hooker.

A clubhouse built in 1935 was described in the local paper as "a palatial one-room retreat overlooking the mighty Fraser River." With the course stretched to par 35, Harry Morrison of Hansard Lake posted a record 31 and Harry Pettis astounded everyone in 1939 with a 64 on nines of 31 and 33.

After the war, with the city booming, the 146 members deserted the soft, sandy greens by the riverside in favour of a new all-grass course at the old airport off the Vanderhoof highway. This course was playable by 1949. When Harold Pretty arrived in 1957 as the club's new pro, the membership had edged up to 160 men and 15 women. By 1966 golf in Prince George was booming with a second nine in play and a new $200,000 clubhouse. The city's population hit 28,000 with another 12,000 in the immediate countryside; membership exceeded 500 men and 120 women.

Pretty, who had caddied and played junior golf at Victoria Uplands before serving four war years in Europe, turned pro at Alberni in 1953. He was followed into the business by his daughter, Kathy, and son, Alan. Kathy turned pro at Williams Lake and later became one of Canada's first female head professionals when she married and moved to the Nelson course as Kathy Bell in 1972. She later returned to Prince George as Kathy Mears. In all, she won 12 of the 17 club championships under three different last names.

Golf came to Williams Lake in 1926. Pioneer merchant Roderick McKenzie presided over the first membership of a course situated on what later became Boitanio Park and Mall. Other founding members were George Bryant, Claude Barber, Major Hart, Claude Huston, Ken Rife, Ed Gaspard and J.D. Smedley, whose son Jack became one of the Cariboo's leading players. Forty years later the membership moved up the hill to acreage purchased from the PGE Railway. Ernie Brown assisted in laying out the first nine in 1966 while greenskeeper Allan McKay handled the second nine seven years later in concert with his father, Gordie McKay, who had built courses at Hope, Chilliwack and Squamish.

Quesnel's original 2,200-yard par-32 course instigated by banker Colin Malcolm opened in 1930 at Charlie China's Flats on Quesnel River benchland. It was named in honour of Lord Willingdon, Canada's Governor-General, who drove the first ball on opening day. Lord and Lady Willingdon, who also played, were in Quesnel as part of a goodwill tour of the country.

Urban growth pushed golf into suburbia in 1959 after railway expansion displaced the original Willingdon Links along the Pacific Great Eastern right-of-way. The new course was developed eight kilometres east of town on the Spring Farm Ranch off Blackwater Road. When the PGE reclaimed its downtown property, a syndicate of 12 men led by Lloyd Harper, Bill Willis and Harry Keen put up $2,000 each to purchase the present site. The course opened with nine sand greens that were converted to grass by 1961. The 1983 completion of the second nine through a rugged, densely treed ravine is a tribute to the determination of the members. Noel Pumfrey, who became club manager, won the course's primary event, the Quesnel Jewellers Open, a record seven times. Little has changed in this area, partly due to declining populations.

Now called the 108 Resort Golf Course, the original 108 Mile Ranch course, a par-71 18-hole layout, was completed in 1970 by brothers Arthur and Henry Block as part of a 650-acre recreational haven. Stan Leonard was instrumental in designing the friendly layout on the rolling Cariboo landscape. In February 2009 arson destroyed a large part of the 62-room hotel at the resort which ended up in receivership. At time of writing it was back up and running.

Eligibility for the Northern British Columbia championships, which began at Smithers in 1932, was restricted to amateurs who resided between Prince George and Prince Rupert and anywhere north of the CNR line. The tournament was undertaken specifically to create sufficient golf interest and justify the extension of the Smithers course from five to nine holes.

President Charlie Reid edged club secretary Norman Kilpatrick to win the first Northern BC title on the Smithers course—three kilometres west of town on Highway 16—the same year the airport runway was built. Now 18 holes, the 6,500-yard Smithers course plays host to the Northern Open every Labour Day weekend. And there are no restrictions on a player's residence.

The story of golf north of Kamloops would be incomplete without turning to Haida Gwaii and the two courses at Sandspit and Masset. Bill and Marg Mathers of Sandspit started the Willows course on their family homestead in 1971 with the assistance of Bill Maxwell, a Crown Zellerbach engineer, and the volunteer labour of founding members. Mathers's pioneer British relatives established a seaside dairy and beef farm on the flat land beside Copper Bay Road which, uniquely, was converted into an 18-hole course with nine double-greens. Today the course features a combination of oceanfront and forest terrain and hosts a popular mixed tournament every August.

At the top end of Haida Gwaii, a shorter nine-hole course with 18 different tee boxes called Dixon Entrance was built along Tow Hill Road around a huge antenna that's central to the Canadian Forces Communications Base at Masset.

Regular golfers include service personnel from the national defence base and from Port Clements, about 30 miles to the south. The course is normally open from mid-April until the final Tombstone tournament played in early October. In the grand tradition of rural integrity, local literature states that the "clubhouse is unlocked from 8 a.m. to 8 p.m.," and "payment is by the honour system."

THE INTERIOR
HEDLEY AND PRINCETON

The fervour for gold and golf went hand in hand with the rush to Nickel Plate Mountain in the Similkameen Valley. The game was played in both Princeton and Hedley. A course on barren benchland immediately west of town existed in 1909, a year before the Great Northern Railway reached Hedley City and months before the completion of the mining town's first hospital, with its five-bed ward, two private wards and an operating room.

Four-horse freight teams and stage coaches were still the mode of transportation when several townspeople armed with picks, shovels and rakes cleared the scrub and rocks from Pinto Flat in April with the encouragement of the new owner, J.L. Merrill. Merrill, head of a New York syndicate, had recently acquired options on all the Hedley camp holdings and just happened to be an ardent golfer—and a southpaw into the bargain. Hedley's population of about 400 counted perhaps a dozen

A Christmas Day match at the new Hedley mines course in 1909 included town druggist Louis Rolls, second from right with putter. DOUG COX

would-be golfers, including Jack Fraser who laid out the course on furrowed rangeland on the outskirts of town. Without water or grass, and named after a local native known only as Pinto, the golf grounds were adorned with nothing but clumps of sage and a few lonely jack pines.

As one of the province's earliest and richest gold mining developments prospered, the town boomed. Hotels, churches, brothels and bars that never closed couldn't be built fast enough. The population rose to 1,500. By 1914, the height of Nickel Plate's first bonanza, the golf club had 22 members: 14 men and 8 women. Three played to scratch: Louis Rolls, Paddy Murray and A.W. Jack. That year, during a November competition for the Merrill Cup, the *Hedley Gazette* reported that "after finding Louis Rolls and Frank French opposition tougher than Princeton beef," W.K. Pollock defeated Emily Jackson one up while "conceding a seven-handicap to his fair opponent." Emily's father, John Jackson, had built one of the town's six hotels, the New Zealand, in 1905. Harry Barnes, a town lawyer who later wrote an account of Hedley's early history, received an inscribed gold coin for winning the second flight.

As in most other towns, golf at Hedley was affected by the First World War. A postwar labour shortage added to golf's woes when the mine closed briefly in 1921. Likewise, golfers in Princeton who had first been seen practising at Sunflower Flats established a dusty course next to the graveyard. But the lack of water soon prompted a move to an Allenby Road site almost two miles from town where a steady flow of spring water was the main attraction. The land was thick with bunchgrass, though, and in 1928 the members moved to the present course skirting Highway 3.

Hedley-born Gerald Burr recalled regular inter-club matches between the towns. A scratch player who caddied for twenty-five cents at Princeton's first courses, Burr joined the army after winning the 1940 Interior Golf Association trophy. "I probably wasn't the best golfer," he says modestly, "but the hotshot visitors couldn't putt those sand greens as good as I could." Burr was club president in the late 1970s when Don and Eleanor Porter were hired to manage the course and clubhouse.

Meanwhile, Hedley's course, like most others, was virtually deserted during the Depression and the Second World War. One day, with no golfers in sight, Chinese townsmen collecting firewood inadvertently chopped down a featured pine on the seventh hole known as Needle's Eye. Despite their claim that they had permission from the local First Nation, the tree cutters were admonished by the grounds committee and ordered to make reparation by constructing several bunkers. By 1955 mining had ceased on Nickel Plate and the course fell into disrepair. Andy Winkler, whose father, Anton, ran the Grand Union Hotel, played golf at Hedley. "With the mine being phased out, not many people were left to golf," recalled Winkler, who later settled in Keremeos. "The Indians fenced it off for grazing. Johnny Holmes, I think, put his cattle on the course and it wasn't long before the sand greens were ruined."

The first two bonanzas from Nickel Plate and the neighbouring Mascot properties yielded more than 1.5 million ounces of gold, 190,000 ounces of silver and 4 million pounds of copper. Golf has been dormant at Hedley for more than 40 years, but Giant Mascot later revived open pit gold mining on Nickel Plate—and it's prospering.

Golf is alive and booming in Kamloops—although one of the area's early golf sites turned into a ghost course and another became a cemetery.

Walhachin is now a ghost town 17 kilometres east of Cache Creek but in the years prior to the First World War it was the BC Horticultural Estates, the dream community sponsored by US dreamer Charles E. Barnes and British aristocrat the Marquis of Anglesey, who enticed many British families and young adventurers to join him in the promised land. Amenities in the colony were to include tennis, golf, a charming hotel and a climate suited to leisure while cheap labour worked the 3,000 arable acres that surrounded them. For a few years the plan started to take shape although no sign of its mysterious golf course was ever found. When 97 of the community's 107 male residents returned to Europe to enlist in 1914 the project was doomed. A storm destroyed the vital irrigation flume and all settlers drifted away with the sagebrush.

If the Walhachin course ever did exist it was a forerunner to a $500 course that 40 people started in 1914 in the bush and gullies of A.W. Johnson's McGill Road property south of Kamloops (now the Sahali subdivision). Membership increases encouraged a move in 1923 to a more spacious but hilly site near the RCMP offices. Following some difficult times for the club, the city purchased the course in 1941 for a graveyard and it became the Hilltop Cemetery. In return the members leased 171 acres adjoining Fulton Field in Bracklehurst. With former mayor Bob Affleck as president, the club bought the property for $1,550 and eventually sold 50 acres to Royalite Oil Refinery for $30,000. The Kamloops Golf and Country Club was on its way.

The principal organizers in 1946–47 were hotel owner Affleck, Judge Russ Kennedy, Stan Leonard's cabinetmaker brother Bill and Les Paterson, a truck driver. Their best decision was to hire Rod Palmer in 1951 from Shaughnessy's greens crew.

"We took Rod because he was so enthusiastic, though there was no water near the property," says Paterson, who got into real estate and presided over the BCGA in 1957. "He was a quiet, small man who worked seven days a week, 14 hours a day. When we decided to grow grass greens, we had to raise the annual fees five dollars and we lost 63 members." As BCGA president, Paterson travelled at his own expense throughout the province and rated about 75 courses. His love of the game and contribution led directly to a job and 30-year career as a sales representative for Slazenger.

Prior to his move to Kamloops, Rod Palmer, a Winnipeg-raised Englishman, served as an army cook in Newfoundland and ran a Legion cafeteria on Burrard Street in Vancouver when he wasn't tending to Shaughnessy. "After the war I didn't have a club in my hand for 10 years," recalled Palmer, whose daughter, Marilyn, won 10 BC championships. "We had to bring water in tank trucks from the river, but we opened nine holes in 1952. It was almost 10 years before we had 18 done. We borrowed a truck to move dirt, and with no machinery we did everything with shovels and rakes."

The Palmers lived for almost 18 years in a house next to the old Kamloops pro shop, which Rod tended through 1971 when he retired at 66. While his brother Ernie was two-time Manitoba champion, Rod's only claim to fame as a player was beating Point Grey amateur Jack Grundle in a playoff for the 1962 Ogopogo Open title. In the spring of 1992 Palmer was still playing several holes before breakfast almost every morning, weather permitting. The successor to the man who turned the Kamloops course green was, appropriately, Mike Graas from Point Grey's pro shop.

Bill Bilton's dream in the late 1970s—to create a golf community beside the South Thompson River—started to become reality when he hired Robert Trent Jones Sr. to build a masterpiece. The course opened in 1982 to rave reviews and in 2011 Rivershore Estates and Golf Links was the host of a Canadian Tour event in the form of the Western Championship when Roger Sloan from nearby Merritt won his first Canadian Tour event. In addition to this inaugural event, the highly rated and picturesque course has hosted the Canadian Mid-Amateur Men's Championship, Canadian Men's Amateur Championship, Canadian Ladies' Amateur Championship, Canadian Senior Men's Championship, Canadian Tour Qualifying School and the PGA BC Championship.

Another acclaimed riverside Kamloops course is the preserve of internationally recognized Graham Cooke. The Dunes, PGA BC's 2005 golf facility of the year, is situated on ground that was once part of the North Thompson riverbed. Billed as "nature's golf course," it has the feel of an Irish links setting, and a generous dose of wheat grass and wild fescue encourages players to stay on the fairways. Cooke won recognition for his work both at The Dunes and at nearby Sun Rivers Golf Course, an expansive desert course set in the rolling hills of the Thompson Valley. Both courses won runner-up honours from *Golf Digest* as Best New Canadian Course when they first opened.

Unfortunately, it appears that an oversupply of quality golf in the Kamloops area caught up with Tobiano Golf Course in the fall of 2011 when its closure was announced. It was a sad day for the Thomas McBroom layout that had been recognized as *Golf Digest*'s and *SCOREGolf* magazine's best new course in 2008 and was deemed BC's Best Public Course in 2009 and 2011 by the latter. The course was constructed on the original site of the historic Six Mile Ranch on picturesque terrain above Kamloops Lake. Doug Roxburgh called it "one of the most visually captivating and stunning courses I've ever played in 50 years of golfing." At time of writing the fate of the course remains uncertain.

Other area courses that opened before 1992 are Eagle Point and Aberdeen Hills, a nine-holer south of Kamloops. Eagle Point opened in 1991 and co-hosted with Rivershore the 1992 Canadian Seniors championships. Founded by Dolores and Hans Schlang and Michael Exner, the 6,792-yard course was designed by Robert Heaslip.

The semblance of a course existed at Merritt in the late 1920s, but it was almost 60 years before modern golfers there had a place to play. Until 1984 most Merritt golfers travelled 25 kilometres to play the Nicola Valley course at Quilchena. Merritt's flat but pleasing nine-holer was created on 40 acres by Jack Reimer and the volunteer work of local enthusiasts.

Nicola Valley's short, flat course at Quilchena came many years after the historic Guichon family home, built beside Nicola Lake, was converted into a 14-room hotel. The land next to the ranch's hotel-restaurant, turned into a course in the late 1960s, once was the scene of rousing polo matches and quarter horse racing.

The real head-turner for golfers in this area came when former PGA Tour player turned course co-designer Dick Zokol announced his Sagebrush Golf and Sporting Club in the Nicola Valley. Unique in its concept, it was named by the *SCOREGolf* panel as the Best New Golf Course in Canada for 2009. Sitting above Nicola Lake and surrounded by a vista of rolling ranchlands, the design embraces its natural environment and has evolved with little interference, thanks to the founders' minimalist design philosophies.

"Ours was a different approach, but one that we strongly believed in," said Sagebrush Golf and Sporting Club co-founder Terry Donald. In harmony with the links designs of Scotland, the course features sweeping fairways and rugged, fescue-topped bunkers. And like the original links courses, there are no rakes and little sign of mankind. The greens are huge and multiple tee boxes can stretch the course from 4,934 yards to 7,372 yards. One local rule notes that there are no tee blocks; the winner of the previous hole presumably chooses the tee-off spot; there is no posted par and in the founders' minds they have created a place where the game can be played as it was intended. At Sagebrush the golf experience includes a Mongolian-style yurt off the 12th green where you are encouraged to enjoy the seclusion and pause for a spell of fly fishing during the round. It is like no other golf experience in North America. Like many Interior courses whose openings between 2007 and 2010 ran up against overbuilding and an economic downturn, Sagebrush is currently re-examining its business model.

REVELSTOKE

At the opposite corner of the BC Interior golf zone sits the community of Revelstoke. The women of Revelstoke were prominent in the development of the town's course at Columbia Park, a racetrack site from 1905 until the First World War. The Revelstoke Turf Club built the track, grandstand and stables on acreage that had sat deserted until 1924 when a group of golfers was granted a lease from the city to create a course.

Dr. A.L. Jones and his wife were primary movers of the Interior's most popular course. While Vernon, Kamloops, Kelowna and other courses all started with sand greens, Revelstoke members enjoyed the luxury of grass surfaces from the outset—a feature that made the course unique in the region until the early 1950s. As a result, Revelstoke became a popular weekend destination for players from other centres.

Volunteer labour created the course, with six fairways coming into play on the racetrack. The oval is still discernible on the original nine. The women, 13-strong the first year and numbering 29 the second, converted the Agricultural Hall into a clubhouse. They raised funds with afternoon teas in the King Edward Hotel, suppers in the clubhouse and bridge parties at their homes. Their annual club dance in the old Masonic Hall was a highlight of the town's social calendar. They raised money for a new veranda, an electric stove, a fireplace, fuel, wiring and clubhouse insurance, and to pay wages for course improvements. In 1939 the women were each assessed a dollar to purchase curtains; in 1940 it was fifty cents for a new sink. Ten years later they gave up the upstairs lounge for use as the club's licensed premises.

Architect Norman Woods planned and supervised construction of Revelstoke's second nine on diked lowland in a bend of the Columbia River. The 6,200-yard course opened on June 12, 1976, against a spectacular backdrop of the Selkirk and Monashee mountain ranges. The century-old clubhouse with its distinctive cupola and lookout tower that dates back to its horse-race origins has been restored and refurbished as a heritage building.

A nine-hole course on Creston Flats existed in the 1930s and the town now boasts a modern 6,400-yard layout with spectacular vistas of the Kootenay River and the flats. Relocated in 1957, it was extensively reconstructed and expanded to 18 holes, including three new holes by Les Furber's Golf Design Services by 1991.

One of the club's oldest trophies, the Arlen Cup, was donated in 1936 by actor Richard Arlen while he was in Revelstoke filming the movie *The Silent Barrier*.

Proud of its wildlife, which includes the odd cougar as well as deer and basking turtles, the course literature notes that during the 2004 BC Ladies' Amateur Championship, play had to be suspended briefly when a large moose stood its ground as competitors approached the 14th green.

KELOWNA

The turn-of-the-century prophet who proclaimed that golf in Kelowna would rival orchards and vineyards as a fruitful enterprise presumably was a doctor named Jack Carruthers. An unsigned 1899 tournament report sent from the Okanagan city to the Victoria press concluded with, "We anticipate Kelowna will some day be as well known for golf as for tobacco, cricket or any other game or vegetable."

Dr. J.B. Carruthers introduced the game to the Okanagan and claimed that he conducted the first competition on the mainland of the province. Prior to Kelowna's 1899 Dominion Day tournament, there's no record of an event at the Jericho, Brockton Oval, Moodyville or Moody Square courses on the mainland. Carruthers set nine holes along the lakeshore north of town, near the present city hall.

The good doctor wasn't without experience. He had arrived in Kelowna the winter before from Vancouver, where he played to a scratch at Jericho. A proficient cricketer, he also golfed at Brockton Point and helped direct construction of the Moodyville course in North Vancouver.

Seven residents joined Carruthers for Kelowna's inaugural event. Other golfers were in the area but it seems that holiday picnics proved a stronger attraction for some bachelors. Only Carruthers had more than a month's acquaintance with the game—as was reflected in the scores. Barred from the prizes because of his handicap, Carruthers shot 99. James Houston's 127 stood up as the next best round. Hugh Rose and Alex Gammie tied for longest drive of 129 yards; E.R. Bailey had low net of 94; and P. Spicer had the day's best approach shot, which, a report noted, "shows that in Kelowna, as elsewhere, aptitude for golf is not exclusively the privilege of the youngest players."

Carruthers was 72 when he died in 1925, a year before the Interior's first 18-hole course opened on the present Kelowna Golf and Country Club site. It was known as the Woolaston property.

Lionel Taylor, an Irish-born orchardist from South Africa, managed a second course in the Bankhead Orchard area during the First World War. It never achieved the required 50 members, at ten dollars for men and five dollars for women. One year, membership subscriptions and golf ball sales amounted to only $291.

Kelowna's first pro, James Gourlay, came from St Andrews by way of England in 1917 and returned to his native Scotland 15 years later. For seventy-five dollars monthly, he worked as pro and greenskeeper from 8:00 AM to 6:00 PM daily, after which he was "allowed" to give lessons at City Park. Gourlay had remained when the Bankhead course was abandoned in 1920 in favour of the Woolaston project which was initiated by a provisional committee of Elisha Bailey, G.R. Binger, G.E. Seon, Dr. G. Campbell and E.J. Maguire. On the first board were president P.B. Willits, E.A. Taylor, Grote Stirling, K. MacLaren and W.E. Adams. Stirling was subsequently elected club president and Yale's Conservative member of parliament for 23 years.

By 1926, with Royal Bank manager H.E. Rees as president of the 216-member club, Kelowna expanded to 18 holes. Jericho pro Alex Duthie designed a second nine, including the signature ninth green that jutted into Eagle Pond in a hollow below the clubhouse. It was familiarly known as the "thousand-dollar hole" or "Duthie hole."

In the early 1950s some club property was sold to the city to finance an irrigation system and grass greens. They now had a verdant course, but room for only nine holes. Within the next decade adjoining property was acquired and a new 18 over 120 acres opened in June 1962. Popular with tourists, the well-manicured course is home to the annual Ogopogo Open that attracts leading players from throughout the province.

The BC Amateur first visited the Interior in 1964 at Kelowna, which has also been the venue for two Canadian Junior championships. The 1969 Junior winner, Dale Tallon, became better known as a Vancouver

Kelowna's longest-serving pro, Dave Crane, wore an army uniform during the Second World War. The Duncan native started under Victoria's Phil Taylor, went overseas and then spent 21 years at Kelowna until his retirement in 1975. Crane died in 1991.

Canucks first draft choice when the team joined the NHL. Local product Brad Newman-Bennett prevailed in 1988.

Among local legends, Chester Owen won his seventh club championship in 1942 while Anne McClymont took the women's title 17 times, Melba Fairholm took it 10 times and Joan Campbell 9. Touring pros Dave Barr and Gail Graham are the club's most celebrated members.

Planned as a resort–dude ranch, Gallagher's Canyon has never lived up to that billing. However, the course originally named Kelowna Pines earned a reputation as a championship layout right from the beginning. In 1979 oil magnate Angus Mackenzie and associates purchased 350 acres from Kelowna businessmen Dan Kitsul and Roger Simoneau. The architectural firm of Cornish & Robinson transformed it into a course worthy of selection for the 1988 Canadian Amateur, the Canadian club championships, Canadian Tour qualifying, BC Seniors and BC Lefthanders.

Pro-manager Dick Munn, an enterprising partner in Gallagher's, also brought considerable attention to the course, to Kelowna and to BC by arranging first-class exhibition matches. As early as 1981 Munn had Arnold Palmer and Hale Irwin playing Canadian pros Dave Barr and Dan Halldorson at the McCulloch Road course. Fuzzy Zoeller and Andy Bean came in 1984 to face local amateurs Grant Barnes and Dean Claggett. Meg Mallon, Cindy Rarick, Hiromi Kobayashi and Kelowna's Gail Graham were whisked to Gallagher's for a match following the 1991 LPGA du Maurier at Vancouver Golf Club.

The MacKenzie group sold the course and adjoining property (412 acres in total) in 1990 to Burrard International of Vancouver. The company revamped Gallagher's Canyon moderately and developed residential sites on its perimeter.

Less than a month after the historic Kelowna tournament in 1899, the *Vernon News* reported that "links are being laid out west of town by a party of visitors who are staying at the Kalamalka [hotel]," and that "this popular game has never been introduced in this section, but it is probable a club will now be formed."

It took 14 years for the Vernon Golf and Country Club's original course to materialize in a drive led by local customs broker H.G. Nangle. During that time both cattle ranching and grain farming flourished and developers started to look beyond the city core. Land values soared from one dollar per acre to $150. In 1907 the Land and Agriculture Co. of Canada, a Belgian syndicate, bought 14,606 acres and built the area's first major irrigation canal to accommodate fruit orchards. Vernon was fast becoming the Okanagan's leading trade centre with some 3,000 area residents, when Nangle's group purchased a 110-acre tract in the BX Valley off Silver Star Road from the Belgians for $16,500. While en route from the west coast, noted Chicago architect Tom Bendelow agreed to lay out Vernon's course. The Aberdeen native, credited with several hundred courses throughout the world, mapped out a par 36 of 3,265 yards that included irrigation for greens. In the first recorded tournament on July 31, 1913, Maxwell Allen's net 50 took the Nangle Cup.

By this point Europe was quivering with rumblings of war and builders were putting the finishing touches on the Vernon Armoury where the 54th Kootenay Battalion was mobilized. The area's population swelled with over 10,000 recruits during the First World War and the new golf course lay fallow.

According to club historian Douglas Cole, the *Vernon News* carried few mentions of golf during the war. We have only sketchy details about the East Hill course near the present high school that was developed by 1920 to replace the B.X. original. Two years later six holes were playable on a second course off Kalamalka Lake Road, the current club site. Agitated by controversy and turmoil over the years, club members opted for expansion in 1969 with Ernie Brown handling the redesign. A long, bitter debate about the merits of relocating to Coldstream Ranch had concluded with the decision to stay put and to use a government grant to install an automatic sprinkling system. Today towering Lombardy poplars and majestic weeping willows characterize this classic course.

PENTICTON

About 50 Penticton volunteers created nine holes in 1917 on the present site of Memorial Arena and Queen's Park. One skimpy report indicated that before a series of oxbows in the Okanagan River were channelized, residents crossed from the foot of Fairview Road on what was then known as the Red Bridge to play on Indian Reserve land.

James J. Warren of the Kettle Valley Railway suggested the first course to the Penticton Board of Trade. The enthusiasts shared a soggy site with a half-mile racetrack and baseball diamond, hauling sand from the beach for the greens and tees. Member Tommy Syer formed flagsticks by melting lead purchased from the CPR, and his wife sewed flags from flour sacks.

By 1921 a second site southeast at King's Park had become home for a 50-member club. J.R. Mitchell was elected president and C. Thornton, who had learned the game in Scotland, offered his services as instructor. It too was boggy property. The members finally moved in 1925 to higher, drier land—too dry as it turned out. They received a city grant and sold $100 debentures at 7 percent interest to purchase Munson Flats on the Skaha Lake Bench near Pineview Road. Jericho's Alex Duthie designed a sporty nine-hole course of 3,160 yards. The site had two drawbacks. While golfers could walk to the old course, vehicles were required to reach Munson Flats. More seriously, the water shortage was critical and remained so even after a well was drilled in an effort to save the course. It was time to move on.

With $2,000 from the sale of the Munson property and a $300 city grant, the hardy members returned to the King's Park area where a new $8,000 course on 50 city-leased acres took shape in 1936. Significantly, an adequate water supply allowed the construction of grass greens and the clubhouse was moved from the former site. With a 20-year lease, the club hired Henry Schmelzel and his wife as managers and Ron Jamieson as first pro.

By the end of the Second World War, both Penticton's population and the number of golfers had almost doubled. Other leases with the city and First Nation band were obtained in 1952 and 1961, and in 1957 the course of the adjoining river connecting the Okanagan and Skaha lakes was altered. Four years later an 18-hole course was completed, followed by an ambitious $100,000 clubhouse.

In 1964, former hockey player Bill Carse, Penticton pro of nine years, was succeeded by long-time amateur star Bob Kidd. Kidd played infrequently while serving a membership that grew from 75 to 600 and worked closely with greens superintendent Don McLeod on course improvements. Kidd retired in 1985.

OTHER COMMUNITIES

The underlying factor that linked the success of courses in smaller communities was the willingness of enthusiastic members to roll up their sleeves and pitch in so they could play the game. The Oliver course, Fairview Mountain, is a classic example of the effort and perseverance required to realize a seemingly impossible vision.

The Oliver Golf and Country Club members can proudly boast of their course in the sun-parched hills directly below the old gold mining camp at Fairview. But their dream course didn't come easily or quickly. Forty-five years after the course was founded they were still putting on sand greens. In the meantime, the challenge of acquiring water prompted some members to abandon their roots and build Cherry Grove, an alternative course, in 1961. Paul Eisenhut Sr. and Don Coy developed Cherry Grove after negotiating a 40-year lease with the Inkameep Band on property less than a mile from downtown Oliver. Paul Eisenhut Jr., a qualified draftsman, designed a course lined with 250 cherry trees.

Cherry Grove, a nine-hole layout located on slopes above Tucilnuit Lake, has most recently re-emerged as the widely praised Nk'Mip Canyon Desert Golf Course, a $3 million expansion to 18 holes that winds through the original cherry grove, vineyards and a desert canyon. *Nk'Mip* (pronounced Inkameep) roughly translates as "flat-bottom land at the mouth of the river" but the spectacular development funded by the Osoyoos Indian Band Development Corporation includes broad practice facilities and an award-winning restaurant.

Meanwhile, nearby Fairview Mountain's hard-core members soldiered on. They refused to surrender to the tundra that their namesake premier, Honest John Oliver, and his benevolent government had made available to the zealous golf residents in 1925. The 200 acres of sagebrush, dreaded speargrass and cacti were too high and dry for use as anything else.

The first president was the club's finest golfer for many years, Sandy MacPherson, a village merchant. Other founders were a group of five novice orchardists who were employed as part of the provincial government's Southern Okanagan Lands Project that opened the area for settlement following the First World War.

Bob Robertson, a Scottish golfer who resided at Dog Lake near Okanagan Falls, helped lay out the original nine holes. Nine members volunteered to care for one putting surface each, fencing them with wire strands to divert grazing cattle. Without funds for mowing, summer golf was suspended until the dry grass could be burned off for fresh green fairways by fall.

John Mars and another founder, Cosmo Bruce, were coerced by their companions into a nine-hole challenge, with the loser to provide a floor for the clubhouse. Bruce, who owned the local lumberyard, conveniently lost and all his golfing pals reaped the benefits.

After struggling through some lean years, Fairview was the area's first course to reorganize following the Second World War. With a heavy influx of newcomers to the valley, it became popularly known as the Triple O Club as members came from Oliver, Osoyoos and Oroville, just south of the 49th parallel, in Washington.

The Oliver Golf and Country Club, alias Fairview Mountain and Triple O, finally got a full irrigation system in 1970. Members installed the hundreds of feet of pipe and 20 years later also helped local contractors to expand and renovate to 18 holes. The $1.5 million project initiated by club president Terry Kehoe and his 1985 executive was aided by a $282,000 GO BC government grant.

Fairview Mountain counted 160 faithful members in 1985; six years later it approached 500 with room for only 150 more regulars.

Golf flourished throughout the Okanagan, and was most often championed by a few local activists who loved the game. The Kettle Valley course opened in 1927 through the efforts of Major Rupert Gray, ranchers H. Douglas Hamilton, Arthur Roberts, postmaster G. Heaven and the fire warden A. Roheslie. The 70-acre, nine-hole course, remodelled in 1988, has had grass greens only since 1991—and ball-stealing crows ever since the club's historian, Lynda Dennill, can remember.

An orchard now stands on the site of Osoyoos's original course fashioned by Raymond Fraser and R.H. Plaskett. It was arid rangeland at the foot of Osoyoos Hill, or Anarchist Mountain. There might be no boulders or dust on Osoyoos's modern course, but rattlesnakes have been sighted on the lush premises and July hailstones have sent players scurrying for cover. The lushness comes courtesy of an effluent-treatment plant adjacent to the course, where 9 holes were playable by 1973 and a full 18 by 1980.

Courses in the Summerland area have existed on and off since 1929. The original course on Paradise Flats, tended by Andrew Fenwick, was deserted by the 50 members during the war but restarted in 1946. It has been said that the first vice-president, Reverend Solly, wore plus-fours under his vestment so he could make his tee-off time after Sunday service. The club's postwar revival was brief, however, as too many members were attracted to nearby Penticton's grass greens.

The Sumac Ridge nine-holer was developed on an estate winery in the 1960s before Lee Hodgson re-established the Summerland Golf and Country in 1978 on the original benchland site about five kilometres from town. Some 150 people joined the resurrected Summerland course and eventually built a clubhouse through a government grant and $500 assessments. By 1986 they were playing 18 holes and by 1991 had a waiting list with 650 members.

Former Quilchena pro Alf Tate and Tom Dawson purchased the Ponderosa course at Peachland from Peter Spackman in 1985 and expanded it to 18 holes. A demanding hillside challenge that overlooks

Lake Okanagan, the Ponderosa course was known for its disti
clubhouse. Constructed in 100 Mile House and reassembled
was one of the largest log structures in the province with 7,600 ...
feet on the main floor and 4,000 on the second.

More recently, the course has given way to a grand real estate vision known simply as Ponderosa. A new Greg Norman–designed 7,100-yard course that embraces the natural terrain above lakeside Peachland has overcome the economic slowdown and is now scheduled to open in 2013.

Owner John Moore designed the Shannon Lake course outside of Westbank that first opened in 1985 and remains a popular track. A second course, Sunset Ranch, opened six years later and now anchors a popular gated community that is part of the steady growth pattern in the entire Okanagan region over the past 20 years.

In 1990 Norm Keglovic and Bob Calder completed their course on a 120-year-old ranch first settled by William "Scotty" Donaldson. Scotty Creek, which runs through Sunset Ranch, pays tribute to the founder.

THE KOOTENAYS

This southeast region of the province includes courses concentrated near Golden and Radium Hot Springs to the north and from Fernie west to Christina Lake near the US border.

Few 18-hole courses existed outside of Vancouver and Victoria until well after the Second World War. In the nooks and crannies of mountainous areas, in communities such as Cranbrook, Kimberley and Fernie, hockey and curling were the popular recreational pursuits.

FERNIE

Curling executives met in Fernie in April 1918 to discuss a golf course. By July a crude layout existed north of town thanks to donations that totalled $500 and incalculable hours of volunteer labour. The Crows Nest Pass Coal Company provided tangible corporate support from the beginning and over the years donated the pipe to convey water for the fairways. It was 50 years before the course had its first grass greens thanks to a debenture program, donations from Crows Nest, Kaiser Resources and local equipment companies. The $30,000 project included the purchase of equipment necessary to maintain the new putting surfaces.

By 1973 the present clubhouse was completed, and the decision to expand to 18 holes came 10 years later. With additional land donated by Crows Nest Industries, president Dan Cox's expansion committee retained Alberta course architect Bill Newis to design the course and supervise construction. Three holes from the original nine were eliminated and incorporated into the development of 12 new holes. With government grants, bank loans, corporate assistance that included equipment supervision by Nohels Logging's Terry Sharpe and volunteers, the course opened in early 1986.

TRAIL

Near Trail, golf had been informally practised around 1900 on a reported five-hole "course" created on Tadanac Flats by engineers at Cominco, the world's largest lead and zinc smelter. But it wasn't until 1922 that the Rossland–Trail Club was formed on the old Floyd dairy farm between the neighbouring centres. Cominco donated the land, with company general manager S.G. Blaylock becoming the club's first president.

Four years later, due to insufficient water supply, the club relocated on hilly farmland up Trail Creek Valley after Cominco made the Endersby farm property available for the development of a longer course. Endersby had been one of 52 area farmers who claimed and received damages from Cominco for sulphur-laden smoke damage to crops. The company gave a sum payment for smoke easement and purchased four farms outright. Years later smoke easement compensation for crop damage would lead to the development of the current 18-hole Birchbank course. For many years the course was known for its rustic log clubhouse and for the unique motor-driven rope tow that pulls players up the precipitous fifth fairway.

Reg and Roy Stone arrived in Trail in 1937 and soon became a big part of the Trail sports and recreation scene in both winter and summer. The curling exploits of the brothers brought as much distinction to Trail as the city's world champion hockey Smoke Eaters of 1938. That same year the golf course was expanded 800 yards to beyond 3,100 yards, which suited the Stones just fine. They were golfers first and curlers second.

The Stone brothers, Reg (left) and Roy, were fixtures at Rossland-Trail for over 40 years until Roy retired as club pro in 1978. BC SPORTS HALL OF FAME 6911.13 AND 611.4

Born in Nanette, Manitoba, Reg and Roy grew up in Chilliwack and caddied at the original Fairfield Island course. "We lived near town and it was seven miles to the course. We'd walk with clubs in hand, hitting shots through the fields and down streets," says Roy. "The longest hole we played was a mile and a half. I forget what we set for par."

Reg won the Fairfield club championship at 16 and before his 19th birthday he owned his own bakery in Chilliwack. With the Depression in full swing the three-time Fraser Valley Amateur champion sold Reg's Bakery to McGavin's. With his older brother's bakery gone, Roy, who had worked for Reg, joined 4X Bakery in Vancouver. He was transferred in 1937 to Trail, where he also worked as a plumber and candy-maker. Reg followed. In 1940 Reg took over as pro-greenskeeper at Rossland–Trail and his wife, Ruby, operated the clubhouse. During the war, Roy helped cut the fairways and greens after his early bakery shifts. Reg supplemented his winter wages by managing the Trail ice rink. When he was appointed superintendent of parks and recreation in 1949, a position that included managing the new arena, Roy succeeded him at both the golf course and the old curling rink.

The Stones organized the Rossland–Trail Open in 1947 and played host to the first major provincial championship staged outside Vancouver–Victoria, the BC Open of 1951. Chuck Congdon of Tacoma won top money of $450 but was more taken with the hospitality and his bonus prize of flies crafted by Curly Wheatley, a hockey referee renowned for catching trout that he would give to friends because he never ate them.

Congdon whipped the field of 90 by shooting a 10-under 278 and three-putting only once on the tricky greens. Stan Leonard, champion for the previous two years, received $300 in second place, nine strokes back. No one else finished under par.

In 1962 the golf course was on the move again, this time to the flat picturesque Birchbank property north of town which overlooks the Columbia River. Like the previous sites, it was an orchard blighted by sulphuric smoke from Cominco's smelter stacks. Reg Stone and Pete McIntyre designed Birchbank. McIntyre, the Cominco personnel manager, was an accomplished left-handed golfer, as were Buzz McGibney and Tommy Ross. The sons of greenskeeper Bob Donaldson, Art and Harry, were also leading players.

Today the mature course sits along the banks of the mighty Columbia River with spectacular views of the Selkirk and Monashee Mountains, and is known for its manicured greens and contoured fairways.

Roy Stone retired as club pro in 1978 and got to keep a BC Seniors trophy after winning it five straight years. Reg Stone, who waited six years for reinstatement as an amateur, retired as parks superintendent in 1974. The Stones were inducted into the BC Sports Hall of Fame in 1984 for their curling accomplishments, but they contributed significantly to golf. They were also advisors in the design and remodelling of courses at Christina Lake, Castlegar, Elkford, Nakusp, Rock Creek and Salmo.

Cominco also contributed to making golf available in Nelson and Kimberley, among other Interior centres where the company had operations.

In 1951 the Rossland–Trail course became the first inland course to host the BC Open.
ARV OLSON COLLECTION

NELSON

Golf travelled to Nelson in 1919 with Blaylock, now Cominco chairman, and a course full of company employees from the Trail–Rossland area. Blaylock built a mansion at Three Mile during the Depression and many of his underlings purchased property for summer homes along the shoreline of Kootenay Lake. The boomtown of about 10,000 was the main railway terminus for the Kootenays. Products were barged on the lake to Kaslo and Creston, and hotels were everywhere.

A 1919 editorial in the *Nelson Daily News* strenuously advocated that

> a course is absolutely essential in any town that has any pretentions of being up to date and such an attraction will undoubtedly be of the greatest possible benefit to Nelson. It's safe to say 96 percent of the touring public are golfers and that almost a universal query is what are the opportunities for enjoying golf.

Charlie Lipinski, seen here, and Charlie Blunt shared greenskeeping duties at Nelson 1935.
JIM LORMAN

With a panoramic view of the lake and Selkirk mountains, the hillside course on the Rosemont farm-orchard land offered seven holes by 1920. Original memberships cost thirty-five dollars but with only 20 founding members, capital for equipment was lacking. Farmers leased the property for grazing sheep, which kept the fairways reasonably trim, and members harvested the fruit trees and set out roadside sales stands. Fittingly, the first club secretary was an insurance agent named Clement Appleyard. The par-31 course measured only about 2,000 yards, with room for a clubhouse and courts for the West Kootenay Tennis Association.

One of the founding members, Eddie Benger, was known as Sparky or Lightning—and for good reason. Playing on a July 1980 afternoon with his wife, Iris, and son Jim, Benger lived to tell about the most shocking experience of his life.

> We were at the sixth tee, waiting for the group ahead
> to clear. The rain started suddenly from dark, passing

clouds. Iris broke out her umbrella and Jim was standing, club in hand, on railroad-tie steps to the tee. I was sitting on the bench, next to Jim's propped bag, behind the screen fence that protects people from being hit by balls coming off the second tee.

The next thing I remember was waking up in the hospital. The bolt of lightning had cracked the top of a nearby fir, ricocheted to piping in the wire fence, knocked Jim over through his club and then smacked me.

Jim's clubs next to me were totally destroyed and I was thrown about 15 feet backward through the screen and into a pile of rocks. People on the second green got an ambulance in a hurry. I spent a week in hospital with two broken ribs and a deep gash in my head from hitting the rocks.

Charlie Blunt arrived in Nelson from Moose Jaw, first as greenskeeper in 1935 and then as pro and secretary-treasurer. "In those days being a pro had nothing to do with golf ability," said Blunt, who received fifty cents for half-hour lessons. "It had to do with repairing golf clubs." Charlie and his wife, Zilla, were honoured with lifetime club memberships for their long service.

In 1972 Kathy Bell arrived in Nelson as Canada's first approved female club professional. The daughter of Prince George pro Harold Pretty had previously worked at Williams Lake but without membership in the PGA. "The PGA didn't know what to do with me when I applied for membership," said the 24-year-old redhead who arrived in Nelson with a 20-month-old son, a husband and a four handicap. "They'd never received such an application before." Bell twice reached the BC Amateur semifinals.

In 1989 at Castlegar, Brian DeBiasio came within two strokes of bringing home the Bostock Trophy as BC champion. The high school teacher, who also played a fair game of hockey, tied Qualicum Beach's Stephen Watson for second, a stroke behind winner Doug Roxburgh.

An early vista from Nelson's course above Kootenay Lake, now known as Granite Pointe.
NELSON MUSEUM OF ART AND HISTORY 1844

Between them, DeBiasio and Ed Clem captured Nelson's Labour Day Open 18 times by 1992, with the ex-Nelson Maple Leaf forward reigning after 10 long weekends.

From 2,000 yards and its original seven holes, the club expanded in 1993 to an 18-hole course and was renamed Granite Pointe. Architect Bill Newis was brought in to design the 6,300-yard track that sits on over 150 acres. The property contains an acre that the struggling club had sold in 1946 for $1,000. The repurchase price 44 years later: $80,000.

KIMBERLEY

The big Sullivan lead-zinc mine was the life-blood of Kimberley, where players first golfed in 1924. Cominco was behind the construction of six holes on company property along the banks of the St. Mary's River. Company machinery was used to construct the course and an old miners' bunkhouse served as a clubhouse.

One of BC's earliest resort courses was built at Radium Hot Springs in 1957 and was a precursor of destination golf as a popular summer pastime in the province. Doug and Bruce McIntosh expanded the Radium spa resort's original nine-hole course to 18 by 1979. The area gained even more appeal after 1988 when the longer, more challenging Springs course, yet another Les Furber design, attracted considerable attention and a new reason for tourists to put the Springs on their travel route. This course is perched beside the Columbia River and is constantly ranked in Canada's Top 100 lists.

Three holes were added on adjoining swamp land largely through the efforts of Ted Nagel, a Kimberley sportsman who tired of playing the course three times to complete one round. Kimberley's first pro, Jim Woods, tended to course duties between fur trapping and summer employment as a Cominco axeman. The course was expanded to 18 holes in 1980, an addition designed by Norman Woods.

CASTLEGAR

The founding members of the first 18-hole course in the Kootenays were, in essence, squatters from the village of Castlegar. Sixteen enthusiasts met at Ralph West's Castlegar Department Store in May 1958 and decided to create a course on land previously cleared and farmed by early Doukhobor settlers. Located above the airport, the property is ironically near the confluence of the Columbia and Kootenay rivers. Why ironic? There was a constant struggle to obtain water for the course.

The course development was a tribute to the community's tenacity. In 1959 the club had 40 members, a bank balance of $125.23, sand greens and sparse fairways chiselled out of buck brush and tall grass. By September 1968 Castlegar had opened six months ahead of nearby Birchbank, making it the Kootenays' first full course. Several years before, Birchbank proponents had coaxed some Castlegar members into joining their project while predicting failure for Castlegar. Castlegar's golf pioneers squatted on the 183-acre tract until legally purchasing it for one dollar an acre from the government in 1963. It was designated parkland.

Like many early courses, Castlegar's original seventh hole features a sand green. MARY MARTIN

The founding members were store owner West, Bank of Montreal manager Cy Onions, district school inspector Barry Harford, Herb Binnie, Walter Jacobson, Jim Kelly, Tom Lampard, Earl Leroy, Otto Walker, John Miros, Charlie Blunt and Mike Verzuh, a Cominco fertilizer plant supervisor who had settled in Kinnaird. West had recommended the area where he used to hunt for the course. While mapping out nine holes, someone suggested hitting a few shots. Given the honour, Harford proceeded to drive into a big boulder near the teeing area. The ball boomeranged back toward the players but missed everyone. Only West's ego was bruised. By 1958 there were nine holes but the discovery of well water led to the completion of a brand new nine with grass greens in 1966, and Verzuh took over as club pro from Al Tomiuk, who went to Christina Lake.

The club slogan was "Built by the working man for the working man." However, big business eased the task of Castlegar's working men and women. Assistance came from Boyd McMillian, project manager of Foundation Bravo, builders of the Keenleyside Dam, Sam Walker of BC Hydro, Celgar's Arnie Simms, Columbia Breweries and Trail pro Roy Stone, who helped in the design.

Denny McArthur, from West Vancouver's Gleneagles, was hired in 1974 to replace the retiring Mike Verzuh as club pro. Superintendent Nick Sherstobitoff needed all his expertise to save the course when well-water levels dropped dangerously low one summer. The club eventually installed a $50,000 system to pump water from the Brilliant Dam to course holding ponds.

The demanding 6,560-yard course was the first in the Kootenays to play host to the BC Amateur, won in 1980 by Sandy Harper. Doug Roxburgh fashioned his 10th BC title in 1989 at Castlegar and Birchbank.

GOLDEN

Another community that persisted in getting its own course was Golden. The first club committee came together in 1935 and seven years later opened their first five-hole golf course south of town near Reflection Lake. However, local golfers had to cross Roger's Pass and play the Revelstoke course to record official tournament rounds.

There was a failed attempt to develop a different golf site in the 1970s before a serious fundraising effort got underway in the early 1980s. One famous fundraiser occurred in the first week of fall in 1984 when "The Longest Hole" was played. Four players teed off in Parson and played a 33-kilometre long hole that ended in Golden. Roger and Mike Ross, Lil Dewar and Muzzy registered 271 strokes and claimed a Guinness World Record for the longest golf hole ever played at the time. (The record has since been broken.)

The original nine-hole golf course opened to members the next year and has since been expanded to a 6,325-yard joyride from the mid-tees, with nary a building in sight for most of the journey. Word of mouth has made it a must-play course among avid golfers travelling in the Kicking

Horse Pass area. In addition, the surge of courses south of Golden along Highway 95-95A through Kimberley to Cranbrook has made this one of BC's most attractive golf routes.

The comparatively short nine-hole Nakusp Centennial course on the east side of Upper Arrow Lake also has a Keenleyside Dam connection. The original clubhouse, purchased for $100, was an old farmhouse removed by BC Hydro as part of the clearing process for the dam's reservoir. Townspeople met in May 1965 to form a club, purchasing M. Fraitzl's flat 38-acre Leverington property in the heart of the Selkirk Mountains. Bill Dupuis chaired the first board of directors, assisted by Fred Sellers and Bill Defoe. An on-site cairn and plaque honour the club's most remarkable volunteer, Myrna Abbey.

Kokanee Springs, a breathtakingly scenic course at Crawford Bay, experienced growing pains in its infancy but it became a true golf resort in 1992, opening an on-site 26-unit lodge. Architect Norman Woods had started shaping the course 25 years before on 120 acres of Ken Jennings's expansive land holdings. The Calgary oilman subsequently took on Oklahoma partners. However, by 1971, after all the greens had died in successive springs, company vice-president Ed Moore was forced to close what was jokingly called "the Kootenays' million-dollar hay field."

After being fully reopened by 1975, the course was purchased five years later by Redfield Developments of Alberta but the remoteness of the course continued to challenge its feasibility. Claude Gallinger, one of Redfield's original principals, formed Kokanee Springs Resort Ltd. and bought the course out of receivership in late 1988. Come summertime the course continues to display its classic good looks with the Kokanee Glacier and ever-appealing backdrop. The lodge has been expanded to 56 rooms.

RECENT DEVELOPMENTS: 1990 ONWARD

The Kootenay region, like the neighbouring Okanagan region, enjoyed a surge of new golf course development in the early 1990s. With Golden and Radium Hot Springs gaining new fans, the route to follow became Highway 95 south to Fairmont, Invermere and Panorama. The skiers had fabulous powder snow in the winter and golfers were discovering dramatic new golf venues at an alarming pace. And, of course, it has always been a mecca for fly fishers.

The Invermere area is a good example of a dual-season recreational region. From a golfer's perspective, one of the highlights has to be the par-70 course at Copper Point which was designed by Gary Browning and opened in 2004. Great terrain above Lake Windermere has been used rather than abused, with undulating greens and many strategic bunkers. More recently the par-62 ridge course playing to about 4,000 yards from the middle tees may be a sign of the future. The latest trend in course construction seems to be toward shorter layouts that can be played in less time at less expense.

At Eagle Ranch the atmosphere is more akin to that of a resort community, with a quality 18 holes and access to Lake Windermere as the drawing cards. Surrounded by the Rockies and Purcell mountains, this is another development enticing well-to-do Albertans to spend their leisure time in a BC recreational sanctuary.

West of Invermere beside Toby Creek lies the magic of Greywolf. The young course designed by Doug Carrick has been recognized by *Golf Digest* as one of the best 100 courses in the world outside of the United States. Known for its memorable collection of par-three holes, it shares with other regional courses a simply spectacular landscape.

Ironically, most of these courses do not see Vancouver as a primary market when it comes to advertising dollars. It seems that only time and the state of the Alberta economy will determine their economic future. Both the par-66 Windermere Valley course and the more upscale Fairmont Hot Springs made it onto the golfing map in 1988 when the latter opened its first 18-hole layout, the Riverside Course. Enlisting the headwaters of the Columbia River as a primary feature of the course, this layout set a standard that has inspired many of the more recent creations. A second course, Mountainside, was added as traffic flow grew and both courses are normally open from the beginning of April to late October.

Near Kimberley, Les Furber's Golf Design Services created Trickle Creek, an alpine gem on the slopes of North Star Mountain, near the ski resort that opened in 1992. Like most Furber courses this one accommodates all levels of golfer.

Golf was first played in Cranbrook as early as 1915 on a long-abandoned course. The current course opened in 1951 and has hosted a number of provincial championships for both senior and junior golfers. In 2004 Cranbrook was the proud host of the RCGA Senior Men's Match Play Championship. The well-manicured course is very walkable and boasts that it is blessed with the most hours of sunshine of any course in BC.

Les Furber came to Cranbrook at the turn of the millennium and in 2001 *Golf Digest* magazine included his St. Eugene Golf Course in the top three Best New Canadian Golf Courses. The course is bordered on the north and west by St. Mary's River, and the dramatic shape of Fisher Peak can be quite a distraction for golfers on the homeward holes.

The latest planned community in the area, Shadow Mountain, is home to Shadow Mountain Golf Course, north of Cranbrook off Highway 95A. *SCOREGolf* named this one of the Best New Courses in Canada in 2010.

Cranbrook is also home to three shorter course layouts, each with its own personality. Mission Hills Golf Course has a total of 21 holes creatively set out in three different configurations. Will-O-Bend is a nine-holer with inviting water on six of them. Way-Lyn Ranch is a par-62 family course with holes ranging from 100 yards to 275 yards.

CHAPTER 8
THE BLACKS: FATHER AND SON

Possibly the most famous father-son duo in the history of BC golf, Davey and Ken Black were different in many ways. However, both were major contributors to golf at the national and provincial levels.

Ken Black was born into golf. His playpen was a golf course. A cleek, mashie, mid-iron and putter were his first set of toys. Throughout his infancy and boyhood, in Montreal, Ottawa and Vancouver, his front yard was a putting green and out back was the practice area.

Ken Black's father was a golf professional, as were six of his uncles. He had an intrinsic passion for the game, and he came to idolize Bobby Jones in an era of larger-than-life sports figures named Ruth, Grange, Cobb and Dempsey. But it was his father, the man he worshipped fervently, whom Ken Black strived to emulate. David Lambie Black was widely liked and respected, first as the "Little Man of Iron" and then as simply "Wee Davey." He was a squat, resolute man with deep roots in the seaside turf of Troon, in the west of Scotland, where golf was part of the landscape and nature was the architect of the links. Davey Black was the ultimate sportsman and gentleman. It was often said there was never a better loser nor more gracious winner than Davey Black.

No taller than five-foot-five, Wee Davey was one of nine boys in his family, six of whom left Scotland. John emigrated to California along with brother Bob. Jim went farther afield, to Manila, while George settled in Chicago and Willie landed at Royal Colwood in Victoria before discovering Bellingham. Davey ended up at Shaughnessy Heights in Vancouver after serving six years as an apprentice club maker at Troon, where he worked under master craftsman Willie Fernie, who played well enough to win the 1877 British Open.

In his only British appearance as a pro, Davey acquitted himself well. He was 17 when he tied Andrew Kirkaldy for 10th in an event at Bogside, won by none other than six-time British Open champion Harry Vardon. Kirkaldy, once described as the best player never to have won the Open, succeeded Old Tom Morris in 1910 as St Andrews pro.

Wee Davey had eyes only for America, and followed his brothers across the Atlantic in 1905. He was 22. Almost as soon as he arrived he caused something of a stir in Montreal. In an open event he tied for first with Charles Murray, who became Canadian Open champion the following year. The quiet, young expatriate served at Outremont and St. Lambert before going to Ottawa Rivermead in 1911. The same year, when the eighth annual Canadian Open was played nearby, at the Royal Ottawa Golf Club, he was runner-up to Murray, the Royal Montreal head pro, losing by two strokes. After the two-day event finished, Davey was one of about 24 pros present who met and founded the Canadian Professional Golf Association, at the time only the second PGA in the world. The British PGA preceded it by a decade and the US PGA would be formed five years later.

Prior to the First World War, Davey finished sixth, fourth and third in Canadian Opens and won his first of four CPGA titles. During this period he would escape the harsh Canadian winters and join his brothers John and Bob in California. He taught annually near Sacramento for over a decade, through 1919, and fell in love with the west coast. In the 1916 Southern California Open he was second to brother Bob.

When the Shaughnessy job became available in February 1920, Davey didn't hesitate to apply. His guaranteed salary made him one of Canada's best-paid pros. The Black family had resided in quarters next to the club-house at Ottawa Rivermead; at Shaughnessy a long, low building behind the stately clubhouse served as their home for more than a decade, until they moved into a house on 37th Avenue near the sixth tee.

Davey Black put Shaughnessy Heights firmly on the national golf map when he came west to be the club's pro from 1920 to 1945. BC GOLF HOUSE 007.128.186

The other on-site resident was Charlie "Big Mac" MacDonald, a bear of a man who also growled like one. MacDonald, the city's most famous caddy master, and Davey were polar opposites in stature but they were both firm and feared. Big Mac weighed more than 350 pounds and in his final years he was virtually blind.

MacDonald directed traffic with an iron hand while camped on a small but sturdy seat near the putting green. His sight and mobility were known to improve dramatically when favourite foursomes approached

Born into the game, young Ken Black first swung a club at Rivermead
in Hull, Quebec, where father Davie was the pro for almost a decade
before moving to Vancouver. BC GOLF HOUSE 007.128.196

the 18th green and he would join them in the locker room to share "a
couple of drams."

Wee Davey wasted little time impressing his new employers. Soon
after arriving at Shaughnessy in 1920, he played the 6,590-yard course
in a record 67. Later that year he made a triumphant return to Ottawa,
winning his second successive Canadian PGA at Royal Ottawa. He was
the only man to break 70, shooting 68 and 67 to distance the runner-up,
George Ayton, by 10 strokes. A Shaughnessy legend was born.

Davey won the CPGA tournament again in 1921 and following his triple, P.E. Ross of the *Ottawa Journal*, the man who had funded the original championship trophy a decade earlier, thought the feat was so remarkable that he presented a replica of the trophy to the Little Man of Iron. Later, at a formal ceremony at Shaughnessy, club president E.W. Peters honoured Davey in the presence of 1,000 spectators and Old Country pros Jock Hutchison and Long Jim Barnes. The visitors then went out and defeated Davey and Alex Duthie of Jericho 5 and 4 in an exhibition game.

Several of Davey's brothers played their best golf in the early 1920s. John, four years Davey's senior, threatened to pull off the greatest conquest. He led the 1922 US Open for two rounds at Skokie, Illinois, before falling one stroke shy of a virtual unknown, Gene Sarazen. John Black, described as a 43-year-old grandfather from Oakland, eventually tied Bobby Jones for second. The next year Jones started to stockpile his fantastic record of major victories.

The Blacks were unmistakably brothers, with and without a golf club in hand. On the course, their diminutive size forced them—even the relatively tall John—to stand further from the ball than normal and employ natural, so-called flat swings. With extra-long wooden shafts, they generated club head speed using their trademark short, sweeping swing. Hardly classic form by today's standards, it nevertheless was surprisingly durable in the days of unsophisticated techniques, instruction and equipment.

Davey played the game expeditiously, without fuss or delay. Rarely squatting to survey putts, he excelled on the greens. It was a given that he would get down in two from 30 feet or thereabouts, and it was likely he'd hit the cup with his first putt. An apostle of the pendulum stroke, he clicked his heels at address with his left toe pointing at the hole as if it were a directional arrow.

Blessed with a typical Scottish temperament, he viewed the game rather stoically, accepting both good and bad breaks as part of the game. His fine sense of dignity and wry humour endeared him to the golfing community. Davey thrived on steadiness, accuracy and putting, playing aggressively but not recklessly. He was never one to enthuse about his own game.

An avid golfer, President Warren Harding drew a large crowd to Shaughnessy in late July, 1923, little knowing it would be his last game. He died in San Francisco after suffering a heart attack on August 2. w.j. MOORE, CITY OF VANCOUVER ARCHIVES SGN943.23

In the 1922 Northwest Open Davey finished three strokes clear of his brother Willie, then Colwood pro. In a 1924 visit to Everett he took the Washington State Open.

During this time Davey first exposed his young son, Ken, to competitive golf. He and Phil Taylor, the pro at Victoria Golf Club whose son was named Allan, staged informal father-and-son two-balls in home-and-home matches in Victoria and Vancouver. The two precocious boys, not yet in their teens, would soon attract considerable press attention and galleries. Allan, a year younger than Ken, developed into a fine player and played on BC's 1933 Willingdon Cup team, but it was Ken who turned the most heads. From the outset, the peering spectators never seemed to faze him.

Davey never gave Ken a formal golf lesson and he never pressured the boy into playing, but Ken received constant inspiration from his mother. He quickly came to appreciate golf's subtleties while caddying, attentively watching and listening to the members and to the patriarch of Shaughnessy, his father. He dutifully shagged balls for his father whenever Davey found time for practice. Caddy Ken regularly went out with members Walter Ferrie, Harry Lochyer and Walter Hepburn. He also enjoyed carrying for Harry Jones, a leading amateur who was 1924 BC champion

Ken's most memorable day as a caddy was July 29, 1923, when few people were permitted in the gallery at Shaughnessy. The president of the United States, Warren Harding, stopped in Vancouver on his return from an Alaskan visit and played golf with CPR president E.W. Peters and club president Tom Fletcher. Davey attended to President Harding's clubs and Ken carried Peters's bag. After the match the president gave two new US dollar bills to the club pro's wide-eyed son. It was President Harding's last game of golf. He died four days later of an apoplectic stroke in San Francisco.

As the Roaring Twenties were winding down, Ken Black was shaping into a fine shot maker. He was destined to challenge the top players—his father included. By age 14 his handicap hovered between four and five. He was beginning to shoot underpar golf and the other caddies were no match for him. The only youth competitions were for caddies, usually on summer Monday mornings, and the first time the modest youngster came home after winning, he only produced the trophy after being questioned at the supper table by his parents.

While a 16-year-old student at Prince of Wales High School, Ken discovered how much he enjoyed competitive golf when he accomplished the improbable by reaching the semifinals of match play in the 1928 BC Amateur only to lose to the eventual winner, the seasoned Tom McHugh of Seattle.

Shaughnessy finally formed a junior club in 1929, with Jack Bourne, Buster Ryan, Ken Newbury, Joe Greer, Lol Killam, Bill Cameron, Ken Black, Arnold Cliff, Ralph Fletcher and Roddie McRae among the fledgling members. Sam Randall and W.L. Keate put up trophies, but only Fletcher played well enough to challenge the pro's son.

About that time, as an uninhibited, fast-developing player, Ken "acquired" a putter that looked almost incongruous in his bag of shiny irons. The putter that would serve him well for many years originally belonged to his uncle, the University course pro Harry Winder, who was married to a sister of Ken's mother. After Ken tried the putter, Uncle Harry never saw it again.

Like his father, Ken didn't have classic form. He perfected a quick three-quarter, flat caddy swing. The flat swing plane gave him a tendency to hood the club on impact, causing many hooks. The flaw moved some skeptics to observe that Ken would never turn into a champion. How wrong they were.

Ken became so proficient on the greens the press tagged his putter Calamity Jane, which was the pet name of Bobby Jones's putter. Ken's putter had a worn leather grip bound at the top by electrical tape. More than half the shaft was tightly wrapped in splicing cord, garnished artistically in bands of yellow and black. The toe of the blade curled upward to a point, rather like a sabot. Significantly, the blade was slightly lofted, though not quite as pronounced as a cleek or two-iron. It was deadly in Ken's hands.

The year 1929 was when the stock market crashed. It was also the year Ken's obsession for golf heightened. He was an impressionable 17. His father and Phil Taylor were the best players in the province, and Ken was enraptured with the phenomenon that was Bobby Jones. Enrolled at King Edward High for senior matriculation, he began to practise seriously for the first time. But he still found time to be class secretary and play both rugby and hockey.

Ken Black's diligence in golf was like that of many leading golfers—he actually preferred practising to playing. His regular routine was to rise with the sun and hit balls in solitude at Shaughnessy's two "orphan holes," the fifth and sixth par-four holes that sat isolated across Oak Street, between 33rd and 41st avenues, now the site of Eric Hamber Secondary School. He hit shots with all irons for hours before school, well before the day's first foursome of members approached the fifth tee. He practised from the rough of those holes and chipped to the greens. "I came to expect to make at least one of every three chips," he said modestly.

The inaugural Open championship of BC, in 1928, belonged to

Davey Black, but his son's day was not far off. Still spritely, Davey ran away from everyone at his home course for a winning 292, no fewer than 13 strokes ahead of runner-up Dunc Sutherland. Phil Taylor was beaten by 15 strokes and Fred Wood, a promising young amateur from the wilds of Vancouver Golf Club, came sixth at 317.

Taylor took the second BC Open at his home links in 1929 but Davey regained the title a year later by closing with 67 at Point Grey for 281, two strokes better than Don Sutherland. Taylor was another shot back.

While Bobby Jones was doing his slam-bang in 1930, and Davey Black was back to his winning ways, Ken Black came within a grass-blade of capturing the BC Amateur title as a junior. He had opened the season by winning the City Junior and a wristwatch for two 75s at Langara. Eight strokes back was a fiery 15-year-old caddy from southeast Vancouver, Stan Leonard.

The amateurs trekked to the Vancouver Club in Coquitlam for the BC championship and Ken served notice by reaching the finals. His semifinal victim, Bon Stein, was a Seattle veteran who had won the title five years earlier. But Ken faced an imposing opponent for the trophy in Wood, who had cultivated a superlative putting stroke while growing up on VGC's greased-lightning greens.

After eliminating Dave Ritchie of Quilchena and Glenoaks's Bill Leonard—Stan's older brother—the 23-year-old Wood added a crowning touch to his amateur career. The man who would replace Davey Black in Shaughnessy's pro shop 15 years later trampled Ken 10 and 8 before 1,500 spectators—the largest crowd to watch an amateur match in BC.

Eighty years later, no one has matched Ken's next accomplishment of capturing both the provincial Open and Amateur championships within a calendar year. He was 20. Playing to a modest four handicap in September 1932, Ken became the Open's first amateur winner. Rounds of 69 and 70 on the final day at Jericho overcame Vancouver Club pro Sutherland's 287 total by one stroke. Another shot back were Davey Black and Leonard, who earlier that summer had set a precedent of his own by winning the Amateur at 17 years of age.

But in April 1933 at Victoria Golf Club, Ken snatched Leonard's title with a resounding 7 and 6 drubbing of veteran Alex "Sandy" Watson of the home links. Before the end of the decade, Ken Black would become a folk hero in Vancouver.

● ● ●

The sky over Shaughnessy was laden with dark rainclouds early in the second week of July 1933 for the first National Amateur championships west of the Rockies. The qualifying scores clearly reflected the wet, heavy conditions. The course couldn't play much longer or more difficult. The only sub-par round was a 71, by Point Grey's Don Gowan. Those who shot 158, a whopping 14 over par, qualified for championship match play. By the end of the long week Ken Black and Albert "Scotty" Campbell had survived to play for the title on one of the hottest days of the year.

Ken had qualified with 75 and 74 and in the semifinal defeated an eminent opponent, Harry Givan of Seattle. Barely advancing with 80 and 77, Campbell got to the final by stopping Leonard 6 and 5 and Glenoaks's Cec Coville, who had earlier provided the week's upset by knocking off 1929 US Amateur finalist Dr. O.R. Willing of Portland.

Three down to Campbell after the morning 18, Ken tied the match soon after lunch to the delight of 2,000 spectators. The irony of Ken's eventual 3 and 2 loss was that Campbell had borrowed two irons from Davey Black's set and used them both with deadly accuracy. Only the second American to win Canada's championship, Campbell repeated the feat in 1934 at Montreal.

Wee Davey's prodigy secured his first full-time job at 18, handling stock in the storeroom of A.G. Spalding Sporting Goods on Hastings Street. By 1934 he had been promoted to Western Canada sales rep and made several business trips to the company's headquarters in Chicopee Falls, Massachusetts. He was in the right place at the right time.

Ken Black's idol was a vice-president of Spalding, a designer and consultant for the firm's line of clubs that bore his name. Bobby Jones had retired from competitive golf in 1930, having won the era's four major tournaments 13 times in seven seasons, capped by the Grand Slam

Bobby Jones retired at 28 after winning the Grand Slam in 1930, and visited Shaughnessy Heights in 1934 for an exhibition shortly after coming out of retirement to play in the inaugral Masters tournament at the famous course he build in Augusta, Georgia. BC GOLF HOUSE 007.131.058

that year. With no other worlds to conquer, Jones decided it was time to concentrate on earning a good living. Business included promotional tours and that fall his westcoast junket brought him to Vancouver.

Ken Black, the young executive, was put in charge of Jones's visit. Jones and two other Spalding reps, pro Horton Smith and amateur Johnny Dawson, arrived by CPR ferry from Seattle. Ken was there to meet them and take them to the Vancouver Hotel, where he had stocked their rooms with the finest of blends. The next day, in a charity exhibition at Shaughnessy, taking Jones as his partner, Ken played a best-ball against his father and Don Sutherland.

The Shaughnessy exhibition occurred on a late November day, gloomy and dank, but there was no mistaking Jones. He stepped to the first tee right out of a magazine advertisement, wearing grey plus-fours, a dark blue turtleneck and a defined part in his dark hair. In his golf bag was an arsenal of 22 irons and 6 woods.

As he stared down the hill from the first tee, Jones pulled out his driver and with an effortless pass at the ball, he dissected the fairway. The excited spectators, estimated at 2,500, murmured and applauded politely, in awe of the man's elegance. Jones's swing was as quiet and impeccable as his demeanour.

No one broke par that day. The veteran pros won when Davey made a 16-foot putt to birdie 18. Davey and Jones both shot par 72, Sutherland 74 and Ken 75. The gate proceeds of $2,000—$200 more than a similar exhibition in Seattle netted—went to the local welfare fund.

Less than a month later Ken received one of his most prized possessions. It was a personal letter from Jones, postmarked Atlanta, Georgia.

Dec. 22, 1934:
I have finally settled down again after doing some more travelling after I returned from the Coast. Having done so, I want to say to you again that I think you did a splendid job of making the arrangements for our meeting in Vancouver. Everything seemed to go off in fine style.

I am particularly grateful for the thoughtfulness you displayed in looking after my every convenience. I certainly enjoyed meeting you and making the acquaintance of a number of your friends. Please remember me most kindly to your father and mother, and especially tell Dave that I am practicing up on my putting. With kindest regards, yours sincerely.

Ken Black remembered Jones as a reserved, unpretentious man who talked to the spectators and grilled him about the city. "He was very serious, but friendly and curious," recalled Ken. The following year Ken went with Canada's Commonwealth team to Britain, where he spent six weeks playing all the great courses. They spent four days at St Andrews, where five years earlier Jones had made the British Amateur the first triumph of his grand slam. Ken counted a 69 the first time he played the Old Course. The second time the wind came up and so did his score—81. He made it to the quarter-finals of the British Amateur.

Ken Black had played a round with Bobby Jones and he had played at the home of golf. What more could he possibly want? What more could he ask? He was obviously profoundly influenced by his close encounters with greatness, for in 1936 he exploded to the forefront. He captured his second BC Amateur title by beating his friendly arch-rival, Leonard, 3 and 1, while approximately 20 under par for the week's eight rounds at Shaughnessy.

While it was gratifying to have beaten the world's best pros, Ken had another world to conquer—the world of amateurs. He was determined to win his country's National Amateur championship.

Returning in 1937 to Ottawa for the first time since he was eight years old, Ken fell short of his goal when beaten 2 and 1 in the semifinal by Phil Farley, the cagey two-time Ontario champion.

Bad luck followed Ken and his Willingdon Cup teammates the next year at London's Hunt Club. Ken, Jimmy Todd of Victoria, Don Gowan of Point Grey and Frank Willey of Glenoaks combined to retain the interprovincial team trophy by four strokes. However, they were later disqualified when Gowan reported to officials that he had inadvertently played two shots from beyond out-of-bounds markers during the second round. Ken's trials and tribulations that week were far from over. On the eve of the Amateur championship's first round, a caddy walked off with his clubs. With a borrowed set, he lost to a noted Ontario hockey player named Marvin Wentworthy.

In 1939, Ken attained his personal goal. He had lost the PNGA final that year to Jack Westland of Everett on the first extra hole at Royal

Colwood. But he won his third straight City title, followed by a third BC crown with a 3 and 2 decision over an all-star rugby player from Victoria named Ted Colgate.

Finally that year, Ken became the first westerner crowned Canadian Amateur king. A hero's welcome awaited him when he stepped off the plane from Montreal. In the crowd of greeters were Percy Williams, who had sprinted to two gold medals at the 1928 Olympics, and a number of regular Shaughnessy foursomes and former mates in the caddy shack.

From the airport he was paraded downtown in an open convertible with his bride of one year, Mayme. The procession of automobiles was met at Smithe and Granville by the B.C. Electric Bugle Band and the Firemen's Band. They raced down Granville, through a shower of streamers and tickertape, to Hastings and then via Richards and Pender to the Pacific Athletic Club for a testimonial dinner.

Presenting a bookcase to the new champion, Capilano president W.C. Woodward told the 200 guests, "We've all appreciated the gentlemanly manner in which Ken has always conducted himself." It was a definitive summary of Ken Black's character that his exemplary deportment was significant as his success. His golfing friends presented him with a shotgun inscribed with a gold plate.

In Montreal, Ken had at last matched one of his idol's achievements by winning his country's championship. In the first all-western final he overwhelmed upstart Henry Martell of Edmonton 8 and 6 at the parched Mount Bruno course. His 67 in an early match play round unofficially equalled the course record that Leo Diegel had established 15 years earlier during the Canadian Open.

By this point in his career Ken was the pride of Capilano. The year before—1938—the lure of a new course in the pristine forest had taken him to West Vancouver. He was member 001. His regular playing partners were Clayton "Slim" Delbridge, Harry Jones and Bill Kelly. One day another good Capilano friend, George Lindsay, made a locker room bet that reportedly climbed to $200. Lindsay bet that Ken could beat the best-ball medal score of Delbridge, Bill Scharfe and former Shaughnessy club champion Harry Butler. Ken shot 70 with a lost ball; the trio had a 72 best-ball.

The Royal Canadian Golf Association had no choice but to rate the westerner No. 1 in their 1940 rankings, with Victoria's Colgate 15th.

Golf and everything else was pushed aside, almost forgotten, during the war years. Ken Black became Lieutenant Ken Black and served with the Pacific Coast Militia Rangers, who formed the first line of defence for any invasion of Canada's shores. He went from Spalding's on Hastings to Boeing at the airport, where in the hammer shop he created spare parts for airplane wings. He also participated in some exhibitions for war charities in Vancouver, Portland and Seattle.

When peace returned, Ken Black was enticed in 1946 into the printing business by his father-in-law, J. Gehrke. He also had a second appointment with Henry Martell in the Canadian Amateur finals. This time at Mayfair, Martell's home course, Ken was handcuffed 6 and 5 by the big Edmonton policeman. One-up at the lunch break, Martell blitzed Ken with a seven-under barrage for 13 holes, including the first hole-in-one ever scored in a Canadian Amateur.

Earlier in the year Ken had won his fifth City Amateur in the rain at Capilano, shooting 74 and 71. He had also taken the 1941 title at Point Grey, beating Jack Ellis of Marine Drive and Hugh Morrison.

Ken's illustrious father, Davey, retired in 1945 after 25 years as guardian of the Shaughnessy pro shop. Almost immediately, Ken followed in his father's footsteps one last time. Upon returning from Edmonton, he decided to retire from competition—at the age of 34. He had won the Provincial Open and Amateur and National Amateur, and he had represented his country in Britain and his province in nine Willingdon Cup matches.

In the ensuing years the Blacks enjoyed many days of casual golf in West Vancouver, many in the company of Capilano pro Jock McKinnon and his father.

Ken vividly recalls his father once turning Capilano's corner in 2-3-2 birdie-eagle-birdie on holes 9, 10 and 11. Davey regularly shot under his age in his late 70s. Lamentably, he never once played the new Shaughnessy course. He died in his 91st year—1974—a decade after the old course off 33rd was declared too central and valuable a property for golf.

Family and business commitments didn't press Ken Black to retire prematurely, though his children—Donald and Barbara—were priorities. He simply decided that 15 years of competitive golf were sufficient. He admits that he might have been tempted to play pro golf, albeit not for the money but for the challenge.

In 1987 Ken joined his father in the Canadian Sports Hall of Fame. They were the first father and son enshrined. Bobby Jones would have been proud of them.

CHAPTER 9
VIOLET POOLEY SWEENY, VERA HUTCHINGS AND SUCCESSORS

This chapter looks at some of the women who have contributed significantly to the status of golf in BC.

VIOLET POOLEY SWEENY

Many female golfers have graced British Columbia's fairways but none was as influential or revered as Violet Pooley Sweeny (née Violet Pooley). The oft-acclaimed Queen of Northwest Golf established standards and set the fashions of her day. Whatever Sweeny scored was the women's par for that course; whatever Sweeny wore was in vogue; whatever Sweeny did was considered acceptable.

Sweeny reigned supreme in golf for the better part of two decades, starting in 1905 with her first of seven Pacific Northwest and nine BC championships. No one has matched her prowess, although she was followed by many marvellous provincial champions such as Vera Hutchings, Kathleen Farrell, Margaret Todd, Babs Davies, Dorothy Herbertson DeGirolamo, Gayle Hitchens, Marilyn Palmer, Lisa Young and Dawn Coe.

Her English-born father—for a time the Speaker of the House—wasn't an especially keen member at Macaulay Plains in Esquimalt, but her brother, Harry, was instrumental in the formation of Victoria Golf Club.

Within a few years of her early triumphs, Sweeny's game progressed so dramatically that she was one of the few women in the world who played to a scratch handicap. She was an intimidating presence, with the size and strength to do a man's work and to drive a golf ball as far as many men could. And she didn't hesitate to raise either eyebrows or hemlines. She was neither indifferent to protocol nor rebellious in a puritanical society, though; she simply did her own thing.

She also smoked in public—something that wasn't considered proper for a woman at that time. She chain-smoked on the course, often playing shots with a cigarette stuck in the side of her mouth. But she was never taken to task for any impropriety.

She was no doubt a proponent of reform when it came to alleviating the difficulties of the day's dress for women golfers. With skirts that touched the turf, elastic waistbands had to be pulled down to the knees to allow ladies to see the ball for putting. White-sleeved, collared shirts with black ties were also part of the day's costume—and not always conducive to making a comfortable swing. The voluminous skirts were gradually raised a foot above the fairway, much to the delight of Sweeny, who became one of the first to flash her ankles.

Several years before her death in 1965 at the age of 79, Sweeny had told *Province* writer Roland Wild that she "never feared I would be ungraceful by raising the club above my shoulder." In fact, she took such a full, generous cut that the club head touched the small of her back on the backswing.

Throughout her career, she used the first set of wooden clubs she owned, a favourite "slammer" spoon, gooseneck putter, cleek and five other clubs. "It was no trouble taking them on the streetcar to Jericho," she said. A superlative shot maker, she was of the opinion that a good golfer should learn to play all types of shots—full, half and quarter shots—with the same club. "That's what the game's all about, isn't it?" she often remarked.

Sweeny's finest golf was probably played in Britain. While details of early competitions overseas are sketchy at best, it's obvious that she rated as one the world's leading players. She reached the fourth round of the 1911 British Amateur at Royal Portrush in Northern Ireland. Two years later, at St Anne's, the accomplished Canadian defeated defending champion Gladys Ravenscroft before losing in the semifinal to the eventual winner, Muriel Dodd, who also won the Canadian title that year.

Violet Pooley Sweeny was in a class by herself in the early days of BC golf. BC ARCHIVES 98212-4

Her promising golf career was interrupted by the First World War. At age 28, she had won her fifth BC title in 1914 after missing three local seasons while golfing abroad. She also captured the first provincial championship following the armistice, in 1920, as a member of Jericho and a married woman. In 1915 she had married S. Campbell "Bimbo" Sweeny, a charter member of Capilano. Bimbo Sweeny refused to golf with his wife, if only to preserve his ego.

Prior to Sweeny's dominance, multi-winners of the BC title were Edith Combe, T. Drake and Mrs. Walter Langley. Combe won the first four competitions, in which there were as few as four entrants, through 1898, and nine years later in 1907. Drake won three titles and was runner-up three times through 1903, while Langley's last of four championships came in 1912.

With only six entries in 1909, Sweeny retained the Flumerfelt Cup with a 4 and 2 victory over Nora Combe Paterson, the daughter of

The two foremost golfers of their era for 30 years, Violet Pooley Sweeny, (right) and Vera Hutchings dominated women's golf in BC. From 1905 onward they won a combined 16 BC Amateur titles. BC GOLF HOUSE 007.139.019

Harvey and Edith Combe. Paterson was no flash in the pan. She won the prestigious PNGA title in both 1910 and 1911.

Sweeny's seventh provincial championship, in 1922 at Shaughnessy Heights, was the first conducted outside of Victoria. Her ninth and last title, back at Victoria in 1929, preceded her loss in the PNGA final to Jericho clubmate and rival Vera Hutchings. She had lost the 1928 BC final at Jericho when stymied on the green of the first extra hole by 18-year-old Marion Wilson of Victoria.

Though she twice won the Vancouver title during the mid-1930s and was a beaten semifinalist in the 1935 Canadian Amateur at Jericho, Sweeny's game was never the same after she fractured a hip in 1937 when she slipped on a running board while exiting an automobile. After breaking the same hip again a short time later, she was left with one leg slightly shorter than the other. Undaunted, she continued to play in club competitions and focused her attention on golf's administrative level and a favourite hobby, breeding terriers. Sweeny served as vice-president of the Canadian Ladies Golf Union (CLGU) in 1924 and as its first BC president from 1933 through 1946.

She became the eighth golfer inducted into the BC Hall of Fame, in 1974, joining Davey and Ken Black, John Johnston, Stan Leonard, Walter McElroy, Bill Mawhinney and Margaret Todd.

VERA HUTCHINGS

At the age of 16, Vera Ramsay from Surrey made England's 1913 national team. She then went to war in the motor transit service and came out of it engaged to a soldier from Winnipeg named Harold Hutchings.

After their marriage, the couple moved to Winnipeg in 1919, the same year she had her first child prior to returning to competitive golf. The Hutchings had moved west for business reasons and Vera discovered that the asthma attacks she'd suffered for years weren't as extreme on the coast.

In 1924 Hutchings became the first western Canadian resident to capture the Canadian Closed championship at Toronto. She also won her first BC title by dethroning Violet Pooley Sweeny 5 and 4, and lost in the PNGA only after she and her opponent were disqualified for skirting the rules by agreeing not to play stymies. She had won the match 6 and 5.

Later that year, she and her husband divorced and she moved with her three toddlers to her mother's house, which was within sight of the Jericho course.

Dominant in BC and at PNGA tournaments throughout the Pacific Northwest,
Vera Hutchings withdrew from competitive golf in 1935 at the peak of her career.
BC GOLF HOUSE 007.139.013A

The conditions for the 1927 BC championships at Victoria Golf Club reminded Hutchings of her years in Winnipeg. It was mid-April and a driving blizzard whitened the links during the final. She was denied a fourth straight title by a one-time winner, Margaret Sayward, who dropped a 10-foot putt on the first extra hole. Snow had to be cleared off the green before they could attempt their putts.

Hutchings swept both majors—PNGA and BC—in four different years, the last double in 1933. That same year she married C.B. Ford of Seattle, but he died only three months after their wedding.

In 1934 she won a second Canadian Closed title at Scarborough, Ontario. In her final major tournament, in 1935 at Seattle, she reached the PNGA championship for the eighth time only to lose to the Californian Barbara Thompson. She retired from golf that fall, and moved from Seattle to Duncan.

In 13 tournament years in Canada, the Dublin-born, English-raised war bride had captured seven BC titles and the Canadian Closed twice, as well as the six prestigious PNGA crowns. Between them, Sweeny and Hutchings captured all but three BC championships between 1920 and 1933.

KAY FARRELL

Kathleen "Kay" Farrell came from a prominent family and was an imposing figure and adversary. The daughter of William Farrell, one of the founders of B.C. Telephone Co., had already revealed signs of her prowess several years before she defeated Mrs. W.M. Silcock in the 1934 BC final.

A fierce and fearless competitor, she had been humiliated by Vera Hutchings in the 1930 final at Point Grey. She was swamped 13 and 12. But four years later at her own course, Farrell claimed her first of three titles with a two-up victory over Quilchena's Silcock. She took the measure of Violet Pooley Sweeny in 1936 at Shaughnessy, winning 2 and 1 after leading seven-up with 16 holes to play, and then stopped Rena O'Callaghan 6 and 4 at Marine Drive in 1938.

Farrell was elected president of the BC branch of the CLGU, serving until 1957 and attending national meetings in Toronto at her own expense. She was also national president in 1949 and 1955.

MARGARET SUTCLIFFE TODD

Following the hiatus of tournament golf during the war, a Victoria woman emerged as the ascendant player. In her BC championship debut as a 10-handicap, Margaret Sutcliffe Todd (née Margaret Sutcliffe) reached the 1946 semifinals but lost to the formidable Farrell 3 and 2 at Shaughnessy.

From 1947 to 1952, Margaret Todd reached the BC Open Final
six straight years, winning the first three. VICTORIA DAILY TIMES

"That week I was a basket case," she said. "I had to stay by myself at the Vancouver Hotel and I was scared out of my wits. The night before the semifinal I had the trots and couldn't sleep. I didn't dare phone home because I was afraid I'd start crying."

A boyfriend introduced Todd to golf in 1938. Using her Aunt Nelle Clark's old hickory-shafted clubs at Oak Bay, she prompted her beau to facetiously suggest she stick to track and field. Instead she joined Uplands and took lessons from pro Walter Gravlin, who espoused a mechanical swing popularly known as the Gravlin drag.

Golfers whose parents didn't belong to private clubs weren't eligible for membership until age 21. The following year Todd turned 21 and, with a 13 handicap from Uplands, joined Oak Bay. She reached the Victoria championship final only to lose to that year's BC champion, Isabelle Dowell, but then won her first of 11 City crowns in 1940.

She ventured to Tacoma in 1946 especially for lessons from Chuck Congdon, who told her to "hit the ball, don't swing at it." She remembers Oak Bay pro Phil Taylor admonishing her for displaying overt excitement after holing a long putt in a competition. "Don't be so emotional," the sage advised her. "Let your opponents think you make those putts all the time."

Husband Jack Todd, once a 10 handicap, perceptively recognized and helped to correct flaws that crept into her swing. An effortless long-hitter, Margaret Todd was unbeaten in BC for three years and by the early 1950s was one of the few women in Canada playing to a plus handicap.

In the 1947 and 1948 BC finals, Todd defeated Rena O'Callaghan, the five-time Vancouver champion. Dowell and Babs Davies of Marine Drive were her nemeses. Once Dowell was dormie-five and beat Todd; she set two stymies, made two long putts and prevailed when Todd blew a short putt and then topped her drive at the extra hole.

There was no question that Todd would win the 1949 BC championship at Oak Bay. She triumphed 5 and 4 over Marjorie Todd, her sister-in-law, during a match in which winds of up to 50 miles per hour lashed the links.

BABS DAVIES

Babs Davies ended Todd's three-year reign as BC's golf queen when she took the title on the 36th green at Point Grey in 1950. But in their rematch the following summer, Davies trampled Todd 8 and 7 at her home course.

Davies, who later moved to San José and then worked in Bob Kidd's Penticton pro shop, had caused a stir in 1949 by winning the Canadian Closed in an upset at Capilano. Todd, six months pregnant with her third son, David, came fifth. In the ensuing week's Canadian Open she became a quarter-final victim of eventual champion Grace DeMoss of Oregon. DeMoss was five under par when the match ended on the 13th green. In her best Canadian Open, Todd lost in the 1961 semifinals on the 19th hole at Point Grey to Judy Darling of Quebec. Darling stopped teenager Gayle Hitchens two-up for the title. But the daughter of Capilano assistant pro Bob Hitchens fought back into the national final the next summer and became the first British Columbian ever to win it.

Gayle Hitchens Borthwick was the first BC woman to win the
National Junior title. In 1962 she became the first to win
the National Amateur. BILL CUNNINGHAM

DOROTHY WILKS

The arrival of Hitchens fell within the "Dorothy era" overseen by the
most durable competitor and dominant winner in the history of the BC
championship. Dorothy Herbertson of Victoria Gorge Vale won the
1954 and 1955 titles. Dorothy DeGirolamo won in 1960 and 1975.
Dorothy Wilks was runner-up in 1991 after previously winning three
Senior crowns. The Dorothys, of course, were one and the same, with a
37-year competitive span between her first win as a junior and her 1991
runner-up finish following her third BC Seniors crown.

From 1954 through to the 1990s Dorothy Wilks won
BC championships in all age classes. VICTORIA DAILY TIMES

"There's no question Dorothy would have won even more times had she not had to work," observes Margaret Todd. "She dropped out of competition entirely to have four children. She's been an exceptional player and competitor for many years."

MARILYN PALMER

For her second straight BC title, Hitchens handled a shy, studious 15-year-old from Kamloops, Marilyn Palmer, in the second round and the experienced Todd in the 36-hole final. Palmer's first love was figure skating but golf was inevitable. Her father, Rod Palmer, wore three hats as the Kamloops course developer, greenskeeper and pro, and the Palmers lived at the new course next to the airport.

"I'd come home from school with nothing else to do, so I hit golf balls," recalls Marilyn Palmer O'Connor, who played her first tournament in Vernon at 12 and was the 14-year-old winner of the BC Interior championship in Revelstoke. "Almost from the beginning, I loved practice over playing."

Palmer was 15 when she and Barb Renwick of Marine both broke 80 for the first time, at the Canadian Junior in Winnipeg. She was so good that few women at the Kamloops Country Club would play with her.

Born in Vancouver, where her father was a greenskeeper at Shaughnessy Heights, Palmer returned to the big city to obtain a teaching degree at the University of BC. She was quickly embraced as a member at Marine. After losing to future teammate Renwick in the 1964 final at Penticton, Palmer turned back Susan Brown at Shaughnessy to claim her first of 10 BC titles. Her last victory came at Salmon Arm in 1989 while on vacation from Calgary with her husband, Don, and sons, Ryan and Sean. In a 14-year period, 1964 through 1977, the quietly intense elementary school teacher won eight BC titles and finished second another four times. She also won the Alberta title five times and the Saskatchewan championship once.

O'Connor's most satisfying triumph came at Saskatoon in 1986 when, at 39, she was finally crowned national champion. "That was special because it was my first and I had been close so many times," she says. "I needed that victory for myself. I guess wanting it so badly after all those years made it harder to get."

She has represented Canada nine times and she retired internationally after going to Venezuela in 1986 for her sixth appearance in the World Amateur team championships.

OTHER WOMEN PLAYERS OF NOTE

Many other women players distinguished themselves in BC circles—among them, Gail Moore, Dale Shaw, Helen Marlatt, Katie Duff-Stuart,

The 1962 BC Women's Amateur Team featured Shirley Naismith, Colleen McCulloch, and Marine Drive stalwarts, reigning National Closed champion Janet McWha and Gayle Hitchens, who won the National Amateur title that year. BC GOLF HOUSE 007.121.029

Colleen McCulloch, Joan Lawson, Winnifred Evans, Holly Botham, Suzanne Foulds and Susan Brown.

Shaw, the strong but erratic player from Victoria, was the harbinger of a modern breed of women professionals when she successfully turned to teaching the game. Now almost every pro shop has a woman behind the counter who's qualified to give lessons, a welcome contrast to the 1980s when golf instruction was basically a man's domain.

While Shaw couldn't make a living as an LPGA tourist, the 1980s produced Dawn Coe of Cowichan Bay, Lisa Young Walters of Prince Rupert and Jennifer Wyatt of Quilchena in Richmond.

"Today's players hit the ball so much stronger and the teaching techniques are more sophisticated," observed Margaret Todd at the time. "In our day the game wasn't approached so scientifically. We didn't have the same instructional advantages. We played from innate knowledge, learning shots from pure feel and experience." In the 1950s and 1960s, more women played regularly, although there were seldom more than five or six who were capable of winning. Today, of course, women's lives have changed and many more of them go out to work than in past decades. They have less time for golf. "Most women with young children in my time didn't have jobs but babysitters allowed them time for golf. It was more difficult when the children were in their early teens. They were too old for sitters and too young to leave alone."

Coe, Walters and Wyatt had much in common. Each won the BC championship at least twice, played at US universities on golf scholarships and scored their maiden LPGA victories in 1992.

Coe, born in Campbell River, grew up in the logging village of Honeymoon Bay on Lake Cowichan. An all-star high school basketball player, she won her first of two successive BC Junior titles in 1978, won the BC Amateur in both 1982 and 1983 and turned pro later that year after winning the Canadian Women's Amateur title at Oak Bay.

A protégé of former March Meadows pro Norm Boden, and now married and a Florida resident, Dawn Coe-Jones has long returned home with her family to sponsor the Dawn Coe Junior tournament at the Honeymoon Bay course. She also credits her family and Lamar University coach Pat Park for influencing her game and career. During the summer of 1992, her ninth season on the LPGA Tour, Coe passed the $1 million mark in official earnings. She played another 16 years, winning three more times on tour, including an LPGA Match Play championship and the 1995 Tournament of Champions where she bested runner-up Beth Daniels by six strokes. Coe finished in the top five in four different LPGA major events, including a third place finish at the 1993 du Maurier Classic. She collected official earnings of over $3 million during her illustrious career.

Lisa Walters, nine months older than Coe, moulded her game in Prince Rupert. She was the 1977 provincial Junior winner and captured three straight BC titles before losing to Coe in the 1982 final.

Walters joined the LPGA Tour with Coe after attending Florida State University where, like Coe before her, she earned all-American laurels. She also finally found her winning form in Hawaii a week after Coe's maiden victory, and won twice more on tour in 1993 and 1998 despite severe knee problems that plagued her during the late 1980s.

Dawn Coe, seen here between 1978 Junior Girl teammates Lynn Akert and Jill Johnson, would go on to become BC's most successful LPGA member. In retirement she sponsors an annual junior event at her childhood course, March Meadows, in Honeymoon Bay. BC GOLF HOUSE 007.131.018

The Vancouver-born Jennifer Wyatt qualified to play the women's pro circuit in 1989. She also attended Lamar after playing her formative golf at Quilchena in Richmond. Wyatt ranked as the country's top-ranked amateur for three years, winning the BC title in 1986 and 1987 and the New Zealand Amateur in 1987. Pros Alvie Thompson, Al Kennedy, Jack Westover and Sandy Kurceba all instructed Wyatt, as did Lamar's Pat Park and Quilchena's venerable Tom Hunter. After leaving the LPGA behind and playing mostly on the west coast she won the PGA BC Women's Championship six times between 2001 and 2009.

Pat Wyatt never doubted her daughter would succeed. "When Jen took a 12 on the first hole of her national tournament debut, the junior in Winnipeg, and came in with a 92, I knew right then she was going to make it," said Pat.

Katie Duff-Stuart never won a provincial or national title, but she was a remarkable woman who won the Vancouver and District tournament twice and several Senior championships. She was a terror at Shaughnessy, where she won her first club championship in 1937 and repeated as winner of the 1968 final.

Putting was never her strength. "I learned to play golf from Davey Black, but he was never able to teach me to putt like he did. He used to say 'miss 'em quick.' But I miss them at all speeds."

CHAPTER 10

STAN THE MAN

*In the 1950s Stan Leonard burst onto the international
golf scene as a formidable force in spite of his age and lack
of high-level competitive history. In BC his skill level was
well known; the rest of the world was in for a treat.*

Long before he left boyhood, little Stanley Leonard was seduced by drives
that rocketed over the horizon and by putts that disappeared for birdies.
Making golf balls vanish was pure magic to his eyes. Leonard dreamed of
becoming the Mandrake of golf, a wizard with clubs.

Smaller than most boys his age, he knew he would need to be
something special to summon up the power and finesse required of
a champion. It helped that he was the grittiest kid in the neighbourhood. The early discovery that he could hit a golf ball straighter and
farther than almost all the bigger, older boys fuelled his ardour. He
delighted in taking to the fairways and beating all of them. His greatest attributes were tenacity, cockiness and a spontaneous flair for the
game. Little Stanley vowed that one day he'd be the best damned golfer
in the whole world.

Leonard learned early on from his father and older brother that self-
confidence was essential to succeed in any endeavour, and especially in
an individualistic game like golf. A person with natural talent, his father
often told him, couldn't begin to win if he doubted his own capabilities
and didn't apply himself.

William Leonard's second son probably would have made a tremendous boxer. Stanley was spunky and scrappy, and he always seemed to be

looking for trouble, fearing no one. He taunted bullies and he turned his back on authority figures if he thought they had wrongly admonished him.

Leonard grew up distrusting people in power. The administrators, the rule makers, alienated him and they considered him too cocky and outspoken. He was as subtle as a sledgehammer, even in his youth. It was his habit to say out loud what he was thinking and too often it came out sounding flippant and spiced with sarcasm. And he didn't mellow with age. At one point he turned crusty and embittered, as if blaming everyone but himself for not embarking earlier on a particular tour.

But he was living proof that the son of a blue-collar worker could learn to play championship golf without the advantages of a private club membership and a full set of fancy clubs.

The golfer who became World Cup champion and was known throughout the golf world as Stan the Man discovered the game at the age of nine. He used crude sticks to wildly whack stones down a dusty, gravel street that dead-ended in the bushes of southeast Vancouver. He developed an early hook, getting into all sorts of trouble by shattering the windows of new houses on Woodstock Avenue. Later, it brought him his share of grief on golf courses. Building contractors soon encouraged Leonard and his pals to play in the surrounding open fields or in the Van Horne schoolyard.

Born in February 1915, the second son of William and Elizabeth Leonard, who had emigrated four years earlier from Aberdeen, Scotland, Stan came to cherish his brother, Bill, almost four years his senior. On the golf course Bill was bigger and stronger than Stan, more even-tempered and easier to like. The Leonards and other southeast Vancouver kids, including Joe and Henry Mitchell, Les Bevan, Norm Will, Dewey Greatrex, Billy Main, Harry Pryke and the ill-fated Tick Willey regularly hiked or biked to caddy at Shaughnessy Heights.

In the evenings they'd all jump the fence and play the isolated holes east of Oak Street until the street lights came on. It was a rare night when they weren't chased off the course by greenskeeper Mr. McRae. They ran away gleefully, a mischievous band of boys who knew they wouldn't be apprehended or punished. The only men they really feared were the two who could affect their livelihood: caddy master Charlie "Big Mac" McDonald and pro Davey Black.

During the late 1920s pennies and potatoes on the kitchen table counted. Caddies at Shaughnessy earned fifty cents a round, sixty cents if they were lucky enough to get a generous member. Sometimes their payment was forty cents and a green streetcar ticket to get home.

Leonard recalled once getting a dollar from Sid Miller, whom he likened to King Farouk. Another member, Jack Fraser, who played on BC's first Willingdon Cup team in 1929, was a "bag" whom they all wanted. Fraser sometimes took his caddies downtown and filled their bellies with Chinese food. Leonard's first regular, Fred Townley, packed as many as 22 clubs. The bags were light canvas but the 14-club limit still wasn't in effect.

When shooed off Shaughnessy, the caddies romped around Langara public course as junior members of the Glenoaks club. Education was not high on their list. Bill Leonard set a pattern for his brother, leaving John Oliver High before he reached the 11th grade to work as a streetcar conductor. Bill next went into the golf club manufacturing business with another Aberdeen transplant, Dave McLeod. Stan also learned the art of club making under the expertise of McLeod, whose sporting goods store on south Granville Street was probably the first golf factory in western Canada. Opened in the early 1930s, it subsequently became B.C. Leather & Findings, Pro-Made, Golf Craft and, finally, Titleist.

Bill Leonard left the amateur ranks, took his first pro job in the mid-1930s at the Calgary Country Club and later became Calgary Earl Grey's original professional. When McLeod decided to go to Old Quilchena as head pro he took the younger Leonard and ever-aspiring caddy under his wing, teaching Stan some of the finer fundamentals and etiquette of the game. During regular rounds together, however, the old pro never managed to harness the youngster's short fuse. Stan threw clubs and temper tantrums like no one else.

The year he became a teenager, in 1928, Leonard had won his first tournament, the Shaughnessy caddy championship, with a 73. While he received rudimentary instruction from McLeod, Leonard gleaned the subtleties of the golf swing through his observations as a caddy.

Technical knowledge and professional advice weren't readily available, but he developed a style of his own and executed it with flair and reckless power. His was a designated caddy swing: flat, choppy and inelegant. He gripped the club with an extremely strong left-hand position. His hook swing had more waggles than a happy dog's tail.

Two years after beating all the city caddies, Leonard was the 1932 champion of all amateurs in the province. It was the first time that the BC Amateur was conducted mid-season rather than over Easter and the result was better weather, bigger galleries and improved scoring. Harry Jones, the 1924 champion, celebrated the fair weather by introducing a new fashion for the links. He wore short sleeves and was noted in the press as the "bare-armed qualifier."

Leonard, the upstart public course teenager with the wild hook and matching temper, attracted attention early on at Point Grey by winning medal honours with rounds of 74 and 72. He played with homemade clubs he had shafted and customized—a noteworthy enterprise for a boy of his years. Two strokes behind were Don Gowan of the host course, Quilchena's Junior champion Arnie Powell and Harold Nicholl of Penticton, who was playing for the first time on grass greens. The defending champion, Harold Brynjolfson, failed to qualify for the championship flight after two rounds of 82.

The challenges of the match play rounds to follow would go beyond the course itself as the ruddy-faced caddy champion ploughed through the competition wearing a cockiness excused only by his eager adolescence. In the semifinal Leonard had few fans cheering as he defeated Shaughnessy's Ted Charlton, much to the disappointment of many club members and in particular the loser's father, Bill, who was the BC Golf Association president. At that point, the tournament committee, some thought in an act of desperation, submitted an enquiry about Leonard's age while pointing out that those who caddied beyond the age of 17 were deemed professionals.

The bureaucratic inquisition of an innocent boy infuriated Elizabeth Leonard. On the eve of the final she obtained from Victoria absolute proof that her son would not be 18 until the following February. Birth certificate in hand, Leonard went out the next day and beat Don Gowan

3 and 2. The unfortunate incident did nothing to cure Leonard of his natural suspicion of authority.

An earlier episode with the elite regime had already alienated Leonard. After winning the 1930 caddy title, Shaughnessy gave him a three-year junior membership. But the patriarchal pro, Davey Black, didn't permit Leonard to compete in the club's junior championships, ruling that he was only an honorary member.

On the day of the tournament, club president L.M. Diether noticed Leonard loitering outside the caddy shack and asked why he wasn't participating. The boy explained his exclusion and when the pro was confronted by a dismayed Diether, Black denied Leonard's explanation. The animosity between the rebel caddy and the venerable pro never did abate. Both stubborn and proud, they remained distant over the years and played together only when they were drawn in the same tournament foursome. Diplomatic draw makers avoided pairing them.

Leonard was three years younger than Black's son, Ken, whose 1932 BC Open victory was as stunning to the golf establishment as Leonard's Amateur win. The barrier between Davey Black and Leonard didn't prevent the two younger men from becoming and remaining friendly rivals.

In 1933, Ken Black captured his first of three BC Amateurs. Leonard's game had faltered noticeably and he returned to the friendly confines of Glenoaks at Langara to play with Jim O'Neil, Charlie McCadden and other old pals. More comfortable at Langara, he promptly bettered the course record by three with 65 in a monthly medal competition.

Back on track, he lost the 1934 BC Amateur when Quilchena's Dickie Moore canned a spectacular chip over a bunker for a decisive birdie. In 1935 Leonard finally repeated as provincial champion but was deprived of the National crown in Hamilton where he was beaten on the 37th semifinal hole by Sandy Somerville. The next day Somerville claimed his fifth Canadian title.

Leonard and Ken Black met one more time in the BC final, in 1936, the year before Stan joined his brother, Bill, as a pro.

Leonard's final amateur victory was his second City crown. He shot two 71s at Quilchena with club junior champion Ernie Brown as his caddy.

Brown recalled that Leonard's drives "were keen and his mashie-niblick did everything but wash round behind the ears." Earlier in 1936, Leonard had won the PNGA title after a course record of 67 at Point Grey.

The most remarkable part of Leonard's game was his prodigious driving. Often described as the pro with the Popeye arms, a shade under five-foot-nine and never more than 160 pounds, Stan kept fit throughout his life. Initially, all his attention went to the strongest, most satisfying aspect of his game and he was rarely out-driven. In a tournament created during the lull of the war years, the Lions Gate Open, Leonard was prodded into a "slugging bee" with a notorious basher from Hollywood, "Mysterious" John Montague.

Montague was left in the lurch, usually by at least 25 yards, and he was mystified by how the little Canadian launched a 345-yarder off the fourth tee and banged one 352 off the 11th. The sport-hungry crowd of 2,500 saw Lloyd Mangrum run away with victory, sandwiching 66 and 65 between a pair of 69s for 269. Leonard was fifth at 284; Montague missed the money.

With his strong grip and blacksmith arms, Leonard was unpredictable off the tee. His alarmingly frequent, recklessly hooked drives brought on fits of frustration and fury that affected his entire game. He eventually recognized that he couldn't compete consistently without altering his troublesome grip. He convinced himself that he could sacrifice distance by changing his left-hand positioning, a cure-all that erased his fear of turning the ball over.

Confidence on the tee enabled Leonard to focus on other significant phases of the game he had been neglecting. He was now developing his finesse. No one ever accused Leonard of skimping on practice time. He maintained his extraordinary length off the tee, strong or weak left hand, with Spartan training. Through his final tournament years he kept fighting trim by regularly pounding a punching bag in the basement of his home. He became a decent putter by switching to a reverse overlapping grip which he claimed lessened the margin for error. Leonard portrays himself as an impatient radical who "wanted to get there yesterday" and who "didn't care who got in my way in the drive to get ahead."

He maintains that while his explosive temper was a drawback early in his career, it served to propel his determination. "In my latter amateur years, there wasn't a better club thrower around anywhere," he admitted. "A lot of folks tried to correct that, yet I believe my temper helped make me a better player. It kept me fighting mad. Being angry, I could never get complacent."

Leonard didn't really come to control his temper until the early 1950s, just before he embarked full-time on the PGA Tour. "I guess I stopped acting up as my game matured," he said. "My guiding light was my brother, though it took me quite some time to see how Bill kept things in proper perspective. I was always flying off the handle for one reason or another and it got me into some trouble."

Leonard turned pro in 1937 under Bill Heyworth at Hastings Park where he had often played with Jack and George Creighton. After about 18 months he followed his brother, Bill, to work for Jack Cuthbert at the Calgary Country Club and returned to Vancouver at the outbreak of the war. Adept with his hands, he took a tool-and-die-making job as a machinist with an engineering firm and was exempt from the draft. In December 1938, he married Christine Main, a telephone operator at the Hudson's Bay store off Granville and Burrard. They honeymooned in California, allowing Leonard to play several tour events. Chris was Leonard's faithful pillar, his mainstay through the good years and the bad.

During the war people had little time, money or desire for golf. Leonard's duties at the machine shop left only evenings for golf. When Jimmy Huish departed in 1940 to work in a munitions plant, a Marine Drive committee headed by George Norgan and Monte Hill appointed Leonard the new pro. After the war, Huish worked as a club maker for Fred Wood and Ernie Brown and then retired.

During the early war years, Jim Brodie and Robert Roxburgh—future grandfather of champion Doug Roxburgh—attended to Marine's pro shop on weekdays. Leonard finally took over full-time in March 1942, the year his daughter Linda was born. When peace and normalcy returned to the world, Leonard was hungry for tournament golf. He requested time off from his club duties during the dank winter months and the directors of the city's most active club obliged him. Leonard was permitted to play for five or six weeks of the winter tour that started in California and ended in Phoenix. He entrusted the pro shop to his assistant Fred Dornan.

In 1946 and 1947, Leonard did well if he made expenses but he was cultivating invaluable experience. In those years more time was spent behind a wheel than on the driving range and the costs of travelling by car often permitted only one pre-tournament practice round.

Leonard believed he was ready to play pro after winning the Pacific Northwest Open at Jericho in 1937 while still an amateur. Later that year, as a pro, he captured his first of nine Alberta Open titles and over the next decade firmly established himself as the nation's best golfer.

Leonard rues an errant drive during the 1946 Canadian Open at Montreal Beaconsfield as the costliest stroke of his career. His old nemesis off the 16th tee, a hook, left his ball behind an old stone barn, forcing a wasted stroke to get back to the fairway. He missed the playoff with winner George Fazio and Dick Metz by one stroke. It was the closest a Canadian-born player had come to winning the Canadian Open since 1920, when Charles Murray of Montreal lost a playoff to Douglas Edgar of Atlanta. "That bad drive more than anything else convinced me to give up distance for accuracy," Leonard admitted later. "That summer I threw out my heavy woods and got a lighter set. I had been averaging about 275 yards off the tee, but I quickly found that drives of 250 to 260 were long enough to play any course."

Leonard didn't play especially well in the 1947 Canadian Open at Toronto Scarboro, where Bobby Locke won. The South African with the floppy swing played a 16-match exhibition series in his homeland against Sam Snead later that year. He won 14 of the matches.

After his first of four British Open titles in 1949, Locke made a similar Canadian tour with Leonard. "I think the results were about even, and the exhibitions made money," mused Leonard. "Bobby got 60 percent of the net and I got 40." A decade later Leonard and another noted South African champion named Gary Player toured western Canada on behalf of Carling.

Leonard noted that

> My performances on those tours and the Hopkins Cup
> matches kind of told me I could beat the top players in
> the world. The Hopkins matches were the forerunner to
> the Canada Cup, which then became the World Cup,
> with eight Americans against eight players from other
> countries.
>
> I had Chris's total support whatever I decided to do.
> Being competitive in that company while I was still a club
> pro was the encouragement I needed in my own mind. I
> needed experience against the day's best players and the
> confidence I could play as well as they could.

However, Leonard's performance in the first Canadian Open staged west of Toronto, in 1948 at Shaughnessy Heights, was frightfully disappointing. His brilliant 65 on the last day went almost unnoticed as he finished far behind the winner, Chuck Congdon, his old rival from Tacoma. Congdon's 280 total was three better than Ky Laffoon and Vic Ghezzi.

In contrast, Leonard was untouchable in the 1949 BC Open at Point Grey when he embarrassed the field with a record 271. Fred Wood was runner-up at 290 while a bright, young amateur named Bill Mawhinney came in with 294 and the clowning Ed "Porky" Oliver, then a club pro at Seattle Inglewood, posted 297.

The year 1950 told Leonard he was a potential tour winner. He captured his third Canadian PGA title and also won the BC, Alberta and Saskatchewan Opens, and finished on Congdon's heels in the Washington State Open. He was named Canada's outstanding athlete of the year. He kept his CPGA crown with a gritty performance in 1951 at Hamilton. Playing with a high fever, he collapsed on the ninth green during the second round. After a five-minute rest from his near blackout he managed to finish at 71. Still groggy from the suffocating heat wave the next day, he reached down and found a brilliant 65 in reserve and staggered in with a 206 total, winning by five.

Sporting a full range of golfing attire, this 1950s foursome includes
Walt McElroy, Stan Leonard, Ken Black and the dapper Fred Wood, all
future members of BC's Golf Hall of Fame. BC GOLF HOUSE 007.121.003

By the early 1950s Leonard was well known throughout the golf
world, although he hadn't yet won a major event outside of Canada. As
CPGA champion he was a regular at the Augusta Masters every April and
he was a familiar figure at winter tour events in Arizona and California.

Leonard also became a close friend of Ben Hogan, if anyone can
consider himself Hogan's close friend. When Leonard was still minding
Marine's pro shop, it was Hogan who recommended that the Canadian
be included in the Fort Worth Invitational. Playing with Hogan was a
privilege. If he spoke to you, it was an honour. In a winter tour event
Leonard recalls making birdies on each of the first two holes, the second
prompting Hogan to acknowledge, "Nice second shot." Hogan smiled
when Leonard chipped in to birdie 17 but said nothing more. "The next

day Hogan went out of his way to come over and say how much he had enjoyed playing with me," said Leonard, smiling. "Coming from him, that was a confession."

When Leonard left his pro shop and migrated for the 1954 winter tour, he landed on a perch at the Phoenix Open. He equalled the course record of 63 at the Phoenix Country Club and totalled 275, only three strokes behind the winning Ed Furgol. At the Crosby tournament he tied for fourth, six strokes back of Cary Middlecoff's 209. They were extremely encouraging tournaments.

Back home that year he won the BC match play title for the fourth time, defeating Langara pro Ben Colk 4 and 3 at Shaughnessy before 4,000 spectators. Leonard collected $302.50, Colk $217.50. Then, in the Canadian Open at Point Grey, won by Victoria-raised Pat Fletcher's 280, Leonard faltered before the home folks once again. Much to his chagrin, he failed to break 72 on any of the four days and finished 17 strokes behind Fletcher. Disappointment, however, turned to elation in the first Canada (now World) Cup at Laval, Quebec. He won the individual title by two strokes over Jimmy Demaret, a performance that opened the door to his affiliation with the resort at Lachute.

Leonard has struck many memorable winning shots but perhaps the one he remembers most vividly was the three-iron he launched uphill to Laval's 18th on the final day of the Canada Cup. The ball came to rest within a foot of the hole.

Winning at Laval was a big feather in my cap. It gave me a lot of publicity and a great deal of self-confidence. I had played well enough overall that year to give up the security of steady employment and try the tour as a regular.

I hadn't felt I was being honest to myself. I knew I could compete and I wanted to give myself a fair chance. Besides it wasn't fair to the club, leaving so often to play. I couldn't wear two hats and do justice to either job. With invitations coming from the Masters, Tam O'Shanter and Colonial, I was asking for more and more time off to play. I couldn't turn down those invites so I decided to be a part-time regular on tour rather than a part-time club pro.

The prognosticators, noting that Leonard was beyond 40 and suggesting he was beyond his prime, wrote him off as a player who invariably had one bad round every tournament. They publicly forecast a pratfall for Stan the Man.

A lot of people, including some of my own members, said they thought I was crazy thinking I could go down there at my age and make a living. I was putting all the chips on the table. I still had to buy groceries for my wife and daughter and I had a mortgage. But I couldn't rest until I tried it and I knew time was wasting. My only regret is that I didn't do it five or six years earlier.

His 1955 debut was a reassuring tie for eighth in the San Diego Open. He earned $513 for shooting 280, six strokes behind winner Tommy Bolt. He collected money in 9 of 10 starts, including a fourth with 272 in the Canadian Open that Arnold Palmer captured with 265 at Toronto Weston.

That year many tour pros were enticed to the BC Open at Shaughnessy. Lumber magnate Poldi Bentley lured them here via the US Open in San Francisco with a $5,000 purse and a promise of hooking into salmon. Leonard closed again with 65 but it was barely noted; tour newcomer Dow Finsterwald won the $2,400 top prize with 270, one ahead of Bud Holscher. Leonard took home $170 with 282.

Leonard's affiliation with the Lachute course came around 1956 when he took time off the tour to win the Quebec PGA. The Lachute connection was a windfall he didn't expect; the offer to represent the club on tour came after his decision to resign from Marine.

Gilbert Ayres, who made his millions out of woollen blankets, had developed the resort at Lachute, about 60 miles north of Montreal. He made Leonard an irresistible offer: a three-year contract that virtually underwrote all Leonard's tour expenses. However, the association was terminated after one contract as Leonard couldn't agree to make his permanent home in Lachute, which Ayres requested.

He was home for the 1956 BC Open only as a spectator. While repairing the roof on his southwest Vancouver house, he fell off a ladder and suffered a broken right foot. But his natural resilience got him into 13 PGA tour events before the year was out. Paycheques from 12 of them totalled $8,831, which ranked 33rd on the money list.

The next year he finally hit the jackpot by succeeding Sam Snead as champion of the Greater Greensboro Open. The victory total of 276 was three better than runner-up Mike Souchak, and earned him $2,000. Stan the Man had finally arrived at the age of 42. "With that win I knew I belonged and ended some of the skepticism that prevailed when I left Marine to play the tour," he says. "Some people figured I was too old for tournament golf and I must admit I wasn't too sure myself."

When Leonard came home for a respite in late May 1957, he was duly recognized with a tribute dinner at Point Grey. More than 150 people attended the ten-dollar-a-plate function, including head table guests Mayor Fred Hume and PGA BC president Jock McKinnon. Leonard had made believers out of a lot of doubters and he delivered a humble, grateful speech to the diners. Later that year he cashed in a prize Chevrolet for $2,500 after scoring one of his 11 career holes-in-one during the Western Open.

The Greensboro triumph qualified him for the 1958 Tournament of Champions, which he made his second tour victory. He shot 275, a stroke better than Billy Casper. The $10,000 bonanza anchored a season in which he earned $22,827 in only 15 starts. Arnold Palmer led the way that year with $42,607 and Bob Rosburg took the Vardon Trophy with a 70.1 stroke average. Leonard placed among the leaders with 70.8 for 58 rounds.

Leonard's 1958 statistics were enhanced by his play in Canada. His 270 at Edmonton Mayfair was three behind Canadian Open champion Wes Ellis and he finally enjoyed a satisfying major tournament in his own backyard. This time his Sunday 65 was noted, though few in the crowd of 14,000 saw any of his shots at Point Grey in the final round of the BC

Centennial Open. That day, Jim Ferree hogged the spotlight by shooting an 11-under 61, the lowest round of the tour year. Ferree went on to win with 271. Leonard finished fifth at 274.

In 1959, the Metropolitan Golf Writers of America recognized Leonard in New York as its player of the year and the Greater Vancouver Tourist Board honoured him as the city's goodwill ambassador for the year as a direct result of his individual triumph in what was then known as the Canada Cup and eight years later would be re-christened the World Cup. Aussie Peter Thomson had paired with Kal Nagle to take the team honours but lost to Leonard in a playoff at Royal Melbourne. For his individual performance Stan was awarded the International Trophy.

Despite the honours, 1959 wasn't an especially good year financially for Leonard. He again made 12 of 13 tour cuts but his official money of $6,767 didn't cover his expenses. Leonard's best showing included what he considers one of his finest tournament rounds, a 67 at Augusta. He and Palmer shared the Masters lead through three rounds, but both were bypassed by Art Wall's closing 66. Leonard came fourth, three strokes out. The previous year Palmer had won with 284, two better than Leonard.

Leonard drove away from the Western Open in 1960 with the championship trophy and $5,000. His third tour win in four years came at the age of 45 in a playoff over Wall, then 37. They had tied at 278, with Leonard closing with a 68 and then holing a six-foot putt to birdie the first extra hole. Few players of Leonard's age managed to win more than once on tour those years. The exceptions included Sam Snead and Julius Boros.

This was Leonard's final productive year on tour. He counted $14,141 from 16 starts in 1960. A graph of his subsequent play at Augusta is revealing. He was a respectable seventh in 1960 and 1961, eight shots behind Palmer and nine behind Gary Player. But he skidded to 19th in 1962, 41st in 1963, missed the 36-hole cut in 1964 when he earned only $5,200 for the year, and wasn't eligible for a Masters invitation in 1966.

During the early 1960s he had several victories on his own territory, but Leonard's tour days were numbered. His nerve ends were finally wearing thin; snap hooks crept back into his swing and he was jerking short putts. He claimed his fifth and final BC Open title in 1962 at New

Seen here in April 1960, Stan the Man poses with the daily
newspaper at the Newsmen's Club of BC where he was named
"British Columbian of the Year." BC GOLF HOUSE 007.85.35

Shaughnessy when he defeated Rod Funseth by chipping in on the first
extra hole after the two touring pros had tied at 290. A sixth title eluded
him the following year at Point Grey as he pulled his drive into the trees
at the second extra hole and lost a playoff to Al Feldman's par.

Leonard wasn't a factor at New Shaughnessy in 1966 when the
Canadian Open returned west for the last time. He missed the 36-hole cut
of 151. The following year he flirted with victory in the BC Open, actually taking home top money by shooting 203 for three trips around the
familiar Marine course. But another Marine Drive player, amateur Johnny
Johnston, prevailed by fashioning 200 with his exquisite short game.

Stan Leonard still stands as BC's most successful professional. BC GOLF HOUSE 007.85.23

Even though he won the 1975 Canadian Seniors at the age of 60, Leonard's decline had started soon after his encounter with Rod Funseth and after he had kicked his 30-year smoking habit. He was a confirmed addict, normally puffing through two packs of cigarettes a day. "Smoking was a crutch and without it my nerves were so bad I was actually unable to play some days," Leonard confessed. "Fear started creeping back into my game. My short game in particular suffered. I became a basket case with the putter. I went to cross-handed. When I tried the Senior Tour in the early 1980s, I was double-hitting some putts. I was that bad."

His last tournament was in 1982, the Legends of Golf, a best-ball event at Austin, Texas. "I thought it was going to be a new career, but I was never able to adjust to tournament play again," he remarked. "My nerves were as bad as ever, worse than I expected. Ironically, one of my last tournaments was at Calgary Earl Grey, where my brother was the original head pro."

Leonard turned instead to the business world. His first business venture was Golfcraft where he became the figurehead of the company whose principal shareholders were Jack Sim, Frank Welters, Jim Moynes and Gordon Southam. In 1974 he was offered the position of golf director at Desert Island, a Palm Springs golf resort crowded with Canadians. Leonard's presence attracted many other Canucks, primarily from the prairies.

Turning to course architecture in the early 1980s, he and Phil Tattersfield designed a course in the heart of the Cariboo, at 108 Mile Ranch. He was also a consultant for the development of several Calgary courses. After concluding that he wasn't cut out for either business or architecture, Leonard reverted to what he knew best and enjoyed the most: teaching. He retired in 1982 and returned to Desert Island as pro emeritus, teaching through 1991.

Leonard had initiated the novel PGA BC Junior Golf College in 1963, a concept that unfortunately was abandoned after five years. There were 108 youngsters at the first college at Chilliwack's Meadowlands course and they beat up 5,000 practice balls.

For a time Stan Leonard made his city the capital of the golf world; for a time he was the best damned golfer in the whole world.

CHAPTER II

PIONEER PROS

BC golfers owe a lot to the club professionals who nurtured the game and have set high standards for course management in British Columbia.

Professional golfers have competed, taught the game and been instrumental in developing quality pro shops at courses across the province for more than a century.

Golf's first professional has been acknowledged as Scot Allan Robertson. The descendant of the clan that for generations traditionally manufactured golf balls at St Andrews also became the first golfer to break 80, in 1858. Naturally he performed this feat with one of the family's gutta percha products.

The distinction of developing a new phase of club manufacture also belonged to Robertson. He was the first to run up shots to greens with a cleek, an ancient Scots word meaning "hook."

One summation of the Victoria Golf Club history mentions that a Mr. Jacobs was hired in the dual role of club professional and greenskeeper for twenty-five dollars per month in 1902. He was to teach golf from nine to five and "the rest of the time had to be devoted to tending the links."

The first dedicated pro to take up residence in BC was Jack Moffat of Musselburgh, the site of another famous early Scottish course. Moffat became Victoria Golf Club's pro in 1905 and was succeeded five years later by his brother, Willie (aka Bill). Almost every ship that left British waters to cross the Atlantic thereafter had a consignment of golf balls and clubs, choice brands of liquor or human cargo from Scotland.

By the early 1900s pros in the United States were earning an average of $750 annually plus board. Fashioning clubs and balls and repairing them provided their main income, and charging one dollar for a nine-hole lesson supplemented it. Some pros returned home during the winter or took jobs in more temperate southern coastal climes.

The diligent Scots also dominated as architects and greenskeepers. They kept clannishly close in the land of opportunity—the early championships were the private preserve of Scots and English players. Most early westcoast golfers were gentlemen of considerable means and influence, and they hired the funny-talking foreigners to teach them the secrets of this new game.

The Moffats were followed in 1907 by Albert Kam who served the revived links at Vancouver Jericho, and by Harold Edmunds at Macaulay Point in Esquimalt.

Macaulay Point's members enticed Carnoustie pro Alex Duthie from Waverley to succeed Edmunds in 1909 but Duthie, a shrewd business-man, stayed only three months as he couldn't resist the opportunity on the flourishing mainland when Kam vacated Jericho. Duthie was recruited by Hall C. Chiene, a long-time Jericho member who served as BC Golf Association president and as a BC Racing Association steward. He remained at the Vancouver course until the property off English Bay was reclaimed for national defence reasons in 1946.

When Bill Moffat replaced his brother Jack at Oak Bay in 1910, he brought with him the restless Jimmy Huish. Huish also spent time at the United Service Club course near Macaulay Point and would soon become the first pro at Royal Colwood when it opened for play in 1914. Troon's Willie Black came through that revolving door in 1918 to replace Huish, and in turn was succeeded by Edward McInnes from Surrey, England, in 1923.

Charles Locke had come from Tacoma in 1911 to set up shop in the pristine premises at Vancouver Golf Club and was there until Tom Gallop took over during the war for a couple of tough years. Jimmy Huish must have felt he was gathering moss on Vancouver Island because he started a five-year residence at Vancouver in 1920.

Meanwhile, Walter Gravlin, BC's first province-born pro, started at the United Service Club in 1919. The promising Victoria baseball player had served his apprenticeship at Victoria Golf Club under Jack Moffat. After Gravlin took over at Macaulay Point he bided his time while members worked to build the new Uplands course. He relocated there and spent the next 40 years, through 1963, at Victoria Uplands.

The immigrant golf professionals that came to BC were expert tradesmen, their own swings reflecting the part of their homeland they came from. Some were widely emulated players, although most of their long hours were spent in workshops making and fixing clubs. Creating equipment was far more profitable than teaching others to use it.

Golf form espoused by Scottish pros was the fashion of the day. A wide variety of swings was taught to and adopted by eager protégés. The so-called caddy swing was popular at windy links such as St Andrews and fitting at Victoria; the club was taken back flat and came down abruptly, turning well before the end of the follow-through. This was designed to pull shots under the prevailing winds and out of following winds.

At the Royal Liverpool Golf Club at Hoylake, beside the Irish Sea, a flatter three-quarter swing that was considered safer and more reliable, though it relinquished distance, was all the rage. Accentuated by taking the club so far back it almost grazed the heel of the left foot, the swing resulted in left to right ball flight.

The first local pros graduated from the caddy yards as assistants to the game's masters who were readily recognizable in plaid, white shirt and tie, cardigan and plus-fours. The likes of Shaughnessy Heights' Davey Black and Jock McKinnon at Capilano a decade later were seldom seen without such togs.

Willie Black was recommended to Colwood by his more illustrious brother, Davey, whom the Victoria course had attempted to lure from Ottawa's Rivermead. Davey Black eventually would come west too, taking the Shaughnessy Heights post in 1920. His predecessors at Shaughnessy were William Bowden and Alf Blinko, an Englishman from Enfield.

With the gradual grooming of BC-born or raised professionals, the migration from overseas petered to a trickle during the 1930s.

FRED WOOD

Among the first homegrown pros were Fred Wood, Ernie Tate, Stan Leonard, Harry Winder, Dave Dixon, Hal Rhodes, Ben Colk, LaVerne Johnson, Bill Watson, Ernie Brown, Doug McAlpine and Roy Heisler.

If golf aficionados of the 1930s and 1940s were polled to determine the province's best all-time putter, the overwhelming choice would have been Fred Wood. Regrettably, Wood's reputation on the greens detracted from his being appreciated and applauded for his skills as a shot maker.

Wood eventually became a favourite at Shaughnessy Heights, and succeeded Black as the pro in 1945. But the Burquitlam product hadn't been given his due in the press while making his way to the prestigious, enviable position of pro at Vancouver's finest course. Wood was an exceptional golfer who played in the shadows of Stan Leonard and Ken Black.

Davey Black's son, Ken, and the brash, explosive Leonard were local youngsters bursting with charisma and unbounded exuberance, qualities that appealed to journalists. In contrast, Wood was seen as the phlegmatic, homely putting marvel from the sticks of Vancouver Golf Club who couldn't possibly putt that well and remain competitive.

Wood had learned early in life not to be discouraged. After saving his caddy fees to purchase his first set of clubs, young Fred returned from school one day to find that his father had broken his hickories in two over the back fence. Fred W.A. Wood, a gold miner among other things, wanted his son to be a pharmacist, not to waste his time on golf.

The self-disciplined Wood preceded his two younger adversaries on the local scene by several years. At the age of 15, in 1922, he won his first VGC caddy tournament, shooting a 94 with a 24 handicap. He repeated his success two years later in a playoff against another future pro, Ernie Tate.

Wood's first of four successive Vancouver Club championships in 1926 preceded his first triumph off his home course, the City Amateur. In the inaugural BC Open of 1928, Wood finished a creditable sixth at Shaughnessy Heights, behind Davey Black, the man he would succeed 17 years later.

Wood repeated as City champion in 1930, and also claimed his only BC Amateur crown by trouncing (10 and 8) Ken Black, then 18, at

VGC. Leonard was 17 when he won the provincial championship in 1932, with Black taking the first of his three titles the following year.

The day's leading amateurs also contested the Open championship and, after winning in 1930, Wood resumed his battles with Black and Leonard as a professional. He worked for five years each at Peace Portal, Fraserview and Old Quilchena before securing the Shaughnessy plum spot in 1945.

The Shaughnessy directors were obviously impressed with Wood's credentials as a player—he won the BC Open in 1935, 1938 and 1939, beating Leonard the last two years—as well as his qualifications as a club pro.

Wood's dedication to his job, combined with the tournament lull during the war years, precluded his winning many more events. His wife, Annie, made sure the family and his Shaughnessy duties were his priorities. "Mom put the kibosh on Dad's tournament golf," says son Bryan Wood, who worked almost three years in Shaughnessy's back shop. "When Stan Leonard started playing the tour golf a few months every winter, he'd always be calling Dad, trying to convince him to give it a whirl. I remember Leonard saying he thought Dad could do well down there."

He didn't give it a whirl until 1957. While on vacation with the family, Wood diverted from the Okanagan to Spokane, Washington, to play the inaugural US Seniors championship for players aged 50 and over. He was the only Canadian entrant. He won.

With son Bryan caddying for him, the 50-year-old Wood tied the legendary Gene Sarazen at 270 after 72 holes. Sarazen, then 55, had signed his final scorecard and believed he had won the title as he was told the only player with a chance to tie him was "some Canadian no one had ever heard about." Sarazen watched in disbelief as Wood rolled in a cross-country putt on the final green to force the playoff. The old master putter won fittingly, on a 12-footer to par the first extra hole.

"Gene putted awfully fast," recalled Wood later. "While I was picking my ball out of the cup I could see out of the corner of my eye that his ball was already on the way." The rattled Sarazen, a winner of three major titles from 1922 through 1935, had reached the green in regulation but proceeded to three-putt from about 20 feet, missing a four-footer to prolong the playoff.

When Wood retired from Shaughnessy in 1972 he was royally feted at a black-tie affair. For his 27 years of loyalty, the members presented Fred and Annie with a month's vacation in Hawaii and $10,000. He died of heart failure in his 78th year in 1984.

JACK MCLAUGHLIN

When Wood died, Jack McLaughlin had been at Shaughnessy for almost a decade. A kindly gentle giant of a man, he was the professorial pro; golf education engrossed him. Before a sudden heart attack took his life at the age of 57 in January 1991, McLaughlin had initiated a teaching program for pre-juniors aged 5 to 11 that snowballed across the country. He started by cutting clubs down to size for about a dozen youngsters at Shaughnessy. Nationwide enrolment in McLaughlin's junior-junior classes surpassed 10,000 in 1991.

"One of the reasons Dad left Toronto Bayview was that the club was losing its practice range," says Jim McLaughlin, one of three sons who followed Jack into the golf business. "He had to have a proper place to teach and Shaughnessy had a first-class practice area."

McLaughlin and the late George Knudson, who had won more PGA Tour events than any Canadian, collaborated on developing a manual to unify teaching concepts in Canada. McLaughlin coached the Canadian Ladies Golf Union's most promising team players. Some of the touring pros under his wing were Brent Franklin, the three-time Canadian Amateur who captured the Canadian PGA title before embarking on the Japanese Tour, and Ray Stewart of Abbotsford and Steve Chapman of Prince George.

McLaughlin had come to Shaughnessy in 1974 and spent many hours on the practice fairway with members or visiting pupils.

ERNIE BROWN

For the better part of 60 years, Ernie Brown's unmistakable profile has been prominent in BC golf. Wearing his hat as a course architect, he himself would consider his "a signature schnozz."

Ernie Brown (right) caddied for Stan Leonard in the 1930s, enjoyed a 20-year career as a pro in the Lower Mainland and then turned to course design where he had a hand in 22 of BC's course layouts. Leonard (left) also turned to design after leaving the pro tour. BC GOLF HOUSE 007.144.006

The skinny kid with the hook for a nose and slice for a swing couldn't play a lick for the longest time. Many caddies played for nickels in the twilight on the five holes east of Oak Street. Brown, among the worst players, didn't enjoy being ridiculed. He saved his nickels and caddy fees and took lessons from Langara pro Nat Cornfoot.

Brown improved through determination. He also developed an astute perspective of the game, an awareness that earned him Stan Leonard's bag for the Amateur. "It was a great honour, being asked to pack Stan's bag," he recalled. "I knew his game pretty well. I could club him better than anyone. He listened to me, trusted me. Oh, he'd argue with me over club selection. I'd hand him a six-iron and he's say, no, it's a five, give me a five, but I'd refuse and walk away with the bag."

Brown persevered in his pursuit of a career in a game he loved. He kept his nose to golf's grindstone and he distinguished himself as a caddy, club maker, professional, instructor, course architect, club official, innovator, tournament starter-scorekeeper and provincial champion. He helped shape courses, improved golfers and administrated and conducted events. Yet his most satisfying accomplishment was the handicap service he initiated for golfers who didn't, and couldn't afford to, belong to clubs.

As a pro, Brown served the members at Jericho, Old Quilchena and Seymour, from 1938 through 1957, before turning to course architecture. He apprenticed under Alex Duthie at Jericho and while at Quilchena came under the influence of Stanley Thompson, the renowned course architect whose BC credits include the widely acclaimed Capilano. His first experience with course design and earth moving was with Roy and Don Gleig and Gordie MacKay in Chilliwack. He subsequently designed, remodelled or extended 21 other courses in the province. Burnaby Mountain and the Sunshine Coast course at Roberts Creek both bear Brown's trademark.

By 1965 he was finally reinstated as an amateur, after having applied eight years earlier, and played at McCleery, which he has served as president.

"I got to the club championship final one year and had to play Bert Ticehurst," says Brown, who won the Old Quilchena club title by beating Jackie Reynolds in 1944. "I was seven down to Ticehurst after the first 18, shot 66 the second time around and picked up only three holes." The young man who had carried teenager Stan Leonard's bag during his 1932 Amateur triumph was crowned a champion, claiming the provincial Seniors title in 1972 and 1973.

While waiting to regain his amateur status he established Ernie Brown Services, a system first conceived in California that compiles certified handicaps for non–club members. Brown's computation of scores qualified individuals to enter national and provincial events for which they'd be otherwise ineligible without membership in RCGA or BCGA-affiliated clubs.

Brown, who handicapped as many as 500 customers in a year, explained,

> When I applied to do it, I pointed out that a survey showed only 10 percent of Lower Mainland golfers belonged to clubs. Thus, 9 out of every 10 golfers couldn't play in their own provincial championships as non–club members and were unable to get a necessary handicap. It was discrimination in a sense; people were deprived from playing because they couldn't afford to join a club. Peter Bentley, then president of the BCGA, recognized the need for the service and pushed to get it through.

BEN COLK

In spring 1939, with a fascist named Hitler posing a growing threat across Europe, Wood was primed to become the first man to win successive BC Open titles and Ben "Nipper" Colk got to run his own pro shop.

The time wasn't opportune for selling anything other than food and war bonds. Even ardent golfers were preoccupied with invasions and bombings and a gloomy future. However, they still used golf as a temporary refuge from the distressing inevitability of a war, and it was business as usual at popular Langara. Colk's first job as a head pro presented the challenge of keeping the public course at least viable for the CPR through the lean times that lay ahead.

At age 30, Ben Colk was enthusiastic in the face of war. As Nat Cornfoot's successor, he developed into an excellent shot maker though he never reached the level of Wood or Leonard. Few did. But Colk eventually became one of the area's most sought-after golf instructors. Adept at articulating the complexities of what he often described as basically a simple game, Colk's reputation attracted advanced players from other clubs to Langara's practice fairway. His championship protégés included future brother-in-law and Canadian Amateur winner Walt McElroy. Other notable students were Bob Kidd, Kevin Riley, Walt McAlpine, Laurie Roland, Alvie Thompson and his successor at Langara, Lyle Crawford.

Laurie Roland, three-time BC Junior champ, tees off at Marine Drive in an exhibition fundraiser for polio while partner Bill Mawhinney (left) looks on. Behind them, their opponents Ernie Brown and the club pro, Stan Leonard, wait to play. BC GOLF HOUSE 007.129.193

Born in 1909 in Duncan, Colk was one of seven children of George and Mary Ellen Colk. He was an athletic child, most proficient at soccer and baseball, who discovered golf by chance while walking along railway tracks that ran through the heart of a course at the Cowichan Station townsite. He also discovered that he could earn a quarter by shagging balls for the pro, a soft-spoken Englishman named Bill Heyworth who gave Ben his first club, an iron.

Colk won Cowichan's Junior championship in 1924, taking the measure of brothers Noel and Dave Radford and Dave Day. Noel Radford would become a badminton professional; Colk became a golf pro five years later.

For the princely sum of forty dollars a month, he followed Heyworth to the year-old Hastings Park nine-hole course on the Exhibition grounds, where the man who would become welterweight boxing champion of the world, Jimmy McLarnin, played regularly with Slim Delbridge, George and Murray West, and George and John Crighton.

Colk's BC Open debut, in 1931 at Oak Bay, was auspicious; he tied for eighth. After spending almost a year under Harry Winder at University, he went to work in 1936 for the venerable Alex Duthie at Jericho. "By going to Jericho I became the highest-paid assistant in the city," stated Colk, then in the prime of his playing form. He captured the 1936 Northwest Open after finishing second the previous year to Ken Tucker of Everett. "Top assistants were getting sixty dollars. I got seventy-five dollars plus a full meal every day at the Duthie house located right on the course."

It was his apprenticeship under the unassuming Heyworth's patient guidance that gave Colk a solid foundation as a teaching pro and a growing reputation as a teacher. Colk earned his keep, giving six half-hour lessons for five dollars and tending to the needs of Jericho members. "After the final round of the 1936 Open at Marine Drive where I tied Don Sutherland for third overall and as low pro behind winner Russ Case, I had to hike up the hill to catch a streetcar," he said ruefully. "I had to get back to Jericho to clean and buff the members' clubs. It was certainly a learning experience for me. Duthie was a gentleman's gentleman and his wife was a wonderful cook."

On April 1, 1939, 10 years to the day after turning professional, Colk went to Langara in his first job as head pro. His first assistants were LaVerne Johnson and Billy Leask; he also hired his brother Fred for a time.

Langara was always crowded with good players who belonged to the social club within the course, Glenoaks. "During one of my first years there I remember it took 77 to be one of 32 club championship qualifiers," exclaimed Colk. "It was some kind of record. It would be pretty darn good anywhere today."

One of golf's greatest inventions, the refined pull-cart, was introduced in BC at Langara, according to Colk. "Functional homemade carts first came here from California in the early 1940s, devised by Clay Puett. He invented the mechanical horse-racing starting gate in 1933. He later came here as a race starter."

An 1897 "trolley" was the forerunner of the ubiquitous modern pull-cart. It was pushed aside with the introduction of unpopular motorized carts. Motor carts were initially scarce at Langara and other public courses. Too expensive for the blue-collar workers and minority groups who frequented the green-fee courses, they were frowned upon by traditionalists who believed courses were meant to be walked.

"Anyone who could afford a cart could rent one and anyone could play at Langara," said Colk.

During and immediately after the war years, "Nipper" Colk played in exhibitions and charitable competitions.

Colk also served a diverse clientele at a time when prejudice was more prevalent than today.

Quite a bit of discrimination existed in golf, just as in other sports. At Langara Japanese players were designated to tee off starting at 6:00 AM. Jewish people started at 7:00 AM and the Glenoaks members went off at 8:00. They paid the same green fees but seldom mixed. It was the same at other courses.

In those days I don't believe private clubs allowed anyone to play who wasn't white or gentile. We'd get quite a few celebrity types, musicians and such, because blacks and Asians couldn't play most other courses. I remember giving lessons to Ray Brown, who was singer Ella Fitzgerald's husband. Bill Kenny of the Inkspots was a Langara regular after settling in Vancouver.

In 1959, before the CPR sold Langara and the adjoining property to the city, Colk went to the new Richmond Country Club where he stayed until his retirement in 1974. "Richmond's membership was almost exclusively Jewish. I convinced the board of directors to ease up on their membership restrictions and let anyone join their club. In time Richmond became a golf club, not a Jewish golf club. It's become a highly successful club."

Colk retired to Vancouver Island, settling north of his birthplace near Nanoose Bay. There the man so frequently called the wily veteran acted as advisor in the development of the Les Furber–designed Fairwinds course. As fate would have it, another retiree to that area was the ebullient Art Donaldson, former greenskeeper and a competent golfer in his own right. With Colk volunteering his teaching time at the Fairwinds range and Donaldson acting as starter at the first tee, Fairwinds members enjoyed rubbing shoulders with two of BC's great golf gurus until their passing. Today the club's main watering hole, named in Colk's honour, is known as Ben's Lounge and in the pro shop a beautiful soapstone sculpture of his trademark hat pays tribute to Donaldson.

BILL HEYWORTH

Bill Heyworth, the thickset, unobtrusive pro from Eastby, Yorkshire, had briefly apprenticed in course construction with Tom Vardon, second in the 1903 British Open to his famous brother Harry. Tom Vardon, fourth in the following Open, was beaten by James Braid in the 1905 PGA Match Play final.

Prior to turning pro at Duncan in 1923, Heyworth helped develop the Cowichan course as club secretary, and drafted plans for and supervised construction of the expansion to 18 holes at Hastings Park. Heyworth had served in both the Duncan and Nanaimo pro shops on Vancouver Island before moving to the Hastings Park in 1927. He remained there until it was closed for construction of the Empire Stadium and a massive parking lot for the 1954 Commonwealth Games.

The first green fees were fifty cents for 18, three dollars for a monthly ticket and twenty dollars annually. Heyworth loved teaching the youngsters who patronized the affordable and readily accessible public course, and looked the other way if an eager boy didn't have a quarter to play. Heywood began vigorously promoting junior golf in 1945; alarmed by diminishing interest in golf, he offered youngsters free lessons.

When the Hastings course closed, Heyworth briefly advised his son, Miles, at Gleneagles in West Vancouver. Miles, his father's assistant at Hastings during the two previous years, decided after about six months that he wasn't cut out for the golf business and became a private investigator. Bill Heyworth passed away in 1961 at 76; Miles Heyworth, who hiked as a youth from his North Vancouver residence to play at Hastings Park, eventually returned to the game as a director of the BC Golf Association.

LYLE CRAWFORD

Lyle Crawford's six years as a leading player were six years too many for golf administrators. The swaggering young man behind the dark glasses had few equals during the 1950s. He was brash, pretentious and rebellious. No one told Crawford what to wear or what not to say. Propriety was a foreign concept to the loud kid from Vancouver's east end. He also happened to be a helluva golfer.

Crawford's cockiness didn't fade away as a pro. Prior to a City Match Play Open round, he introduced himself to an opponent by blurting, "Good luck, fella. I hope you can play half decent. I've never seen the back nine of this course."

He was good and he let everyone know it. But no one ever found out how he manipulated shots so well with his unconventional staccato swing and carefree carriage.

A wife, two kids and a mortgage precluded a competitive career during his prime. Had his mentor, Colk, remained one year longer in Langara's pro shop, Crawford might have had the opportunity to fulfill his promise. But when Colk departed to Richmond, Crawford couldn't refuse the Langara promotion. "If Benny had stayed on, I probably would have gone back down south," said Crawford, who took the pro job at Saanich's municipal Cedar Hill course in 1978. "I could've been a

In May 1960 Lyle Crawford, two-time BC Amateur champ and defending BC Open winner, is congratulated by his wife on winning the Vancouver City Match Play competition.
VANCOUVER PUBLIC LIBRARY 44045

pretty good player. When I won that Canadian bursary to play the 1957 US tour, I made every cut. Eventually I ran out of money. I needed more time, maybe another year, to prove I could make it."

Crawford never lacked confidence. While he didn't become national champion, he was a finalist and semifinalist in successive Canadian Amateurs. He twice won the BC Amateur and the Open, and keyed his province's 1955 Willingdon Cup team victory by firing a pair of 67s at the Calgary Country Club. He would have missed the event if teammate Walter McElroy hadn't also opposed authority. The BCGA used to hand-pick the four-man interprovincial teams and Crawford, the rebel, was named alternate after dominating local events. Public course players were often overlooked during a time when choosing a Vancouver Islander was a given, even if the player wasn't as good as the number four mainland candidate. "He [Crawford] goes or I don't," asserted McElroy, the 1951 national champion. Crawford went.

When Hastings Park succumbed to bulldozers in 1952, Crawford went to Fraserview. A few months after Crawford won the 1955 Kelowna Ogopogo Open in the company of Colk, the veteran encouraged Crawford to turn pro. Crawford remembered that

> We'd play a lot of cards and jack around on rainy days at Langara. Still, I worked hard on my game. There were big trees along both sides of a practice area behind the pro shop and I'd take about 75 balls and hit them there all day. When I missed hitting one between the trees, I'd retrieve them all and start over again. It was great training. You'd learned how to bear down if you only had five or six balls left. I wouldn't stop until I hit every one between those trees or until it got so dark I couldn't see.

Crawford fared well with his patented three-quarter swing, but like many superb shot makers he never putted consistently well.

Crawford and Len "Scotty" Taylor eventually bought Western Golf Sales, which originated in Marpole in 1968 as a club repair shop for local pros. When it branched out to Vancouver Island, Crawford took over the Victoria store and replaced Bill Goldsworthy at Cedar Hill.

JACK WESTOVER

Jack Westover was arguably the province's most successful teaching pro. No one else has converted as many novices or juniors into national and provincial champions. A deliberate, discerning instructor, the phlegmatic Westover took great pleasure in developing young players. His devotion to his students is exemplary.

Westover's early graduates played at Marine, where he worked as an assistant pro before teaching at driving ranges throughout the mainland. His disciples followed him wherever he went.

He started in 1957 by helping Barb Renwick become BC's women's champion. He also taught fundamentals to Wayne Vollmer, Dick Zokol and Tom Moryson, and guided Holly Botham, Paula Phillips, Val White, Lynn Cooke, Liz Culver, Jennifer Wyatt and Kim Cowburn, helping them earn a host of championships along the way. Doug Roxburgh became his prize student.

CHAPTER 12

DOUG ROXBURGH:
THE CONSUMMATE AMATEUR

Harvey Combe and Doug Roxburgh brace golf's first century in this province like bookends of granite. British Columbia's greatest amateur champions played the game with austere, regal reverence: Combe as the course-blazing pioneer and Roxburgh as the enduring craftsman.

Dominance was the common denominator for Doug Roxburgh and Harvey Combe. Roxburgh surpassed Combe's once seemingly unreachable record of nine BC Amateur championships in 1989. Since Senator Hewitt Bostock donated the trophy in 1895, only James Lepp of Ledgeview in Abbotsford has won it more than three times. He was BC champion for four straight years, 2001–04. Both Roxburgh and Combe made it into the record book: Roxburgh with 13 victories and 5 seconds, Combe with 9 triumphs and 3 runner-up finishes. Combe was an established bureaucrat of 35 in Victoria when he first captured the title in 1897. Roxburgh first accepted the trophy in 1969 as a shy, precocious 17-year-old Vancouver high schooler.

At the turn of the century, worthy opposition for Combe was limited and the tournament's fields at Victoria Golf Club were comparatively small. He was the absolute tournament ruler through 1909. During his 13-year reign of supremacy, Combe missed the springtime event at least twice to visit his native England. Conversely, the studious, diligent Roxburgh forged his victories while coping with an endless parade of talented, young challengers, many of whom turned professional over the years. Roxburgh's endurance at the championship level has been remarkable. Few golfers anywhere have won any tournament of the calibre of the BC Amateur in four different decades. Roxburgh accomplished that feat with his win in 1991. Since 1969, the unassuming accountant has only once gone for as long as four years without winning the title.

All of Combe's victories were at the Oak Bay links during a period when other courses existed only at Macaulay Point in Esquimalt, New Westminster, Kelowna and the Vancouver area where the original Jericho members moved between three different venues. Players outside Victoria rarely contested early championships and Americans weren't eligible to play for the Bostock until after the First World War. Combe wasn't afforded the opportunity or didn't aspire to compete nationally or internationally. He had a lust for golf but only as a recreational player who, at his advanced age, found contentment playing his home links. Roxburgh has won everywhere, including twice at Capilano, Castlegar and Shaughnessy and at several other courses. By the time he had reached the age of 35 his golf prowess had taken him throughout the world. At that age, he was on the verge of matching Combe's record nine BC titles and he was one year removed from capturing his fourth Canadian Amateur title, at Gallagher's Canyon.

In the eyes of his peers, Doug Roxburgh is the consummate amateur. Few people in BC golf have commanded the respect and recognition earned by the son of Mac and Mary Roxburgh, and his influence has extended well beyond triumphs and titles. The game he painstakingly started to craft as a boy has been widely admired and so has his unwavering presence. He has led by example, by his modesty, implacability and clean-cut manner.

Ward Stouffer, one of a legion of Roxburgh worshippers, couldn't restrain himself the day he noticed a certain player anxiously studying the scoreboard at Gorge Vale Golf Club in Victoria. "Now I've seen everything!" Roxburgh's Marine Drive clubmate exclaimed for all to hear. "I've seen Doug Roxburgh hanging around to find out if he's going to make the cut."

It was late in the second day of the 1984 Amateur. Roxburgh had already checked the ferry schedule. He had shot 80 at the Gorge and

77 the day before at Glen Meadows in Sidney, where he bogeyed the first five holes and the last five. He missed the cut by a stroke. The only other Amateur cut Roxburgh failed to make was in 1967. He was 15, at Shaughnessy for his Amateur debut. In 1996 he became BC Amateur champion for the last time.

Decades before the Roxburgh kids—Doug, Bob and Margo—followed their parents to Marine Drive, the course was a magnet for quality players. An ongoing array of leading players on the membership roll created a fiercely competitive atmosphere at the shortest of the Lower Mainland's private courses. "At Marine, you get conditioned to good competition. If you don't stay at top of your game, you don't last long in the club championship," says Roxburgh. "You get over the first-tee jitters as a junior for casual matches or you won't be able to compete. Marine's a course where you can shoot some good scores . . . it gets you excited about the game."

The club's tradition of turning out young prospects was upgraded when Len Collett was employed as professional in 1966. The classy Winnipeg pro and his assistants, Jack Westover and Irv Taylor, initiated regular junior clinics.

Roxburgh, born in the Dominican Republic on December 28, 1951, first went down to Marine to caddy for his father and later regularly toted the bag of lumber baron Poldi Bentley. His mother and his uncle, Murray Roxburgh, took him for his first rounds to old Shaughnessy Heights where the Park Board operated the 11 remaining holes before the grand course's inevitable termination. Collett, who later went to Shaughnessy and Gallagher's Canyon as pro-manager, recalled:

> I remember him at group classes. Doug was just one of the boys. Then one day all of a sudden, like wow, he was special. Every time you looked up, there he was in the practice area. It would be pouring rain but Doug would be there pounding balls, chipping and putting. He probably enjoyed hitting balls more than anyone I've ever seen. He reminded me of George Knudson, who I saw turn himself into a great golfer through hard work.

Following introductory group lessons, Doug and his brother, Bob, decided to continue with more advanced instruction from Westover. A fundamentalist who subsequently made a career out of teaching at driving ranges, Westover has been Roxburgh's only tutor. Westover has been responsible for instructing many other fine players, including his own son, Keith, who won the Canadian Junior before turning pro. Jack Westover turned himself into an accomplished ambidextrous golfer, attaining a four handicap with left-handed clubs. In systematically shaping Roxburgh's game, Westover applied a composite of Sam Snead and Arnold Palmer techniques. Constant guides were Snead's hand position, eight-millimetre films and photograph sequences that Westover took of his prize pupil.

Hardly a day went by during his teens that Roxburgh didn't play at least one round or practise for a few hours. Westover designed self-stimulating contests for Roxburgh that kept him focused while practising. He also convinced the youngster to log his practice time and routine. Those logs remind Roxburgh that he devoted more hours to hitting balls than putting them.

"If there's such a thing as a natural swing, Doug had it," says Collett. "He developed a simple, basic swing which has never changed over the years. It wasn't manufactured; it was a natural action he's been able to repeat for all these years."

The bashful, free-swinging 15-year-old with the dark hair and spectacles remembers qualifying to play all medal rounds of his first two Amateurs and that John Russell, the smooth veteran who lived across the back lane from West 46th Avenue, won both.

Roxburgh wasn't remotely close as one of the eight qualifiers for championship match play in 1967. But he got to slog twice around Shaughnessy with Mike Zichy and Normie Reid under a relentless rain that final day of qualifying. Mike Reasor of Seattle was the medallist and Point Grey's classy John Russell—Roxburgh's neighbour—took the title over Bud Bird. On the way home from school or the course, Roxburgh would see his neighbour pitching shots to Montgomery Park off a cocoa mat on his front sidewalk. In 1968 he got to play all four rounds again. But he missed the top eight at Victoria Gorge Vale and watched Russell repeat over another inelegant opponent, a cigar-chomping former pro and greenskeeper named Art Donaldson. By 1969, eagerly practising for the coming season and his third BC Amateur, Roxburgh was a seasoned 17-year-old. He had already competed in two Canadian Junior championships and his first Canadian Amateur. And he had experienced stage fright. "I had the jitters playing in front of all those people for the first time," he recalls in reference to his Canadian Junior debut. At a tender 15, he lost in the national final to Jason Paukkunen, who later moved west from Ontario and became a successful driving range teaching pro. "After that I've never been really that nervous playing before crowds anywhere."

That period produced many players for a youngster to admire: Russell, Ticehurst, Johnston, Kidd and Vollmer. Roxburgh was in the audience whenever Leonard came down to hit balls, in awe of the venerable former Marine pro's rhythm and aura.

Roxburgh, quick to develop an acute comprehension of the swing, dwelled on basic mechanics and constantly experimented with technique. When Westover took a teaching position at the Grandview Driving Range, his protégé could often be found there. If a hitch crept into his swing, the analytical Westover was present to repair it. The perceptive youth recognized the importance of course management and he learned to apply himself accordingly. The trait has served him well over the years.

Roxburgh became such a methodical, pure ball-striker that he didn't need to rely on putting to score well. But titles aren't won without putting proficiency and Roxburgh was no exception. While not rated superb on greens, he was surely better than average. Roxburgh hasn't been confronted by as many par-saving putts inside the length of the flagstick as the next player. Stroking for so many birdies, it wasn't as essential for him to stalk putts.

In 1969 Harry White, the sleepy-eyed, angular Marine Driver, earned medal honours in the Amateur while munching on bananas and raisins for energy between shots at baked, breezy Richmond Country Club. Ron Fratkin, his nose sun-blistered, delighted the home members by finishing second among the eight qualifiers. The 17-year-old Roxburgh and another young clubmate, big easy-going Mike Buckley, tied for third at 293.

Doug Roxburgh wins the 1969 BC Amateur at 17, his first
of 13 spread over four decades. ARV OLSON COLLECTION

Roxburgh drew a character, Terry Wiens, in the opening quarter-final match. After pitching stiff to the first green, he was flabbergasted when Wiens conceded the hole without even attempting his third shot from the rough. He won 4 and 3 over the North Surrey high school basketball star who seemed completely satisfied after winning a bet that he could qualify. The next day Roxburgh faced White, who confessed he would never concede anyone a birdie, not even a tap-in. White forced extra holes by making four out of the sand at the par-five 18th, which Roxburgh three-putted. Roxburgh won at the second extra hole by tapping in a two-foot birdie putt. John Morgan, a 27-year-old engineer from Quilchena, virtually disappeared from the competitive scene after losing the final 4 and 3. Roxburgh was the tournament's youngest champion since Leonard's 1932 victory.

Roxburgh learned an unforgettable lesson the following year at Pitt Meadows. He progressed as medallist, shooting par 288, and drew the wily Ticehurst in the first round of match play.

I eagled the 10th to go four under par and four up in the match. Then I drove right up the middle of the 11th fairway and Bert hooked into the water. I figured I had him right where I wanted. He took a drop and got a half by matching my bogey. Then he won the next three holes and 16 when I missed a short putt. We went back to the first tee and he reached the green with his second shot and two-putted for a birdie to beat me.

When invited to address junior clinics, Roxburgh emphasizes the significance of maintaining composure, patience and determination. "I tell them to never give up, that strange things happen in golf, especially in match play." Roxburgh cites as examples two British Amateur matches that he won after it appeared he had been hopelessly beaten.

As family and business commitments took precedence over practice time, Roxburgh's deteriorating precision ball-striking intensified pressure on his putting stroke. His putter deprived him of his most glorious opportunity to capture the one local tournament he's never won, the BC Open. On his home turf in 1977, he seemed comfortably in control at 10 under par through 44 holes of the then 54-hole championship. He three-putted the 45th, then missed putts inside seven feet on four of the last seven greens and lost by a stroke to Dave Barr. Roxburgh had still led after hooking off the 17th tee. The ball struck the rear of spectator Ernie Drake, a member who a week later was still showing off the welt in the shower room. Roxburgh's self-inflicted bruise came on the green, where his five-footer for par refused to drop, before Barr managed to extract himself from two green-side bunkers, including the dreaded Big Bertha. The tournament was lost when Roxburgh bogeyed 18 by pushing his seven-iron pitch and then lipping out from about three feet. Uncharacteristically, Roxburgh vented his anger by ripping up his scorecard and heaving his golf bag into the locker room.

It was one of his biggest disappointments. He had expected to play well enough to win. He knew the course better than anyone else and he knew exactly how he was going to play it. "I've always prepared mentally for tournaments well in advance," he says. "I run through the type of required shots in my mind, how I want to approach each hole. Before I go to a tournament I like to have a definite plan in mind and I try to stick to it."

Roxburgh had known, sight unseen, how he was going to approach Winnipeg Niakwa for the 1974 Canadian Amateur. His greatest fan, his father, had played the course years before and habitually kept the scorecard. "From studying the yardages on that card, I knew exactly how I was going to play Niakwa. In my mind I was ready to play it before I got there. I didn't have to worry about how to play a totally strange course. I just knew I was going to have a good tournament." The result: his second national title in three years. His confidence was equally buoyant 14 years later when he headed to Kelowna in search of his fourth national championship, at Gallagher's Canyon Resort. With a game perfectly suited for his favourite course, he also practised overtime. "My local knowledge on that course was worth three, four shots and I knew it. I would have been terribly disappointed with anything less than a win."

Two days before the opening round, Roxburgh was in bed with severe stomach flu. Without a practice round, his struggling 72 opener was washed out when heavy rain prevented the late starters from even teeing off. The sun's appearance the next day rejuvenated him. He cruised around the pine-framed premises in 66 and never looked over his shoulder.

In August 1992 Roxburgh returned to Riverside in Saint John, New Brunswick, for a replay of the 1975 Canadian Amateur in which he finished second to clubmate Jim Nelford. He had never revisited the course and his duties as project manager of Fort Langley's new Belmont course didn't allow him time for proper preparation. Arriving on the eve of the event, Roxburgh relied on his recall and shot 68 for the first-round lead. His inactivity eventually caught up with him, though he still finished a respectable fifth.

Golf has taken Roxburgh throughout the world many times, to the Canadian Open five times and to the British Amateur twice. He has represented BC in every province except Newfoundland and Labrador. He has represented his country in four South American nations and in

New Zealand, Sweden, South Africa, France, Fiji and Portugal; in the fall of 1992 he made his seventh World Amateur Team appearance in his own playground.

He regrets not having competed more frequently in the US Amateur championships. He vividly remembers one of his two appearances, in 1976 at the Los Angeles Bel-Air Country Club course. "It was 7:15 in the morning and I was on the putting green getting ready for my third-round match. I guess I recognized the voice, but when I looked up I couldn't believe it was Mr. McLean who was greeting me."

Next to Mac Roxburgh, Doug's greatest visible supporter was the ubiquitous Alexander McLean, a neon-sign writer. A regular golfer at Fraserview, McLean rarely missed any of Roxburgh's local rounds for several years and was often accompanied by his wife and his son, Rob. He also scheduled holidays to California and Alberta around events in which Roxburgh was entered. Also known as Mac, he died in August 1992.

Roxburgh couldn't see McLean in the huge galleries at Glen Abbey in 1983. He had qualified for the Canadian Open as a result of winning his third National Amateur the previous summer. Roxburgh was the only amateur to make the 36-hole cut at Glen Abbey, acquitting himself well with rounds of 74, 73 and a pair of weekend 75s. He's proud of never having shot over 77 at the Canadian Open site. Professional golf never entered his mind, though. The simple pleasure he derives from playing the game would be lost for him on the hectic, high-pressure pro tour where many of his contemporaries have reaped small fortunes. "If I turned pro I think all of the fun would go out of golf." A confirmed homebody, he couldn't tolerate the steady diet of golf and travel. "My family gave me tremendous support. My parents, my brother and sister, and then Lorna, they've always been behind whatever I've decided to do. They never put any pressure on me to turn pro or go to school. It was always my decision."

Roxburgh accepted a partial golf scholarship to the University of Oregon where he majored in commerce. He enjoyed two years on the Eugene campus but took a year out after missing a month's classes while representing Canada in Argentina and Brazil. An ensuing trip took him to South Africa and he returned all golfed out. Roxburgh's father found

The 1979 Willingdon Cup team was Doug Roxburgh's 10th in 11 years and included (L to R) Steve Berry, Rick Gibson, Jim Bruce (alternate), Roxburgh and Kelly Murray. His last Cup team in 1991 was his 19th. BC GOLF HOUSE 007.121.009

him work at the BC Sugar Refinery and in the fall of 1973 he resumed studies for his bachelor of arts at Simon Fraser University in Burnaby. His commerce degree took him to Canadian Pacific Bulk Systems, where he became controller.

In the first round at Royal Troon in 1977, Scottish international Ian Carlslaw led four-up with five holes to play. Roxburgh won the last five, when Carlslaw bogeyed twice and Roxburgh birdied the last three. He reached the British semifinals in 1979 at Hillside after a gritty overtime win over England's David Whelan at the Southport course adjacent to Royal Birkdale. He was one down and playing the par-five 17th. With

Whelan five feet from a birdie, Roxburgh pitched strongly into thick, knee-high grass 60 feet from the hole. Upon finally finding the ball he turned to his caddy and shrugged, "I think I'll just pick it up."

"No, you won't. Play it," retorted his caddy and new bride. Roxburgh and the former Lorna McPherson, a fine junior golfer in her own right, were on their honeymoon. Roxburgh swung his wedge as hard as he could. Almost miraculously, the ball popped out and alit on the back apron. Still away, he audaciously holed the 20-foot downhiller for par. Utterly taken aback, the incredulous Englishman failed to convert his birdie putt. Roxburgh lost in the semifinal to Jay Sigel, who stopped fellow American Scott Hoch for the title.

A year after the Amateur format was switched to straight medal play Roxburgh embarrassed the 1972 field by playing brilliantly at Royal Colwood. His 279 total distanced Russell, in second place, by 11 strokes, a gap that still stands as the tournament's largest victory margin.

Incredibly, Roxburgh's highest finishes through 1992—save 1984 when he missed the cut—since the change from match to medal were 10th in 1971 and 8th in 1990. He has averaged 71.2 strokes per round while finishing among the top three in 18 of 22 years through 1992.

Roxburgh's closing 82 at Nanaimo in 1990 was his worst round in the event since he was 16. The 56 players who bucked the nor'wester that gusted to 40 kilometres an hour averaged 82 that day; winner Rob Anderson shot 73, Dan Douet had 74 and the next best was 77. Roxburgh's record in the Canadian Amateur has also been extraordinary. In 22 appearances at 24 Amateurs through 1992, he placed among the top five 12 times with an overall stroke average of 72.4 on many of the country's most challenging courses.

Of his 5 national and 13 provincial Amateur titles, Roxburgh rates his first and 10th BC championships and his last Canadian title as the most satisfying triumphs. "The first is always special and so was winning the Canadian Amateur in 1988 because Gallagher's a favourite." The next year at Castlegar and Birchbank, he was relieved to eclipse Combe's nine championships. Roxburgh repeated at the Castlegar and Birchbank courses in 1995 and the following year had his name engraved on the

Bostock Trophy for the last time, turning aside Kurt Cassidy by four strokes at Shaughnessy.

When he turned 60 on December 28, 2011, Doug Roxburgh retired after serving Golf Canada for 12 years as director of National High Performance Players. However, fly-fishing idyllic lakes where only the call of a loon or splash of a jumping trout interrupt the solitude will have to wait. The province's premier amateur for two and a half decades still has unfinished business to attend to, beginning with brushing up his neglected game. Five years late in getting started in senior golf, he plans to play provincially and nationally. He's anxious to try Pacific Northwest events and courses and is set to play the 2012 BC Senior Amateur at Nanaimo Golf Club. Roxburgh noted that his timing to play in the Senior was not perfect. "Yeah, over at Sandy Harper's backyard in Nanaimo," he told the *Vancouver Sun*'s Brad Ziemer with a laugh. "He's a senior for the first time at his own club. He's already licking his chops." Doug also plans to enter a minimum of five more BC Amateur championships, giving him an amazing run of 50 consecutive starts in the province's leading amateur event.

The trout will still be there when the time comes.

CHAPTER 13

BARR, ZOKOL, RUTLEDGE
AND THE NEW BREED

Over the past 35 years BC golf fans have grown used to
following a few of their home-grown pros on the PGA
tour and other professional circuits worldwide. Names like
Dave Barr and Dick Zokol stayed in the hunt for Sunday
glory through the 1980s before the name Weir began to
dominate. Slower off the mark but willing to play anywhere
was the youthful Jim Rutledge, possibly now, at 52, with
his best years still ahead of him on the Seniors Tour. And
then there is BC's "new breed." A band of merry young
men who are still in the minor leagues but showing much
potential on the Nationwide tour. Who will be the next
"real deal" and a BC superstar on the international stage?

DAVE BARR

What you have to understand about Dave Barr is that he considered the
golf course his office, the place where he made his living. Easily irritated
by his own mistakes or by nearby spectators jingling loose change in their
pockets, he rarely appeared to be enjoying himself. Even away from the
forbidding rough and the tormenting greens, away from the office, Barr
wore a stoic look and could be aloof on his best of days. Looks, of course,
are deceiving; his acquaintances know him as a pleasant, unpretentious,
caring individual. They'll tell you he's a friend you can count on, that he's
as loyal to Canadian golf as anyone in the country.

Like him or not, and at times he made it easy not to be a Barr fan, the big, surly-looking Kelowna golfer has achieved tremendous success with an unconventional swing and notorious personality. Until Mike Weir and Stephen Ames came along Barr had earned more prize money from golf than any other Canadian. Barr insisted that he played the game only for the money and not the prestige. He underlined that assertion in 1985 with his indifference over bogeying the final two holes to lose the US Open. He had led by two strokes with six holes to play. To win one of the majors is every pro golfer's dream, but Barr was never driven by the prospect of records, glory or a place in history. He was disappointed not so much with losing the US Open, but with failing to get the 10-year tour exemption that goes with a major victory. An unforgettable catastrophe to others was an experience Barr promptly dismissed. Conversely, he claims that the second-place tie inspired his best tour years in the late 1980s.

The second son of Allister and Christine Barr was born on March 1, 1952, and grew up in a modest house on Richter Street in downtown Kelowna. Dave's father was a mechanic at the General Motors dealership and his mother worked in a food-packing plant. Both parents encouraged their sons to play sports. Baseball and hockey were Dave's favourites; he was good enough to skate for Kelowna's junior team.

When their neighbours, the Newtons, moved to Glenmore Drive across from the Kelowna Golf and Country Club, 12-year-old Dave came to hunt balls with chums Arden and Alan Newton before caddying on weekends. Dave and his brother, Jim, the Newtons and Paul and Kirk Snook bicycled or walked to play the more accessible Mountain Shadow course, now Central Park. Dave was at a distinct disadvantage; he was natural southpaw and left-handed clubs were unavailable. That first summer, golfing until dark almost every night, he played crosshanded with clubs he and Jim borrowed from their father's aunt, Blanche Popham. When they joined Kelowna as juniors for fifteen dollars the following year, Jim got brand new clubs and Dave got to use Aunt Blanche's set. He deserted the cross-handed grip—after all, no one else did it that way—and used the clubs as if he were at bat.

"I always felt better gripping clubs with 10 fingers and it worked for me, so why change?" says Barr. "My baby finger never felt comfortable or natural on the overlap." In his third year, he was beating not only his five friends but all the local juniors. He was 15 and he had a three handicap.

Barr was a self-made golfer. Initially he took group lessons from Kelowna pro Dave Crane and putting instruction from Irv Taylor, another former country-club pro. Through experimenting, he quickly learned to allow for hooking the ball; his strong right-hand grip overpowered the left. Undismayed, he took the hook with him to college. Ted Gellert of Kelowna had gone to Oral Roberts University (ORU) in Tulsa, Oklahoma, on a baseball scholarship, switched to golf and got Barr enrolled there too. As a freshman he was second man on a team that included three other BC boys: Gary Scramstad of Kelowna, Rob Laing of Prince George and Dave Donaldson of Victoria.

No one at ORU tried to convince Barr to come to grips with his swing. In his sophomore year of 1971, he was more exasperated with three-putt greens than hooked shots. After Barr putted terribly in a casual game, teammate Gary Lee took the liberty of flinging Barr's bullseye putter into a lake. "Our coach, Myron Peace, gave me his putter—a McGregor blade—and I'm still using it," said Barr 20 years later. In 1972 he was second to Roxburgh in the Canadian Amateur and earned a trip to Argentina for the World Amateur team championships.

Competing against many outstanding college players who also graduated to the PGA Tour, the determined Barr tied for fifth behind winner Ben Crenshaw in the 1973 National Collegiate Athletic Association championship at Stillwater, Oklahoma, and won second all-American team honours and the Oklahoma State Amateur. The results encouraged Barr to try pro golf.

He was second-guessing himself after two Canadian Tour seasons during which he was financed by Kelowna supporters, assembled by his accountant brother, who called themselves Red Ink Inc. Barr plugged the flow of red ink in 1975 when he won his first prominent pro tournament, the BC Open, worth $4,000. But consistency, particularly with his putter, plagued his progress. That winter he put his clubs away and worked in the SunRype plant in Kelowna making orange and apple juice when he wasn't on the graveyard clean-up shift.

In 1976 Barr married schoolteacher LuAnn Busch of Kelowna, whom he had had a crush on since they were in elementary school, and his career went fast-forward. LuAnn brought home the room-and-board money while Dave continued to pursue a tour career. "She was the breadwinner, working the whole time I was struggling to make it as a golfer. LuAnn made ends meet; any prize money I collected was a bonus."

Blessed with a tolerant, supportive spouse, Barr went to the 1976 PGA Tour qualifying school out of curiosity. He didn't get beyond the first phase. But he was chosen to play on his first World Cup team and, after making more than expenses on a 1977 Arizona winter mini-tour, he basked in the sunshine of a tremendous season. He earned almost $19,000 while capturing the Quebec, Alberta, BC and Washington State Opens and chased George Knudson to the Canadian PGA title. His crowning achievement was qualifying for the PGA Tour. The top 25 players and ties made it; Barr's final-round 78 at Pinehurst tied him for 25th. Fighting his hook, temperament and a putting stroke that wouldn't behave, Barr barely retained his card and sanity in 1978. Fortunately he had another group of sponsors from Kelowna, Calgary and Vancouver.

If there's a turning point in his career, it would have to be when he reached the eighth extra hole at Oakwood Country Club at Coal Harbor, Illinois, in 1981. He endured a five-man playoff at the Quad Cities Open, a victory paved with a four-year tour exemption, then slumped badly the next year to $12,474, which without his exempt status would have relegated him to the Canadian Tour. But he progressed dramatically in 1984, jumping from 166th to 62nd on the money list. Barr approached 1985 optimistically, knowing he couldn't afford to falter with his exempt eligibility expiring. When June came, he was in top form for the US Open at the famed Oakland Hills course in suburban Detroit. Entering the final round he was perfectly placed behind a golfer whom he didn't know, Tze-Chung Chen of Taiwan, and Andy North, who counted the 1978 US Open title among only two wins in 12 tour years. On the Sunday morning Chen stood at 203, jump-started by a 65 that included the first double-eagle in Open history; North was 205 and Barr 208, on rounds of 70, 68 and 70. Chen opened the door for a horde of pursuers by double-chipping and inflicting a two-stroke penalty to take a quadruple-bogey eight at No. 5. From that moment on he was known as Two-Chip Chen.

Barr birdied the hole and in one fell swoop caught the immortalized Taiwanese. Tied with North at the 17th tee, Barr pondered his club selection and the stiff cross-wind. With 204 yards to the flag, he pulled out his three-iron and waited for the gallery around the nearby 16th green to settle after North had putted. "I was unlucky having the honour on that particular hole with the wind gusting," he recalls. "I would have taken a four-iron had I seen [playing partner Rick] Fehr's shot first." Barr pulled his tee-shot through the green, the ball settling in deep rough directly behind a huge hump in the green, 40 feet from the cup. A bump-and-run shot into the hump called for allowing a 20-foot break.

> There was no way I could get the blade on it cleanly for that type of shot . . . I had no choice but to play a flop-shot. I flopped it three feet short of perfect. The ball veered off the mound, away from the hole, and left me still about 40 feet away. I two-putted for bogey.

Barr figured that a birdie on the 450-yard final hole was almost impossible.

> I played it for a par and possible playoff. We were still into the wind and I tried to drive just left of the bunker on the right, 260 yards out. But the ball faded and missed carrying the sand by three feet. I gambled with a four-iron to clear the lip of the bunker. I just clipped it, taking everything off the shot, and came up 100 yards short of the green.

Barr's superb pitch stopped eight feet directly behind the hole, but he lipped out with the par putt that would have forced North into a playoff.

While lasting fame as US Open champion evaded him that afternoon, Barr went about his business as if it had been just another tournament and not a major setback. "That week was reassuring for me. It told me I could still be competitive in that company."

Beaten by Corey Pavin in a playoff at the 1986 Milwaukee Open, Barr blitzed the 1987 Atlanta Classic field with a personal best 23-under total for his second tour victory. The following year he lost a Hartford Open playoff to Mark Brooks and went to bed that Sunday night as the Canadian Open's clubhouse leader.

> I'd finished at 11 under when the weather turned ugly and things were finally postponed with several guys still on the course, including Ken Green at 12 under through 12. The conditions weren't much better when I woke up the next morning, but they got to finish up. Green played those last holes one under to win with 13 under.

In addition to Barr's two PGA tour wins, he finished second on four occasions and had 37 top-10 finishes. Barr remained a supporter of many Canadian events and eventually won 12 times on the Canadian tour between 1975 and 1988 when he won the TPC title. In 2003 he became the first Canadian to win a Champions Tour event when he won the Royal Caribbean Classic in Florida.

Through 2011, Barr had $2,404,793 in official PGA Tour money. Combined with his winnings elsewhere in the world, including the Canadian Tour and special events, he's collected about $4 million since turning pro in 1974. He won $300,000 in the early days of the Canadian Skins game and has represented his country in 11 World Cup competitions.

Barr teamed with Ontario-based Jerry Anderson in 1983 to finish second at the World Cup and won individual honours. Two years later, playing at La Quinta in California, the result was even more fulfilling when he teamed with buddy Dan Halldorson of Manitoba to become the last Canadian tandem to win the World Cup.

Dave Barr, seen here during a practice round at the 2005 Canadian Open, played at Shaughnessy in Vancouver, was inducted into the Canadian Golf Hall of Fame in 2000 and last won the Canadian PGA Seniors Championship in 2007.
GOLF CANADA ARCHIVES 34001

In an arena of fashionable purists, Barr deliberately forged an unorthodox, but remarkably efficient style that television commentator Peter Allis once described as "a caddy swing." Barr's disposition has always overshadowed any critique of the quick, wristy swing he quietly perfected over the years. "When you think about it," the late Shaughnessy pro Jack McLaughlin said after Barr's Atlanta victory, "it's really amazing what Dave has done with a swing most people thought couldn't stand up under that kind of pressure. He's been great for Canadian golf." During his playing career there were many who would not concur with McLaughlin's assessment. But those who have been intimidated and appalled by Barr's scowling, pouting and bellyaching were not familiar with the man away from his office. He was incapable of performing at ease in an intense atmosphere that commanded his full concentration; he even appeared uncomfortable in the relaxed romp of the televised Skins games. He never pretended to be a showman and never hesitated to bare his volatile emotions or to speak his mind.

Beneath the surface, Barr's devotion to his family and loyalty to the game and his country is beyond reproach. Time permitting from his hectic tour schedule, Barr readily supported junior golf and various charities without fanfare. He also had a strong allegiance to the Canadian Tour, never forgetting the value of his four-year apprenticeship. Nagging back problems and erratic putting eventually took their toll on him, limiting his time on the fairways. The upside was that the spinal discomfort led to more time at home in Richmond with LuAnn and their children, Brent and Teryn, who came along in 1980 and 1982. LuAnn Barr has always said that her husband has never brought his frustrations home with him and in 1986 she characterized him as "nicer than the guy I married."

Dave Barr now lives in the Okanagan and in 2007 proved that he can still compete when he won the Canadian PGA Seniors Championship. By then he had been a member of the Canadian Golf Hall of Fame for seven years and of the BC Golf Hall of Fame since he was first eligible in 2003.

DICK ZOKOL

This story comes covered with dust, from Dick Zokol's modest early years. The year, 1971 or 1972, isn't pertinent. The scene at Marine Drive's practice area: an impressionable teenager of 14 or 15, watching from a distance, mesmerized by the familiar figure rifling balls like Robbie Robot.

Even then Zokol's mien, the intensity in his dark eyes, suggested a special latency bursting to get out. Joe and Elsie Zokol's unruly youngest of four children was a feisty striker who could run all day on the soccer pitch and an all-star Little League pitcher with a wicked fastball. Golf and discipline didn't come to him quite as easily.

He was born in 1958 in Kitimat, where his father had gone to practise dentistry directly out of school in Portland. Joe Zokol, who had caddied at Langara in the 1930s when he wasn't driving a taxi, took up golf at Kitimat's Thornhill course and joined Marine Drive upon returning to

Vancouver. The Zokols resided on a street above the flatlands course, an easy hike for Dick. He caddied regularly for Poldi Bentley but travelled with a bad crowd and Dr. Joe discovered he had a 13-year-old on marijuana. "I laid down the law right then; I grounded him for the whole summer, the only place he could go was the golf course."

When he wasn't caddying, cleaning clubs in the back shop or working as a bus boy in the dining room, Dick Zokol was playing—and paying attention to the players in his midst. The single-minded youngster knew from watching Doug Roxburgh practise that he faced a mountain of work if he hoped to be one of the club's better players.

Zokol and his best pals, Russ Jordan, Peter Radiuk and Chris Rivers, would stay through dusk, hitting the precious balls jammed in their shag-bags. "We'd pretend we were Roxburgh, trying to imitate his swing," recalls Zokol, who never did capture the club championship. "We couldn't believe how he routinely landed all those two-iron shots so close together. We were in awe. We'd never use range balls either. We got good practice balls, just like Roxburgh, and we treasured them as if they were gold. They made you concentrate on every shot; you didn't want to spray them in fear of losing any."

In his desperation to beat Jordan, Kelly Murray and other older juniors, Zokol unwittingly drove himself to elevate his standards. It was a constant motivational factor which has taken his career well beyond anyone's expectations.

> Learning the game in that intensely competitive environment was so stimulating. Watching Roxburgh, trying to emulate him, probably was the biggest impact on my game. Everyone admired Doug for his ethics and behaviour. There was total affinity to him as a pure ball-striker. I wanted so badly to be a part of the fraternity of good players at Marine. I realized I'd have to work hard to belong. I was proud of the club's tradition. I wanted my name with all those others on that plaque of champions in the clubhouse.

Zokol had chosen to be a golfer. Scheduled to pitch for the Kerrisdale All-Stars, he told the startled coach he couldn't play because he had to caddy for Marine assistant pro Westover in the Sun Match Play Open. Except for soccer at Magee, he had stopped playing all other sports by the time he was 15.

Westover gave him formative lessons and he later had instruction from Marine pro Alvie Thompson. He got a strong sniff of success in the 1976 BC Junior by tying Jim Rutledge for second place, a stroke behind winner Joe Limoli of the host VGC. During his last year in high school, Zokol decided he wanted to follow Marine member Jim Nelford to Brigham Young University in Utah. He brazenly wrote to BYU coach Karl Tucker about possible enrolment with a golf grant but, with no record to speak of, he wasn't given any consideration. More determined than ever, the slightly built 17-year-old captured the 1977 City Amateur title at Seymour that June and followed by beating Roxburgh, Steve Berry, everybody again, in the Greenacres Amateur. He went to Kamloops for the BC Amateur, brimming with confidence.

Zokol was paired in the first two rounds with Nelford, the Canadian Amateur champion the previous two summers. He led going into the fourth round, but inexperience cost him a late double-bogey as he finished behind winner Roxburgh and veteran Garnett Lineker, the local reinstated amateur who had once worked in Marine's pro shop.

Nelford saw enough potential and competitive fire in Zokol to recommend him to Tucker. The day after returning from Kamloops, Zokol asked to borrow his father's car and drove 24 hours to Provo. After hitting shots on a campus field for Tucker, he carded 69 in a trial round. Zokol was assigned to room in a dormitory with a freshman whom he'd never heard of. Unknown to Zokol, Bobby Clampett was the most heavily recruited golfer in America. "It bugged me that Clampett was so much better than I was, which I guess Coach Tucker was counting on when he roomed us together. It made me all the more determined to improve and make the team."

After his first semester Zokol received a partial scholarship. He was aghast when he saw his swing for the first time on videotape at BYU. "I thought I had a pretty good swing, but I was totally shocked at how bad it was." But the resolute BYU walk-on adapted quickly and developed well enough to earn the team captaincy in his senior year. With other future tour pros Keith Clearwater and Rick Fehr as his 1981 teammates, Zokol led BYU to its first and only NCAA championship. Later that summer, Zokol achieved major success on his own by winning the Canadian Amateur on the first hole of a sudden-death playoff against Blaine McAllister, yet another future tour pro, at Calgary Golf and Country Club.

In the fall Zokol went to the PGA Tour qualifying school and came home from Florida with his diploma. His passing grade, like Barr's, was a tie for the last available spot. Q-School is without doubt golf's most dreaded, torturous test of nerves and the sometimes skittish Zokol put himself through the agonizing grind of it five times in his first 11 years as a touring pro.

Zokol frequently refers to himself as a "slow learner, someone who takes longer than most people to adapt and develop." He didn't win a noteworthy tournament until he was almost 18, didn't hit the college jackpot until he was a senior and made the Canadian championship his final amateur start. And it took him more than a decade to win on tour. Comparatively few tour winners are under 30. The experience of first contending is virtually essential, and so is winning secondary competitions. Zokol won the 1982 BC Open with an exquisite closing 64 at Point Grey and two years later he won the Utah Open. As a rookie he shared the lead at the Greater Milwaukee Open with four holes to play and before 1992 he counted several top-10 finishes, including seconds in Chatanooga and Hawaii.

Zokol attracted considerable attention at Milwaukee in 1993. It was where he was first noticed wearing a Walkman headset between shots to soothe his turbulent emotions. He tuned in to FM music and news, and tuned out negative thoughts and distractions. It was where he became Disco Dick. He led after each of the first three rounds by shooting 65, 69 and 70. On Sunday he encountered some static and finished fifth after 75.

A 22-year-old Dick Zokol raises the Earl Grey Cup at Calgary Golf and Country Club as the new 1981 Canadian Amateur champion. GOLF CANADA ARCHIVES 26743

Two summers later, the headset discarded, Zokol met the most significant man, in his opinion, to step into his career. Dr. Richard Lonetto, a University of Guelph psychology professor, convinced Zokol that he needed to control his anxiety levels to play better golf. Zokol's unique pre-shot routine, a deep-breathing bio-rhythm procedure, was designed to govern his heart rate. In addressing each shot, he lifted the club shoulder-high, pointing it to the sky while taking a deep breath and deliberately exhaling. Before going into his backswing, he took his right hand off the club and extended his arm from his side. The exercise reduced his heart rate for a calming effect during address and maximized it at impact.

His 1992 earnings surpassed $300,000, buoyed by victories at Hattiesburg, Mississippi, and the city in which he was christened Disco Dick. The Greater Milwaukee Open triumph opened all sorts of doors to Zokol, including a two-year exemption and 1993 starts in the Masters, Tournament of Champions, World Series and PGA. Dick had 20 top-10 finishes during his 20-year PGA career, played in more than 400 events and last won in 2001 at the Canadian PGA, a Nationwide Tour event.

Dick met his wife, Joan Kindrachuk, in Edmonton. She worked in the office of Zokol's agent, Mike Barnett of CorpSport International, whose prize client was Wayne Gretzky. Zokol, a devoted family man, travelled almost half of his tour schedule with Joan and three children in tow. Their twins, Conor and Garrett, were born in 1987, and Hayley came along in 1990. Shepherding three little ones made Dick stand out on tour, Sony Walkman or not. "Some of the guys look at me like I'm crazy or something, on tour with three young kids," recalled Zokol. "But I wouldn't have it any other way. We're a family. Joan and I want to be together with the kids as much as possible. Joan's a marvel at organizing our trips. Things, as you can appreciate, don't always go that smoothly, like when we're delayed in airports with cranky kids and the formula's packed in a suitcase."

An enterprising realist, Zokol turned his interests to the business side of golf and has undertaken a series of entrepreneurial projects over the past 15 years. He always recognized that security for a tour golfer was minimal. He knew that the golf earnings would decline and when they did he would leave the tour. "I don't want to sacrifice my family life to pay the bills," he said 20 years ago. "There are so many players in their 40s out there who have to play, and have trouble making cuts. It's an awful lifestyle and they've got nothing else to fall back on. That won't be Dick Zokol. I want to have a choice."

A few months before he had his big win in Milwaukee in 1993 Zokol had listened to a passionate Ben Crenshaw describe a new golf course that he had designed in Nebraska. It started him thinking. Fifteen years later, closing in on 50 with injuries having long ago convinced him to move on from competitive golf, the Canadian reflected on his conversation with Gentle Ben. "I knew right then that I wanted to build my own course," he told *BC Business* reporter Robert Thompson.

In the summer of 2008 Dick Zokol was on the brink of opening Sagebrush Golf & Sporting Club, a unique facility in the Nicola Valley on rolling lands that were once part of the legendary Quilchena Ranch. The concept stood out from all others and relied on him finding 40 well-heeled sporting enthusiasts who would pay $200,000 for an exclusive membership and then round up a foursome that would kick in $27,500 per year to keep the place well maintained. Even those numbers didn't add up to a profitable venture, so a real estate element was added that would see 37 exclusive building sites spread over about 50 hectares of land.

Zokol found four key investors to fund the entire project and got the first holes open for play in late summer 2008. The course officially opened in 2009 and was named best new Canadian course by both *Golf Digest* and *SCOREGolf* magazines. One of two Mongolian-style yurts acted as the clubhouse and a second, set beside an idyllic trout lake between the 12th and 13th holes near the highest point on the course, was called the Hideout. Golfers were encouraged to settle in for a while, try a little fly-fishing and close out their round with a day of good memories.

Unfortunately the construction delays meant it opened into a very competitive market amid a downturn in the economy. Over the next few years Alberta oil money started to look south to the shattered US sunbelt market where deals on golf real estate were everywhere. Zokol's field of dreams was becoming a quagmire of nightmares.

Early in 2012 Zokol announced that he was leaving Sagebrush amid plans to recapitalize and rethink the business model. In a statement to the Canadian Press he noted, "Needless to say, it has been a very tumultuous time in golf, we all know that." He made it clear that he did not agree with the direction in which the four original investors wanted to go.

Dick Zokol is nothing if not resilient and the life-long overachiever took little time to bounce back onto the golf scene. Within weeks of leaving the Nicola Valley he resurfaced a short distance east in the Okanagan. At the beginning of March 2012 Dick Zokol was introduced as the new executive director of golf development at Predator Ridge. It could be a perfect fit. Zokol is a thoughtful man who persevered as a self-described "consummate PGA Tour journeyman." He has a lot to offer and he knows golf is a very mental game. "There's a zillion people that can teach the golf swing," he told Vernon reporter Kevin Mitchell after the Predator Ridge announcement. "The mental side of the game, to me, is where there is a big void. Literally how you prepare to think and manage, and there is a lot of opportunity there, and it's a direction that I take very seriously."

It sounds like the man has a book to write.

JIM RUTLEDGE

If Dick Zokol knew that you were supposed to give up the tour at some point he never communicated that message to Jim Rutledge. Golfing globetrotter Jim Rutledge has spent a career parachuting to tours throughout the world. Now into his closing competitive years, the laid-back veteran pro from Victoria has touched down feet-first on the game's cushiest garden spot, the exclusive Champions Tour. This is the 50-and-over closed shop that Lee Trevino once described as "the place you get a licence to steal."

The itinerant Rutledge has probably logged more miles than any other golfer on the planet, save Gary Player. You don't ask Rutledge which countries he's visited over the years. You ask him where he's never been. "That's easy," says Rutledge, managing a smile. "Iceland and Alaska. Actually, I've never played in South Africa or South America either."

If there's a tour Rutledge hasn't played, he couldn't find it: the European Tour, Asian Tour, the Nationwide, Canadian, PGA, Australian and several mini-tours in the southern US, and after turning 50 in August 2009 he became eligible for the Champions Tour.

Rutledge has never charted his travels; the only statistics he tracks are tour performances such as driving distance, greens-hit and putting. They're the stats that matter. After turning pro in 1978 he spent much of the next two decades playing golf in Asia during the winter and in Canada in the summer months. "I have no idea how many miles I've travelled to play golf," he shrugs. "Plenty, especially in Asia. I've been using air miles for my fares for quite a while. I've accumulated more than enough for us [family] to travel quite a lot."

Rutledge's schedule kept him in North America exclusively through 2010 and 2011 as he stubbornly earned a living playing 30 events on the Champions Tour. Fighting tough odds to get into that many fields, he achieved this rare success as a *conditional* player, a secondary tour status whereby he drew into Monday qualifiers at individual Champions tournaments. Only through scoring consistently well in the Monday qualifiers or by earning a top-10 finish in the prior event would he join the more established all-exempt players in the lucrative tournament field.

Once he committed to this uphill battle, in any given year Rutledge would become totally exempt for the following season either by gaining an outright victory or by placing among the leading 30 money winners at season's end. The trick has been getting into as many tournaments as possible because only gaining entry into about 60 percent of tournaments makes it very tough to make the top 30 among the world's best senior players at year-end.

As a conditional player in 2010, his "rookie" senior year, Rutledge made the most of 14 starts. He had one sponsor's exemption and had to Monday-qualify 13 times. This is easier said than done, as there are usually 30 to 40 players fighting for only four Monday qualifying spots. Still, he managed to wring $290,000 out of prize pots, making him 54th on tour. Well short of avoiding another qualifying grind, but encouraging. With $39,000 from three Canadian starts and $10,000 for winning the Canadian PGA Seniors he collected almost $340,000 for the year.

In 2011 the gains were marginal but a few of his statistics were phenomenal. He finished 51st on the money list while playing in 16 events with earnings of just under $298,000. But despite grinding it out the hard way to face the likes of Fred Couples, Tom Lehman and Tom Watson, Rutledge was right there in the top five in driving distance and number two in overall driving behind only tour money champion Tom Lehman. Even more impressively, Rutledge led the entire tour in his average final round with an average Sunday score at 69.0. That resulted in him leading another category know as Final Round Performance where he improved his position in the field 93.75 percent of the time, more than 10 points higher than any other player.

Rutledge's road to the Champions Tour has been unique. Wandering golf's tours for more than 32 years, the modest Canadian vagabond has nine victories stamped on his lengthy résumé, including six on the Canadian Tour, three of which were the BC Open (1979, 1981, 1989). He's been surviving quite nicely, thank you. With an even temperament and graceful form, he is an extremely well-rounded competitor. His rhythmic swing—long, languid and upright—mirrors the form of Tom Weiskopf, a tour standout when Rutledge was learning to play at Victoria's Cedar Hill.

Rutledge has fared well financially most years while teeing it up on several tours. After many seasons in Asia and Australia, between 1988 and 1992 he was a member of the European Tour. He qualified for the 1990 Open and made the cut, eventually finishing T-57. He won his first and only Asian title in 1995. Played at the historic Delhi Golf Club, the prestigious Indian Open was the oldest annual international professional sporting event in that country.

At age 41 in 2000, Rutledge concentrated on the Nationwide and Canadian tours. The schedule reduced his long-distance trips as his son, Ryan, was starting middle school. Previously Ryan had accompanied his caddy-mother, Jill, to foreign events for weeks at a time. Then, in 2001, both Jill and her father, Tom Smith, were diagnosed with cancer. Smith passed away in 2003 but Jill overcame breast cancer following surgery, radiation and chemotherapy. This traumatic experience changed Rutledge's approach to life and the game. Jill, a former top athlete who caddied for her husband at different times in his career, has continued to inspire him with her tenacity and courage.

After 2006 Rutledge refocused on the Nationwide Tour, the primary breeding ground for the PGA Tour. Here the top-25 money winners in any given year earn full playing privileges on the primary circuit for the following year. At long last he found himself playing with the big boys in 2007. At time of writing he remains the second-oldest pro to earn the right to a rookie season on the PGA tour.

As the Nationwide's 14th place finisher with $258,000 in 25 starts, he finished well clear of the 25th player's $193,000. The Victorian's year included a rare victory—the New Zealand PGA championship, where he lived up to his title of Mr. Sunday by closing with a 64. He had won the Sunday moniker for consistently posting low final rounds when out of contention and that reputation has carried on to the Seniors tour.

The PGA Tour's bright lights apparently left Rutledge dazzled. "I guess I must have tightened up without realizing it," he says, trying to explain his disappointing season playing courses he had previously seen only on television. Needing almost $775,000 to place among the top 125 and retain his card, Rutledge collected a paltry $62,000. He made just five cuts in 23 starts. "You might say it left me in shock. I've always been a streak putter, but only average," he admits. "You have to be better than average on the greens. Average putters linger in the middle of the pack. Good putters are among the leading players."

Rutledge emphasizes that counting one less putt per round amounts to four less per tournament, a huge difference over the course of a season.

> I putted okay last year but my game was a little rusty at times. I missed about three weeks with a sore bum shoulder . . . that affected my play. But most Champions courses are friendlier than those on the PGA Tour. They're a little shorter, which gives longer hitters an edge on the par-five holes, and the greens aren't quite as firm and fast.

Fellow Nationwide tourist and Rutledge-booster Ted Purdy remains confounded by his friend's failure to win frequently. When Rutledge first started to appear at Champion tour events, Purdy commented, "People are going to be blown away by how good this guy plays."

As this book goes to press Jim Rutledge is playing a full 2012 schedule on the Champions tour. Unlike his previous two attempts, in November 2011, during the tour qualifying tournament, Jim shot a superb 62 in the second round of the tournament and finished tied for second to assure himself full playing privileges in 2012.

It is fair to say that life this year for Jim and Jill Rutledge is finally so much simpler, so uncomplicated. The Victoria pro golfer is guaranteed that he can tee up in all of 30 events. Monday qualifying, sponsor exemptions and weekly uncertainty are no longer part of the game. Finally, he has full exempt status.

THE EARLY ACE MAKERS

According to a study commissioned by *Golf Digest* in 2000, the odds of making a hole-in-one are 3,000 to 1 for a tour pro, 5,000 to 1 for a low-handicapper and 12,000 to 1 for an average player. The longer the hole, the longer the odds.

Alex "Sandy" Duthie, the much-loved professional at Jericho for 32 years, is best remembered as one of the first, if not the first, to score holes-in-one on successive holes. And he brazenly predicted that he was going to make the second one. Duthie's remarkable double aces were accomplished several months after the official opening in June 1911 of the first nine holes at Vancouver Golf Club.

Duthie, a mason from Monifieth, Scotland, who started at Jericho in 1909, made his aces at the existing original third hole of 135 yards and the uphill fourth, then 160 yards to a green situated at the crest of the present fairway. After accepting handshakes from playing companions Harry Taylor and Jimmy Yellowlees for acing the third hole, Duthie teed his ball on a tuft of sand, steadied himself and casually pronounced in an undertone, "Here goes anithin. Watch it!"

They were two of 14 career aces for the man who, at age 23, had left for greener fairways in 1902 after a runner-up finish to Dave Robertson in Carnoustie's Caledonia Kettle Club championship. Duthie later assisted in the design and construction of the VGC's outgoing nine, Jericho's second nine in 1923 and courses in Vernon, Penticton and Kelowna.

Only one other instance of two holes-in-one during the same round in BC was recorded. That was on March 6, 1927, at Langara. Koryo Tanaka, a Vancouver garage operator who regularly played the public course, holed a mashie shot at the 115-yard fifth and made a second by rolling in his tee-shot with a wooden club at the 210-yard 16th. Max Banbury of West Vancouver was one of those who had made successive holes-in-one, at Woodstock, Ontario, in 1952 during a Canadian Legion tournament. Banbury, ironically, once caddied regularly for Duthie.

Unofficially, Mike Turyk of Victoria Golf Club must reign as BC's king of aces. He had 30 holes-in-one over 31 years, 12 of them at the Oak Bay links. "I don't hit the ball far but I hit it fairly straight," said Turyk, whose handicap has been as low as 12. "I guess I'm kinda lucky, too." One of Turyk's aces came at Oak Bay's old feared seventh, where the wind dictated whether a full drive or mid-iron was required. The ocean gobbles up hooked tee-shots to No. 7, since altered to a four-par. It still has a diabolically designed but delightfully challenging green that tilts toward the beach.

One day Turyk, Mr. Lucky, snap-hooked a drive destined for the briny. The ball bounced off a beached log, plopped up to the green and rolled into the cup! Seven behind in the ace race, Dr. George Bigelow claimed—and who was going to dispute Buck-Buck Bigelow's claims?— he saw every one of his 23 holes-in-one. "They've all been good ones, no flukes," the former Saskatchewan Open and Amateur champion said adamantly. "There aren't many 18-hole courses with six par-three holes. I've done them all in one shot. According to *Golf Digest* magazine, I've been only the second person to ace six holes on one course."

Of the thousands of holes-in-one recorded in a century of golf in this province there are untold numbers of phantom aces. The shots that never actually happened were claimed at holes with greens that weren't visible from the tees—for example, the old 14th at Marine Drive and the 8th at Shaughnessy Heights.

At Marine, balls struck reasonably close at the uphill 14th would be surreptitiously kicked into the cup by pranksters while the unsuspecting golfers made their way to the green. The youngsters hid from view in trees and, stifling their giggles, delighted in watching the golfers' reactions when they discovered the ball in the hole. There was material motive for similar dastardly deeds at Shaughnessy. Caddies sent to the green to chart blind tee-shots occasionally pulled the caper to increase their chances of a gratuity from a happy hole-in-one shooter.

Not one, not two, but three Albert Selinas have aced the 15th at Royal Colwood. Alberta Selinas III, at 19 years old, started the run on November 7, 1978. His father, Dr. Albert Selinas, 51, matched his son's feat on August 18, 1982. Then Albert "Pop" Selinas, 74, followed his son and grandson into the hole with one stroke on November 4, 1985.

The most unusual shot that didn't count as a hole-in-one was a believe-it-or-not par at Marine Drive's fourth by Jack St. Mars. St. Mars shanked his tee-shot at the 142-yard hole flanked on the right by the north arm of the Fraser River. The ball landed directly in a passing barge heaped with sawdust under tow. Hitting three off the tee, St. Mars proceeded to fly his next shot directly into the cup. He had scored a par-three without a ball having touched the ground!

Former Langara and Richmond pro Ben Colk said he had "over 20" holes-in-one, including five in one year. Many of Colk's aces were scored at Hastings Park, an abbreviated nine-holer that counted four par-threes and two reachable par-fours while he was assistant pro at the course. "Most of the aces weren't on holes I would have liked to have made them on," confessed Colk, who dropped his fifth dodo of 1935 on December 29, which was believed at the time to be a record for most aces in a year.

Marine's members have a slight advantage over players at other clubs. It has five par-three holes on which Ernie D'Amico has bagged 15 of his 17 aces. "You don't make holes-in-one, they just happen," shrugged the long-time Marine Driver who played to a handicap of two to six for 30 years. "The more you play increases your chances and I've played a lot in my day." D'Amico's last ace happened on February 5, 1990, and it was special. It was the 700th at Marine since the club had started tracking them in 1954. He made his first ace at Langara in 1949.

Hole-in-one insurance at Marine evaporated frequently, and the year's aces began to be celebrated en masse with a gala season-ending dinner. "Rather than everyone drinking what was left in the hole-in-one kitty, we decided to do something different," said member Ken McKenzie, originator with Bob Sampson of the special dinner and its only chairman. "The dinner has become a tradition at Marine. Next to myself and Ernie D'Amico, I'd say the man who attended more of the dinners than anyone else was Al McLellan, the promotions director at the *Sun* who used to help us with it."

Personally I witnessed three holes-in-one in 35 years of covering golf for the *Vancouver Sun*. The most memorable was the irrepressible Johnny Johnston's four-wood at Marine's difficult sixth hole during his semifinal victory over clubmate Bob Kidd in the 1959 Canadian Amateur.

Sheila Bentley's hole-in-one at Seymour's second, now the fifth, came during the women's championships, and I was playing in Marty Zlotnik's group when he holed a wedge to Beach Grove's old sixth during the Fraser Valley Open pro-amateur. With luck and talent ebbing like my hairline, I have yet to witness one of my own tee-shots finding the hole.

A.J. Finch, the club captain, proved in 1925 to fellow Penticton members that his first ace at the 130-yard third was no fluke. He holed out at the same hole a few days after celebrating the first. The honour of the first hole-in-one at Cowichan's regular course belonged to J.G. Somerville, a former member of the Duncan course. While on vacation from Nanaimo, he dropped an iron shot into the cup at the 158-yard third hole in the company of Dr. Kerr. According to the *Victoria Daily Colonist*, Oak Bay pro Bill Moffat made only the course's second hole-in-one at 14th in April 1914. "Only once has this feat been accomplished. Mr. Challoner, a member, having holed out in one some seasons ago," reported the newspaper.

GREAT PLAYERS ALONG THE WAY

Amateur golf success does not necessarily lead to fame and wealth as a professional. Some players, like James Lepp, simply opted out. Others, like Brent Franklin and Jim Nelford, suffered serious injury away from the course. Fine players like Rick Gibson ended up on foreign soil for most of their career. The largest group would be those who lived their dream trying to scratch out a living on the satellite tours before settling into a more stable life as a club pro or general manager, or working with a club manufacturer.

Years from now, when they look back at BC golf in the first decade of the new millennium, those who knew him will no doubt say there was only one James Lepp. As the poster boy for BC golf's new generation of outstanding prospects, in 2005 James Lepp would do things on a golf course that no other Canadian has ever matched. By the end of his US college career he had established glittering credentials and broad predictions for the professional career that lay ahead. Lepp's success soon filled the dreams of younger contemporaries such as Nick Taylor, Eugene Wong, Adam Svensson, Adam Hadwin and many others. While Lepp could have been the leader of this "new breed" he had other plans.

After earlier winning two Canadian Junior crowns, Lepp won his fourth consecutive BC Amateur championship in 2005, touring a tough Gorge Vale course in Victoria at 13 under par, four strokes clear of his closest competitor and only one of four to break par that week. The streak even surpassed the best of legendary Doug Roxburgh who had 13 provincial victories over his career.

That year Lepp also became the only Canadian and the first Washington Husky golfer to ever win the coveted Individual NCAA championship. He topped off the fabulous year by being the US Amateur medallist, and was named the Pacific Northwest Golf Association's male golfer of the year. In the next two seasons he added several Amateur titles and two Canadian Tour events, the first before turning pro. Then swish, to the surprise of absolutely no one who knows him well, the sensation and long-time pride of Abbotsford's Ledgeview course stepped away from a pro career in his very own customized new golf shoes.

Lepp, then 26, scrapped, temporarily at least, potential tour riches and endorsements—and became a shoemaker! Rather than competing with the likes of new, young pros such as Rick Fowler, Luke Donald, Jonathon Vegas and Rory McIroy, Lepp put his heart and soul into becoming an entrepreneur. As founder, CEO, marketer and warehouseman of Kikkor Shoes, he's now challenging the giants of the golf footwear industry, Foot-Joy, Nike and Etonic.

He's created fresh footprints. With a couple of business partners, the unpredictable Lepp closeted his golf clubs and was soon off and running, developing an innovative brand of shoe. In a video promo, he's the boss in blue jeans and backwards golf cap chipping balls into shoes off the cement floor of his warehouse—just keeping in practice. Influenced by the culture of skateboarders and snowboarders, he designed a distinctively bold, colourful shoe that's advertised as comfortably different. His shoes are described as a unique alternative to traditional golf footwear. Golf, says Lepp, needs to be cool again. It's supposed to be fun, isn't it?

While at Washington, Lepp majored in business with a focus on entrepreneurship, so he was always thinking of new business ideas. He is a man who has always walked to his own drummer. He says and does things on a whim and apparently no one ever tinkered with his golf swing; if they did, he wasn't paying attention.

Lepp might be missing a most effective pitch as an enterprising salesman by not establishing himself as a PGA Tour leaderboard regular while sporting and endorsing his own product. He realizes success as a tour-familiar player would help sell himself, and his shoes. But he does things his way. On the market since 2010, his shoes aren't sitting in unopened crates in the warehouse. Sales, he reports, are "pretty fair so far." He said he's played only a half dozen rounds since getting into new shoes. "I started playing left-handed a little bit, and it reminded me how golf used to be—new, fun, enjoyable," he told *Vancouver Sun* golf writer Brad Ziemer. "I've only played four rounds lefty, and I'm already down to a 3.5 index. At that rate I might be on the PGA Tour by the end of next year!"

Apparently fully content with his unpredictability Lepp adds, "My right-handed scores were 77-78, and my left-handed rounds were 86-75-73. Golf is confusing. I'm confusing."

Brent Franklin dominated amateur golf in Canada from 1983 to 1987, winning two junior national titles followed by three men's titles before turning pro and spending much of his career playing in Asia. GOLF CANADA ARCHIVES 26743

Don't misunderstand Brent Franklin, please. He wasn't snubbing golf by refusing to attend the Canadian Sports Hall of Fame banquet in 2010 to be recognized for his achievements. In fact, given his current frame of mind he likely won't be present at the Golf Hall of Fame of BC for induction in 2015 either!

The former whiz kid of Canadian golf has nothing against Hall of Fame awards. He just disagrees with all the pomp, expense and ceremony of the selection process. Franklin said he would have attended a casual function in 2010, but not an expensive evening with pricey tickets and all. "That's not my style."

Franklin came to Vancouver with his family from Barrie, Ontario, as a teenager and became a member of Shaughnessy with his father. He was taught golf by the late Jack McLaughlin and quickly made a statement about his game in 1981 when he won the Vancouver City Match Play Championship as a 15-year-old amateur, which would make him the youngest champion ever in that event. Two years later he started his "championship tear" by winning both the Canadian and BC Junior titles in 1983 and 1984. He then followed by capturing the Canadian Amateur three straight years in 1985–1987. During the same span he made All-America teams all three years while attending Brigham Young University on a golf scholarship. He was a member of the Canadian team that won the 1986 Eisenhower Trophy at the World Amateur Team Championship, played in Caracas, Venezuela. When Franklin turned pro in 1988 he won the Canadian PGA crown in his first season and won Rookie of the Year on the Canadian Tour. He seemed destined for stardom on the PGA circuit.

However, Franklin opted to play the Japanese golf tour in 1989; he played 112 events over seven years. He lost once in a playoff and had three other runner-up finishes but never won. He had plans to play the PGA in 1996 but never made it as he was seriously injured after being hit cycling in Japan. He recovered but never fully regained his form during a return stint on the Canadian tour.

His ignoring the hall-of-fame honour didn't sit well with some people but no slight was intended. "It [the championship run] means everything to me, don't misunderstand," he told Barry Sharpe of *BC Golf News*. "But I've had my day . . . now I'd just like to fade into the background. They could send the plaque to me." He doesn't want people to think he's ungrateful about being selected for the Canadian award, but "I haven't played in a tournament for 15 years. That's in the past."

Franklin won't be eligible for induction into the Golf Hall of Fame of BC. He resides in Boulder, Colorado, where he's an assistant coach for the women's golf team. He is most probably unaware that proceeds from the BC Golf Hall of Fame banquets go toward operating expenses for the BC Golf Museum. If and when the day comes, Franklin's friends in and around Vancouver might enjoy attending and applauding Brent Frankin for his accomplishments. Individuals are worthy of acclaim and the winner that night would be the museum foundation.

● ● ●

Jim Nelford possibly suffered the most unlucky bounce in the history of the PGA tour, even though the ball in question was not his.

In 1973 Nelford was BC's high school champion and BC Junior champion and joined a list of BC golfers who played for Brigham Young University's varsity team winning two All-American selections. He crossed Canada in 1975 to win his first Canadian Amateur in Saint John, New Brunswick, and returned north from school in the summer of 1976 to win his second Canadian Amateur at Royal Colwood.

Nelford turned pro in 1977 and spent a decade on the PGA tour. A highlight away from the tour occurred in 1980 when he teamed with Dan Haldorson to win the World Cup. He earned a living on tour but his best finishes were seconds in 1983 and at the Bing Crosby Pro-Am where he lost in a playoff in 1984. That was a day that Nelford would never forget. He had fashioned a brilliant closing round at Pebble Beach and stood in the clubhouse with only one golfer, then looking down the 18th fairway, able to tie him.

Sports Illustrated called what happened next "the ultimate testament to how anything can happen in golf."

The golfer on the 18th tee of one of the most picturesque golf holes in the world was 15-time tour winner and two-time US Open winner Hale Irwin. Usually cool under pressure, Irwin pulled his tee-shot badly and grimaced as he watched it sail toward the rocky shore of the Pacific Ocean. "Incredibly, it hits some rocks and bounces back onto the fairway; he makes birdie and forces a sudden-death play-off with Jim Nelford,"

His promising career shortened by a boating accident, Jim Nelford
was denied a PGA victory by one of the luckiest bounces in the
history of the game. BC GOLF HOUSE 007.128.184

Sports Illustrated would report in their next weekly with Irwin gracing
the cover. "Both golfers par the 15th, the starting hole. Then Irwin laces
a 2-iron from the fairway bunker on the 16 to within 9 feet of the cup.
He sinks the birdie for the win."

Pebble Beach still treats the outcome as one of the most memorable
finishes in the course's history. One website rendition of the event stated,
"Irwin was the beneficiary of a remarkable ricochet. His ball not only
avoided the out of bounds area, but also put him in position to make
his birdie, which he fatefully did. Irwin won the playoff and sealed an
indelible memory at Pebble Beach."

Nelford suffered crippling damage to an arm when it was badly sliced by a propeller blade in a waterskiing accident in September 1985. He recovered but never regained top form on the PGA Tour. Shortly before the accident he co-authored *Seasons in a Golfer's Life* with long-time golf journalist Lorne Rubenstein. Nelford went on to a career as golf analyst with ESPN.

● ● ●

Rick Gibson chose the Asian Tour as centre stage for most of his playing career. Like Zokol, Nelford and Franklin, he went to BYU where he won All-American recognition in 1984. He came home to win the BC Open in 1985 and five years later reigned as Canadian PGA champion.

Over the next two decades Rick played primarily in Japan and Southeast Asia. He won in Japan in 1991 and 1995 and claimed both the Malaysian Open and Philippines PGA titles while at his peak. Gibson's last win was his only official Asian Tour victory, the Philippines Open in 2002. He has recently relocated back to Vancouver Island and is aiming to claim a spot on a Seniors tour.

THE NEW BREED

With the exception of James Lepp's performances in university and at the national amateur level, there seemed to be a lull in player development in BC in the early 2000s. Ironically, if Lepp did inspire new talent it seems to have occurred right in his own backyard with the emergence of Adam Hadwin and Nick Taylor. Like James Lepp, Taylor and Hadwin learned the game at Abbotsford's Ledgeview, which, at about 6,100 yards from the back tees, is sometimes called the longest short course in the Fraser Valley. Obviously underrated, in part due to limited practice facilities, Ledgeview boasts a recent history that outdoes any other BC course in terms of grooming quality players. The trio of Lepp, Taylor and Hadwin was preceded by two other alumni who both reigned as provincial champions—Glenn Bannister and Andrew Smeeth.

As the quirky shoemaker was making his dramatic career change, Nick Taylor, who had followed Lepp to the University of Washington,

After a promising amateur career, Nick Taylor has found the shift
to pro golf challenging. His supporters believe that it is just a
matter of time. CHRISTOPHER MCGRATH, BRITISH COLUMBIA GOLF

capped a brilliant university golf career by achieving international status.
In 2009, over a seven-month period, the comparatively conservative
Taylor took honours as the Royal and Ancient's choice as top-ranked
amateur in the world. He announced his credentials by shooting a 65 in
the second round of the 2009 US Open. It was the lowest amateur round
in the history of the Open and helped him finish as the low amateur in
the tournament. Taylor was named Canada's Top Amateur Golfer in both
2008 and 2009. In 2010 he earned the coveted Ben Hogan Award as US
college player of the year and graduated from Washington after setting
records with four tournament victories and 17 top-10 finishes at college.

Nick was drawn to competitive golf at the age of 11, after watching Mike Weir win his first PGA tournament. "I remember watching the Air Canada championship on TV, when Mike holed out to win," Taylor recalled in an interview. "But being that kind of high-profile event and to win the Masters [as Weir did in 2003], it's just something you want to do. If you're a Canadian, you want to follow in his footsteps and have that kind of success."

Late in 2010 Taylor turned professional and prepared to play the Canadian tour the following summer. He had two top-10 finishes in seven events. The transition to professional golf has not been easy. Mike Weir knows Nick's game and suggests that Canadian fans should bide their time. Speaking of Taylor and other young pros, he told Robert Thomson of *Canadian Golfer*, "I see the drive in those guys and it gets tougher all the time. Every year the ability to separate from the pack is tougher than it was when I started, and a lot tougher than 20 years ago."

Weir reminded readers that it took him seven years to get to the tour and another five before he won the Masters. "It takes time and it is a tough game . . . Everyone wants instant gratification. And golf, maybe more than any other sport, takes patience."

When it came to turning pro, Adam Hadwin didn't show much patience. After one year of university at Louisville where he majored in business management and earned an academic scholarship, Adam followed in his father's footsteps and turned pro. Only six months older than clubmate Nick Taylor, Hadwin took to the professional game with gusto. It turns out that the son of Morgan Creek teaching pro Jerry Hadwin was a late bloomer, experiencing only moderate success in local amateur golf.

Hadwin was starting competitive junior golf when James Lepp began his run of four-straight BC Amateur titles (2001–04), followed by the NCAA championship (2005). "I never really knew James. We were four years apart," says Hadwin. "But I sure knew all about him, of course, and looked up to him as a young member at Ledgeview." Asked what he thought of Lepp's choice not to pursue tour golf, Hadwin was candid. "With all that talent, yes, I was surprised he gave up pro golf to go into his own business. But tour golf's a different lifestyle; it's not for everyone."

After his showing in the 2011 Canadian Open, Adam
Hadwin became BC's biggest hope as an emerging star
capable of filling the British Columbia void on
the PGA golf tour. VANCOUVER GOLF TOUR

By 2009 Lepp knew enough about Hadwin to have an opinion. "I wouldn't be surprised if Adam continues to progress toward the PGA Tour," observed Lepp. "I played with him in Victoria a couple of summers ago. His ball-striking was tour-esque."

Hadwin didn't survive the 2009 PGA Qualifying School and turned to the Canadian Tour. There, in 2010, he placed second on the money list with $88,000 that included an early victory and two seconds while finishing out of the top 10 only twice. He earned another $57,000 in other events, including $17,000 for an impressive tie for 37th in the Canadian Open. He was low Canadian in the event after an eye-catching second-round 65. But that was only a teaser of what was to come.

Continued putting improvement was Hadwin's primary focus in his second full season of tour golf in 2011. "Putting has always been my downfall, so I knew I had to work on my short game," he readily admitted. "I developed consistency on the greens last year. Better putting made a huge difference to my confidence." And confidence is a critical asset in golf. Still, Adam Hadwin makes absolutely no pretence about who he is. "I'm a Canadian tour player. I'm not a PGA Tour players; at least, not yet, anyway."

By the end of August 2011 he was the poster boy for the "new breed" in BC golf. He had played in 10 of the 11 scheduled Canadian tour events, winning once and ranking seventh in the money list.

What you have to like about this 23-year-old is his candid self-confidence. It is cocky, brash, composed and refreshing, all rolled into one. Pro golfers can't succeed without it.

What Hadwin did when the Canadian Open returned to his home province at Shaughnessy Golf & Country Club in the summer of 2011 was unthinkable. The willowy kid from Abbotsford Ledgeview beat all but three players, ending in a tie for fourth only two strokes behind tour veteran Sean O'Hair and a burly rookie pro named Kris Banks who played the first playoff hole like a truck driver, taking double-bogey six to lose to O'Hair's five.

Hadwin had the nerve, the guts, to flirt with history in only his third PGA Tour start—all of them national Opens where he has made the 36-hole cut each time. On paper, he simply does not have the credentials to suggest that he is capable of this accomplishment and his startling 2011 result. But maybe he is one of those performers who respond to the bigger stage. Maybe, although he is a proven supporter of Canadian Tour events, he has problems getting excited about the Times Colonist Island Savings Open in Victoria or the Dakota Dunes Casino Open near Saskatoon.

In taming the 7,011-yard monster of a course called Shaughnessy and coming agonizingly close to a Canadian Open victory, Adam Hadwin earned $230,000—easily the largest cheque of his young career. His high finish qualified him to play in the PGA's next event even though it was a continent away. Hadwin was on the flight for West Virginia on the Monday morning to spend the last week of July not only making another cut but adding $32,500 to his bank account with a 68-68 finish at the Greenbrier Classic.

But it was in Vancouver that the young BC pro gained a whole new level of respect. Hadwin had handled himself with exceptional poise on a course set up like the US Open with gnarly rough. They allowed it to grow up to four inches deep in places, framing the 25- to 30-yard-wide fairways, and perilously close to miniature greens. There were volunteer ball-spotters lining the fairways. It was severely criticized by some competitors, but by the end of the week it had literally grown on them in more than one way. World number-one ranked golfer Luke Donald had reportedly said that he could tell the rough looked tall even as his private jet approached the nearby Vancouver International Airport.

According to one writer, Hadwin showed he "had a lot of game" by moving up to the top three with two late birdies out of that rough. At Shaughnessy birdies were never easy to come by.

Six years earlier, Mark Calcavecchia had only one birdie during the final weekend of the 2005 Open at Shaughnessy, but his rounds of 71 and 72 were good enough to stave off Ryan Moore and Ben Crane by a stroke with a five-under 275 total. That event had marked the return of Canada's national Open championship to western Canada for the first time in nearly 40 years dating back to Don Massengale's three-stroke victory at Shaughnessy in 1966. The club had also played host, albeit at its original nearby location, to Chuck Congdon's Canadian Open triumph in 1948. "Shaughnessy is the type of old-style traditional course that players on tour absolutely love to play," said Calcavecchia when he returned for the 2011 Open. "I remember back in 2005 the players couldn't say enough about how great the golf course was. I think the players would agree that it's going to be one of the best golf courses we play in 2011."

Narrow fairways, severe rough and Shaughnessy's smallish greens had confounded the field in 2005. Besides Calcavecchia, only eight other players finished below par. Eight players also broke par 280 in 2011, with Hadwin finishing two-under with rounds of 72-66-68-72.

Before he graduates from Surrey High in June 2012, Adam Svensson will have a file of scholarship enquiries from American universities and

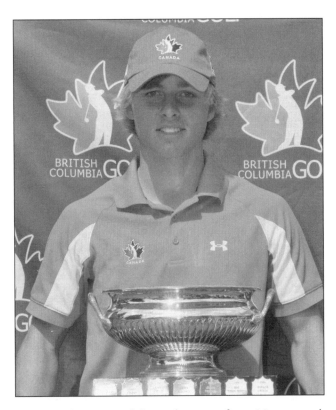

Adam Svensson has continued the steady stream of promising young players with the potential to emerge from amateur golf and succeed in the professional arena. CHRISTOPHER MCGRATH, BRITISH COLUMBIA GOLF

memories of tours of major campuses. Svensson is expected to be one of the most heavily recruited golf prospects in North America off his glittering achievements since he became a teenager.

The strapping youngster was regularly breaking 70 before he turned 13, twice won the Canadian Junior and in 2008 at 16 became the youngest BC Amateur champion in history, younger even than Stan Leonard and Doug Roxburgh. Svensson won the 2010 BC Amateur by five shots at Castlegar. He finished eight-under on rounds of 67-71-68-70, a wire-to-wire winner at 276. This was his third golf victory in as many weeks; the week before he had served notice to the golf community by winning the Callaway Junior World Golf crown in San Diego, California. That made Svensson a member of an exclusive club of five, along with Doug

Eugene Wong has continued to thrive in US college golf, most recently being named the PAC-12 Men's Golfer of the Year for 2012. CHRISTOPHER MCGRATH, BRITISH COLUMBIA GOLF

Roxburgh (1969), James Harper (1982), James Lepp (2002) and Eugene Wong (2008) as double Amateur champions. Eugene Wong of North Vancouver, BC, received the Men's award; Christine Wong of Richmond received the Women's award; Svensson received the Junior Boys' award.

In 2010, Eugene Wong became the latest young BC golfer to raise eyebrows at a Pac-12 university. As a member of the University of Oregon Ducks golf team he collected two individual victories and five top-5 finishes, and finished ninth in the NCAA Championship. He was co-recipient of the Pac-10 Golfer of the Year and an NCAA First Team All-American. Even better, he was named the 2010 NCAA Jack Nicklaus Award Winner, an honour given to the Division I Collegiate Player of the Year as voted by golf coaches throughout the United States.

CHAPTER 14

IN THE BACKGROUND: CADDIES AND ARCHITECTS

Where would the early players have been without their caddies, many of whom went on to become accomplished golfers? And how would the courses look without the expertise of the course architects? This chapter pays tribute to the caddies and architects who helped BC golf become the success it is today.

CADDIES

Caddies are—alas—a vanishing breed. These days you're as likely to see a caddy as you are to see a pro playing in plus-fours and a long-sleeved white shirt and necktie. As long as at least one foursome of former Shaughnessy Heights bag-totters was alive and able, however, there was a caddies' tournament on Labour Day weekend at Gallagher's Canyon Resort in Kelowna. Angus Mackenzie's annual celebration for his former sidekicks in the caddy shack was a wonderful event. The reunion was a social gathering of men from all walks of life—rich and poor, prominent and ordinary, doctors and lawyers and candy-stick makers, men who trudged Shaughnessy's fairways and those who followed with someone else's golf bags over their shoulders.

Mackenzie made his fortune in the oil business, but he never forgot his roots or his boyhood in Vancouver, where he pocketed his first dollars as a caddy at Shaughnessy Heights. "During the tough times of the Depression, we somehow knew things were going to get better,"

"For many years after 1979, successful oilman Angus Mackenzie (third from
right, standing) brought together all ex-Shaughnessy caddies in an annual
reunion held at Gallagher's Canyon in Kelowna. ARV OLSON COLLECTION

he recalled. "I guess they couldn't get much worse. Some of us had to
get lucky." Mackenzie chose to quietly share some of his good fortune
with his former fellow caddies. He never knew many of them, never met
them, but he genuinely cared enough about them to create a unique
fraternity. Through the modest Mackenzie's generosity, friendships and
acquaintances were renewed every holiday weekend in September starting in 1979. The final reunion was held before his passing in 2010.

When Burrard International negotiated to purchase Gallagher's
Canyon, Mackenzie as majority owner insisted on a peculiar provision
in the sale agreement. It stipulated that the course be reserved for the
ex-Shaughnessy caddies every Labour Day as long as a few were still alive.
He provided everything for as many as 30 weekend golfers—airfares,
hotel rooms, green fees, car rentals and prizes. The first-class affair was
launched after the genial host had casually enquired about the where-
abouts of some caddies to Dick Munn, the Point Grey pro who became
Mackenzie's most significant associate in the development of Gallagher's.
When told that many caddies still resided in BC, Mackenzie suggested
the reunion tournament.

A tall, elegant man with a bushy moustache and mild manner, Mackenzie was a caddy from Vancouver's Main Street area and a fair golfer. His father, a stone mason, immigrated to Grand Forks from Scotland.

After serving in the air force during the Second World War, Mackenzie developed a successful oil business, basing his company in Calgary. He also played golf well enough to win the Central Alberta Amateur prior to the participation of notable champions named Doug Silverberg, Keith Alexander and Bob Wylie. Mackenzie's caddy tournament was organized and run through the efforts of Munn and two former caddies, Les Paterson and Ernie Brown, who both subsequently forged golf careers. The nostalgia was intense at Gallagher's every Labour Day and the camaraderie was wonderful. The 26 former caddies at the 1991 reunion were a mixed bag, comprising retired executives, a judge, a detective, an engineer, a fireman, golf pros and pensioners. They came with an assortment of golf implements, rusty clubs in musty bags and the latest in costly modern equipment. They came from vastly different worlds, though they'd lived mere miles apart. Many hadn't seen one another for decades, others since they were caddies or since the September before. At Gallagher's Canyon they again shared common ground and common experiences.

Ted Ingram first caddied at Shaughnessy Heights in 1918 when he was 11. He was one of only six regular caddies at the course. For 18 holes, they received fifty cents, or fifty-five cents and a green streetcar ticket if they were lucky. Among the first Shaughnessy caddies in 1912 were Ed Day, Jim Pollock and Merv Boucher. During the Depression Ingram ventured south and became a tour caddy. He recalls riding a freight train with Johnny Goodman a few years before the amateur from Nebraska won the 1933 US Open. He was the last amateur to win it.

Wages and jobs were more plentiful in the post-Depression and war years. Ingram returned to work on greens crews at Beach Grove, Old and New Shaughnessy, Seymour, Kokanee Springs and Arbutus Gardens. The old caddies laugh about hiding from the caddy master when the four-bitters arrived and they remember Sam Snead as one of the cheapest visitors. Shaughnessy members who avoided the frugal Snead included Jake Palmer, the John Oliver school principal who used a cane to support a bad leg, and Walter Hepburn. No one wanted to pack bags for a frugal player.

They bribed the forbidding caddy master, Charlie "Big Mac" MacDonald, with cigarettes for preferred or early bags. The gambit enabled them to avoid the four- and six-bitters and to get in a second round. Speed was key to earning the choice bags on weekdays. "It was a race out of school to the course," said Bob Hamilton, who became a postmaster. "The first ones there got the golfers furthest along in their rounds and they'd usually get paid for a full 18."

Hamilton caddied from 1928 until the war, drawing Johnny Bulla's bag for the 1936 Jubilee Open. He was pro Bob Hamilton's caddy in the 1948 Canadian Open and took a week off work to pack for Hugh Royer, the first-round leader of the 1966 Open at New Shaughnessy.

Bob McLeod earned fifty-five dollars as MacDonald Smith's "boy" in the Jubilee tournament while Bob Anderson and Jack Hamilton both got $37.50 caddying for Byron Nelson and Jimmy Thomson respectively. Ernie Brown couldn't recall how much he was paid by Ralph Guldahl, who took amateur Jimmy Todd under his wing after the Island southpaw won the 1937 BC Open at Oak Bay. Brown did remember, however, that it was financially beneficial to shag for pro Davey Black's lessons rather than caddying. "We'd get twenty-five cents a lesson, less a nickel for each ball we lost in the bush—which was more profitable than spending at least three hours caddying for six bits [seventy-five cents]."

Black was a stickler for rules and deportment. When he snapped his fingers, the boys in the caddy shack jumped to attention. Brown commented,

> We owe a lot to Davey, though we didn't realize it at the time. He taught us the rules and how to behave. He'd appear on his pro shop porch from time to time, waving his little yellow Dunlop rulebook. He'd call us by name and ask us a certain rule. If we didn't know the answer he'd say "Down the road you go, laddie, and come back tomorrow knowing that rule." We'd learn a lot listening to him when he gave lessons. If you didn't obey his rules, and he was strict, you were gone.

Many Hollywood sportsmen came to BC in the 1950s, for both salmon
fishing and golf. Clark Gable is seen here at Shaughnessy Heights in 1960.
STUART THOMSON, CITY OF VANCOUVER ARCHIVES CVA99-2790

Most caddies in Brown's day lived in east Vancouver, from 25th and
Main south. Some pedalled bikes to the course, others trekked three or
four miles over Little Mountain, which was bush. On Mondays, some
members such as Reg Milroy, Jack Fraser and Don McLean kindly
allowed caddies to use their clubs on day-long adventures to play Peace
Portal at the border. Fraser, a 1925 City champion and four-time club
winner who was a Union Oil salesman, often picked up caddies at 25th
and Cambie, en route to the course.

"We got close-up looks at all the celebrities who came to town; they all played Shaughnessy," recalled Lorne Muir, a late-1920s caddy who joined the Vancouver police after the war. "We'd get to pack for some of them. Clark Gable was a regular, a pleasant man and pretty good golfer. Randolph Scott and W.E. Fields also played there. One day I got lucky, I thought, when I was assigned to caddy for Prime Minister Arthur Meighen. I figured I'd be getting at least two or three dollars. He turned out to be a six-bitter."

Virtually all the good amateurs came from the caddy ranks. Among those who worked at Shaughnessy were Norm Nixon, Stan Leonard, Henry and Joe Mitchell, Les Harvie, LaVerne Johnson, Babe Goodfellow, George Booth, Les Beavan and Jack Whalen. Nixon, from the class of 1930, remembers caddying for Bobby Jones. He received five dollars, which was paid by the club.

Bright and early on Saturday mornings, as many as 100 boys camped on the benches, waiting for Big Mac's signal. The caddy master had his favourites and discouraged youngsters he didn't particularly like. In 1924, 12-year-old Harry Plumsteel determined there was more money in caddying than delivering 20 newspapers for a cent each. He lived near 12th and Oak and went to the nearest course, Shaughnessy Heights. Plumsteel recalls:

> The caddy master caught me talking too loudly once and sent me home so I had no alternative but to find another course. It was quiet Monday to Friday at Marine Drive. The usual fee was a dollar and the younger caddies got stuck with the four-bitters. Chris Spencer, part owner of Spencers Department Stores, took a shine to me. He'd play only nine holes and never gave me more than twenty-five cents. The members were pretty kind to us, though. They organized a tournament for us every year with prizes, donuts and pop and everything.

Shaughnessy easily had the largest contingent of regular caddies. But Bill Bain, Max Banbury, Bruce Yorke and Ab Sweeny were among those who did well at Jericho. Bill Morgan and future pros Wood and Tate started as caddies in the 1920s at Vancouver Golf Club. Brian and Ron Hopkins, Bev Davidson and George Crass were budding young players who also caddied at Marine. Morgan, a long-hitter who later played Marine, reportedly shot 66 at the Burquitlam course in 1921 while playing with only a cleek.

Point Grey boasted potential champions in Bob Watson, George and Ed Ireland, Bruce Firth and Reg Arkell. Pro Dave Ayton's daughter, Florence, and Dorothy Mole were competitive with the caddies.

A teenaged girl named Margaret Wadey created labour strife among Peace Portal caddies in 1935 when she packed for a Mr. Ball. The boys went on strike, avoiding the course for a week. Wadey caddied for three years and was followed by Naomi Anderson, who developed into a good player.

Almost all the caddies who worked Qualicum Beach during the 1920s summers were from Victoria, Vancouver and other bigger towns. A "Cheapskate List" posted in the Qualicum caddy shack identified players who didn't pay the going rate of fifty cents for 9 holes and one dollar for 18. The caddies refused their bags. At other times they would be all too anxious to draw a celebrity. Qualicum's tudor-style luxury hotel, built with the coming of the railway in 1914, had been used as a convalescent hospital for amputees during the war before being restored to its original grandeur and becoming a popular vacation destination for fishing and golf. It attracted such stars as Spencer Tracey, Errol Flynn, Bob Hope, Bing Crosby and Shirley Temple. The caddy master was Fred Westnedge, who gained the role as a 20-year-old and earned sixty dollars per month, plus room and board. He had first gone to Qualicum with his parents on summer vacation.

At Prince George, Bobby Foot held three caddy distinctions in 1935. He was the shortest, carried the biggest bag and was the only one with enough gumption to complain to club executives that he wasn't paid sufficiently for honest services rendered.

Junior programs didn't exist when Shaughnessy staged the first city caddy championship in 1923. The tournament was a competitive launching pad for future champions. Golf's original professionals sprang from the corps of the St Andrews caddies and with the exception of tour golf, the only colonies of regular caddies still in existence are at the traditional Scottish courses.

Caddies were relieved of burdensome bags in 1937 with the introduction of the 14-club rule. Previously, there was no limit and bags could be jammed with as many as 25 to 30 clubs. The limit wasn't established to alleviate the caddy's load, but to reduce delays that resulted from players deciding which club to use.

When functional pull-carts appeared in the late 1940s, only the most dogged caddies endured. The first prototype pull-cart, a Rover *circa* 1900, had small, hard wheels. They were difficult to navigate on hilly courses, especially since they didn't have proper handles. The caddy's fate was sealed by the war and motorized golf carts. A caddy shortage developed during the war when youngsters discovered easier ways of making money than strapping golf bags over their shoulders. And after the war, affluent golfers made many pull-carts obsolete when they began to favour the motorized carts introduced in 1948. The first motorized cart was a modified three-wheeled military unit called the Arthritic Special. It spewed too much smoke and made too much noise. In the mid-1950s Cushman finally came out with a quiet, clean electric cart.

Former caddies at Gallagher's Labour Day weekends rode the roller-coaster fairways playing golf courtesy of Angus Mackenzie. During an early Labour Day event, Arnold Palmer and Hale Irwin were at Gallagher's for an exhibition. They marvelled at the special reunion that embraced

Caddy is a derivative of *cadet*, meaning little chief, which translated into a porter or street loafer who ran errands and did odd jobs. Some refused to work for a peon's pay. A few years before the Second World War, Jericho caddies went on strike for two days after caddy master Jack Stone reduced pay a dime to sixty-five cents.

The golf term *fore* emanated from *forecaddie*, a boy sent ahead to track expensive feathery balls. When players hit wild shots, they alerted the ball-hawks with shouts of "fore caddy," which later was abbreviated to fore.

caddies from as far back as seven decades. "This," Mackenzie told Palmer proudly, "is one tournament you don't qualify for."

William "Tish" Walsh, who became probably the oldest active caddy in Canada, was so diminutive he could hide behind most bags at Victoria Golf Club. He stood a grass blade above five feet and weighed about 110 pounds. Walsh caddied at Oak Bay for 40 years. At age 81, in 1957, he went to New York and stumped the panel of the TV show *What's My Line?* In a modest autobiography published in pamphlet form in 1961, Walsh claimed to have bettered his age at Cedar Hill. He carried the clubs of many notables over the years, among them Edward, Prince of Wales and later singer Bing Crosby and comedian Bob Hope. Walsh claims he wasn't paid by the prince but that he cherished the honour. He remembered receiving five dollars for toting Crosby's bag for 14 holes. "He had to leave early because he wanted to go fishing at Campbell River," Walsh wrote.

After serving in the British army, Walsh had come to Canada in 1919 with his wife and four children. He first worked as a deckhand on the S.S. *Princess Royal's* Vancouver-Victoria run. Later, to supplement his wages as a school janitor, he discovered he could make fifty cents caddying between his morning and late-afternoon duties at various Victoria schools. Walsh died in his 88th year on August 27, 1964. His body was found in waters off Oak Bay's fifth fairway. An autopsy revealed he had suffered a heart seizure, though exactly where and when he died remains a mystery.

The last of the caddies, at least on the Lower Mainland, was Ken Jones. Caddying was becoming increasingly unusual in the province, except at tournaments. Easier, better-paying employment was becoming available to youngsters as the fast food business took hold. Old regular caddies died off or could no longer trudge the fairways. And golfers who once used caddies now use power carts, preferring not to walk 18 holes.

Ken Jones, however, carried on. Quiet and inconspicuous, like a good caddy should be, Jones existed for the better part of 25 years on welfare and carrying someone's golf bag. He has been employed in the back shops of Point Grey, Capilano and Seymour, and he has been called on to caddy for touring pros and other high-profile personalities visiting Vancouver's top courses over the years. Jones's most nerve-wracking and most memorable job was caddying for the prime minister of Japan at Capilano. Security was airtight for the prime minister's foursome. A helicopter hovered over the course and 20 security men patrolled the wooded fairways. "Extra power carts were used for supplies of drinks, chocolate bars and cigarettes," said Jones. "If anyone hit a ball into the woods, and almost everyone did, security guys threw them back to the fairways. No one was permitted to tee off an hour before or after the Japanese foursome."

Jones's expertise also earned him the bags of Gene Sarazen, Mike Bonallack and Bob Panasiuk, among many other distinguished players. Bonallack, a great English amateur before achieving renown at the administration level of the Royal and Ancient, was a "real gentleman" according to Jones. Sarazen, the fabled US champion, was described as "a dour individual whose clubs were at least triple-X . . . so stiff they were like boards."

In 1974, Panasiuk was as hot as the midday sun in Osoyoos when he arrived at Point Grey for the Open. He had won the Alberta and Saskatchewan Opens and he was chasing a stranger from Texas, Jim Barker, in the last round.

Jones tended the cavalier Windsor pro's bag that week:

> Panasiuk knew he needed a birdie-eagle finish to force a playoff. He hit an eight-iron shot about three feet away to deuce 17 and murdered his drive off 18, a short par-five hole. He only had a pitching wedge left and put it 12 feet from the cup. But he missed the putt and got $2,500 for second. I was paid eighty dollars. Almost every player gave their caddies the going rate of twenty dollars a round, plus 5 to 10 percent of their winnings.

THE ARCHITECTS

The most indelible golf imprints on this province's landscape have been branded by two men of entirely different eras: Arthur Vernon Macan and Les Furber. Numerous people in a century of golf have been influential builders, administrators and supporters in boardrooms, courses and practice fairways. But, with the passage of time, their intangible contributions have been regrettably forgotten, unlike the lasting, visible creations of Macan, Furber and other noted course architects. Macan and Furber have been BC's most prolific course creators. However, not all of Macan's artistry during six-plus decades has withstood change and some of Furber's designs will also be modified in due time. Furber, today's master craftsman, has designed, built, renovated and remodelled courses not only in Canada but also in the United States, Cuba and several European countries.

Macan's trademark graced many early coastal courses from Nanaimo to San Francisco. The Irishman from Victoria was in great demand after his original effort, Royal Colwood. In the experimental years of course architecture, Macan proved to be a progressive technician and innovator. Courses he didn't design were handled by members of clubs that couldn't afford architects or by wily club pros such as Alex Duthie and Davey Black. Duthie rearranged Jericho's original nine holes in 1910 and 13 years later he was responsible for the design and construction of the expanded course. Several Interior clubs engaged Duthie in an advisory capacity, while the University course was constructed under Black's supervision.

Other professional players have also been aspiring architects, Stan Leonard and Ernie Brown among them. Brown, Duthie's assistant at Jericho, became a course architect-consultant after leaving Seymour's pro shop in 1957. Brown was influenced by Stanley Thompson, whose many legendary creations across the country include Capilano, Banff Springs and Jasper Park. Thompson's American counterpart, the distinguished Robert Trent Jones Sr., also trained a generation of course designers. Among them were his sons, Rees and Robert Trent Jr., Bill Robinson of White Rock and Furber. It was R.T. Jones Sr. who said, "The Lord put a million golf courses on the earth. Our job is to find them." He found one on the banks of the Thompson River east of Kamloops. He described links-style Rivershore as one of his best creations on straightforward property. R.T. Jones Jr.'s first BC project, the Chateau Whistler, opened in late 1992.

Bill Robinson, who attended Penn State on a golf scholarship, designed Gallagher's Canyon in Kelowna and collaborated on other northwest layouts with transplanted Canadian Geoff Cornish. Norman Woods, another Thompson protégé originally from Toronto, eventually settled in Penticton and was responsible for more than 300 courses, many in western Canada. Woods's most magnificent BC layout was Kokanee Springs at Crawford Bay in the Kootenays. His other credits included remodelling New Shaughnessy, Gorge Vale and Lake Point in Fort St. John.

Furber's company GDS is most probably the busiest course developer in BC. Two of Furber's partners, Jim Eremko and Craig Ewanchuk, also learned under Robert Trent Jones Sr. Furber—who once boasted a six handicap—got into the business purely by accident while vacationing in California. He worked for Jones for 14 years, including 9 years in Europe and on the Rivershore project. If there's a signature or philosophy to GDS's architectural styling at courses such as Predator Ridge, the Springs at Radium, Fairview Mountain, Storey Creek, Mayfair Lakes, Fairwinds, Morningstar and Northlands, it's a distinct visibility of hazards and framework of contoured greens and mounding. Predator Ridge, near Vernon, gave GDS its first opportunity to fashion an authentic links-style course. "The owners gave us freedom, a mandate, to create something different," says Furber.

Don Kitsul and Jack Reimer, who both trained under Woods, have constructed or renovated innumerable courses in the province. Kitsul first worked with Woods on Willow Park in Calgary. He also moved and shaped earth at Guildford, Surrey, Burnaby, Lake Padden, Shaughnessy, Whistler, Nakusp, Invermere, Prince Rupert, Vernon, Cowichan, Burquitlam, North Vancouver, Gabriola Island and Kamloops. Kitsul built Gallagher's Canyon, which opened as Kelowna Pines in 1980. "Bill Robinson did the original design," said Kitsul, who sold the property to Angus Mackenzie and partners.

CHAPTER 15

THE GLAMOROUS EXHIBITIONS

Exhibition golf was part of the barnstorming era when famous sports and entertainment celebrities first crossed the continent to demonstrate their skills with assured payment from local promoters. The charisma of Bobby Jones and others made them popular draws in Vancouver and Victoria. Before the mega-money of the US tour, and before commercialism and television turned professional golfers into highly visible millionaires, exhibitions were the staple of marquee players.

The attraction of tournaments between the two world wars wasn't the prize money, it was the notoriety that came with winning.

Few big money winners from 1920 through the early 1950s grew rich from tournaments. The purses were scant and shallow. Hacking a livelihood solely out of tour golf was impossible without consistently placing among the leaders. Yet club jobs, and regular paycheques, were abandoned for the sake of fulfilling dreams—and those who managed to satisfy their stomachs were considered fortunate.

Lucrative endorsements and corporate outings that supplement the income of today's tour regulars weren't available to fringe players until well after the Arnold Palmer boom of the 1960s. The major winners until then—Walter "The Haig" Hagen, Jones, Sarazen, Snead, Nelson, Hogan—were the box-office attractions. With only newspaper photographs to help them recognize the stars, fans swarmed to see them close up when they came to town.

One-day exhibitions in cities never touched by tour golf provided easy, guaranteed money between tournaments or when none were scheduled. The glamour players commanded appearance fees frequently greater than first-place tour cheques, and they were treated like royal visitors wherever they went.

The barnstormers usually travelled in pairs to facilitate best-ball challenges against two of the best local pros. With well-groomed courses, well-heeled supporters and tolerable winter conditions, Vancouver and Victoria were popular destinations during off-seasons for the itinerant pros. The proceeds from exhibitions aided war efforts and various charitable causes, and the exposure stimulated the status and popularity of the game and its courses.

Local opponents for the midweek matches were perceived as volunteers who played the roles of straight men for the celebrated visitors. But on occasion the public was delighted to discover that the home pros were more capable than had been thought. This served to boost the esteem of the local players, all while they gained valuable experience in performing before large crowds.

An automatic choice to face any visitors was Davey Black. He was still at Ottawa Rivermead in 1913 when two famed globetrotting golfers hit the west coast for an exhibition. The second nine at Shaughnessy Heights had been opened for play earlier that year, making the 5,231-yard course the choice over nine-holers at Jericho and Burquitlam as the stage for British Open champions Harry Vardon and Ted Ray.

Vardon and Ray were at the end of a barnstorming US tour on behalf of the *London Times*. The tour had been punctuated at Brookline, Massachusetts, in September by their playoff loss for the US Open championship to an unknown ex-caddy of French-Canadian heritage named Frances Ouimet. Vardon, the supreme stylist and perfectionist, had already won four British Opens and the 1900 US Open. Ray, a hulking man with a bushy moustache, wielded clubs like an angry giant, a pipe forever clenched between his teeth.

The visitors commanded $400 for their appearance against Alf Blinko, the resident pro, and Jericho's Alex Duthie, with Shaughnessy providing

From left, Ted Ray, Biggerstaff Wilson, A.V. Macan, Harvey Combe and legendary
Harry Vardon prepare for an exhibition match at the Victoria Golf Club in 1913.
ARV OLSON COLLECTION

$200 and the other two clubs $100 each. Vardon shot two 68s, the best
score since Blinko's opening-day 70, and Ray recorded 69 and 71. The
visitors won going away, 10 and 9, as Blinko had 78-80 and Duthie 80-77.

The gallery, limited to 300 because of the fragility of the new nine,
marvelled at Vardon's fluid, effortless swing. The equally enraptured press
lauded the elegant Vardon's precision, exaggerating enthusiastically that
he could literally play shots on the second round from divots he left
during the morning 18.

Vardon and Ray also played at Victoria Golf Club in a Saturday match,
where they received another $200 each for beating Willie Moffat of the
host course and Seattle pro Robert Johnstone. Ray collected a fifty-dollar
bonus for bettering 68; he matched the course record 67 on the strength
of an incoming 32. He had opened with 72 while Vardon posted 145,
Johnstone 143 and Moffat 156. On Sunday morning Victoria threw

three well-regarded amateurs at Vardon in a match where the best ball among the three locals would be pitted against Vardon's ball. Nine-time BC Amateur champ Harvey Combe, and the two 1913 BC Amateur finalists, A.V. Macan and Biggerstaff Wilson, were a stout contingent but Vardon prevailed in a tight match, one-up.

Shaughnessy and Victoria were two of only six courses in Canada that Vardon ever played. He described Oak Bay as "quite a good test . . . most of the play was through openings in rocks" in his 1933 book *My Golfing Life*. While strolling the streets of 1913 Victoria, Vardon recalled passing a newspaper office and laughing at the headlined sports page in the window: "British golfers beat locals 5 and 3—whatever that means?"

In his second season at Shaughnessy, Black and Jimmy Huish combined for an overwhelming 8 and 6 victory over Australians Joe Kirkwood and Victor East before 600 spectators at Huish's Vancouver Golf Club course. Two days later, Black took the measure of Kirkwood at Shaughnessy 3 and 2.

East was Australia's leading amateur while Kirkwood had tied for second in the Canadian Open after claiming both the Australian and New Zealand Open titles in 1920, but he earned his fame as a trick-shot artist.

Kirkwood returned the following November accompanied by Hagen, and also toured extensively with Gene Sarazen, enlivening proceedings with his remarkable dexterity.

However, it was The Haig whom everyone came to see at Shaughnessy and the dapper, freewheeling New Yorker who won major titles 11 times from 1919 through 1929 didn't disappoint. Hagen toured Shaughnessy, sight unseen, in 68 during the morning as he and Kirkwood handled Black and Huish 6 and 5.

After lunch Kirkwood dazzled the spectators with his canny control of ball and club. He commenced by stymie-hopping with a mashie and putter, negotiating the shot right-handed with a left-handed club. He drove balls 250 yards—teed off a bag, a club shaft, his caddy's toe, under the caddy's foot and off the face of a wristwatch, from which he once holed a shot.

Shaughnessy pro Davey Black, lower left on grass with son Ken, and touring Aussie amateur champion Victor East watch trick-shot artist Joe Kirkwood exhibit his form in 1921.
ARV OLSON COLLECTION

A caravan of players from Chicago featuring Long Jim Barnes and Jock Hutchison visited Shaughnessy and Royal Colwood in 1925. Barnes—the Englishman who defeated Hutchison in the first PGA championship of 1916 and took up residence in California—and his partner drew Black and Point Grey pro Dave Ayton before 1,000 at Shaughnessy. In a second match, Chick Evans and former Irish champion Ernest Carter defeated local amateurs Cec Coville and Eddie McCadden 5 and 4.

At Colwood, Barnes and Hutchison were 3 and 2 winners over Black and Oak Bay pro Phil Taylor while Evans and Carter defeated Victorians Frank Thomas and A.V. Macan. In a third exhibition before 500 spectators, Americans Joe Novak and Keefe Carter won 6 and 5 over Colwood pro Alex Marling and Victor Price, the 1921 BC Amateur champion from Uplands.

A colourful autumn quintet assembled at Point Grey in 1929. (L to R) Dunc Sutherland, Davey Black, referee Jimmy "the Hush" Huish, and barnstormers Horton Smith and Walter Hagen make up one of the most entertaining exhibition squads ever assembled in BC.
BC GOLF HOUSE 007.121.011B

During the presentation ceremony after the Barnes-Hutchison appearance at Shaughnessy, Hutchison baited—and hooked—several members by remarking that he'd bet he could reach the first green in two shots with a putter! The downhill hole measured more than 500 yards. Ears perked and several gentlemen, 1920 BC Amateur champion Reggie Symes among them, put up $500 to wager that Hutchison couldn't do it.

They were suckered. The slightly built St Andrews native actually swatted two shots beyond the green using a No. 10 Mills aluminum mallet putter that had an over-length shaft. Hutchison deliberately drove to a dip on the left side of the fairway, leaving himself an advantageous uphill lie for his second "putt."

Hagen's troupe returned several other times. In 1926 he showed up at Uplands in a starched white collar and tie and shot 75 to match the best-ball of three members, the left-handed Price, Percy Edmunds and John Savident. In the rainy, wintry November of 1928 he toured with US Open champion Johnny Farrell, playing at Langara, Colwood and Tacoma Fircrest.

Hagen and Quilchena amateur Monty Hill won 2 and 1 over Farrell and Vancouver Golf Club amateur Fred Wood before 300 drenched fans at Langara. A steady downpour also greeted the visitors at Colwood, where Hagen and local amateur Harold Lineham finished even against Farrell and Bon Stein, the ace Seattle amateur.

The most memorable Hagen visit was to Point Grey in October 1929, in the midst of the stock market crash that saw investors lose 40 percent of their portfolios in a matter of weeks. Hagen and young Horton Smith were upstaged 3 and 2 by Black and newly appointed host pro Dunc Sutherland before a crowd of 2,000, one of the largest local crowds of the time.

It was only the sixth defeat in more than 80 matches of Hagen's western tour. The man who once said, "I never wanted to be a millionaire; I just wanted to live like one," went away empty-handed that day. Hagen, then 37, and Smith had accepted a side bet from brave local sportsmen for the sum of their $500 match guarantee.

In a previous match at Edmonton, Sutherland recalled losing his composure and the match after Hagen had needled him.

> On the 16th tee Walter casually remarked how well I had been driving all day and that I hadn't hit one slice. I proceeded to push my tee-shot into trouble.
>
> When I drove him to the train station later than night, he asked me how much I had been paid for the exhibition. After telling him I hadn't received anything, he reached into his pocket and slipped me fifty dollars.

After the Point Grey victory, Sutherland and Black were invited to tour Portland, San Francisco and Los Angeles with Hagen and Smith.

England's Joyce Wethered broke 18 course records during her 1935
North American tour, including an impressive 73 at Jericho. Bobby
Jones said of her, "I have not played golf with anyone, man or woman,
amateur or professional, who made me feel so utterly outclassed."
STUART THOMSON, CITY OF VANCOUVER ARCHIVES CVA99-1836

The smooth-swinging Smith, who led the 1936 tour with earnings of
$7,682, created bold headlines across the width of Vancouver newspapers
on August 19, 1937.

More than 4,000 spectators, a throng which hasn't been seen at
University since, saw Smith break resident pro Harry Winter's course
record by firing seven birdies for a 64 during a season-long series with
Lighthorse Harry Cooper, Jimmy Thomson and Lawson Little. After
shooting a 66 in Smith's shadow, Thomson said he had travelled "40,000
miles during the past year and played a tournament or exhibition round
on 361 of the 365 days." Little was par 71, Cooper 73.

The Depression forced Joyce Wethered to turn pro and tour North America with Gene
Sarazen, Horton Smith and Babe Didrickson Zaharias, whom she bettered on a regular basis.
BC GOLF HOUSE 007.141.068B

Black also was privy to the remarkable shot making of Joyce Wethered,
the Bobby Jones of women's golf. In these hard times, Wethered forfeited
her amateur status to tour North America with Sarazen, Smith and the
big-hitting Babe Didrikson Zaharias, whom she consistently outdrove
and outscored.

In 52 matches during the summer of 1935, Wethered broke records
at 18 courses, including Jericho where she shot 73 in the company of
Toronto's Ada Mackenzie, Black and Duthie. When Vancouver official
Dave Manley informed the Englishwoman that 1,500 spectators were
expected for the match, she replied, "In that case I expect I shall have
to be rather good, shan't I?" Duthie couldn't recall a woman ever having
broken 80 at Jericho.

The pros had magnanimously spotted a three-up advantage to
Wethered and Mackenzie, fresh from her fifth Canadian amateur title
at Jericho. It appeared a foolhardy gesture early in the exhibition before

1,500. Mackenzie birdied the first hole. After Duthie hit a career drive off No. 2, Wethered—whose length was comparable to that of a scratch male player—was the last to play her approach. She pitched weakly but dropped a 50-foot downhill putt, forcing Black to follow in from 12 feet for a half.

The women eventually gave way by losing four successive holes on the back nine and the match finished even. Black shot 70, Duthie 76 and Mackenzie 83.

With the outbreak of the Second World War, exhibitions became fundraising events. In October 1939, soon after his first of two US Amateur triumphs, Marvin "Bud" Ward agreed to venture from Olympia, Washington, for best-ball matches on behalf of the Canadian Fund for air-raid victims. About 1,000 Islanders paid one dollar to see Victoria's Taylor and Davey Black defeat the curly haired 26-year-old Ward and Ken Tucker, the Everett pro who was the Northwest Open champion.

The Point Grey billing was a 36-hole duel of the year's National Amateur champions, Ward and Ken Black. Ward led at the lunch break after taking two holes with stymies. The players agreed to forgo stymies in the afternoon and to slow down after playing the first 18 in 2 hours, 10 minutes. Under an unrelenting drizzle Ward prevailed, winning one-up.

Ralph Guldahl, the US Open champion in 1937 and 1938, and Johnny Revolta came in May 1940. They beat the Victoria twosome of pro Joe Pryke and amateur Ted Colgate at Colwood and then lost to Ken Black and pro Fred Wood when Black ran in a 35-footer downhiller at the 17th green.

Revolta, who had led the 1935 tour with $9,500, substituted for Sam Snead, who had been called home for his mother's funeral. After Black's putt, Guldahl told the green-side spectators that "the last time I was here, old Davey scored a hole-in-one . . . it must run in the family."

Some 1,500 fans were at Shaughnessy in the fall of 1944 to see Ken Black match Ben Hogan's 69 that raised $7,000 for the Air Force Benevolent Fund. Hogan and Taylor combined for a 3 and 2 win over Wood and Stan Leonard at Oak Bay. The Milk for Britain Fund match was refereed by Premier John Hart, an avid golfer and supporter of the game.

Byron Nelson made a number of visits to BC to play exhibitions
and would have won the Jubilee Open in 1936 had it not been
for the heroics of Ken Black. BC GOLF HOUSE 007.85.26

Hogan returned in October 1945, accompanied by Snead, prior to
the Seattle Open. They combined for a one-up verdict over Leonard and
Wood before about 2,500 onlookers at Shaughnessy. Snead carded 70,
Hogan 72, Wood 71 and Leonard 73.

Only 1,446 tickets were purchased, however, indicating that about
1,000 of the spectators had neglected to contribute a dollar despite
Hughie O'Callaghan's efforts as a circus barker. There wasn't much left
for the local pros or the PGA BC's promotional fund after $396 went to
income tax and $665 to Snead and Hogan.

Babe Zaharias, one of the finest female athletes ever, came to Victoria in 1949 for
a fundraiser at the urging of Marjorie Todd. A prodigious hitter, she told the crowd,
"I just loosen my girdle and let everything fly!" BC GOLF HOUSE 007.141.066

Byron Nelson monopolized the tour during 1944 and 1945 and his
perennial runner-up was Harold "Jug" McSpaden. Known as the Gold
Dust Twins they also toured together, twice teaming up to defeat Leonard
and Wood. They fired 65 and 67 at Marine Drive in 1943 and, in a
benefit for the Prisoners of War Fund before a record Quilchena crowd
of 3,500, won again the following year as Nelson took an eight on the
10th hole.

Bobby Locke, the South African with the unorthodox style, took
the 1947 tour by storm after whipping Snead 14 times in a 16-match
exhibition series in South Africa. After winning the Canadian Open and
finishing second only to Jimmy Demaret with over $20,000, Locke faced
Leonard in a fall Western Canada series. Playing for a $1,500 fee at Marine
Drive, Locke beat Leonard 2 and 1 while doing wonderful things with his
brassie and an ancient wooden-shafted putter for 4,000 witnesses.

Lloyd Mangrum, the first of the postwar champions, attracted
about 5,000 spectators for a clinic prior to the 1948 Canadian Open at
Shaughnessy. A twice-wounded war hero who was awarded the Purple

Heart after serving under General Patton at the Battle of the Bulge, Mangrum had beaten Nelson in a playoff for the 1946 US Open. Three years later he led the tour by earning $26,000. But it was Hogan and Snead who dominated the early postwar years, when purses escalated sharply and spelled the decline of exhibitions.

Leonard and Wood made a five-day promotional tour of the BC Interior in 1951 to promote the game on behalf of the PGA BC. They played in Kelowna, Kamloops, Penticton and Revelstoke. In Kamloops they played with Bob Affleck, the town mayor and club captain, and Leonard's brother, Bill. Stan and Trev Pickering shaded Wood and Monke Steele one-up at Kelowna. Wood fired a 67 at Revelstoke, Leonard 68. Al Nelson, assistant to Vancouver Club's Ernie Tate, partnered Wood while left-hander Ken Granstrom teamed with Leonard.

The legendary Babe Zaharias, who had first visited Victoria three years earlier, came to Shaughnessy in May 1952, when she and Wood lost to Leonard and Jock McKinnon 5 and 4. The greatest female athlete of all time had lost her putting touch but amazed the 3,000 spectators by frequently outdriving all but Leonard. "Why don't you put on a dress?" Zaharias quipped after her drive carried beyond the ball of McKinnon, who was known to play wearing a kilt. She underwent major cancer surgery the following year, returned to win the 1954 US Open and died in 1956.

Leonard's next appearance was at Marine Drive, his home course, in 1953. The occasion was Beat Ben Hogan Day, the forerunner to National Golf Day, and Leonard smashed Marine's newly lengthened course with a 30-32-62 onslaught while accompanied by members Reg Foulds, Harry Haddock and Frank Pateman. In all, 23 Marine members beat Hogan, who had 71 in Texas. No one's net score topped Leonard's. Leonard was the Davey Black of the day, the man everyone wanted for exhibitions and appearances—especially after his first two of three US tour victories. In 1958 Canadian Al Balding played a five-stop BC Centennial series in Kamloops, Kelowna, Penticton and Victoria and at Marine. Leonard started like a rocket, firing a course record seven-under at Penticton, and closed with a 67 at Marine. He was 17-under for the five rounds, collecting a $500 bonus for $2,700 overall to Balding's $2,300.

Stan Leonard and Al Balding ruled Canadian men's golf for over a decade, winning a combined four times on the PGA tour in 1957 and representing Canada at international team events including the Canada (World) Cup. BC GOLF HOUSE 007.128.197

Leonard's most unforgettable exhibition was captured on film in 1964 at the picturesque Capilano course. Almost 5,000 people were in the gallery for Leonard's *Shell Wonderful World of Golf* television match against George Knudson. The television production spanned the globe matching the world's best in a format that was widely viewed through the 1960s during a decade that averaged nine matches per year.

The tedious, yet thrilling production was staged over two days, a curtain of dusk falling on the 15th fairway the first day. Everyone in the gallery was urged to return for the closing holes the following day wearing the same clothes.

Leonard made up a stroke on each of the last three holes to match Knudson's six-under 66. They both earned $5,000 for the most protracted 66s in BC golf history.

Gallagher's Canyon Resort in Kelowna treated the public to two exhibitions involving leading US pros. Resort director Dick Munn's timing was exquisite when he brought in Fuzzy Zoeller and Andy Bean to play local amateurs Grant Barnes and Dean Claggett in 1984. Zoeller had won the US Open the month before.

Munn's entrepreneurial luck continued in 1991 when he whisked in four LPGA pros the day after the du Maurier Classic at Vancouver Golf Club. Earlier that year he had enlisted Meg Mallon before she captured both the US Open and LPGA championships. She joined Cindy Rarick, Hiromi Kobayashi and Kelowna's Gail Graham.

The Women's Pro Challenge event was decided by a chip-off, with Mallon beating Kobayashi after they had both toured the course in three-under 71. Mallon collected $5,000—the same amount that Joanne Carner had received 20 years earlier for winning the US Open.

THE WAR YEARS

During the world-war years, tournament golf in BC unceremoniously ground to a halt. Bullets and bombs suddenly supplanted the levity of birdies and bogeys.

Golf was virtually forgotten from 1914 through 1918 and almost all championship events were cancelled from 1941 through 1945 while the Allied Forces fought Germany and Japan.

During the First World War the exigencies of war created operational problems that resulted in the requisition of some clubhouses and even golf courses by the federal government. Sacrifice was the order of the day and many enthusiasts relinquished their memberships in fear of government reprisals for playing the game in wartime. Publicity for golf vanished with cancelled tournament schedules.

The postwar years weren't easy either. Alf Blinko, a young Englishman who was appointed Shaughnessy Heights pro in 1913, went to war and upon his return from France resigned his position. Nat Cornfoot, the St Andrews–born first Langara pro, was wounded while serving with the Cameron Highlanders and famed architect A.V. Macan's left leg was shattered from the knee down.

Vancouver Golf Club directors decided in March 1919 to extend full privileges from April through August to all returning servicemen and women. The free invitations were offered, the club announced, to provide the veterans with light exercise and open-air recreation to help restore their health. Golf was considered rehabilitation for both mind and body. For many it was a welcome relief that became a passion. "War is just like golf," humorist Will Rogers said in 1925. "Once a fellow takes it up, he won't let nothing interfere with it. "

Recreational golf came to another virtual standstill in 1940 as people of all walks of life rallied behind the war effort at home and abroad. Even private clubs were empty on many sunny summer weekends.

Pro shop shelves were empty soon after the declaration of war, as the raw materials used to manufacture golf clubs and balls went into the production of weaponry and ammunition. When the ball supplies were finally exhausted, old retrieved balls were repainted in the back shop and resold.

The rationing of gasoline also severely affected golf as it curtailed travel to some outlying courses. With so many members at war and those at home restrained from golfing, clubs were forced to lay off pros, greenskeepers and clubhouse staff. In many cases members had to assume the responsibilities of maintaining courses and providing clubhouse amenities.

One of the last prewar tournaments in Vancouver was the short-lived Western Canada Open, which Fred Wood won in 1940 at Capilano. While regular events remained in limbo through 1945, pros were encouraged to play exhibitions. The competitions were a welcome diversion from the pall of war and also stimulated war-bond drives. Several pros went into military service, of course.

Any collections from golf tournaments or functions staged during times of war went to the war effort. Clubs across the country held Spitfire Days competitions and collected more than $19,000 to donate to fighter plane construction. The women's section of the Ardmore club in Sidney managed to triple their fundraising goal; they raised $123 to help in the purchase of a Spitfire aircraft.

Women golfers also contributed to the Red Cross, and sent thousands of knitted clothing and bedding articles to Britain, and socks and cigarettes to the fighting forces.

On the home front, many pros left their shops to work in shipyards and aircraft plants. Stan Leonard toiled in a tool-and-die shop on weekdays and at Marine Drive on weekends. Quilchena pro Dave McLeod did intricate precision work at the Sea Island plant of Boeing Aircraft Ltd., where LaVerne Johnson of Hastings Park operated a yoder hammer, Langara pro Ben Colk was in charge of tooling in the hammer shop, Shaughnessy assistant Jack Cummings handled jig maintenance and amateur champion Ken Black was an expediter in the hammer shop.

In the difficult early years after the war, people were indifferent about resuming frivolous interests such as golf and other leisure activities. They were too busy trying to return to normal. The golf business suffered as few new courses were built. However, construction that had started on a course in Prince George before the war was completed in 1946; Castlegar and Dawson Creek were opened in 1947; Mount Brenton in Chemainus was playable in 1948; Cowichan's new course followed in 1949 and Quesnel had a course by 1950.

Many clubs in the bigger cities advertised membership drives, inviting newcomers at ridiculously cut-rate entrance fees. It was a prime time to join a club.

Military service had taken many leading players from the US tour, though most of them remained in the United States in the Special Services—a military euphemism for playing golf with the brass. Byron Nelson, exempted from the service because he had a form of hemophilia, cleaned up on the curtailed circuit. He hogged the headlines and prize purses in 1945 before many players, including Ben Hogan, were discharged from the service late that summer.

Nelson's marvellous run of 11 straight victories helped restore golf's impetus to that of the late 1930s. Golf fans everywhere were hungry for competition and their appetites were satisfied on the Lower Mainland.

The void of springtime tournaments was filled thanks to the creation in 1946 of the City Match Play Open. It was great spectator sport and a great boost to public morale, as reinvigorated people came out with the daffodils and daisies.

CHAPTER 16

BC'S AMATEUR AND OPEN CHAMPIONSHIPS

Both amateur and professional golf have a storied history
when it comes to province-wide competition, which has
often served as a breeding ground for young golfers who
later either joined the Canadian Tour or expanded their
golf horizons internationally.

THE BC AMATEURS

A December 1894 issue of the *Province*, then published in Victoria, reported,

Golfers had a very enjoyable day at the Oak Bay links last
Saturday when the championship of British Columbia
was contested for. It looked at one time as though a dark
day and unfavourable weather would spoil sport, but the
clouds lifted and nothing interfered with play except darkness coming on early as it does at this season.

Mr. W.E. Oliver was the winner with a score of 102,
Mr. W.A. Ward next at 112 and Messrs. H. Combe and
C.C. Worsfold, 113. In the handicap Mr. Worsfold was
the winner at 103, receiving 10 strokes. Sixteen entries
were received but none from the Mainland, which is much
to be regretted.

An agreeable surprise was in store for the members
when . . . Mr. Hewitt Bostock generously donated 50 dollars for the purchase of a championship cup.

The 100th anniversary of the amateur golf championship of British Columbia actually fell in 1994 but organizers dismissed the inaugural competition when setting their centennial celebration for the following year. The first competition concluded without the presentation of silverware in 1894, so it is possible that they only began recording the tournament when William Edgar Oliver, a 28-year-old lawyer, became the first recipient of the Bostock Trophy in 1895.

Oliver's name was the first engraved on the Bostock Trophy after he beat 13 challengers with 87, eight better than Combe and Worsfold. Oliver repeated in 1896 by defeating a scratch player from Duncan named Fred Maitland-Dougal 85 strokes to 90. That year, the entry fee for the nine contestants was fifty cents.

Starting in 1897, and every year thereafter until the beginning of the First World War, the tournament adopted a match-play format to determine a champion. That shift would prove that Oliver obviously preferred medal play, as over the next five years he reached the final only twice, losing both times. After the format changed to head-to-head competition, Harvey Combe, who played to a five handicap, thrived. Combe's record of nine BC championships was considered untouchable until Doug Roxburgh came along in 1969, claiming the first of his 13 provincial victories spread over a 27-year period.

The tournament was conducted exclusively at the Victoria Golf Club until its post–First World War renewal. Players from Vancouver and Tacoma, however, participated as early as 1898 when Dr. Jack Carruthers of Jericho shot 84 to lower Oliver's course record by a stroke and L.B. Keyser of Vancouver lost to Combe in the semifinal.

Oliver won the 1900 handicap open with 81 before A.H. Goldfinch took the first of his two successive Bostocks. While beaten by Goldfinch in the 1901 final, Oliver prospered off the course and invested wisely in real estate. He served eight years as reeve of Oak Bay between 1906 and 1916.

Only Charles Prior, another golfing barrister, could stop Combe during the next five years, winning in 1905. Combe, who shot a record 72 early in 1907, was visiting England when 18 entrants, including Mr. Waghorn from Vancouver, competed with Victoria physician R.H. Stirling. He scored the most lopsided victory in the championship's history at 11 and 10. His victim, Jack Rithet, could be excused to some extent as he was only in his second season of golf.

While Combe won twice more in the next seven years, so did newcomer A.V. Macan, who won tight final matches that went to the final hole in both 1912 and 1913.

Upon resumption of the championship in 1919, Bob Bone emerged as the first mainlander to claim the Bostock Cup. He had gone to Victoria after winning three straight Vancouver championships. Only three other mainland players were in the 24-man competition— A.C. Stewart, Bone's Vancouver Golf Club mate, and the Shaughnessy Heights duo of Alfred Bull and William Ward, a veteran originally from Victoria. In the end Bone prevailed 6 and 4 over a courageous Macan, who had limped home from fighting in Europe only days before the tournament.

The first Amateur championship venue off Vancouver Island was conducted at Shaughnessy Heights in 1920 when the event started to alternate annually between the Victoria area and the mainland. That year April showers fell as snowflakes, delaying the start for the 49 competitors. To make up lost time the scheduled 36-hole semifinals had to be reduced to 18. Co-medalists with 78 were A.E. Mountefield of the host club and H.P. Gardiner of VGC. Macan followed with 81 while defender Bone took 87. Two players who shot 95 were the last of 32 qualifiers for the championship flight. Under skies cleared by brisk winter-like winds, Shaughnessy club captain Reg Symes claimed the Bostock by defeating Gardiner on the first extra hole.

The intrepid Macan returned to the final in 1921 only to lose at Royal Colwood to Victor Price, a lefthander from the United Service Club, who had earlier that summer won the inaugural Victoria City Amateur. In 1922 Bone regained the trophy in an all–Vancouver Club final at Burquitlam. He turned back Jimmy Yellowlees, the grim, old campaigner who had qualified by firing a course record of 76 on the heels of 92. Biggerstaff Wilson of Victoria, future president of the BCGA, was a medallist with 161.

Jimmy Yellowlees, complete with pipe and wristband, was the 1912 Vancouver Golf Club champion, and runner-up that year in the BC Amateur. COQUITLAM 100 YEARS

Golfers from the Seattle–Tacoma area dominated until the 1930s, save victories by Harry Jones of Shaughnessy in 1924 and young Dick Moore of Victoria in 1927. Bernie Schwengers, Victoria's top-ranked tennis player, was no match for Chuck Spiers of Seattle in 1923; tall Bon Stein, a leading Northwest player, turned back Vancouver's Cec Coville; and Chuck Hunter of Tacoma took the measure of future politician Jack Westland and 18-year-old Norm Wallace of Victoria in 1929. Stein had lost the year before to Tom "Babe" McHugh, also of Seattle.

The durable Moore became 1927 champion by beating Bill Davidson of Seattle during a hailstorm at Oak Bay. After moving to Vancouver, Moore won again at his new home course, Quilchena, by upsetting Stan Leonard in 1934. In 1958 Moore reappeared in the final, 31 years after his first victory, only to lose to then Marine Drive clubmate Bob Kidd.

Ken Black and Leonard were, of course, major figures during the 1930s. Black's introduction to championship golf in 1930 was a rude awakening at VGC. He was blitzed 10 and 8 by Fred Wood, the fair-haired protégé of Burquitlam pro Jimmy Huish. In six of the next nine championships, either Black or Leonard was a finalist, but Islanders Harold Brynjolfson and Ken Lawson prevailed at Uplands in 1931 and 1937. In the last major event at Jericho, Don Gowan of Point Grey defeated Frank "Tick" Willey of Langara for the 1938 crown. A year later Black counted his third and last title at Victoria, 3 and 2 over Ted Colgate, a local tire salesman.

Seattle's Harry Givan won the last prewar Amateur, beating fellow American Gerry Bert in 1940 at Marine Drive before a five-year hiatus. In 1946 Lyle Hurschman—a big, chain-smoking, future tugboat captain who played out of Langara—followed Leonard as only the second public course player to win the BC Amateur when he upset Ken Black at Point Grey.

The all–Marine Drive final of 1947 at Uplands went to hard-hitting Hugh Morrison, 4 and 3 over Monty Hill. Controversy ruled the day, however, when an incensed Roy Stone, who had ventured to Victoria from the Rossland–Trail club where his brother Reg was pro, had his amateur status questioned. In the semifinals against Morrison, Stone, who enjoyed a four-hole lead at the clubhouse turn, was informed by his caddy that he had overheard officials questioning his amateur status. Irate at the city folks questioning his integrity, Stone later said that he deliberately lost four of the next eight holes. Morrison postponed Stone's plan to self-destruct by three-putting 18 but Stone took no chance on the first extra hole. "I was so cheesed off being investigated as pro, I purposely chipped one-handed over the green at the first extra hole and Hughie made a four-footer to win," recalled a still-angry Stone many years later.

The Amateur's first "working man's final" matched the unlikeliest of 1948 characters: Percy Clogg and Walt McAlpine. Clogg, a wiry unemployed bookkeeper, had been reinstated as an amateur in 1947 after three pro seasons. A delightful man, he frequently wore a silly grin, gaudy flowered shirts and a white peaked cap, and constantly whistled "Bluebird of Happiness" while sauntering between shots. McAlpine, a 35-year-old fireman from Langara Glenoaks, had narrowly beaten his clubmate Hurschman on the seventh extra hole before losing 3 and 2 to Clogg at VGC.

Preparing for the long ride to Quebec City for the 1947 Willingdon Cup, BC team (L to R) alternate Bill Mawhinney, Hugh Morrison, Jim Robertson, Percy Clogg and Walt McElroy pose on the Trans-Canada Airlines staircase in Vancouver. BC GOLF HOUSE 007.128.028

Clogg defended successfully in 1949, by which time the tournament was no longer alternating between Vancouver and Victoria courses and stayed instead at Quilchena. Whistling Percy took three days off as an Exhibition Park parimutuel clerk and persevered in the final by laying a clinching stymie to beat Austrian-born Hans Swinton 2 and 1 in a sloppy match.

In 1950 Jim Squire emerged from Oak Bay as a one-tournament flash, the first Islander to win since Ken Lawson's 1937 triumph over Russ Case. Squire beat 19-year-old Bob Fleming of Gorge Vale at the 37th hole. The enigmatic Fleming also lost the 1951 final in extra holes, at the 38th to Bill Mawhinney. Mawhinney repeated in 1952 by clipping the adversarial Walt McElroy one-up at Marine Drive before Bob Fleming finally got the job done in the 1953 championship match, 4 and 2 over Jackie Reynolds at Royal Colwood. Fleming was never heard from again.

After the end of the war Walt McElroy and Bill Mawhinney played on
a total of 10 Willingdon Cup teams, three times as teammates. In the
1952 BC Amateur, the lanky Mawhinney prevailed in the final
over McElroy at Marine Drive, one-up. BC GOLF HOUSE 007.85.128

The next source of excitement was the back-to-back victories of Lyle
Crawford, the cocky, talented eastender, who first iced the iceman, Bob
Kidd, and then in 1955 took care of popular fellow public course player
Babe Goodfellow. Spokane's Rod Funseth defeated unassuming Gordon
MacKenzie in 1956, right at the beginning of the "Kidd era," when Bob
Kidd reached the BC final six for the next eight years, winning three
times. His first two finals victims were seven-time Vancouver Club cham-
pion Frank Proctor and his veteran clubmate Dick Moore. In 1958 the
29-year-old had reached the final by defeating medallist Doug Bajus on
the 19th and then Bert Ticehurst, a respected local lacrosse star.

Ticehurst then fell in the 1959 quarter-finals to 23-year-old Ron
Willey. The nephew of 1938 finalist Frank Willey then disposed of two
Bobs—lawyer Bob Plonuner and the perennial favourite Bob Kidd—
before taking his girlfriend dancing.

Before disappearing from competitive golf, Bob Fleming won both the 1953 BC Amateur at Royal Colwood and the Pacific Northwest Golf Championship, the only golfer to ever accomplish that double in the same year. BC GOLF HOUSE 007.144.015

Dick Munn and Joe Jeroski, two promising young players, were beaten in the next two finals, falling to Laurie Kerr and Kidd, who won his third and final Amateur in 1961. The next year a flamboyant 23-year-old from Victoria named Billy Wakeham stopped Kidd's bid for a fourth win; he then repeated by trouncing Blake Cramb of Powell River 5 and 3. At Richmond against Cramb in 1963, Wakeham became the first Islander to be awarded the Bostock on the mainland. Wakeham later also won back-to-back BC Open crowns—the first and only man to ever successfully defend both championships.

The first Amateur staged outside Victoria-Vancouver went to Ticehurst at Kelowna Golf and Country Club. The memorable 1964 match was Kidd's farewell appearance as an amateur.

John Russell of Point Grey was then set to inherit Kidd's place in the

Long-time McCleery teaching pro and 1962 Canadian PGA champion Alvie Thompson is surrounded by three BC Amateur champs, Johnny Johnston to his right, with Lyle Crawford and John Russell to his left. BILL CUMMINGHAM

hierarchy. He lost the 1965 final at home to Canadian Junior champion Wayne Vollmer, and made his first of a record 11 successive Willingdon Cup appearances. Russell's victims in the 1967 and 1968 BC finals were carpenter Bud Bird and Art Donaldson, a fun-loving former pro turned greenskeeper, notorious for his diabolical tournament pin placements at Capilano where he was course superintendent.

Then, in 1969, Doug Roxburgh arrived. He started that year by besting John Morgan in the final played at Richmond, 4 and 3. One-timer Carl Schwantje had his day in the sun in 1971 before the tournament switched to medal play in 1972 and Roxburgh shot 279 to finish 11 ahead of his neighbour Russell while overwhelming the field at Royal Colwood.

Roxburgh won a stunning 10 of 20 tournaments played over two decades through 1991. When he wasn't winning, the champions were Bob Mitchell, Jim Nelford, Fred Couples, Sandy and Jamie Harper, Steve Berry, Ed Beauchemin, Brian Wells, Gary Puder and Rob Anderson, who all won one each with Roxburgh nipping at their heels to finish second another five times.

Nelford defeated Roxburgh in a 1975 playoff at Nanaimo and the smooth-swinging Freddie Couples, the public course player from Seattle who went on to earn millions on tour, dominated on Roxburgh's home course in 1979. The Harpers of Nanaimo became the only brothers to win the Bostock—first Sandy at Castlegar in 1980 and Jamie two years later at Shaughnessy. Ed Beauchemin, a one-time greenskeeper at Glen Meadows, made his mark in 1984 and eventually turned pro as did Mission's hard-hitting Brian Wells, who won in 1985 when the tournament used both Cranbrook Kimberley layouts.

Gary Puder's 1987 victory at Kamloops Rivershore was a triumph for veterans. His belated first major win came at age 49, making him the oldest Amateur champion in at least 40 years. Ironically, it came on a course widely rated as one of the province's most demanding, especially when a westerly howls up the North Thompson River. The secondary school vice-principal from VGC, who had made a career out of placing second or third, carded three-under 285, two better than Roxburgh and Berry.

Roxburgh's edge was one stroke each of the next two years, at Ledgeview-Pitt Meadows and at Castlegar-Birchbank, before Anderson thrived in a gale at the Nanaimo course the final round of 1990. Anderson birdied the third extra hole against Jeff Kraemer, who literally blew a six-stroke advantage, closing with 79. Only Anderson, with two 73s, and veteran Dave Mick, 70-78, broke 150 on the final weekend. Roxburgh regained the Bostock for the 11th title in 1991 with a one-shot victory over the omnipresent Steve Berry.

Berry and Roxburgh were in final round contention at Chilliwack in 1992, but in the end it was Anderson and Andrew Smeeth, the intense former BC Junior champion from nearby Ledgeview in Abbotsford, who came through. Smeeth's world was temporarily shattered when Anderson chipped in from the 18th fringe for a birdie-three that precluded a play-off. Berry had stayed in contention by, remarkably, scoring eagle-three on the same hole—the 485-yard fifth—on each of the four days. Almost 100 years earlier in 1894, W.E. Oliver would have been thrilled with the four pars during his round of 102 that were good enough for BC's first Amateur championship.

Smeeth took revenge the following year at the VGC course by besting Anderson by two, and the following year Darren Griff bested Bryn Perry by five at Kelowna.

The next two years saw a resurgence of the amazing Roxburgh as he won his final two Amateurs in 1995 and 1996 at Castlegar and Shaughnessy. The tournament then embarked on a five-year journey around the province, playing courses like Predator Ridge, Prince George and the idyllic Storey Creek track in Campbell River. During this time new champions Dan Norton, Kurt Cassidy, Brad Newman-Bennett, Gordie Scutt and Matt Makinson emerged.

And then came James Lepp, the only young amateur to stay on top long enough to claim a legitimate comparison to Doug Roxburgh. Lepp had made his Amateur debut in 2001 at the age of 17. He was prepared for top competition after winning successive Canadian Junior titles and at Royal Colwood he finished third in his first Amateur, four strokes behind the winner, Matt Makinson, and only one fewer than Roxburgh had needed to win there 29 years earlier.

He was well primed for his run of four straight triumphs. Like Roxburgh, Lepp was first crowned at Richmond where, in 2002, he finished six strokes clear of Dan Swanson and Andrew Lovas with a 278 total. The following summer his margin was four over Kent Eger with 276 at Fort St. John's Lakepoint Golf and Country Club. Playing on two courses at Vernon and Spallumcheen in 2004, Lepp bettered by two Roxburgh's 20-year-old tournament record with 270. He closed with 65 and 66. At 22 James Lepp became the first and only player to ever win the BC Amateur more than three times when he topped James Allenby by four at Gorge Vale in 2005.

Lepp had moved on to new adventures in 2006 when Bryan Toth won over the picturesque Golden Golf Club. The following year at Morningstar, near Qualicum Beach, Mitch Gillis beat dynamo Adam Hadwin by three. The emergence of young talent continued into 2008 as Eugene Wong bested Parker Lily in playoff while Hadwin stood alone in third place at Marine Drive.

The next year at Duncan Lakes, Daniel Brown, a father of three from Creston, leaped over Mill Bay's Brady Johnson on the back nine, by going five-under for the day. Meanwhile his rival made a triple at 13 and lost by one.

In 2010 the young blood kept flowing thanks to Adam Svensson, who had won the BC Junior Boys only two weeks before his five-stroke victory at Castlegar. The 2011 winner was David Rose of West Vancouver, who came from behind with the aid of a balky putter in the hands of co-runner-up Richard Jung and Royal Colwood's Kevin Carrigan.

THE BC OPEN

The first official BC Open was actually a closed tournament. It was a mere sideshow to the day's primary events—the Pacific Northwest and provincial amateur championships.

In the spring of 1928 Davey Black, Phil Taylor and a few other professionals, clannishly close and craving competition with a pot of prize money at the end of it, staged their own little championship. It was open only to residents of the province. The pros graciously decided to allow amateurs to play under their club handicaps "in order to give them every possible chance to show their stuff and get a shot at the prizes."

Two years before, in 1926 at Jericho, the amateur BCGA had staged an open tournament in conjunction with its annual provincial championships. Yakima pro Neil Christian beat the mixed field by shooting 295 over the two days of double rounds. He was six strokes better than Seattle's Bon Stein, the 1925 Amateur champion, and seven ahead of runner-up pro Bert Wilde of Bellingham. Taylor's 305 led the BC entrants.

Without the patronage of amateurs—that is, without their entry fees—the Opens as conducted by the PGA BC would have amounted to nothing more than regular honey-pot competitions among several foursomes of pros. They would have been playing only for their own entry fees. Amateurs still furnish the support required to finance open events such as the BC Open and match-play opens that were organized as supplementary postwar events. The Open wouldn't be viable even today without the lucrative pro-amateur preludes, and match-play tournaments in Vancouver and Victoria couldn't exist without amateurs' entry fees.

When Black and his cohorts put together their own open, corporate sponsorship was still several decades away. In the inaugural official Open of 1928, nine pros were in the field of 49 players who paid five-dollar entry fees. Club donations supplemented the purse, so that six of the pros made the money list and shared $650. The US Open that year offered $2,145. In near-perfect fall conditions, they toured Shaughnessy Heights twice on successive days.

The tournament-tough Black easily walked off with the first Open title over his home course with a 292 total that newspapers described as "only four over par, a remarkable golfing feat." Black finished 13 strokes clear of second-place Dunc Sutherland. Oak Bay's Taylor was the only other player under 310 while Fred Wood took amateur honours with 317. Moore, the 1927 Amateur champion, could do no better than 322.

For four years the tournament was the preserve of Black and Taylor. They alternated winning until Black's 19-year-old son, Ken, scored a stunning 1932 victory by a stroke over Don Sutherland at Jericho. The pros had been forewarned. The year before, an Uplands gallery of 2,000 inspired local amateur Bob Morrison to chase Taylor to victory. Don Sutherland finished second for the third time by losing to Taylor's 286 at his Burquitlam course in 1933. But the unobtrusive Scot had his day a year later at Colwood, where he outdistanced precocious Uplands teenager Ken Lawson for his only BC title. Lawson had been the sensation of the Open three years earlier when, aged only 14, he opened with 72 and shot 309.

On the heels of Ken Black, Morrison and Lawson came two more brilliant youngsters—Fred Wood and Stan Leonard. After powering to his second Amateur championship in 1935, Leonard tied Sutherland for second behind Wood, who had turned pro at Fraser. It was the ruddy-faced

Wood's first of three Open triumphs and the beginning of a runner-up jinx that clung to Leonard like Cariboo mud for six long, straight years. Leonard's closing 66 at Marine in 1936 fell one short of catching Russ Case, a noted snooker player before he took up golf and who became the Open's second amateur winner. Ben Colk, then Jericho assistant pro, and Don Sutherland split the top money, four strokes behind Case's 277.

Case was probably the tournament's most improbable champion. He had gone to war with the First Canada Pioneers at 18, didn't play golf until he was 30 and won the Open at 39. Marine's club champion in only his second year of golf, Case worked as a shoe salesman, dance teacher and special policeman with the compensation board. On the eve of the final round, an amateur psychic had told Case that he couldn't "see anybody beating you." The following summer Lawson beat Case one-up in the Amateur final.

Leonard decided to play for pay in 1937 and made his pro debut by winning the Alberta Open. But at the second and last Open staged at Victoria Golf Club, he lost to Jimmy Todd, club champion of the Oak Bay links. Todd, the only left-handed Open winner, also turned pro soon after and went to New York as a disciple of Texan Ralph Guldahl, the US Open champion in 1937 and 1938.

In 1938 players outside the province were first welcomed to compete in the Open, though Fred Wood's dominance continued both that year and in 1939. He topped Leonard by six strokes at Shaughnessy and by one at Point Grey. He would most probably have added several more titles but for the suspension of tournaments during the war. Upon resumption of events in 1946, his priorities had changed dramatically. Black had retired the year before and Wood's dream job was at hand. He was Shaughnessy's choice to succeed the grand old pro from Troon.

The 1946 formation of BC's section of the Canadian PGA coincided with the Open's first four-figure purse—$1,000—and the emergence of Chuck Congdon. The poker-faced club pro from Tacoma would make more headlines in BC than in the state of Washington.

The Leonard–Congdon confrontations that endured for almost a decade made for the hottest rivalry in BC golf history. They took turns at finishing one-two eight times during a nine-year stretch through 1954.

In 1948, the BC Open was played at Quilchena where Chuck Congdon (centre) bested defending champ Stan Leonard (right) and Bob Bolton. VANCOUVER PUBLIC LIBRARY 84176B

In 1946 Congdon made an uncharacteristic entrance at Uplands. He raced to the Victoria course from the ferry slip, arriving 10 minutes before his scheduled tee-off time. After closing with rounds of 65 and 68, he slipped away with $250 for a three-stroke triumph over Stan Leonard.

Leonard's frustration with being anchored second mercifully ended in 1947 when he dethroned Congdon by two strokes after shooting 277 on the verdant slopes of Capilano in West Vancouver. But the balding Congdon struck back the next year. Already the 1948 Canadian Open champion, a title he had captured at Shaughnessy Heights, Congdon won the BC Open at Quilchena. Leonard, however, won in both 1949 and 1950. With Congdon absent from the first of these two events, the Marine pro humbled the 1949 field by manufacturing 271 in the wind, rain and snow at Point Grey to post a record 19-stroke victory. He also collected $450 first money at Marine in 1950, using his home advantage to beat Congdon by two shots.

In the next three years Congdon topped Leonard by 9 strokes at Rossland-Trail, 3 at Shaughnessy and a whopping 11 at Quilchena. In the 1953 tournament, Quilchena Amateur star Bill Mawhinney made his pro debut where he had learned the game; he collected $200 for placing third behind the two giants.

They returned for a farewell battle at Quilchena in 1954 and Leonard, priming himself for the American Tour, prevented his adversary from a fourth straight title by winning the tournament's first playoff. Tied at 210 with Leonard and Congdon were Portland pro Johnny Langford and Doug Bajus, the gangling amateur stalwart from Point Grey.

Times were extremely difficult and in their wisdom PGA BC sages decided to milk the situation for what it was worth. The officials opted for an 18-hole playoff the next day—a Sunday—rather than an immediate sudden-death affair. Another gallery of nearly 2,000 paying customers returned to Quilchena.

Leonard and Langford, still tied after the extra 18, parred one sudden-death hole before darkness halted the proceedings. The PGA BC asked the unemployed Langford to come all the way back from Portland the following Sunday. Before 1,000 spectators, Leonard took the $450 top-place prize with a 68 to Langford's 71. In what turned out to be the longest Open in history, and possibly the longest extended-play tournament in modern golf history, the original 54-hole event turned into 91 holes being played over an 11-day period.

By 1955 Leonard had left the relative comforts of Marine for the nomadic life of the PGA tour. That same year many of professional golf's premier players were lured to the BC Open because of an expanded prize pool. PGA tour purses averaged $21,700 that year and many leading players were lured to Shaughnessy because the event schedule fell on the heels of the prior week's Portland Open and the US Open, which had been held two weeks before at San Francisco's Olympic Club.

L.L.B. "Poldi" Bentley, the local lumber magnate who was a great fan and supporter of the game, underwrote the $15,000 budget for the three-day July event, which included the added enticement of a players' Howe Sound fishing trip for avid anglers.

Bill Mawhinney's abbreviated swing resulted from a neck
restriction, but it didn't stop him from winning two BC
Amateurs and the 1957 BC Open. BC GOLF HOUSE 007.85.50

Sam Snead, Mike Souchak, Bob Rosburg, Tommy Bolt, Ted Kroll,
Art Wall and Marty Furgol came. So did Julius Boros—who led the year's
money list with $63,121—and a charging rookie named Arnold Palmer.

Another tour newcomer, 25-year-old Dow Finsterwald, left Vancouver
with the top money of $2,400 for his second win of the year. It was a sign
of things to come for the slender, conservative Finsterwald; in the next
five years he finished no worse than third in tour earnings and in 1958
won the PGA title and Vardon Trophy for the lowest stroke average. He
prevailed at Shaughnessy with rounds of 67, 68, 65 and 70, one better
than young Bud Holscher of Apple Valley, California. Holscher missed
forcing a playoff by blowing a 30-inch putt on the 72nd hole.

Snead tied Souchak and Rosburg at 274, four behind Finsterwald. Snead was pacified with his limit of salmon; Souchak was disappointed after practice rounds of 62 and 65; and the surly Rosburg sulked off after holding the halfway lead on rounds of 65 and 67.

A closing 65 for 282 brought some solace and $170 for Leonard. Boros, whose son would be BC champion 36 years later, took an $82.50 share of the last money. Arnold Palmer, who made that year's Canadian Open his first of 61 tour victories, picked up during the final day after rounds of 70, 74 and 68. Congdon's 285 missed the money but he returned in 1956 and beat off the brazen Lyle Crawford for his sixth and last Open title. They played off at Point Grey after tying at 139.

The Open, without a sponsor, was also a mere two-day affair in 1957 and Mawhinney used his muscle at Vancouver Club to beat Willey. Dead-stymied by a waterpipe on the old 18th fairway, the brisk-playing Mawhinney simply flexed his biceps and bent back the pipe rather than waiting for a ruling. He chipped to the green, righted the pipe and made par for a one-shot victory.

Member Walt McAlpine closed with a competitive course record 65 but fell two short of matching Mawhinney's 140.

Tournament organization was still in disarray during the following two years. After being cancelled in 1958 rather than fall in the shadow of the BC Centennial Invitational, the Open resumed in 1959. That year, Crawford got the better of Congdon in a sudden-death playoff at Point Grey.

Crawford and Congdon were both moved aside in 1960 and 1961 by Bob Duden of Portland. After Duden destroyed Marine Drive in 1960, shaky putters throughout the Northwest began experimenting with his croquet-style stroke. His strange between-the-legs method—which was also adopted by Sam Snead—was subsequently banned. He blitzed Marine Drive with rounds of 68, 64, 69 and 67 not because of his putting prowess, but on the strength of hitting 69 greens in regulation figures.

In 1961 Chilliwack had taken on the troubled event through the efforts of pro Roy Gleig and Penfold rep Duncan MacKenzie. Soliciting businesses from Vancouver to Chilliwack, they scrounged up a kitty of $1,200 to keep the event afloat. This Open can lay claim to the most bizarre ending, but one that confirmed the integrity of Chuck Congdon. It happened on the second green adjacent to the main roadway and within earshot of the course entranceway. Duden had made his par-four on the short birdie hole and Congdon was hunched over his 10-footer for a winning three. As the calm veteran addressed the putt, an ignorant motorist burned rubber as he screeched away from the course. Congdon flinched at the obvious distraction and stepped away from the ball. After finally leaving the putt inches short, he offered a congratulatory hand to the startled Duden. Duden, moving toward the third tee, was as confused as the gallery. Returning to the clubhouse, Congdon explained that he had inadvertently touched the ball while addressing it the first time and he called himself on the infraction no one else had seen. "The blade of my putter moved the ball when I backed off it," he shrugged. "Those are the breaks of the game." He never challenged for another Open title and died at the age of 55 in February 1965.

MacKenzie stayed on to manage the Open in 1962 when Tooke/Van Heusen came on board as its first commercial sponsor. Appropriately, the new Shaughnessy course hosted the event; Jack Sim, general manager of Tooke/Van Heusen, happened to be a five-time Shaughnessy club champion. The company sponsored the Open through 1967 and didn't lose its shirt despite the doubters who had witnessed the tournament's decline. MacKenzie, a stubborn but diligent and efficient organizer, proudly boasted that the Open never lost money while he was in charge.

At that time there was still plenty of golf left in Stan Leonard. In 1962 he chipped in to birdie the first extra hole and beat Spokane's Rod Funseth, who lipped out with his birdie chip after they had tied with two-over-par 290 scores on the wet Shaughnessy course. The next year, in a third successive playoff, Leonard hooked his drive into trees at Point Grey's old second hole and lost the 1963 title to Al "Tiger" Feldman, the likeable craggy-faced character from Tacoma who was never without a smile or white Hogan cap. Dick Munn, the youthful host pro, Portland pro Tom Marlow and amateur Gary Fawcett of Vancouver missed the playoff by one stroke.

The colourful Bill Wakeham was a competitor and a club pro with yarns to spin, both on and off the course. BILL CUNNINGHAM

Ken Still, another Tacoma tour pro on the verge of quitting the game, was enticed to the Vancouver Club in 1964 and clipped Feldman by a stroke. Spokane product Al Mengert took the new Chuck Congdon Memorial Trophy in 1965 after winning by three over veteran amateur Johnny Johnston.

At 54, Feldman became the oldest Open winner in 1966 at Point Grey and a decade later the original "Tiger" tied for 12th at Quilchena in his 25th consecutive tournament appearance.

It had been 30 years since an amateur had won when Johnston was victorious at Marine Drive in 1967 after shooting 200 over three rounds on a course that he and Leonard both knew so well. Leonard's 203 took low pro money of $1,400 from the $7,000 purse, with Dick Munn another five back in third.

Carling Breweries sponsored provincial Opens on the Canadian Tour in 1968, boosting the BC purse to $10,000 and then to $15,000 in 1969. Victoria's colourful Bill Wakeham, who had turned pro to accept a prize boat for scoring a hole-in-one at a VGC event, won both Carling-sponsored Opens. He shaded Alvie Thompson by a stroke at Shaughnessy in 1968 and repeated before a frenzied home crowd of 4,000 fans and at least 400 relatives at Uplands the following year. Beer gave way to nicotine as Peter Jackson took over the tour in 1970 and Brian "Buddy" Allin's victory at Richmond provided a launching pad to a PGA Tour career. The decorated Vietnam War veteran from Bremerton, Washington, went on to capture five tour victories.

After tying three others for second behind Allin, a former Canadian Junior champion, Wayne Vollmer found himself in another logjam in the closing holes of the 1971 Open at Marine.

Wakeham, the irrepressible Moe Norman, ex-footballer Tom Nettles and an 18-year-old BC Junior champion from Langley Newlands named Scott Keenlyside were tied in a knot and warming up for a playoff as Vollmer, in the final group, studied his 90-yard approach to the 18th green. The strapping tour pro needed a birdie to join the playoff for the $3,000 top money. About 4,000 spectators watched the flight of the approach shot and roared as one when the ball landed in the hole for an eagle-two and sudden victory.

Visiting strangers who answered to Terry Small, Gary Bowerman and Jim Barker triumphed through 1974 before burly Dave Barr dominated with three victories in four years, a string only interrupted in 1976 by Victoria amateur Cec Ferguson who won at Quilchena on the strength of a four-iron shot he holed for eagle-two at the 14th. Barr, a young man of destiny, had broken through at Quilchena the previous year. He repeated at Marine in 1977, one stroke to the good of local amateur

Wayne Vollmer won the BC Amateur in 1965 and the BC Open in 1971. He played 43 events in a brief PGA career before settling into a career as a club pro. BILL CUNNINGHAM

Doug Roxburgh and Washington touring pro Rick Acton. When tobacco companies collectively started to drop sports sponsorships, Prince George Breweries brought the BC Open north to their home venue in 1978 for the only time in the event's history. Barr triumphed again.

Jim Rutledge, then an enigmatic young talent from Victoria, commanded attention when two Victoria hotels underwrote the event at Glen Meadows, a long, difficult course in Sidney. Rutledge beat Dan Halldorson to win in 1979. The next year at the same venue he lost by one stroke to Don Bies, the classy Seattle veteran. Rutledge then scored a seven-shot win in 1981 when Chilliwack was revisited.

George Williams Moving and Storage took over as the primary sponsor for the next nine years and the tournament stayed at Point Grey for eight straight summers through 1989. That was a strong decade for BC golf. Dick Zokol, Jim Nelford, Sandy Harper and Rick Gibson, locals all,

Watching the true sunset of the BC Open, this crowd at Predator Ridge watches the final hole of a tournament that would be cancelled the following year due to lack of sponsorship.
BC GOLF HOUSE 007.131.004

were champions before American Jim Hallet's one-shot conquest of Barr in 1986. By this point, with Expo 86 thrusting Vancouver and British Columbia onto the world stage, the BC Open was a $100,000 affair.

The quiet, fair-haired Gibson went on to thrive on the Asian tour while Hallet eventually progressed to the PGA Tour, as did 1987 BC Open champion Jim Benepe, a slightly built pro from Utah who caused a sensation by winning in his US tour debut. Portland's Dave Delong followed his Open win in 1988 with the big tour as well.

Rutledge was brilliant in 1989, matching Bob Duden's 1960 tournament record of 268 at Point Grey, two clear of his pal Gibson and Mexico's Carlos Espinosa. The victory brought him his third and final Open conquest.

The monsoon-abbreviated 1990 Open bogged down at VGC as winner Brandt Jobe of Colorado somehow squeegeed a record 64 out of the sopping Burquitlam course. He reigned with 203 as torrential rain washed out the scheduled fourth round.

Williams stepped aside as sponsor in 1991 and Xerox came to the fore as the Open returned to Point Grey. Guy Boros, the jovial son of Julius, was the big winner of the $160,000 tournament but the Open was a big loser at the gate. With many high-profile players known to local followers absent and a purse reduced to $100,000, the Open flopped again in 1992. A feud over sponsorship priorities between the operating PGA BC and the Canadian Tour fuelled adverse publicity that the tournament could have done without. The infighting was resolved but the smallest Open crowds since the 1960s witnessed Perry Parker's victory.

PGA BC tournament director Cec Ferguson and the Open sponsors, Xerox Canada, continued with the troubled tournament but took it to a new market in 1993, the two-year-old Predator Ridge course south of Vernon. Poor late-June weather plagued the event, which attracted only a scattering of spectators and minimal media attention outside of the Okanagan. The winner was a freewheeling blond California beach boy named Eric Woods, who preferred surf to turf. In dire financial straits, the Open was doomed to collapse. Perhaps inevitably, it was discontinued by the PGA BC after the 1993 event.

BC AND THE CANADIAN TOUR

The Canadian Tour as it exists today is largely based on the format established more than four decades ago. After 1970, when Imperial Tobacco was still allowed to sponsor sporting events, the old Peter Jackson Tour pooled up to $200,000 per season to finance seven or eight tournaments played across Canada from coast to coast. After 1978, with new legislation restricting tobacco advertising looming large, the tour folded and only a few regional events were able to carry on. While George Williams brought some stability to BC in the form of the BC Open for a number of years, other parts of the country were not so fortunate.

Within the Canadian Professional Golf Association, touring pros formed the Tournament Players Division. By 1985 they had selected Bob Beauchemin as their president, with the mandate to "build, promote and conduct tournaments of the Canadian Tour to develop Canadian professional golfers to a world-class level." The Tournament Players Association

(TPA) was formed as an independent, non-profit entity; today the TPA is the governing body of the Canadian Tour. It oversees a growing series of summer tournaments in Canada, as well as winter/spring events in the United States and South America. The association represents more than 200 members and is a full member of the International Federation of PGA Tours. The Canadian Tour has proven to be an outstanding training ground for PGA tour success.

Although it took until 1989 for all tournaments to play 72 holes, the Canadian Tour began attracting players from around the world in the mid-1980s. It has gained status as one of only 10 tours where players can earn world ranking points and now attracts players from Australia, New Zealand, South America and Europe. About half the players are Americans and one-quarter are Canadian.

It was here that Mike Weir, the winner of eight PGA tour titles, including the 2003 Masters, earned Rookie of the Year honours in 1993.

In early 2012, the Canadian Tour, facing economic challenges, received financial support from the PGA to aid further development— sure recognition of the Canadian Tour's relevance as a breeding ground for new golf stars. And in BC, at press time, the longest-running Canadian Tour event, played in BC since 1981, was gearing up for its 30th anniversary in June 2012.

Now known as the Times Colonist Island Savings Open, it is currently played at the Uplands Golf Club in Oak Bay. Over the years the event has rotated around courses on southern Vancouver Island and was originally played as the Victoria Open. The original 1981 event saw Dave Barr win for the sixth time on the Canadian Tour at Glen Meadows Golf Club. That same year Barr would make his mark on the PGA Tour, winning the Quad Cities Open in a five-way playoff that included fellow Canadian Dan Halldorson.

After a two-year hiatus, the tournament regained a foothold in the golf world and was known as the Victoria Open through 1991. Only two Canadians prevailed during that time: Windsor, Ontario's Bob Panasiuk in 1986 and Rick Todd in 1991 when he won at Cowichan, the only time that the tournament ever ventured beyond the magnificent Malahat

Drive. Journeyman US players Charles Bolling, Jeff Sanders, Todd Ervin and Kelly Gibson won in 1984, 1985, 1988 and 1989 respectively.

Two international stars-to-be were the victors in 1987 and 1990. Australia's Craig Parry, now a 23-time worldwide winner, won his first event outside of his homeland when he took the Victoria Open played at Gorge Vale in 1987. In 1990, few who witnessed the sweet swing of Steve Stricker would have forecast that he would become a 12-time PGA tour winner who would go on to rank as high as the second-best player in the world. Until then he was little known outside his home state of Wisconsin. His first professional victory was the 1990 Victoria Open, also played at Gorge Vale.

Gasoline then fuelled the sport. Payless Gas—for seven years—then Shell Oil—for three years—stepped in as sponsors, paying out prize cheques to 10 different winners between 1992 and 2001. Three Americans, including budding star Brandt Jobe, won through 1994 before BC's Norm Jarvis and fellow Canadian Arden Knoll won at Uplands and Royal Colwood respectively. Ontarian Rick Todd became the only repeat winner of the event in 1997 when he prevailed at Gorge Vale. By then Todd had won twice on the Nationwide Tour; the win at the Gorge would be his final at this level of competition.

Little-known Jay Hobby won the next year, which was only one of two times the event was played at Cordova Bay. Then two southern boys, Ken Duke and Jason Bohn, followed with wins in 1999 and 2000—first-time career victories that launched both to success on the Nationwide and PGA tours. They share five wins and both are still active at time of writing.

Kiwi amateur magician Paul Devenport, known to entertain spectators as much with his sleight-of-hand as with his golf, made the last Shell Payless event in 2001 the last of his four Canadian tour wins. The following year, Australian Scott Hend enjoyed a brief moment in the northern sun when he won the Victoria Open at Uplands for his only North American victory. American Patrick Damron won in 2003 at Royal Colwood.

In 2004 there was great relief when the *Times Colonist* started to sponsor the golf event that now often launches the Canadian segment of the tour in early June. One of Canada's current big-league stars, David Hearn of Brantford, Ontario, had been the Canadian Tour's Rookie of the Year in 2002 and made the 2004 stop in Victoria his only Canadian Tour victory before winning on the Nationwide Tour the same year. Hearn earned 2010 playing rights through his 2010 performance on the Nationwide Tour and used a strong finish to his 2011 PGA season to retain PGA playing rights for 2012, where he again played well.

Fellow Canadian Craig Taylor won in 2005 before a string of five young Americans won from 2006 through 2010. California buddies Spencer Levin (2007) and Byron Smith (2009) rank as the most notable at this stage, and are now playing on the PGA and Nationwide tours respectively.

The first Mexican golfer to ever win in Victoria, Jose de Jesus Rodriguez, won what is now known as the Times Colonist Island Savings Open in 2011 when the tournament was hosted at Uplands for the fourth year in a row. By the end of 2011, the Canadian Tour was billing itself as the breeding ground of alumni who had won more than 100 PGA tour titles and in excess of $400 million.

In early 2012 the selection committee's eyes turned west as they named Abbotsford's Adam Hadwin their Canadian Male Professional of the Year. He shared the spotlight with Hamilton, Ontario's Alena Sharp at a time when a new breed is beginning to replace some of Canada's most successful players of the past two decades.

CHAPTER 17

VANCOUVER'S CANADIAN OPENS

Vancouver is the only city in BC to host the Canadian Open and it has happened five times over 63 years, culminating in the tension-packed final round of the 2011 event when newcomer Adam Hadwin thrilled a massive gallery on a sunny Sunday afternoon.

1948

The original Shaughnessy Heights course was the venue for the first Canadian Open to come to Vancouver in 1948. The players of the day were Ben Hogan, Sam Snead, Jimmy Demaret, Claude Harmon, Bobby Locke, Cary Middlecoff and Lloyd Mangrum. Other newsmakers of the day were Harry S. Truman who had managed to retain the US presidency, a horse named Citation and a Cadillac with a Hydramatic automatic transmission and tail fins inspired by Lockheed's P-38 fighter aircraft. The car sold for $2,833.

Umbrella sales were brisk in Fred Wood's pro shop early in the third week of that September as the debonair Mangrum and Middlecoff set out on heavy fairways with 129 other entrants to pursue $12,500 and the Seagram Gold Cup.

Virginian Dick Metz stood alone atop the leaderboard at 138 after the second day when hail and driving rain sent scores soaring. Fresh off an opening 67, he pitched in to eagle the first hole of day two and ended his round two strokes clear of fellow tourists Johnny Palmer and Herman Keiser. Fred Wood and Stan Leonard, the local favourites, and Chuck

Long-time pro Hal Rhodes, who had left Fraserview to open the Harrison Resort course two years earlier, won the bravery award at the 1948 Canadian Open by turning in two score cards totalling 178 strokes. BC GOLF HOUSE 007.139.040

Congdon, an unpretentious $20,000-a-year club pro from Tacoma, were within striking distance at 143. Walt McElroy, the promising 21-year-old Shaughnessy Heights member, sat at 145 in his ostensible battle for amateur laurels with Skee Riegel, the 1947 US champion, and Bud Ward from Spokane.

Before the dank day was over, official scorer Billy Thompson called veteran Harrison Hot Springs pro Hal Rhodes "the bravest man in the

Shaughnessy Heights pro Fred Wood eyes the predicament of Second World War vet
Ed "Porky" Oliver. At five-foot-nine and 240 pounds, Porky was one of the game's more
colourful characters. Seen here during the week of the 1948 Canadian Open, he was once
disqualified while tied for the lead of the US Open because he had teed off a half hour early.

tournament" for signing for a second straight 89. Local amateur Jack
Fraser had absolutely nothing good to say about Ward, his playing partner. Fraser picked up during the round after Ward's alleged bad manners
almost led to an argument.

Ward shot 72 for 146 but, good manners or bad, he vanished without
turning in his card after Friday's third round. He had been bitten by the

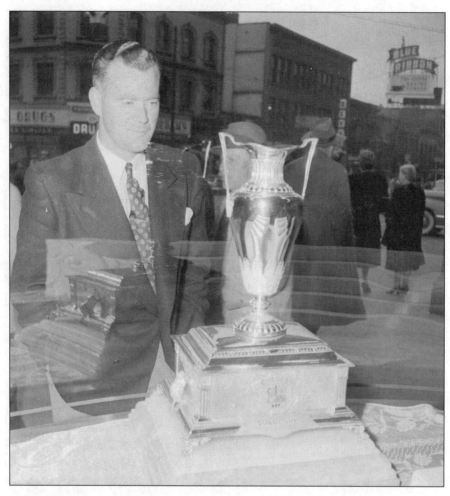

Jock McKinnon of Capilano views the classic Seagram Gold Cup, on display in the downtown Vancouver Birks window prior to the 1948 Canadian Open. VANCOUVER PUBLIC LIBRARY 84181A

deadly little 270-yard 12th hole. Ward took a fat nine after hitting two drives onto 33rd Avenue, finished the round and paid off his caddy.

A third straight sub-par round of 71 left Metz two strokes to the good of Congdon, who shot Friday's low round of 68. The usually happy-go-lucky Ed "Porky" Oliver finished with 74 for 221, and without a putter. He had smashed it in two against a tree after missing a 14-inch putt.

On Saturday, Jimmy Thomson, the Scottish-born pro once considered the game's longest hitter, was an early final-round casualty. Out of contention with 221 starting the day, he, like Bud Ward the previous day, never got beyond No. 12. After hitting the first two tee-shots toward 33rd Avenue, he turned and stomped angrily to the clubhouse.

The balding, taciturn Congdon made his winning statement with a marvellous bunker shot from 150 yards out on the 16th fairway. He made his eight-foot birdie to take the lead, and finished with a final-round 69 and a 280 total to add the National championship to conquests in both the BC Open and Portland Open earlier in 1948.

The sun peeked out on the Saturday when BC's Premier John Hart handed the cup and $2,000 to Congdon, who was three strokes clear of a three-way tie for second between Dick Metz, Vic Ghezzi and Ky Laffoon.

Wood and Leonard were the only Canadian pros in the money—the worst showing by Canadians in tournament history. Wood's 290 tied for 15th, worth $123.33, while Leonard's 293 got a $25 share of the 20th and last pay spot.

The slender McElroy stamped himself as a future champion as the lead Canadian, shooting 73 after 74, 71 and 70 for par 288. He was both low Canadian and low amateur, 10 strokes to the good of Riegel, and tied for 10th overall. A final-day audience of 8,000 enthusiastic spectators qualified the event as a success.

1954

Pat Fletcher's "marriage" to Vancouver Point Grey is an essential part of annual pre-tournament advance stories and will remain so until another Canadian wins the Canadian Open. The story is repeated endlessly during tournament week as long as a Canadian stays near the lead.

Fletcher, a club professional first and then a professional golfer, was the last of his ilk to capture the Open. No Canadian has managed to win the National Open since Fletcher conquered what subsequent observers dismissed as an inferior field in an event far removed from the US tour. Most of the day's big names may not have been at Point Grey in July 1954, but those who competed for the top prize of $3,200 were no match for the flat, tight, tree-lined course—or for Pat Fletcher.

Pat Fletcher's name is still resurrected at every Canadian Open as the last Canadian to hold this trophy, on July 14, 1954. VANCOUVER PUBLIC LIBRARY 44037

Fletcher, born in England and raised in Canada, was good enough to represent Canada four times in the World Cup team championships. He won the 1952 Canadian PGA and finished among the leaders the next week in the Canadian Open at Winnipeg St. Charles. In 1953 at Scarborough, he tied for fourth, four strokes behind Douglas. On three occasions he won the Saskatchewan Open, in which he was runner-up five times, and he had three seconds in the Alberta Open.

Fletcher's golf career began at the Victoria Golf Club links, where he first caddied at age 10. At 17, he won the 1933 club caddy championship and failed to defend when W. Turner, carrying a 20-handicap, shot a 90 for net 70. Fletcher, who played to a three, posted a gross 75. No other entry broke 80.

The enterprising youngster was encouraged by Victoria pro Phil Taylor, who permitted Fletcher to use his own clubs during the years he won the BC Open three times. Fletcher's only amateur victory was Gorge Vale's inaugural Junior championship. As he caddied beyond his 19th birthday, Fletcher was deemed a professional under the rules of the day and found work that summer at Jasper Park Lodge.

He made his pro tournament debut in the Alberta Open at Edmonton only because Ernie Brown was committed to playing Jasper's Totem Pole event. He finished second and his performance didn't go unnoticed. After serving his apprenticeship under Tom Morrison at Edmonton Mayfair, Fletcher secured the pro-manager position at the country club. He then gave the hotel business a whirl while doubling as pro at Edmonton Highlands before going to Saskatoon in 1946 for 10 years. He was at the top of his game, and he crested at the lowlands of Point Grey in 1954.

Two years after winning at Point Grey, Fletcher landed one of the most high-profile club pro positions in the country: Royal Montreal, the oldest (1873) club in North America. While in Montreal, he and son Allan opened a golf repair business that flourished into Fletcher Golf Enterprises, one of the country's largest equipment suppliers.

To play the '54 Open, Fletcher bunked with his friend Stan Leonard and borrowed an eight-iron because he was one club short for a practice round. The two went salmon fishing the day before the opening round and Fletcher, always good around the greens, rolled to an opening 65 while his host, Stan the Man, had to settle for 74.

Fletcher's grand opening, however, was overshadowed by San Francisco pro Bob Rosburg's 63.

Rosburg, who five years later would win the PGA title despite an explosive temperament, was almost a post-entry, arriving only a day before the tournament. Jack Hazeldine, who was Rosburg's then 17-year-old caddy, recalled, "He only had time for practice on the front nine and then went out and shot 63. He hit a big fade and he was a fantastic putter. Off 18 he aimed left at the adjoining first fairway with his three-wood and carved a fade back into the middle. Then he drilled a three-iron close and made eagle."

Fletcher and Rosburg shared the halfway lead after rounds of 70 and 72 respectively. Rosburg faded out of the competition with a third-round 75 that included an ugly shank at the ninth hole. "He broke his nine-iron in two, jamming it into the ground until the shaft snapped," recalled Hazeldine, a Point Grey member. "I thought he was going to stab himself when the club finally broke. I've still got the pieces somewhere in my basement. After missing a putt on the 16th the last day he chucked his putter into the ditch and I refused to retrieve it."

A character from Lower Valley, Washington, Buck McKendrick hadn't helped Rosburg's disposition during the second round. A wayward shot by McKendrick happened to hit Hazeldine. The Washington pro tried to stick Rosburg with a two-stroke penalty but tournament officials ruled against him. McKendrick was among the leaders after rounds of 70 and 71, and shot to 81 and 80 in his final two rounds.

By that time, Lawson Little, in the dusk of a great career, could hold his own in the bar with McKendrick, who liked to drink Scotch and milk. The winner of five major titles, then aged 44, had been a regular contender in the Masters as late as 1951 when he was sixth. But Little didn't break 74 that week at Point Grey and took a fifty-dollar cheque—which didn't begin to match his bar bill, according to his caddy that week, George Drew, who played out of North Vancouver's Seymour club. "He was a nice man, most generous to me though he didn't win a heck of a lot . . . Boy, could he down the whiskey after the rounds. He'd get a beer glass filled with whiskey and drain it like nothing."

Other pretenders fell by the wayside along with Rosburg during the middle rounds. When the field awoke to a bright, warm day for the final round, the week's most accurate drivers were at the head of the pack—the 40-year-old Fletcher and Gordon Brydson, a dapper 47-year-old Toronto pro who was stoked with an abundance of confidence and cigars. Brydson had seized the lead with his second 68 for 207, two better than Fletcher who lapsed with a third-round 74.

Brydson had won the 1948 Canadian PGA title at Point Grey and started the final day like a man possessed. He birdied the first two holes, but the pressure of the occasion got to him by the 10th hole and he lost the lead even though Fletcher could do no better than turn in 39 after a run of bogey, double-bogey and triple-bogey. Fletcher, shaky himself, recovered to birdie 12 after avoiding the out-of-bounds left to Blenheim Street by hitting a huge slice to the adjacent 18th fairway.

Supported by about 6,000 spectators, the Victoria product salvaged several pars with his magical wedge through to the short 17th, where he holed a 30-footer for a deuce and then closed with a routine birdie-four at the easy home hole. It added up to par 71 and four-under 280, four strokes clear of Brydson and big Bill Welch, the former US public links champion from Kennewick, Washington.

Windsor, Ontario pro Rudy Horvath's 285 was matched by a pair of amateurs: Doug Bajus, the tall, unorthodox Willingdon Cupper from the host course, and Portland's Bruce Cudd. The cantankerous Rosburg took $800 with a 286 total.

In becoming the first Canadian since 1914 to win the National Open since Ottawa's Karl Keffer, Fletcher made few miscues with his driver or wedge and, according to his caddy, pulled off a few uncanny shots. Jackie Wilson, a Langara member and himself a good amateur at the time, was perplexed by some of Fletcher's decisions. "The second day he putted three times from about 15 feet off the green," he recalled. "When a player asks you what club to use, it's not unusual. But when he asks you how hard to hit it, well . . ."

Before he retired following the 1975 Canadian Open at Royal Montreal, Fletcher was welcomed into the Canadian Sports Hall of Fame, the RCGA Hall of Fame and the Saskatchewan Hall of Fame. In his retirement he chased birdies as a member of Royal Colwood and he hunted salmon not far from his Cadboro Bay home. He died at the age of 70 in July 1985.

His family and friends established the Pat Fletcher Golf Foundation that has provided financial assistance to deserving young Canadian golfers at the post–secondary school level.

1966

There is little especially distinctive to recall about the 1966 Canadian Open, except that the soggy conditions did not impress much of the field. It was only the third Open to be played west of Ontario in almost four decades.

In this era most pro were independent contractors with limited endorsement deals and no need to accommodate their sponsors. The tempestuous Dave Hill packed up and went home after a practice round on a course he considered too long and difficult; Tom Weiskopf walked away from an opening par 71 because he was lovesick. All of Vancouver fell in love with the ever-upbeat showman Juan "Chi Chi" Rodriguez.

Earlier that year Jack Nicklaus had won his second straight Masters title and his first British Open, Casper beat Palmer in a US Open playoff and Al Geiberger captured the PGA championship. Palmer was not in the field and none of the other three was a factor at Shaughnessy.

Until that point, the three Opens that had been conducted in Vancouver were bound by a common set of numbers. Dial 280 and you get a winner—Chuck Congdon of Tacoma in 1948 at Old Shaughnessy Heights, Fletcher in 1954 at Point Grey and Don Massengale in 1966.

Massengale, a soft-spoken Texan who earlier that year had made the Bing Crosby Pro-Am at Pebble Beach his maiden victory in six years on tour, was truly a model of consistency at the new Shaughnessy. His four successive rounds of two-under 70 totalled three fewer than the ever-bantering, bantam-weight fan favourite, Chi Chi Rodriguez. The amiable Puerto Rican stumbled to a lamentable 75 on the last day.

For the sake of television, the course's nines were reversed and restructured for the Open. The $20,000 prize was Massengale's after he wedged in a 35-yard shot for an eagle at the tournament's 544-yard 16th, Shaughnessy's regular seventh. "It was a perfect shot, a sand wedge from the short rough that took two or three hops right into the cup," according to Gordie Spence, then a 29-year-old Vancouver policeman who took a week's vacation to caddy in the event. Spence, who went to Vegas the following week with his US$500 caddy fee, added:

> I remember Massengale told me to stand to his right while he was playing the shot so I'd block out any gallery movement in his line of sight. He was a quiet guy, easy

In a rare serious moment, Chi Chi Rodriguez wills himself onward in the 1966 Canadian Open. In the end he would finish second to Don Massengale. BILL CUNNINGHAM

to caddy for. He only hit 10 or 15 balls to warm up each morning. He asked me distances but not what to hit. Not when he bogied after I clubbed him.

I knew I had a serious contender after the first round and I told a certain *Sun* reporter as much. I knew he'd be close because he was putting so well. Those bumpy greens called for a firm stroke. I think they were dug under shortly after the tournament.

While a routine par round would have sufficed that day for victory, Massengale needed solid putting on greens made spongy and unpredictable by rain earlier in the week. They were the bane of many players. The phlegmatic Massengale didn't commit his first three-putt until the 72nd hole, when it mattered not. On the difficult par-three 17th, Spence said his man had "chunked" his tee-shot 30 yards short of the green but saved par by pitching to within six feet.

Chi Chi Rodriguez, in the last group with the largest crowd from the overall gallery of 12,000, bogeyed the final two holes for 75 and 283. The week's attendance, estimated at 42,000, disappointed tournament chairman Jack Randall. Ticket sales only hit $115,000, about $10,000 less than the previous year at Toronto Mississauga.

Tied for third at par 284 were Tommy Aaron, Lou Graham, Rod Funseth, Dick Sikes, Homero Blancas and Randy Glover. Graham had bolted into contention on the Saturday by firing 66, which broke Chuck Congdon's course record by a stroke. On the Sunday Graham was penalized when his ball moved while he was addressing a shot on the 12th, an infraction that cost him sole second and about $7,500 in prize money.

Not only the weather hurt the tournament. So did Palmer's absence and the fact that the day's other two "big three" players, Nicklaus and Casper, weren't contenders—neither were Geiberger nor defending champion Gene Littler. Among those who missed the 150 cut, the second highest on tour that year, were Stan Leonard, Ken Venturi and Charles Coody.

Nicklaus, only 26, came to Shaughnessy with his power game as the player to beat. He had already won the US Open and PGA and that year he took his third Masters title. "I doubt if anyone will break 280," Nicklaus predicted after a 70 in the pro-amateur. "Except for Firestone, site of the recent PGA, this is the toughest course we've played this summer. I like this kind of course because you have to play a lot of shots to beat it. It's not like so many courses we play, where putting is so important. All the griping I've heard about the condition of the greens since arriving here, I expected to see rough."

When the tournament started, Nicklaus couldn't break 72 on the 6,907-yard course. He posted 73, 72, 72 and 75, worth $712.50. But he blamed poor putting conditions, not his stroke. "The grass on the greens isn't very good. The traffic and rain have made them pretty bumpy. A putt's liable to go in any one of 30 directions."

Casper, a four-time winner in 1966, was in the midst of a tremendous 14-year run during which he finished out of the top-10 money winners only once—and that was 11th in 1963. But he failed to recover from a 76 opener, though he still tied for 12th at 288 after rounds of 72, 69 and 71.

Many of the visiting pros cried as often as the skies, whining about the greens, the length of the course and the foul weather. Saturday morning rain and the forecast for Sunday showers convinced too many people to stay home and watch the first live telecast of a Canadian Open to audiences in both Canada and the United States.

While other pros cooked up sudden excuses, the volatile Dave Hill pulled out after frankly admitting,

> I'm going home because I'm unhappy with the weather and the course conditions. Don't get me wrong; I think this is a great championship course. But it's too damn wet and too damn long for me. If I missed a short putt out there, I'm liable to throw a tantrum or something. I don't want to get upset and make an ass of myself.

After Thursday's opening round, Tom Weiskopf, Bert Yancey and Jay Dolan followed Hill's path to the airport. The long-hitting Weiskopf, then only 23 and considered the next Nicklaus, told officials he was "sick to the stomach" after a bogey, double-bogey finish for 71. He was only three strokes behind the obscure leader, Hugh Royer, and his sickening round had included two chip-in eagles. In truth he was lovesick. Weiskopf, saying he hadn't been feeling well for three weeks, also confessed he wanted to get home to see his fiancée and parents. His October 22 wedding date was three weeks away and, he said, "That's been on my mind."

Dolan was disqualified after sleeping in and missing his Friday tee-time while Yancey, a three-time winner that season, walked in from the second hole complaining of a sore shoulder. He had started with a 75 and took a 9 at the second after hooking twice out of bounds.

Vancouver woke up to clear blue skies on Sunday but the sun didn't shine on Chi Chi. The jaunty little man in the Panama hat had taken the tournament lead with a 67 Saturday but apologized to his many followers, tongue firmly in cheek. "I'm sorry I didn't have much chance to talk to the fans behind the ropes today . . . I was in the middle of the fairways all day." With his two-bogey finish while surrendering the lead, Chi Chi was more subdued at the end of his Sunday round.

Failing to finish the final day were two of the headliners. The colourful Doug Sanders quit, citing sore hands as the result of playing eight-over golf the first three days. Bob Rosburg, not generally known for being perky, withdrew mid-round, nine over par for 11 holes and 15+ overall. Only his pride was hurt.

2005

There was a 39-year gap after Massengale's 1966 victory at Point Grey before the Ontario-based Royal Canadian Golf Association (now Golf Canada) saw fit to award another Canadian Open to a British Columbia course.

In their wisdom, the Royal Canadian Golf Association commissioned Jack Nicklaus to build Glen Abbey Golf Course in Oakville, Ontario, as the permanent home of Canada's premier golf event. After 1977 it became the dominant site, hosting 22 of the next 25 Opens while Royal Montreal hosted the other three. The Canadian Open has only been played outside Ontario-Quebec nine times: five times in BC, twice in Manitoba, and once each in Alberta and New Brunswick.

Glen Abbey has long been a subject of debate. The Toronto-area course also houses the Canadian Golf Museum and Hall of Fame. Several noted tour players weren't particularly fond of the premises. Tom Watson, for one, never set foot on Glen Abbey. Tiger Woods chose to play the Open there only once; he won the 2000 Open in spectacular fashion while setting a course record, yet he never returned. The event will return to Glen Abbey in 2015.

The Shaughnessy Golf & Country Club hosted the two most recent BC-based events, first in 2005 and again in its centennial year, 2011.

Former British Open winner Mark "Calc" Calcavecchia made the 2005 Canadian Open his 12th career PGA tour win while renewing his love affair with Vancouver. Calc had first won in BC in 1997, taking the Greater Vancouver Open when the short-lived event was part of the PGA tour.

At Shaughnessy, Calcavecchia opened with a superb 65 to share the lead with Lucas Glover and led outright by five strokes after a day of accurate driving and a solid short game helped him fashion a 67 to go eight under par. Glover was alone in second.

The leader got off to a slow start after hitting "an awful iron into the first hole and then another terrible iron into two." He felt he had started "too relaxed" but when he stuck a five-iron two feet from the pin at No. 3 he told reporters, "I really got into the round and played great from the 3rd hole to the 11th."

The next day was not so good as he failed to make birdie, made two bogies and only held on to a one-stroke lead after getting up and down from 60 yards out at the 18th. "The good news is I hung in there and only shot two over . . . the bad news is I was in a position to get to 9 or 10 under and put some space between me and the rest of the guys."

As it was, the Canadian crowd found a new hero to cheer on as the new Canadian citizen and transplanted Caribbean Stephen Ames equalled the course record with a brilliant 64 to move into contention, tied with Vijay Singh and Jerry Kelly, and Britain's Brian Davis, three behind the leader. The zany Swede Jesper Parnevik was only one back after a 67, as was journeyman pro Craig Barlow, who made a six-foot eagle putt at 13 and aced 17 on his way to a 65. Next in line was the 2004 US Amateur champion and now rookie pro from Tacoma, Washington, Ryan Moore.

Sunday was not much better for Calcavecchia as he made only one birdie, but steady play kept the frontrunner in the lead and another superb shot into 18 allowed him to make a two-putt par and earn a popular one-stroke win over hard-charging Ben Crane, who finished with 66, and a steady Ryan Moore, who tied for second. Parnevik faded to 72, alone in fourth, Kelly and Joey Sindelar tied for fifth, and Ames, Singh and South Africa's Trevor Immelman tied for seventh.

Calc pocketed $900,000 for the win—a far cry from the $3,200 that Pat Fletcher had won about 50 years earlier. "I've got to admit I never thought I'd win again, let alone on a golf course like this, in a tournament this big," the bluntly honest 45-year-old said after being told he was the tournament's oldest winner. It was his first win in four years and he admitted to the Associated Press, "I have a lot of self-doubt and a lot of demons that float around inside my head." Looking back on the last hole and the result of a strong drive and great iron shot, Calc joked, "I knew I could two-putt. How embarrassing to lag from six feet."

2011

Inevitably, another Canadian golfer will supplant Pat Fletcher as a national hero of sorts and win the national title. Some great golfers have certainly come close. George Knudson, the Manitoba-born Hogan clone, won eight PGA events between 1961 and 1972 and finished second at the 1969 Masters, yet inexplicably never claimed victory in his own national championship. His best finish was sixth behind Gay Brewer in 1972 and he was seventh twice in 17 starts.

Canada's other eight-time tour winner, Mike Weir, came heartbreakingly close in 2005 at Glen Abbey when he tied Vijay Singh over 72 holes, only to lose the playoff on the first extra hole.

Stan Leonard missed a tie for first by a stroke in his Open debut, in 1946, and had six top-10s through 1961 everywhere but BC. But in 1966, he failed against woefully weak fields at Vancouver Point Grey, a short walk from his front door, and Old Shaughnessy, a course he had known so well as a caddy.

Adam Hadwin from Abbotsford, who arrived virtually out of obscurity as a genuine contender in 2011 at Shaughnessy, posed the main threat to Fletcher's long-standing record.

In 2011 the Canadian Open field faced a layout fit for a National Open: long, rough, narrow fairways and a layout that would yield only a four-under winning score. Only once since the Second World War has a Canadian Open course played any tougher. Yet most of the pros loved it.

The tournament came on the heels of the British Open. To enhance the field a charter plane from Scotland brought a host of big names direct to Vancouver to tee it up. After getting a look at the deep rough, veteran Ernie Els, fresh off a two-under opening round, said, "This is the way a National Open should be played . . . as tough as possible on a very stern test. That's what you've got here."

All in all there were 13 major tournament winners in the international field that included 2011 Masters winner Charl Schwartzel and World No. 1 Luke Donald, who flew his own jet to Canada's west coast.

Els was only a stroke behind the purple-clad, relatively unknown Chris Blanks, a 39-year-old tour non-winner who had a small but dedicated gallery. Tied with Els was Canadian Matt McQuillan, a personable 29-year-old tour rookie who had showed signs of progress on the tour in recent weeks.

The second round brought a new cast member to centre stage when Hadwin shot a 66 and gained the spotlight. Hadwin had announced himself the previous year when, at age 22, he was low Canadian in the 2010 Canadian Open. His best was yet to come.

Hadwin bombed long drives and used only 27 putts as he moved into contention as part of a two-under logjam in fourth place that included Kris Blanks, Schwartzel, Australian Geoff Ogilvy, former teen idol Rickie Fowler and fellow Canadian David Hearn. By the end of the week Hadwin would rank second in the most telling of golf statistics, greens in regulation. Vancouverites had been treated to some outstanding golf and at the halfway point there were still five Canadians in the hunt.

The third round saw Friday's lead trio fade to dark while Hadwin shot a solid 68 to sit second alone, one behind the hefty Oklahoma resident Bo Van Pelt and one ahead of the next great Argentinean golfer Andrés Romero along with the stubborn Kris Blanks. Lurking in the wings at two-under were Ogilvy, fan favourite and ever-resilient John Daly and the day's top scorer, Texan Sean O'Hair, who had birdied the tough 17th to fashion a 66.

On Sunday the back nine was a roller-coaster ride. Hadwin shot himself in the foot early going four-over on the front nine, including his only double bogey of the week on the eighth hole. Romero suffered the same fate. Only Van Pelt held his ground, staying even par for the day—but he had new pursuers at his heels. In the second-last group Daly stumbled to one-over on the front nine while Blanks and O'Hair fed off each other, each going two-under to sit one out of the lead.

Then, as if some miracle script was being played out, Hadwin, who had bogied 11, electrified the gallery as he strung together three straight birdies on 12 through 14. Van Pelt obliged by going four-over on the first five holes of the back nine while Romero also made three birdies along that stretch and was tied with Hadwin going to 15, both one clear of Van Pelt. In the threesome ahead, Blanks was also faltering with two recent bogies but he and O'Hair had actually gained the lead at three-under.

It was the par-five 15th that would end up being the pivotal hole. Both O'Hair and Blanks managed birdies as did Romero behind them. Hadwin, who had failed to make birdie here all week, again settled for par as did Ogilvy who would par in over the last four to tie for fourth. Romero made a great birdie at the 16th but gave it back on 18 after finding a greenside bunker and taking two putts to get down.

Blanks and O'Hair managed to stagger in, their dignity intact until they got to the playoff. There, in a one-hole calamity, O'Hair was the last man standing after his bogey outdid Blanks's double bogey.

In retrospect Adam Hadwin could look back to that mean little par-three eighth hole where he was four-over on the week while all those who finished ahead of him had played it in even par. The game of golf had once again proven that you just never know what part of the course will bite your butt.

That tournament made Hadwin a familiar name to many Canadians. In my opinion he brings a refreshing manner and attitude to the game, complete with self-confidence and raw candour. Throw in some cockiness, brashness and creativity and you have a persona that helps pro golfers succeed. Somewhere between the ages of 18 and 22, Hadwin's college experiences helped him learn to control his emotions, to shrug off poor shots and to blow up holes that had been plaguing his performances. His achievement in the summer of 2011 was unthinkable, rivalled only by Stan Leonard's rookie appearance 65 years earlier. Still, landing a permanent gig as part of the big show may take him longer to reach than he might hope. In the Canadian Open he earned $230,000—easily the largest cheque of his young career—and then added another $325,000 with a 68-68 finish at the Greenbrier Classic the following week. By the end of the season Hadwin had earned a special PGA exemption directly into the final stage of qualifiers because of his stellar performance. His superlative play in the Canadian and US Opens and two other PGA events meant that he collected a whopping $438,800 in the four starts, jumping 118 places in the World Rankings, from 332nd to 214th.

He turned pro in September 2009 and was the Canadian Tour Rookie of the Year in 2010 but six PGA events during 2010–11 have been the extent of his experience in top-level competition.

After a strong opening at Q-school, his momentum shifted into reverse unexpectedly and suddenly. It was a crude awakening for the overnight sensation in his qualifying school debut in which he was expected to comfortably meet the challenge. Hadwin's limited experience with PGA pressure probably factored into his tumble from contention midway through the six-round ordeal at La Quinta, California.

Hadwin was in midsummer form through three rounds. He was sailing along after rounds of 70, 69 and 70, seven under par, in 15th place. He was comfortably positioned to stay with the leaders battling for 27 PGA Tour cards. But the Canadian found rough water directly ahead. He slipped to rounds of 76, 75 and 73, capsizing to place 100th in the 170-man field. The cut for full exempt status was eight-under; he missed it by 12 strokes and was 21 shots behind leader Brendon Todd.

At press time the auspicious young man from Abbotsford who flourished with gilt-edge clubs in 2011 was in a peculiar predicament. He had virtually nowhere to play. Other than possible open qualifying and sponsor exemptions, PGA Tour appearances were now out of the question until 2013. The secondary Nationwide Tour offers limited opportunities. Still, there are a lot of people who are sure he has "the right stuff."

CHAPTER 18
OTHER MAJOR TOURNAMENTS

Several other major tournaments have called in on BC
over the years. This chapter looks at some of the highs
and lows of a selection of major tournaments.

VANCOUVER JUBILEE OPEN

Over the years all three of the major PGA tours have found their way
to BC, and on two occasions significant one-time events have attracted
some of the finest golfers in the world. One of those one-time events was
the Vancouver Jubilee Open, staged in 1936 as part of the city's 50th
birthday celebrations. The purse of $5,000 matched that of the year's
US Open.

The tournament was a supplement to a hit-and-miss tour, as North
America struggled to emerge from five years of economic depression.
Tour golf in the 1930s wasn't a wise career choice. In the aftermath of the
stock market crash of 1929, the game was looked on as particularly frivolous. Many tournaments such as the Jubilee and the $3,000 Evergreen
Open at Victoria Golf Club that followed the Shaughnessy show that
year were rarely repeated. The average purse of 35 PGA tournaments in
1936 was $4,250. Few tour regulars made more than travelling expenses;
fewer had bank accounts.

That week at Shaughnessy, the 92-man starting field included 50
Americans. Eighteen of them were tour regulars who had arrived in town
en masse from St. Paul, Minnesota. They were met at the CPR's Main
Street station by Mayor Gerry McGeer, a golfing enthusiast who seemed

omnipresent in that election year, and by Bill Charlton, Dave Manley and Joe Hatchett of the Jubilee tournament committee.

The luggage that got special attention belonged to Byron Nelson, Jimmy Thomson, Ralph Guldahl, Horton Smith, Lloyd Mangrum, Tony Manero and a husky, fresh-faced rookie who answered to Lawson Little. They were the tour's star attractions.

The July event was a grand success even before its surprising finish. The great Byron Nelson, who would win his first Masters the following year, was the clubhouse leader after finishing a strong final round; some members of his large gallery were ready to raise a glass to their champion. Then word came from out on the course that a charge was being mounted and many of them scurried frantically back on to the links. Other spectators abandoned the 18th green and excitedly backtracked in search of local youngster Ken Black's threesome. They were anxious to confirm reports of the local amateur's astounding exploits, and to cheer him through the closing holes of the Jubilee Open—the pro tour's third-richest tournament of that year.

While Nelson was being congratulated and interviewed as the apparent winner, Black, the young reigning provincial amateur champion, was still eight holes from the finish.

Nelson had been putting out for a brilliant 66 to post a target score of 278 as Black, Thomson and their third, Willie Goggin, were approaching the green of the nearby par-three 10th hole. Reaching for his putter from the hand of caddy Jack Hamilton, Thomson turned to Black and announced loudly: "Kenny boy, we need three birdies each on this nine to tie Byron. Let's get him." Unaccustomed to such high drama, Black nodded and replied tersely, "Okay, let's go."

It had already been a memorable week for Ken Black. It started when he drew Tony Manero, Horton Smith and young Johnny Bulla for a practice round. He was in exalted company. Smith had won the first Masters in 1934 and repeated at Augusta that April, and Manero had been a totally obscure player until winning the US Open at Baltustrol in Springfield, New Jersey, only a month before the Jubilee.

It was a fortuitous pairing for young Black. Manero, the slightly built instant champion, was an amiable man distinguishable by a pencil-thin moustache and slicked-back hair. He had slithered into the US Open field by surviving a playoff among non-qualifiers. Black also drew inspiration from Smith, then in his prime. By year's end, Smith would be leading the tour with $9,000 in earnings and a record stroke average of 71.65.

During his familiarization round on the short but challenging course, Manero offered the local amateur a tip that was to serve him well that week—and for the rest of his career. Black, as was his wont, had nervously pulled his drive off the first tee. As they strolled down the fairway, chatting, Manero casually suggested that Black might rid himself of the hook by adjusting his grip ever so slightly. "He told me my right hand was in a weak position at address," Black recalled. "He recommended I move it on top so I wouldn't have to turn the hand over while hitting through the shot. Manero's advice, I think, was a permanent cure for my hook."

Advice, like everything else, was difficult to come by in those days. Nelson had been winning since 1934, but hadn't been earning enough money to file income tax returns. The Dirty Thirties was an interim time for golf, a period between the Bobby Jones era and a prewar boom. The loquacious Jimmy Demaret noted that the tour was "nothing but a bunch of strung-out conventions where the manufacturers tried to teach club pros on vacation how to sell their merchandise. As a bribe for bringing the convention to whatever town, they got local businessmen to put up $3,000 or so in prize money as a come-on. Nobody fooled himself into thinking he could make a living out there."

In addition to Ken Black, the host pro, a strong local flavour for the Jubilee was supplied courtesy of Davey Black and two of BC's finest young players of the time, Stan Leonard and Fred Wood. Wood emerged as the leader after the opening salvos. The public course pro from Fraserview started with a five-under 67, one better than Texan Ralph Guldahl, who had a machine-like swing.

At 69 were Thomson, the lanky North Berwick basher, along with a grim 46-year-old MacDonald Smith and a pair of unknown Americans, Gene Kunes and Emery Zimmerman. In all, 19 players negotiated the premises under par—including Ken Black. He celebrated his 24th birthday by shooting 70.

The next day another 70 left Black three strokes off the pace at the halfway juncture. Wood also managed a 70 and was now the joint leader at 138 with another comparative stranger, Orville White of Chicago.

A sparkling 66 by the resident pro, Davey Black, went virtually unnoticed as Lawson Little grabbed everyone's attention by fashioning a 64 that easily might have been 58 or 59. Ernie Brown, who caddied for Guldahl, remembers that Little "putted for nothing but birdies and he missed several short ones."

With 1,000 spectators at the course, Little launched his day with an eagle and two birdies that carried him to 29—eight-under—at the clubhouse turn. On the back side he putted for nine birdies and made nine pars.

Little's round broke the course record that Davey Black had established only two weeks before, but he was still five strokes shy of the lead. The chunky two-time winner of both the US and British Amateur titles had stumbled out of the starting gate with 78. With his 66, 53-year-old Davey Black tied Guldahl and was within a stroke of the co-leaders.

On the Saturday they marched double-time, completing the tournament with two 18-hole rounds. Scoring well despite a sore back, Wood felt the burden of packing the lead overnight for two days. In the morning he scratched and clawed for pars, scraping out a 70. His 207 left him well clear of the favourites and one ahead of Zimmerman. Manero was well placed at 210, while MacDonald Smith stood at 211 along with the venerable and surprising host pro. Nelson and Black the Younger matched scores for the third straight day, this time uneventful 72s. They went to lunch tied for eighth, five strokes behind Wood.

With no rain all week and without a sprinkling system at the time, Shaughnessy's sun-baked greens were as slippery as ice and the fairways were firmer than an airport runway. It was considered a thinking man's course where positioning was more critical than distance. From the back tees, Shaughnessy stretched to 6,590 yards. It played nearer to 6,200 yards during Jubilee week. Following his third-round 72, Ken Black held out little hope of winning.

At Shaughnessy, everyone banked on a birdie at the 564-yard downhill first hole and Black had chipped stiff for his. He deuced the 133-yard third by punching an eight-iron to within nine feet and a huge drive set up a two-putt birdie at the 495-yard fourth. Yet another bird came at the fifth where a feathery five-iron shot stopped 12 feet from the pin.

He opted for his five-iron again to approach the seventh and he believed the shot was perfect. But the ball dug into the face of a hump on the front portion of the green and spun back to the apron. With a characteristically bold chip the ball ran four feet beyond the cup and he missed the par-saving putt.

The next two holes were played in par. As Nelson finished and playing partner Thomson set their back nine target, a win still seemed unlikely. Despite long-hitting Thomson's exhortation, Black went to the 11th tee demoralized after missing a "nice easy putt" of about 10 feet. It was his fourth routine two-putt par over five holes, a stretch interrupted by the bogey at the seventh. His auspicious beginning had dissipated.

Later, Black said he had sensed no mysterious presence in his midst, not even after an excellent chip resulted in a 4 at 11 for his first of three successive birdies. At the uphill 270-yard 12th, he smoothed a brassie to the green and got down in two putts. Then he pitched a seven-iron nine feet below the hole at the 370-yard dogleg 13th. Winning still wasn't in his mind. Suddenly, however, he was tied with Nelson.

"But I still wasn't thinking about where I stood. I really didn't believe I could win," Black recalled. He was locked in one of those trances that occasionally enshroud golfers. "I guess I was in sort of a fog, because I don't remember recognizing anyone in the gallery. It helped that Thomson also was going so well. That kind of rubbed off on me."

Black didn't waver at the downhill 14th. Brandishing his nine-iron, he hit a bull's eye into the green and a firmly stroked putt of about nine feet dove to the bottom of the cup. After a routine par coming back up the hill, he stiffed another short pitch and made three at the 360-yard 16th.

Scottish pro Jimmy Thomson played alongside Ken Black as they stormed the back nine at Shaughnessy Heights. He called Black's charge the "greatest nine holes of golf under pressure I have ever seen." BC GOLF HOUSE 007.85.80

With the swelling gallery now cheering excitedly, the young amateur finally caught a whiff of possible victory.

His best shot of the day—of the tournament—was a putt of some 20 feet. The 17th measured 232 yards and Black, pumped up, struck a crisp two-iron off the tee. The ball came in low and hot, running to the back of the undulating green. Black deliberately studied the downhill double-breaker, a treacherous putt he probably couldn't make in 20 attempts. The ball snaked into the heart of the hole. "If I hadn't hit that one right in the middle, it certainly would've been a three-putt. Instead of a four, I made two."

Black played the home hole rather coolly, although he said he still wasn't confident of victory until his approach, again with his trusty five-iron, about 10 feet from his final destination. The crowd was frantic. But with Thomson away they had to hold their final cheers. Thomson boldly made birdie from 20 feet for a 65 that tied Nelson's 10-under finishing total. Almost predictably, Black's putt for a 62 pulled up inches short.

Between them over the final eight holes, Black and the explosive Scot had made eight birdies. Ken Black's 63 that afternoon stands as probably the greatest round of golf ever played in BC.

In a conclusion as unexpected as Max Schmeling's shocking knock-out of Joe Louis the month before at Yankee Stadium, the unassuming 24-year-old son of the resident professional tore into the incoming nine holes with his woods and irons smoking and his putter afire.

After Black's 275 total had clearly beaten all of the day's finest touring pros by three strokes, the stoic Thomson was moved to call the performance "the greatest nine holes of golf under pressure I have ever seen." It was straight out of a storybook.

As 2,000 people burst into applause, the hometown hero's flushed face beamed as he walked off the green to accept the outstretched hand of his proud father. His mother, rosier than ever, was there with the first kiss of congratulations, followed by the embrace from Mayme Gehrke, the pretty, dark-haired girl in the crowd whom Black would marry in two years. Later, in the locker room, Mayor McGeer's eyes were damp as he shook the young champion's hand. "Winning was beyond my wildest imagination," Black said at the prize presentations. "It took a while to sink in. I had a great round. I was a little excited at the end."

The exalted mayor told the crowd that the event had taken about $2,500 out of the city's Jubilee coffers. But he was pleased with the week's attendance of 7,000 and said that the worldwide publicity was worth 10 times what the tournament had cost. "Little's 29 went around the world and Ken Black's 63 would do the same. They will always be linked with Vancouver."

Thomson admitted that he had forgotten his own game while watching in admiration as Black forged his eight-under round on an afternoon

In 1936 Horton Smith (right) defeated the entire Evergreen Open field at Victoria Golf Club, including Ken Black, that year's BC Amateur champ. BC GOLF HOUSE 007.131.001

when only five others bettered par. "If I could putt like that I could have retired a long time ago," the Scot was overheard saying.

While Nelson and Thomson split the first two money prizes, each getting $995, Black left the prize presentation with a new wristwatch.

Little, who earlier in the year had beaten Thomson at the Canadian Open for his first pro win, failed to regain any of his magic of the second round. He closed with 72 and 75 for 289, missing the money by three shots. MacDonald Smith, a great Scottish pro who at 20 had lost the 1910 US Open in a playoff with his brother Alex, rallied with 70 and 68 to tie Manero at 279. They both collected $500 while an Illinois pro who needed a name tag, Terle Johnson, took $350 for shooting 280.

After holding or sharing the lead for three rounds, the frazzled Wood did well to scramble for a closing 74 and 281, worth $300. Zimmerman and Guldahl followed at 283, getting $250 each. Goggin, the other man with Black and Thomson, matched the 285 posted by the elder Black, who returned 73 and 74 on the heels of his 66. Both made $165.

Horton Smith didn't manage to break 70 and shared the last money spots with four others including rookie Ernie "Dutch" Harrison. Smith's eighty-six dollars was barely enough to pay his caddy, Bob McLeod—who got fifty-five dollars for his week's work—and purchase his fare on the midnight ferry to Victoria.

"We'd come here more often if those Black burglars would leave us be," MacDonald Smith smiled, recalling that Davey Black and Dunc Sutherland had beaten himself and Walter Hagen 10 years before in an exhibition for $500.

The following week in Victoria, Smith found the Oak Bay links more to his liking. He took the top prize of $700 in the Evergreen Open by using 269 strokes in four trips around the 5,800-yard course, three ahead of runner-up Byron Nelson. The leading Canadian was Don Sutherland, the quiet Vancouver Golf Club pro who had posted 288 at Shaughnessy. At Oak Bay, he was sixth with 278, good for $180, while resident pro Phil Taylor had 280. Little collected his first cheque as a pro—seventy-nine dollars for carding 281.

Ken Black, the young amateur from Shaughnessy, opened with a 69, counting an eight on the 11th, and closed with 67. In between he could do no better than par and was nowhere in sight of the leaders at the finish. But Black could be excused. He was still numb from triumph. He had celebrated his victory the previous Saturday night by driving to the top of Grouse Mountain with a group of old schoolfriends and golfing companions. "It wasn't a party or anything," he said. "We skiers just decided to go up there to see what it looked like in the middle of the summer." In Victoria, the week after his greatest triumph, he was sitting on top of the world—not a mere mountain.

Before the Canadian Open returned to Vancouver in 1966 another one-time event brought some of the world's top golfers to BC.

THE BC CENTENNIAL INVITATIONAL

Another special anniversary event, the province's 100th birthday, brought the US PGA Tour back to Vancouver in 1958. The $47,800 BC Centennial Invitational came to Point Grey during the last week of August on the heels of the only Canadian Open to ever be played in Alberta at Edmonton's Royal Mayfair Golf & Country Club. Of the 1958 tour's 39 stops, the Centennial ranked as one of the richest—the average purse was $25,750, whereas the Canadian Open offered $25,000.

Among the day's big-name players were Arnold Palmer, Lionel and Jay Hebert, Mike Souchak, Ken Venturi, Dow Finsterwald, George Bayer, Art Wall, Billy Casper and Champagne Tony Lema. And alongside those names was an obscure tourist, Jim Ferree, who hadn't won enough to meet expenses his first two years on tour. He left Point Grey with the top money of $6,400.

"It's like pouring water down a dry well," exclaimed Ferree, a jaunty North Carolinian. Early in the week, Ferree had attracted international attention by destroying Point Grey with a second-round 61, the lowest round on tour that year. Venturi, later one of golf's premier analysts, volunteered that "I think it was the greatest round in the history of golf."

Ferree, using an eight-dollar putter he had purchased two weeks earlier, posted a 270 total for a one-stroke win over Casper. Venturi and Finsterwald tied for third at 274, one better than Stan Leonard, who had won his first of three tour victories earlier that year at Greensboro. Leonard's Sunday 65 was lost in the lustre of the struggle that developed between Ferree and Casper but Stan the Man was playing some solid golf. He had been fourth in Edmonton the week before, three behind Wes Ellis.

In smashing Point Grey's course record of 65, Ferree used 23 putts for his 32-29-61 on the par 37-35-72 layout. About 4,500 people ringed the 18th to see Ferree's downhill 30-footer from the back fringe nestle against the flagstick for an eagle.

Casper, the former sailor from San Diego, began the final day six strokes behind Ferree. After starting the closing round with three birdies, the 27-year-old Ferree had to stave off challenges by veteran Fred Hawkins and then Casper for what would be the only PGA Tour victory of his career.

Hawkins quietly crept to within a shot of Ferree before driving out of bounds at 14 and three-putting for a triple-bogey. Ferree, who later achieved financial success in his second career on the Seniors circuit, cracked at the 16th. He pushed his drive beside an evergreen, topped his second into the ditch that crosses the fairway instead of chipping out safely, and took a double-bogey six.

Casper, playing in the same group, calmly dropped a birdie putt from about 18. The three-stroke swing left Casper only two shots back. "Stupid, that's all I was," Ferree groaned later, describing his travails at the 16th. "I was an egg-headed rebel on that one . . . should've been sent home to walk behind a mule."

After both made par on 17, Ferree's closing drive unluckily deflected off a spectator and left him a partially blocked second shot. He found a greenside bunker, two-putted for par and then sweated while Casper skinned the cup from 12 feet with an eagle putt that would have forced a playoff.

Ferree didn't get to pocket the entire $6,400. In a pre-arrangement no longer permitted on the tour, he had agreed to pool his winnings with three other emerging pros: Johnny Pott, Tommy Jacobs and Tony Lema. Lema earned $950 while Pott and Jacobs both missed the cut. If they had kept their bargain, they each would have earned $1,840.

Of the four, it was Tony Lema who would enjoy a brief meteoric career that included the 1964 British Open win. Two summers later he and his wife died in a tragic airplane accident while flying to a golf tournament.

THE CANADIAN PGA

The first two Canadian PGA championships conducted in BC, both at Point Grey, were restricted to Canadian professionals. Gordon Brydson beat Stan Leonard by a stroke in 1948 and the enigmatic Bob Cox Jr. clipped Ron Willey by the same margin in a 1969 battle of local public course products.

Cox was an exceptional talent whose questionable work ethic and lackadaisical approach to the game prevented his winning many more tournaments and substantially more money. The high-water mark in

Cox's career was the summer of 1969, when he won the PGA, four other tournaments and $24,000.

On a day when only one player broke 70 at Point Grey, Cox "backed in" to the $5,000 victory after labouring to a closing 76 and 280. The animated Willey posted 281, one better than former champions Al Balding and Moe Norman. The eccentric Norman blamed some of the 6,500 spectators for his failure to catch Cox, with whom he was in the last pairing. He claimed fans fidgeted while he missed a birdie putt at the 16th, and that after Cox tapped in for par at 17, "they rushed away, stamping the ground, and caused me to blow that putt from three feet."

After the 1966 Canadian Open and until the mid-1990s, the only occasion on which foreign PGA regulars competed in BC was the inaugural Labatt's International Classic. It was the 1978 Canadian PGA championships, embellished with a $100,000 purse and an expanded field that included 19 international champions and Arnold Palmer.

Relative international newcomers who added lustre to the field at Shaughnessy were Nick Faldo, 21, of England and Bernhard Langer, 20, of Germany, the crowd-pleasing Palmer and Roberto de Vicenzo, a delightful gentleman from Argentina.

By the end of a soggy summer week, the course record and $20,000 top prize belonged to the fast-swinging US PGA champion Lanny Wadkins. Almost 10,000 spectators were attracted to Sunday's final round by Wadkins's play, Palmer's presence and blues skies for the first time during the August tournament. They certainly hadn't come to see a competition. Wadkins ran away from everyone with a record eight-under 64 in Saturday's rain-delayed third round, winning with a 270 total.

His 12-stroke win over South African Dale Hayes matched Palmer's 1962 Phoenix Open winning margin, the widest on the US tour since Hogan, Nelson and Locke dominated the scene in the 1940s. "It's as good a test as any of the courses we played on tour," Wadkins said of Shaughnessy, on which he had only one three-putt in firing 22 birdies while returning cards of 69, 68, 64 and 69. "What I like about the course is that it requires a lot of good mid-iron shots. In my mind, that's a sign of an excellent course."

ALFRED DUNHILL CUP

The brief history of the prestigious Alfred Dunhill Cup matches illustrates the magnitude of Canada's greatest international golf conquest. Initiated in 1985, three-man teams from 16 nations competed in the annual medal-play competition at St Andrews, Scotland. In 1994, the event's 10th anniversary and final year before the matches were changed to a pro-am format, a glittering field of the world's top-ranked players led by Nick Price, Fred Couples, Ernie Els, Bernhard Langer and Tom Kite paraded onto the Old Course. In 1993 Couples had teamed with fan favourite John Daly and Payne Stewart to claim only the second cup for the United States since the event's inception. English, Irish and Greg Norman–led Australian teams had won twice and Sweden was also an upset winner along the way.

Canada had fared so poorly over the years, never having advanced beyond the round-robin preliminaries, that the British bookies sent them off as 33-1 long shots. The lightly regarded trio representing Canada in 1994 were three BC-born underdogs—Dave Barr, Ray Stewart and Rick Gibson. Stewart was a substitute for original choice Dick Zokol, who had a date that week at the PGA Tour qualifying school.

On paper, a most formidable task lay ahead for the Canadians who would have to overcome five far superior pairings in four days. All the members of these premium teams were ranked among the world's top 50 players. Barr, the veteran team captain from Kelowna, was Canada's best-rated competitor, ranked 63rd. Stewart, from Abbotsford-Matsqui, and Victoria product Gibson, who was playing in Asia and living in the Philippines at the time, were not ranked in the top 100. If the Canadians had any advantage whatsoever it was Barr's vast experience at the venerable Old Course. In seven appearances at St Andrews he had the third-best individual match record, 15-6. Also, all three had drawn seasoned Old Course caddies. Barr acknowledged,

> Our caddies were a great help. No matter how many times you play it, you learn something new about the course. The caddies often confirm where you're supposed

to hit certain shots, like at targets in the distance well beyond the course. Because of the prevailing high winds, they use extremely short flag sticks, five or six feet, about half the height of normal pins. Judging distances is also difficult because many greens are the same elevation as the fairways.

It was the first visit to St Andrews for both of Barr's teammates. The fair-haired Victoria-born Gibson, 32 at the time, was a regular on the Japanese tour. Stewart, then 41, the nicest guy this side of Matsqui—or any other side of it, come to think of it—was struggling with his game, trying to compete on the Canadian Tour. Two practice rounds served to introduce Gibson and Stewart to the historic links; Barr, however, knew the nooks and nuances, the grief and gorse, the swales and gales that lay ahead. He had experienced St Andrews in all weather conditions imaginable.

Barr emphasized that the important thing at St Andrews wasn't knowing where to place shots, but knowing where *not* to hit them, which the caddies underlined to their charges. "Let's try to play as well as possible and enjoy ourselves," said Barr. "If we can't win, and most people give us absolutely no chance, let's remember this as an unforgettable experience. If we can take home a few of their dollars, so much the better."

Playing in Scotland in October meant there would likely be the occasional frost delay, though for 1994 the Old Course was reasonably dry. Mid-October on the capricious east coast of Scotland came with unpredictable weather and chilly late afternoons. Tactics often required overnight adjustments. The contestants were greeted on opening day by howling winds and incessant, slashing sheets of rain. Fairways as firm as airport runways turned sodden, demanding shots be kept under the fickle winds. Traditional run-up chips wouldn't run as freely. The blustery conditions called for punched pitches to spongy, dart-board greens. It made for target golf, stick-and-stay golf.

To Gibson and Stewart the widely acclaimed links were initially rather unremarkable. They resembled a bleak, dead-flat moonscape, pock-marked with scrub brush and a broad assortment of perilously cavernous bunkers. Many hazards weren't entirely visible from tees; backdrops were vague. "Caddies told us where danger lurked but they didn't volunteer to club us if we looked in doubt about what to use," observed Stewart. "Where they really helped was making sure we were lined up properly. The wind was difficult to figure out. The caddies also confirmed our thinking when we appeared puzzled by putting lines."

Gibson was given the master of the caddy shack, the amiable Richard Mackenzie, a long-time friend of former Canadian Cup regular Dan Halldorson. Canadians were among Mackenzie's favourite people. He was a tremendous cheerleader and would help settle Gibson down after a nightmarish start. Barr's caddy Stewart Logan, a professional for 40 years in Scotland, was familiar to him. He worked Barr's early appearances at St Andrews and was on the 42-year-old's bag when he won the Atlanta Classic. Stewart had the expertise of another wise veteran and clan member, George "Dod" Stewart.

On the eve of the matches the Canadians didn't rest comfortably as long shots. They shrugged off the bookmakers' golf knowledge. Then they awakened for their first match against Sweden to find a storm brewing angrily off the Firth of Forth. Winds peppered a salty deluge on the course and city, gusting to more than 50 miles per hour. The imposing grey, stone edifice that is the clubhouse seemed to almost waver above the slippery cobblestone streets that take visitors beyond the quaint city to the grand site of Scotland's oldest university.

Speculating during breakfast about what lay ahead, Ray Stewart was moved to quote an old Chinese proverb. "He who expects nothing has everything," he quoted. "We're here expecting to win but in reality we hope to enjoy ourselves and have a great week."

That first day even the hardiest of locals wouldn't have ventured outdoors without good reason. The course was almost unplayable. Competitors struggled to remain balanced while addressing shots. The wind occasionally blew balls off tees. It was disconcerting when balls teetered in the wind as players were about to putt. Only 3 of the 48 contestants managed to match par 72 on opening day, and 15 of them signed scorecards of 80+ rounds.

The Swedes were apparently better acclimatized than Canada's "wet coasters." They prevailed two matches to one, putting instant pressure on the Canadians. One more loss and it was *adiós*, Canada, again. Barr encountered as much trouble pronouncing and spelling his foe's name as he did in the match itself, losing on the second extra hole to Gabriel Hjertstedt. Stewart beat off the best-known Swede, Jesper Parnevik, and Gibson lost to Anders Forsbrand's 81 after posting a frightfully forgettable 85 in the gale. He bogeyed each and every hole on the outgoing nine and was asked to recall the last time he did that. "I can't recall," gulped an embarrassed Rick Gibson, "shooting 85 since I began playing this game."

The weather conditions, and the Canadians, improved dramatically during the remainder of the week. On day two, they faced a team led by the amiable Nick Price, then number-one player in the world and winner of six PGA tournaments that year. After willingly volunteering to take on the world's number one, Ray Stewart stepped aside for the determined team captain. Barr responded by outlasting Price 68-69, the difference a closing 18-foot putt for birdie. There was never more than a one-stroke difference during the entire match.

While Barr took the measure of Zimbabwe's Price, the plucky Rick Gibson provided the much-needed second match victory. He boomeranged from his torturous opener, improving 14 strokes in 24 hours for a 71 against Tony Johnstone. Stewart's loss did the team no harm.

The next day, against Germany, Gibson went two strokes better with a three-under 69 that doused Alexander Cejka while Dave Barr's 69-70 over the great Bernhard Langer set the stage for a most improbable journey.

The back-to-back victories had, for the first time in 10 attempts, qualified a Canadian team for the semifinals against the highly rated South Africans. Suddenly upbeat, they finished the round-robin tied with Zimbabwe at 2-1, but advanced by virtue of their preliminary triumph over the African nation. Surely the British touts were looking a little closer into the form the three BC boys were showing.

Barr had earned two PGA tour victories that year and had already earned a career high $314,000. Stewart had gone in the other direction and, after losing his all-exempt PGA tour status, stood only sixth on the lowly Canadian Tour. Gibson was ranked 42 on the Japanese Tour and was winless that year although he had previously won titles in Malaysia, the Philippines and Japan. He had also won the Canadian PGA title when it was played at Richmond's Quilchena course in 1990.

Against South Africa, Barr finally faltered, losing to a youngster known as The Big Easy for his fluid golf swing. Ernie Els was then reigning US Open champion and rapidly earning a reputation as one of the great match-play golfers in the world. However, the two other Canadians rose to the challenge.

The high-powered, favoured US trio of Fred Couples, Tom Kite and Curtis Strange loomed large as the final hurdle. Between them the Americans had combined for 47 PGA Tour victories including four majors. Couples, looking for a repeat win, came to Scotland ranked sixth in the world while Kite had ranked in golf's top 10 for over three years and had already played in seven Ryder Cups. Two-time US Open winner Curtis Strange had slipped in the world rankings to 47.

The Americans were strong favourites as the final matches started. Knowing the win could be worth a staggering $216,000 to each player, the Canadians set out to dazzle their opponents by arriving at the first tee in pink V-neck sweaters and matching caps.

The stage was set after Barr beat Kite and Gibson gave way to Strange. In the third match Stewart had made three birdies in the first six holes while Couples ran into some bogey trouble. But as they came down the stretch things tightened up and Stewart held a two-stroke advantage on the 18th tee. Then a unique incident, albeit barely noticed by anyone, occurred when Couples arrived at his ball on the green well before Stewart and proceeded to apparently putt out of turn.

> At least I thought I was away by at least a few feet . . . but he decided to putt ahead of me. No, no, he wasn't trying to deliberately unnerve me . . . hoping I might three-putt which would have sent the match into extra holes. But darned if he didn't make the putt! I didn't see it as

Ray Stewart, Rick Gibson and Dave Barr celebrate their victory. BC GOLF HOUSE

gamesmanship on his part at all. Fred's not that kind of guy. He wouldn't go against the spirit of the game. He just wanted to putt first and get out of my way so I could celebrate right after putting.

If anyone noticed that Couples may have putted out of turn, absolutely no one mentioned it later. Stewart admitted that "the whole situation [playing out of turn] would have been entirely different had there been only one stroke difference between us."

The Canadians each finished 3-2 on the week. Barr averaged 71 strokes per round. He took advantage of laser-like long iron shots that consistently placed him among the tour's top-10 hitting greens in regulation. Stewart averaged a solid 72.2 and Gibson 73.8, which was inflated by his opening 85. In his three straight winning rounds he shot 71, 69 and 70. The champions' prize money represented their largest career cheques. Finally claiming the Cup in his seventh attempt was the most satisfying part for Barr.

Besides his seven Dunhill Cup appearances, Barr made 13 trips to the World Cup. Following his best financial year in 1994, he slipped off the tour charts by 1997 after back surgery. Returning for the Champions Tour, he won in his 2003 rookie senior season before losing his exempt status.

For Stewart, Dunhill was a windfall. Losing his consistent form, he seemed unable to keep a putting stroke together for four successive rounds to retain playing privileges beyond the Canadian Tour.

"What am I going to do with all of this money? That's easy," said Stewart, upon his return from St Andrews. "Half is going to Chrétien [taxes to the then prime minister]. My caddy's got $16,000, $5,000 goes to the Red Cross and my wife's getting the rest."

THE PGA TOUR 1996–2002

Other than the five times that the Canadian Open has visited Vancouver, PGA-endorsed events have to date been rare. Unfortunately, the one effort to establish an annual BC tournament as a second regular Canadian event on the tour lasted only seven years, from 1996 to 2002. However, the PGA Tour had previously included a stop in British Columbia in its schedule. Three years before Jim Ferree's victory at BC's centennial tournament, the 1958 Vancouver Open Invitational, Dow Finsterwald won the unofficial 1955 British Columbia Open Invitational.

The Greater Vancouver Open was first played at the Northview Golf & Country Club (Ridge Course) in Surrey, BC, in 1996. Over three years it crowned Guy Boros, Mark Calcavecchia and Brandel Chamblee as champions before a new sponsor renamed it The Air Canada Championship in 1999.

That year's tournament will always be remembered in Canada as Mike Weir's coming-out party. Canada's most accomplished golfer since George Knudson won his first PGA tournament by shooting back-to-back 64s on the weekend for a two-stroke victory over Fred Funk. Weir went on to win eight PGA events, including the 2003 Masters, before a series of injuries started to affect his play.

Two other young players claimed their first tour victories at Northview in 2000 and 2001. South African Rory Sabbatini shot a 65 to win by one, then Joel Edwards showed a brief flash of brilliance with his only tour win, a seven-shot victory over journeyman Steve Lowery. Then Gene Sauers won his last of three tour victories in 2002 before the tour sponsor pulled its sponsorship for economic reasons. Effectively, as at other venues, the PGA's ineffective policies and lack of influence in securing player commitments meant that it failed to deliver quality fields to the event in spite of local efforts and a $3.5-million prize pool.

THE PGA SENIORS AND LPGA

The PGA Seniors Tour has visited Vancouver twice and BC galleries have seen the LPGA Tour visit on three other occasions prior to their planned 2012 event at the Vancouver Golf Club. In addition, there was a special 1976 event at Victoria Golf Club that brought the men and women together.

That year an estimated 10,000 spectators flocked to the Oak Bay links to see eight two-member combinations of leading Senior and LPGA players compete in the two-day $45,000 Lady Scott Invitational. Art Wall and Pat Bradley combined for a 279 total to edge Donna Caponi-Young and Tommy Bolt for a top prize of $5,000 each. Ontario's Sandra Post, playing from the men's tees, established a women's course record of 68 and helped partner Bob Rosburg to a third-place finish.

The Seniors men's competition first came to BC in 1981 when the circuit for pros aged 50 and over was in its embryonic stage. A par on the first extra hole at Capilano gave tour rookie Miller Barber his first victory after he and Gene Littler had tied at 204 in the Peter Jackson Champions event. Australia's Peter Thomson also shot 204 to win at Vancouver Golf Club in 1985 when the event returned to Vancouver as the du Maurier Champions, before the Seniors tour disappeared from Canada for a decade.

Sally Little, in 1988, and Nancy Scranton, in 1991, both posted 279 at the Coquitlam course to capture the highly successful du Maurier Classic, which was recognized as one of the LPGA's four major tournaments until it was replaced by the Women's British Open in 2001. Little won with a dramatic 25-foot birdie putt on the final hole, and stalled big-hitting English rookie Laura Davies's run for top money of $75,000.

In preparation for the 2012 CN Canadian Women's Open, the Vancouver
Golf Club rebuilt the par-3 third hole. VANCOUVER GOLF CLUB

Scranton tied for fourth in 1988 and on her second visit left with a first-place cheque worth $105,000. With four birdies and an eagle-two on the final seven holes, Scranton closed with a 68 for her first victory in seven years on tour. After having barely survived the 36-hole cut, Scranton bolted into contention with a course record 64 during the third round.

The LPGA first touched BC in 1969 when six-foot-three Carol Mann made the Molson's Canadian Open at Shaughnessy her fourth straight tour victory. Mann collected $4,000 from the $30,000 purse with rounds of 70, 70 and 72, three better than Canada's Sandra Post and the great Kathy Whitworth. The year before, Post had beaten Whitworth in a playoff for the LPGA championship in her rookie year on tour.

The last visit of the LPGA to Vancouver was in July 2003 when Beth Daniel capped a 33-victory career with a one-stroke victory over long-time rival Julie Inkster and won what was then known as the BMO Financial Group Canadian Women's Open at Point Grey Golf & Country Club.

The LPGA will be welcomed back to the Vancouver Golf Club in August 2012 for the CN Canadian Open, an event that attracts most of the tour's leading players. Two young Canadians who recently qualified for the tour, Rebecca Lee-Bentham and Maude-Aimee Leblanc, will be joined by a cluster of BC's bright young stars all seeking to emulate Adam Hadwin's exciting charge at the men's event in 2011.

MADE FOR TV: THE SKINS GAME

Although not an officially sanctioned event, one of the more popular annual spectator events in Canadian golf is the Skins Game, an 18-hole shoot-out where four or five of the leading international golfers, now usually including one top Canadian player, compete over two days. The event is always shot at a Canadian course with a live spectator crowd and shown later to a TV audience in edited form. It always emphasizes that any money raised goes to charity. It is a variation of the original PGA-sponsored contest that saw the Big Four of PGA golf—Arnold Palmer, Gary Player, Jack Nicklaus and Tom Watson—tee-up in 1983 with Player taking the lion's share of the purse. Only once in its history has a player swept the board taking all 18 holes; that was Greg Norman in 2001.

In Canada, the summer get-together has been played since 1993. It first came west to the Nicklaus North course in Whistler, BC, in 1997, when Norman dominated a field of four—the other three were Fred Couples, Jack Nicklaus and Nick Faldo.

The following year, tournament policy changed. It became manda-tory to include a Canadian star and so Mike Weir became an annual fixture. Weir played every year through 2002, including the tournament's next trip to BC in 2000. That year Kelowna's Predator Ridge was the stage. Fred Couples continued to display his international dominance to the Skins format, winning seven skins to six over the energetic Spaniard Sergio García. Phil Mickleson, playing from the left side, along with Weir, brought up the rear. All plays took home part of a total purse of $360,000 for one afternoon's play.

Stephen Ames made his first appearance in the Skins in 2005, rep-resenting Canada when Nicklaus North became the first repeat host of

Jack Nicklaus walks the terrain of what would become Whistler's Nicklaus
North Golf Course with Kent Gilchrist of the *Province, Sun* reporter and author
Arv Olson, and course developer Caleb Chan, far right. JEFF VINNICK

the contest. He performed well, topping the money list and tying Jack
Nicklaus with seven skins each. John Daly bagged three skins while Vijay
Singh was shut out as the four golfers agreed to donate the $25,000 prize
that was tied to the final hole and no winner prevailed over an extra
tie-breaker hole.

In 2006 the tournament switched to a popular international theme
whereby five players representing different continents would compete. In
retrospect it was a visionary move as golf entered an era of charismatic
players from around the world bringing a new dimension to the scene.

Golf's favourite bad boy, John Daly, won back-to-back Skins Games
in Alberta and Ontario the next two years while Canada's representative,
Stephen Ames, finished second and third, respectively.

Predator Ridge was the event site again in 2008. The enigmatic
"Spiderman," Camillo Villegas, won female hearts of all ages and the
older gents, Greg Norman and Fred Couples, gave their fans enough
highlights to make the weekend. Both Mike Weir and the acerbic Scot
Colin Montgomerie were shut out.

The success of the BC-hosted events led to their return in 2010 when Victoria's controversial Bear Mountain course hosted a great quintet of Weir, Villegas, Couples and two quality first-timers, South Africa's Retief Goosen and Britain's Ian Poulter. Much to the delight of locals, Weir was able to rekindle some of his Masters magic and prevail by winning 12 skins and three-quarters of the $360,000 pot.

Great tournament golf has prevailed in BC for more than a century now and continues to attract the world's finest women and men golfers to what continues to grow as one of the world's great golf destinations.

A NEW COMPETITION FOR AN OLD ASSOCIATION

When the inaugural PNGA Cup competition took place during the first week of May 2006, at the Seattle Golf Club, it marked the beginning of a now popular four-team golf event that sees four 12-player teams from British Columbia, Washington, Oregon and Idaho use a Ryder Cup format to determine an annual recipient of the already prestigious trophy.

It is the latest success story of the Pacific Northwest Golf Association, which can be traced back to 1899, making it the fifth-oldest golf association in North America. At that time, journalists in Victoria's *Daily Colonist* first wrote of the pending association, which officially came into being on February 4, 1899, in Tacoma and was originally called the Pacific Coast Golf Association. The six founding members included the Victoria Golf Club. C.B. Stahlschmidt of Victoria was elected president and Stuart Rice of Tacoma was elected secretary. At an April meeting in the same year the name was changed to the Pacific Northwest Golf Association.

The association was instrumental in establishing cross-border competitions and has long rotated both men's and women's tournaments, including Junior and Senior events, with play in BC and the northwestern states. In 1962 the PNGA introduced a new logo, designed by Don Sutton of Capilano Golf & Country Club. Depicting the international scope of the PNGA, it features the Peace Arch and the flags of both countries encircled by "Pacific Northwest Golf Association 1899."

The PNGA's annual championship quickly gained stature and by 1905 more than 100 players vied for the title. Many of BC's top amateurs

This 2012 British Columbia PNGA team finished second to Oregon in the annual event played at Gorge Vale in the first week on May. (L to R) Kevin Carrigan, Tony Hatchwell, Christina Proteau, Penny Baziuk, Alison Quinlan, Alison Murdoch, Sandy Harper, Gudmund Lindbjerg, Stephen Watson, Bryan Scott, Ben Griffins, Brent Wilson.
CHRISTOPHER MCGRATH, BRITISH COLUMBIA GOLF

Alison Murdoch of Victoria Club is the only BC golfer to have participated in all seven PNGA Cup events since the inauguration in 2006. CHRISTOPHER MCGRATH, BRITISH COLUMBIA GOLF

competed over the years, led by its great women players including Violet Pooley Sweeny who won seven times between 1905 and 1928, Vera Hutchings Ford who won six times between 1922 and 1935, and Marilyn Palmer who, in 1973, became the first BC resident to win in 38 years. All three women were later inducted into the PNGA Hall of Fame.

A fourth BC golfer so honoured was Margaret Todd. The three-time captain of the Canadian National Team was also the first female golfer inducted into the BC Sports Hall of Fame. In 2010, Todd donated $100,000 to the University of Victoria (BC) for the creation of a women's golf athletic financial award bearing her and her late husband Jack's name. The PNGA Super Senior Women's Amateur Championship trophy is named after Margaret Todd.

The PNGA cup brings together men and women who compete in four-ball, foursome and singles matches in Mid-amateur and Seniors (+55) for men and women and a Masters category (40-55) for men. Alison Murdoch from the Victoria Club has competed in all seven events for the BC team while Craig Doell of Victoria and Sandy Harper from Nanaimo have been mainstays on the men's team over the years.

In the seven competitions for the PNGA Cup through 2012 Oregon has dominated with five wins, including the most recent where they bested the BC team by two points en route to their fifth overall victory, played in blustery weather at Gorge Vale in Victoria. Both Washington and BC have won the event once, the latter's victory occurring in 2009 at the Crane Creek Country Club in Boise, Idaho.

In 2012 the BC team's second day comeback fell short as they finished second to an always-strong Oregon team. The Mid-amateur women's pairing of Christina Proteau from Port Alberni and Uplands member, Alison Quinlan, led the BC team with 5.5 out of a possible 6 points.

THE VANCOUVER GOLF TOUR

While the PNGA Cup is strictly an amateur event, another emerging competition in BC Golf is the Vancouver Golf Tour (VGT), founded in 2006. With the motto "Preparing Tomorrow's Champions," the Tour's goal is to provide opportunities for the region's best amateurs and young professionals to compete in a PGA-tour-calibre environment and learn how to maximize their game as they aspire to play on national and international tours.

VGT has quickly become Western Canada's focal point as a development tour while at the same time working alongside various charity golf events and raising more than $200,000 for charities since its inception. In 2011 alone, more than 1,000 players participated in at least one VGT event. Seven made their way to the final stages of the PGA qualifying school.

Fraser Mulholland, the VGT commissioner, outlined a 25-event schedule for 2012, including the inaugural BC Golf House Tradition Classic. Last year's two closing tournaments spoke to the pace at which the tour is gaining wide respect. The second-last event, played in early September, the Paine Edmonds Vancouver Open hosted by the sponsoring legal firm and the trio of Vancouver Parks courses at McCleery, Langara and Fraserview, featured an exciting overtime finish when Kamloops' Sun Rivers standout Brad Clapp surged from behind with a birdie-eagle finish to tie Adam Hadwin after regulation. Hadwin birdied the first extra hole to take the professional win while junior phenomenon Adam Svensson blew away the amateur field by finishing six-under and sixth overall before returning to the classroom for his last year of high school.

Brad Clapp gained some revenge before the month's end when he took the VGT at Quilchena, or the newly branded QGolf Club as it is now marketed. Clapp, who made his fourth journey from his home course that summer, earned an exciting one-stroke victory, after posting nine birdies in his round.

Clapp accepted his cheque and trophy while noting, "I'd like to thank Fraser and his team on the VGT for putting on such professionally run events. It's a great opportunity to play against such strong fields down in the Vancouver area on the VGT. It is like a mini-Canadian Tour event every time they tee it up. There are so many great players in this region."

And young Mr. Svensson was again present, with another six-under round and an eight-stroke victory over his nearest amateur rival.

The future of the VGT looks bright indeed.

CHAPTER 19

MURDER, MAYHEM AND OTHER ANECDOTES

Not all golf lore involves breathtaking shots on the greens. Beyond the pristine appearance of the fairways lurk sinister tales of misdeeds and mischief.

MURDER

Alf Willey didn't doubt for one minute that his brother, Frank, was a victim of foul play. Frank wouldn't have left town with their mother and sister in Edmonton for an Easter visit. He frequently went on excursions to escape the suffocating crowds but he wouldn't have done so without telling someone, reasoned Alf. He certainly wouldn't have deliberately vanished. The extensive manhunt for Frank "Tick" Willey dominated the front pages as Alberta's most sensational murder case of 1962 and brought him more attention than he had ever commanded as an amateur golfer in Vancouver or a pro in Alberta. Willey hasn't been seen since the April evening he left home to deliver a set of clubs to a visitor from Vancouver. Two men, Raymond Workman and William "Headball" Huculak, were convicted of murdering him, but his remains have never been found. One witness at the trial claimed she saw the suave 44-year-old Riverside course pro two days after he was reported missing. Willey's mother never believed her son was dead because she didn't want to believe it.

Tick Willey's comfort zone was solitude. He was shy and seemed to have an inferiority complex. He definitely had a homemade golf swing with a distinctive baseball grip, and an uneasy manner. However, he had quietly developed into a competent golfer who first gave notice in 1935.

Between victories by Stan Leonard, his illustrious clubmate at Langara and fellow caddy at Shaughnessy Heights, Willey captured the 1935 Vancouver Amateur title. He won with rounds of 71 and 75 at Point Grey.

Three years later, the slightly built public course player was centre stage. He had adopted a more conventional overlapping grip and entered the 1938 Amateur at the top of his game. Willey had averaged 70 in 15 practice rounds at Langara in preparation for the last major event at Jericho. He made it to the 36-hole final. Though unemployed, the dark, bushy-headed Willey appeared resplendent in plus-fours and argyle stockings for the title match against Point Grey's cherubic Don Gowan. Nicknamed the Local Haig for his nonchalance and the aplomb of Walter Hagen, Gowan caught Willey on the rebound from five years of self-imposed retirement. He claimed he sold his clubs for a biscuit then purchased a new set only a year before the Jericho event.

Before a gallery of 1,200, Gowan succeeded Ken Lawson as champion by defeating Willey on the 36th hole. The difference between the players was Gowan's polish and unwavering play. Willey, stronger with a brassie off the tees, was jittery around the greens. From tee to the green on the fifth hole Willey reportedly hitched up his pants 19 times. His undoings were two three-putt greens, the result of under-clubbed pitch shots.

During the war, Willey served with the Canadian army but never went overseas. In 1948 he resurfaced as a golf pro in Calgary. Alberta was an ideal refuge, affording him winters to play tours in California and Arizona, which he continued to do through February 1962. After first working in Calgary and Red Deer pro shops, Willey opened the city-operated Riverside course in 1951. Successive victories in the Alberta Open in 1953–1954 fuelled his confidence for continued journeys south. He rarely survived Monday qualifying rounds and, when he did, seldom made the 36-hole cut.

"Frank could play up a storm around Langara and Riverside," said Alf Willey, who caddied in winter for his brother in the early 1950s. "But he was too nervous to compete on tour." Alf last saw his brother in late 1961 at Riverside, returning the following June to testify at a preliminary hearing. Alf told the court he had met his brother's wife, Paris Willey, and

Workman, one of the accused, at Vancouver's Exhibition Park racetrack in July 1961. He testified that Paris Willey told him she planned to file divorce papers and marry Workman, a bookkeeper. He said Frank and Workman had known one another in Vancouver and had golfed together at Langara.

Another witness for the prosecution testified that Workman and Mrs. Willey had lived together in Edmonton for about three weeks in 1961. In his summation at the eight-day trial, Crown Prosecutor W.K. Shortreed said the motive for killing Willey arose from the familiarity of Workman with Paris Willey. Shortreed submitted evidence to prove that Workman and Huculak planned to lure the pro to a southeast Edmonton house on the pretence of buying the clubs, render him unconscious, hit him with a wrench and make it appear an accident. He said they decided instead to bury Willey's body in the country.

There were blood stains on a golf bag and club head-covers found in the trunk of Willey's abandoned car the day after he disappeared. The circumstantial evidence was sufficient for the six-man jury to find both Workman and Huculak guilty of capital murder after 2 hours 35 minutes of deliberation. It was only the second case in Canadian legal history where a body was never found but murder convictions resulted. Workman and Huculak were sentenced to hang. The sentences were later commuted to life imprisonment and both men were eventually paroled.

A 1963 court order declared Willey officially dead. Paris Willey received $44,500 in life insurance carried by her husband and inherited his car, assets in the Riverside pro shop and their $17,000 house. The Willeys had two children, Frank Jr. and Jan. The Case of the Disappearing Golf Pro has been closed, though Frank Willey's remains have never been recovered.

In his years as assistant pro at Langara, Len "Scotty" Taylor saw and served many peculiar players. But no procession of visitors was more bizarre than the party that marched across Langara's fairways one winter day in 1954. "Billy, the judge, jury and newspaper people all came to view the scene of the crime," recalls Taylor. "Billy was handcuffed, escorted by a Mountie all decked out in his scarlet tunic. Darned if Billy didn't raise his arms and wave to me, smiling, as they passed the pro shop. I'll never forget it. You'd have thought he was going to a party or something."

Billy was William Wakefied Gash and he was headed for the gallows. The unemployed 19-year-old father had confessed to slaying Frank Pitsch near Langara's 13th green on December 10, 1953, to rob him of $100. Head pro Ben Colk described Pitsch, who regularly searched the course for lost balls, as "a surly fellow we frequently chased off the place." Pitsch resided on East 49th, about seven blocks from Langara, but was known to have stayed on the course overnight.

The 45-year-old man's body was discovered by Bob Broome, a Langara regular, beside a rock pile in a cluster of bushes. Pitsch's head had been bashed with a blackjack that Gash had fashioned from a car axle. Billy Gash, who occasionally hunted balls and knew his victim, told police that he had planned the robbery for three weeks but that he "didn't mean to kill him." After bludgeoning Pitsch, Gash rolled up a coat to place under the victim's head and took his wallet. Then, filled with remorse, he dropped to his knees on the grass and wept.

At the trial, the court was told Gash had helped a woman pull a baby carriage through mud adjacent to the course before the fatal encounter with Pitsch. Gash, lanky and stoop-shouldered, was a volunteer wood-work instructor at Sunset Memorial Centre, where he also coached young boxers. His wife was expecting their second child.

Gash was sentenced to hang. But Justice Minister Stuart Garson acted on the all-male jury's "strongest recommendation of mercy," and a 750-name petition drafted by the convicted man's friends and neighbours. Gash's death sentence was commuted to life imprisonment and he was later paroled.

GHOSTS

The Ghost of Oak Bay has provided lively fiction for the news fabricators outside Victoria Golf Club as well as the storytellers inside the hallowed clubhouse.

Dr. George Bigelow, 12-time club champion, earned his place in Victoria Golf Club lore during his first victory in 1947 when his ball inexplicably "jumped" into the hole.
BC GOLF HOUSE 007.139.004A

According to several reported sightings over the years, the spectre of Doris Gravlin has haunted the course's famed Gonzales Point holes since her body was discovered on the beach below the seventh green in September 1936. The 30-year-old sister-in-law of Uplands pro Walter Gravlin was apparently beaten and strangled by her estranged husband, Victor Gravlin, the sports editor of a Victoria newspaper. A month later a fisherman found the remains of Victor entangled in a bed of kelp near the course. The assumption is that he drowned himself after murdering his wife. The apparition of Doris Gravlin has reportedly been seen by local university and high school students, thrill-seekers and neighbourhood people walking their dogs on the course at dusk. In his book *Ghosts*, Robert Belyk relates accounts of several witnesses identifying a misty figure as that of a woman.

Don't try convincing Dr. George Bigelow, a genuine character and fine golfer, that apparitions didn't exist at Oak Bay. Bigelow credited a miracle putt on the second green of the 1947 club championship to an earthquake. But he doesn't completely discount the possibility that a ghost might have been disoriented that morning and mischievously kicked the ball into the hole. The anesthetist with the prairie swing had putted to within two inches of the cup in his match against Don Campbell. As he walked to the hole, the ball fell into the cup. After Bigelow had won his first of 12 club titles, it emerged that an earthquake had shaken the centre of Vancouver Island, creating damage at Duncan and Comox. The quake hit at precisely 10:21 AM, a split second after Bigelow's attempted birdie putt at the second hole. No one at the green had felt a tremor—or sensed a ghostly presence.

While traditionalists like to believe in ghosts and tall tales, agnostics can't comprehend eerie occurrences such as the phantom bell ringer. The bell in question hangs behind the sixth green, which is blind to approaching players. The bell's toll signals that the green has been cleared. Donated to the club in 1923 by J.R. Waghorn, the bell is said to be from the *Duchess of 1862*, a Dunsmuir coaling locomotive. While lieutenant-governor of the province, James Dunsmuir constructed Hatley Park, now home to Royal Roads University. The former mansion is also said to be haunted. Club members attribute the mysterious bell-ringing and shadow-dancing across the foggy links to young pranksters.

THE LIGHTER SIDE OF GOLF

The memorial plaque on the water fountain at Marine Drive's 12th tee isn't a reminder for members to shout "Tibbetts" when their drives hook toward the out-of-bounds trees and adjacent McCleery course, although with many of them it became an instinctive pleading cry. Until his passing, clubmate Bill Tibbetts was famous for his pulled drives invariably deflecting off trees but staying in bounds rather than heading in the opposite direction on to McCleery. He did it so often that his regular playing partners started shouting "Tibbetts" in hopes of getting similar lucky caroms with their hooked drives.

"Years ago three of us playing in Puerto Rico were joined by a local," recalled Mike Tompkins, a close friend of Tibbetts. "The guy hooked a shot and I almost fell over when he yelled 'Tea-Buts.' I asked why he had yelled that. He shrugged, saying he'd heard it somewhere. Another member heard a player shout it in Florida."

Tompkins said the refrain started with a group of regulars: Don Bodie, Alvie Thompson, Dave Edgell and himself. "When Bill was ricochetting those drives from going OB, the trees weren't as thick or high as they are now," says Tompkins. "It was amazing how he would keep hitting those spindly trees and how 'Tibbetts' has spread internationally." The water fountain was inscribed following Tibbetts's death in 1987.

The battleship-grey skies hung low, mercilessly saturating Cowichan golf course. Few cars were in the parking lot, and the one nearest the pro shop belonged to Bill Wakeham. Declaring the dank winter day unfit even for fishing, Wakeham seized the opportunity to stock-take. Alone almost all morning, he heard the door open and close, glanced round to greet a visitor he didn't recognize, and resumed stacking a shelf with sweaters.

"Help you with anything, sir?" Wakeham asked, noticing the man handling several drivers.

"Not really," he replied. "But do you have drivers with stiffer shafts than these?"

"Sorry, I don't." Wakeham's back was turned to the customer as he squatted to open a carton of sweaters. Something, perhaps his acute instincts, alerted him to turn his head. As a result he saw the blur of a shaft coming down at him and moved his head a split second before crashing to the floor from the impact to his shoulder. Wakeham, not seriously injured by the glancing blow, later learned his attacker was related to a female member who reportedly had been in the pro's company long after a half-hour lesson the evening before. "I was lucky," the free-spirited Wakeham joked weeks later. "The guy was a slicer."

Golfers have been expelled from clubs for various indiscretions but Doug Davidson got a bum rap when ordered to clean out his locker at Vancouver Golf Club. He was known to be as reckless and impetuous as his brother the late Al Davidson, a fiery, controversial sportscaster who constantly created static on the airwaves.

Doug spent considerable time at the club, golfing and playing cards in the men's grill and socializing in the lounge upstairs. He occasionally flirted with a particular waitress. Stairs in the clubhouse lead from the men's grill to the lounge-dining room, bypassing an auxiliary area of the kitchen. One evening Davidson decided it was time to quit cards and eat or he wouldn't be in any condition to drive home. Upon reaching the top of the stairs, he couldn't resist surprising a bustling waitress with a playful pinch from behind. Everyone in the dining room heard the shriek. When the woman turned around, Davidson was aghast as the sobering discovery that he had been guilty of mistaken identity slowly dawned on him. The woman he thought he recognized from behind was the wife of a club director. Davidson was suspended from the club for life.

● ● ●

There is no wrath like the wrath of a golfer. Rafe Mair, the former lawyer-politician and radio open-line host, once played to a two handicap at Kamloops and Quilchena. His fits of temper are still recounted at the West Richmond course.

Utterly disgusted with the game and himself one day, Mair threw more than another tantrum. He chucked his bag of clubs into the lake in front of the clubhouse and stormed into the men's lounge. Several drinks later, vowing never to play again, he left the clubhouse, cursing as he fumbled through his pockets. Then he remembered. Before teeing off, he had put his car keys in his golf bag for safekeeping. To the delight of clubhouse onlookers, Mair removed his shoes and socks, rolled up his pants and waded into the pond. He dragged the clubs out with considerable difficulty. Upon removing his keys from the side pocket, he heard someone shout gleefully, "We knew you wouldn't quit for more than 24

Dunc Sutherland's Meadowlands cornfest came complete with prize goats for winning Burquitlam foursome Al Nelson, Al Mather, Ken Matheson and Elmer White. AL NELSON

hours." Mair promptly flung the clubs back into the pond, found the parking lot and drove off.

◦ ◦ ◦

No one could throw a golf party as well as Dunc Sutherland. There was no pro-amateur quite like his annual gathering at Meadowlands, the quaint little country course in Chilliwack. Every fall when the corn was sweet, Sutherland beckoned us to Meadowlands for a fun day of golf.

Following the king-sized spread on Kay Sutherland's banquet table, you sweated out the prize presentations. Everyone got something, a bag full of corn, a gallon of honey, smoked ham and some more lively prizes: rabbits, goats, pigs, geese, anything that Dunc could round up from neighbouring barnyards. His penchant for encouraging all the winners to take their prizes home with them eventually caused some problems and Dunc was forced to discontinue gift-wrapping farm animals. One

September the SPCA was alerted that two men, one brandishing what looked to be a golf club and the other wearing a tam and kilt, had been observed chasing a squealing, runaway pig along the highway.

One year Sutherland regaled grand winner Dave Crane, the Kelowna pro, by appearing from the kitchen, bagpipes blaring and a goat in tow. Crane put Billy the goat into his station wagon for safekeeping and returned to the banquet. Later Crane discovered to his horror that his prize had enjoyed a feast of his own. The goat had dined on the upholstery of Crane's vehicle.

● ● ●

Stan Leonard had been eliminated from the 1934 Amateur at Old Quilchena so his caddy, Ernie Brown, was unemployed for the rest of the week. Hal Straight, who enjoyed covering golf for the *Vancouver Sun* from the men's lounge until play was meaningful, summoned the idle caddy to his table with a job offer. "Hey, kid, here's a pencil and notepad," said Straight. "I'll give you fifty cents if you get me the results of what's happening." Brown dutifully reported the details to Straight. When he requested payment the next day, Brown was promised a dollar if he'd run scores again. Still unpaid starting the third day, Brown vowed to get even with the reporter.

After nine holes of the Dick Moore–Allan Taylor semifinal, Brown sought out Straight in the clubhouse, saying he had a hot scoop. "Taylor's out in 29 and 7 up on Moore," Brown said excitedly. Straight dropped his drink and rushed to the nearest telephone, reporting the partial score for the *Sun's* late edition. The man who eventually became the paper's managing editor was almost fired as a result of Brown's information. Moore, not Taylor, had led by seven holes.

● ● ●

Johnny Johnston was the undisputed king of needlers, notorious for playing mind games with opponents young and old. On the morning of his 36-hole final for the 1966 Amateur championship, Johnston dragged himself to Capilano's practice fairway with caddy Glenn McDonald in tow.

Wayne Vollmer (left) and Johnny Johnston played together on three Willingdon Cup teams in the mid-1960s. In 1966 Johnston denied Vollmer a repeat win in the BC Amateur by defeating him in the final played at Capilano. BC GOLF HOUSE 007.128.187

Wayne Vollmer, his young, determined opponent, was already there, working up a sweat with his one-iron. The dynamic future touring pro stopped briefly and watched Johnston empty a shag-bag containing about a dozen balls. Johnston motioned to McDonald to stop after about 30 feet, wedged the balls into the bag held aloft by the caddy and moaned, "That's enough, Glenn. I've got this horrible Drambuie headache. I'm kind of hungover." Vollmer allowed himself a smirk, and continued his practice a little more confident of victory. Johnston, of course, hadn't swallowed anything stronger than tea the night before when the nine o'clock gun signalled his bedtime. He won 4 and 3.

Golfers can be rather eccentric. Terry MacKinnon was a classic case, intensely volatile and overly proud. Through hard work and determination, the Vancouver radio broadcaster turned into a fair but never satisfied golfer.

After an apparently decent round at Langara one summer day in 1990, MacKinnon was muttering to himself as he stomped to the parking lot. He was cursing his putter. Everyone heard MacKinnon depart. He didn't burn rubber on 49th, heading to Cambie. It was the clankety-clank-clank of the putter he had unceremoniously tied to the back bumper of his Camaro. He dragged it all the way home, punishing it. He lived near 70th and Granville.

●　●　●

Yarns are spun at Oak Bay about George Bigelow's pet seagull, whose squawk sounded more like a cackle following one of the good doctor's waist-high wind-cheating shots. The doc tolerated the cheeky seagull, though it is said that pro Phil Taylor was less than fond of the bird. He shooed it off the roof of his pro shop several times.

One day Taylor and Art Christopher, a money-player from Shaughnessy, were dead-even on the par-four 18th tee. They both drove up the middle, almost equidistant. As they walked up the fairway, the seagull swooped down, plucked up Christopher's ball and flew over the green, dropping the ball two inches from the hole! The seagull-three cost Taylor ten dollars. Years later Christopher showed up at Taylor's 80th birthday celebration and presented him with the ten-dollar bill, mounted and framed.

●　●　●

Like so many golfers, Bill Simmons would go to any lengths to save a stroke or win a match. At New Quilchena, the former Vancouver police sergeant sliced his second shot at the ninth hole. But his ball didn't splash into the lake between the 9th and 18th greens. It startled the ducks and swans by landing on the island in the middle of the lake. He wasn't about to accept a penalty for being unable to play a ball on dry ground, even though it was in a lateral water hazard. The birds were startled and disturbed again when Simmons removed his spikes, threw his wedge to the island, dog-paddled across, pitched to the green and swam back. With his playing companions still roaring with laughter, the sopping Simmons splashed onto the green and two-putted for his par.

To those who knew and loved him, Les Milne indirectly evoked life's enjoyments and experiences every day. He was Mr. Junior Golf in BC. The whimsical, endearing Scot with the snow-white hair touched the lives of hundreds of juniors throughout the province, specifically those at Fraserview, Vancouver Golf Club, Old Quilchena and finally Seymour. Milne passed away in 1977 at the age of 80. In keeping with his requests, he was cremated and his favourite dark rum flowed at his wake at the home of Mel and Tricia White. One evening months later, Milne's non-golfing daughters Leslie and Estelle appeared at the Seymour pro shop with an urn containing their father's ashes. It was pitch black when they were last seen walking toward the 10th green to spread the ashes over the fairway of what apparently was Les's favourite hole, the 16th. Members were puzzled the next morning to find a defined stripe of residue, as if chalk-marked. An approving smile must have adorned Les's face as his daughters deliberately did their duty. In the dark, they drew a line directly down the centre of the fairway. It was an appropriate tribute to a man who did his utmost to encourage everyone to play life, and the game, straight down the middle and to smile while doing it.

At Port Alice, the course with the church between the third and fourth fairways, there was never any doubt who was the guilty party when a ball crashed through one of St. Paul's windows. During the war when equipment was scarce, golf balls were marked for identification purposes, usually by the member's initials. When a lost ball was found, it would be returned to the rightful owner. Murdo Thompson, who did volunteer work on the course and at the town bowling alley, was caught dead to rights one afternoon when he sliced his marked ball through a church window. "The choir was practising," says Thompson, a Port Alice mill machine-tender from 1937 through 1952, "and I blamed them for throwing me off by hitting a high note just as I was in my backswing."

As Qualicum Beach's caddy master while in his early teens, English-born Fred Westnedge dealt directly with celebrities and aristocrats who visited the posh Vancouver Island haven during the late 1920s and early 1930s. "My accent helped me get the job," says Westnedge. "The entire staff in the hotel was very, very English." He remembers serving Zane Grey, Edgar Rice Burroughs, Dr. Davidson and Major-General Francis Arthur Sutton.

Davidson, a Titanic survivor who wore a neck brace, was the only medical man in town. One day a hotel bellhop rushed onto the course to find the good doctor, whose services were urgently required at a nearby road accident. He anxiously asked the foursome at the ninth tee whether his group could play through!

Sutton, a flamboyant soldier of fortune, found his way to Qualicum Beach from Vancouver in 1927 and purchased Portland Island in the Gulf of Georgia. The English adventurer had lost his right arm at Gallipoli during the First World War and became known on the course as One-Arm. "Do you look after things around here?" Sutton enquired of the young caddy master while preparing to debut at Qualicum. "Yes, sir," replied Westnedge. "Well, hold on to this for safekeeping, laddie," said Sutton, removing the prosthetic limb and handing it to the startled youngster.

Walter Hagen anecdotes are legendary. On their 1920 North American exhibition tour the irrepressible Haig and the brilliant young Horton Smith were passengers on a Victoria-bound CPR ferry that collided with a Seattle vessel on a foggy October evening. When the alert sounded, witnesses said Smith, the 21-year-old sensation and winner of nine tour events the previous winter, was one of the first persons prepared to abandon ship. He came on deck with two lifesavers around one arm and his golf clubs over his other shoulder. Hagen, ever the showman, made the most of this impromptu stage. He sauntered out of his cabin attired in a silk lounging robe, oblivious to the panic. He watched the proceedings with the nonchalance of being four down with four holes to play.

ECCENTRIC ENVIRONMENTS

Perhaps the most peculiar golf course ever contrived in BC was located on Savary Island, the sandy pencil-thin paradise off Lund in the Strait of Georgia. Savary Island's sporty links were as capricious as the winds: there one day, gone the next. The lunar table dictated dates for the club's annual championship; there could be no tournament without an ebb tide because otherwise there would be no course.

Whimsical organizers annually improvised a course on the expansive sand-baked shores of Indian Point to determine who would take possession of the Cast-up-by-the-Sea Cup. The championship started in the mid-1920s after, so it has been said, vacationing Victoria Golf Club member John Ashworth found an unusual samovar that apparently had drifted ashore at Indian Point. It was duly presented for annual competition.

Annoyances and hazards were uncommon along the smooth, level sand course, resulting in extraordinary long shots and low scores. Contestants did not actually putt out, but instead completed the hole by hitting their ball within a four-foot circle scratched into the firm sand. It was folly and it was fun. Ernie Roberts of Vancouver Glenoaks took the 1929 championship with a score of 57 for 18 holes. Ashworth's 60 tied Miss M. Archibald for second.

David Jones II of Lillooet would appreciate Sir Walter Simpson's theory on one specific principle of early Scottish golf, as described in his historic missive *Art of Golf.* Simpson wrote,

> A shepherd tending his sheep would chance upon a round pebble; he would strike it away, for it is inevitable that a man with a stick in hand should aim a blow at any loose object lying in his path . . . a shepherd feeding his sheep on the links, perhaps St Andrews, rolled

one of those stones into a rabbit scrape. "Marry," he quoth, "I could not do that if I tried," which nerved him to the attempt.

Was golf born from such beginnings? And when Simpson spoke of hazards, specifically the bunker, were the first "from a natural sandpit where sheep huddled for shelter"?

Appropriately, Sheep Pasture is the name owner Jones chose to call his homemade course on his family's 1,500-acre spread five kilometres from Lillooet. There 150 head of cattle and 235 sheep are his mobile hazards, his automatic grass cutters. They roam the fairways at will. "Golfers make good shepherds," Jones concluded after seven seasons on the course he started in 1984. "They keep away predators with their presence. Before I had the course coyotes used to get 25 sheep every year. The last four or five years I've lost but one." The wary sheep have learned that grazing in proximity to the 60-acre course is reasonably safe, although they're occasionally stung by rocketing white pellets.

"The course's still rough in places but it's comin' around," observed Jones, a Lillooet-born rancher who inherited a fondness for golf. "It's the third one that's been made on this property."

Oswald Jones, his grandfather, purchased the ranch as an investment before the First World War. A surgeon, Jones was the ship's doctor when he came around the Horn to Victoria from Wales in 1906. He liked Victoria so much he stayed and joined the Oak Bay links. In the 1920s Oswald's son, D.C. "Joe" Jones, also a keen golfer, moved from Victoria to manage the ranch and soon charted out a course along the river bench. In 1951 the local Elks Club was allowed to fashion a course of sorts elsewhere on the ranch but abandoned it five years later. Both of these courses had sand greens and little maintenance and ultimately reverted to pastureland.

The viability of a course in Lillooet intrigued David Jones II. The nearest golf was in Kamloops, about 160 kilometres to the east. Jones assessed local golf interest with a petition in a service station. "About 100 signed up saying they'd be interested in joining a club," he noted.

At Sheep Pasture, where hazards are natural, owner David Jones demonstrates that course grooming is not utmost in his mind. STEVE BOSCH

"I figured if I could actually get 50 of them I could make it work." He didn't regret building the 2,625-yard course. For the 1992 season the 130 members paid annual dues of $175, ensuring Jones wouldn't lose any sleep over counting his sheep.

Twenty years later the course remains a golfing centre that doesn't take itself too seriously. Its website describes the course as "home to the local mixed-breed sheep herd who tend to keep the course well fertilized, nicely grazed and the golfers amused." A change in management in 2004 helped sustain the course which is nestled along the banks of the Fraser River with few frills. Bring your own food and beverages and heed the invitation to "ditch the cell phone and come up and hang out with the sheep at Lillooet Golf Course."

Mount DuBose Golf and Country Club must have been the most exclusive course in the province. It was surely the most isolated. Sand greens awaited golfers in Kemano, a remote community that Alcan created for a hydro-electric power station that serves Kitimat's aluminum smelter at the head of Douglas Channel. No roads led to Kemano, with its fluctuating population of approximately 300. In its heyday, Alcan's 40-passenger vessel arrived twice weekly from Kitimat with supplies that likely included a few sleeves of golf balls. The company town, originally built in the 1950s, closed down in 2000 and many of its buildings were burned as part of a province-wide training exercise for select fire departments. Any leftover golfers in the region now look to the 18-hole Hirsch Creek course in Kitimat, where the fairways can be shared with assorted wildlife including black bears, grizzly bears, moose, deer, eagles and the club's pesky mascot Red Fox, a famous ball thief.

Glacier Greens used to be one of the best kept secrets in Comox Valley, a private course that was restricted to Canadian armed services personnel and guests. Originally called the Base Golf Course, Glacier Greens was built on the orders of Colonel K.C. Lett and opened in 1971. The base commander in 1968–69 was obviously an ardent golfer and recognized the need to provide personnel with easily accessible golf. Captain Bob Sherrat, a navigator with the 409 Squadron, sketched a 3,000-yard layout over 70 dormant acres and the course was developed almost entirely by on-base volunteers. In his design Sherrat captured the vista of magnificent Forbidden Plateau from the fifth and sixth fairways. Glacier Greens, now open to green-fee players, was expanded to a full 18 holes for 1995 and has become a popular mid-Island course.

At Salmo, where they've golfed since the mid-1930s, visitors were alerted to give oncoming traffic the right-of-way on the third and fourth fairways. The Salmo District Golf Club was advertised as North America's first golfport. Although Salmo is not BC's busiest airport, club members—about 100 strong in 2012—learned to be wary of incoming airplanes, helicopters and skydivers. The airport came first, built to provide employment during the Depression. Skinny Anderson, a founding club member, recalled golfers playing before the Second World War but that a course wasn't launched until 1942 after Japanese citizens, housed at a nearby internment camp, provided the labour force to complete the course. The club leases the property from Transport Canada and the third and fourth fairways still cut directly across the golfport's only runway.

Wayne Lindberg said his ambition in life was to own a golf course. The former Vancouver high school teacher bought two abandoned courses, remodelled and reinvigorated them, and claims he was content to make a living off green fees from his course in Langley and Ruskin. Lindberg turned doomed Shamrock at Langley into Tall Timbers in 1979 and salvaged Ruskin's notorious Iron Mountain layout by rechristening it Eighteen Pastures. This unique course is noted for its red clubhouse and for greens fees as low as fifteen dollars (only on Tuesdays) not including the lost golf balls. Lindberg brought both old and new fans to the course with distinct fun events that included a series modelled on a boxing promotion variation. "So you think you can golf" days drew a horde of masochists to the course for a tournament in which the course was made diabolically difficult. Over the years millions of dollars have gone into the 210-acre site. The original speculators went bankrupt and a second owner, Larry Messier, forfeited his hold on it after announcing plans to develop an obesity treatment facility on adjoining land. With the course going to seed, Lindberg came to the rescue and in 1987 took it off the hands of the municipality of Mission, which zoned the property parkland.

CHAPTER 20
SPONSORS, CHARITY AND VOLUNTEERS

From the very beginning, golf has been heavily reliant on the goodwill of volunteers, whether they donated time, money or expertise. This chapter recognizes some of the people and organizations who have contributed to golf's growth and endurance in BC, as well as the charities that have benefitted from the generosity of golf enthusiasts.

SPONSORS

A 17th-century author named Robert Smith Surtees must have had George "Sonny" Williams in mind when he coined the phrase "full o' beans and benevolence." Anyone who knew Williams wouldn't have found it difficult to believe the anecdotal account that led to his involvement with the BC Open. It's a graphic illustration of the man's caring and giving, of his love for people and golf.

A new member at the Vancouver Golf Club, Williams experienced his first pro-amateur competition in the 1982 Open at Point Grey. He loved every minute of it. With an ugly duckling swing, wildly fast and pell-mell, he seemed to relish self-destructing on the golf course. The cussin' truck driver from Vancouver's east end wore a smile all day, as permanent as the cigarette in the corner of his mouth. Williams had enjoyed himself in his tournament debut that day in part because of a playing companion. He had drawn Seattle's classy Don Bies, who had won the Open two years earlier, as his pro.

A few weeks later, Williams was holding court at VGC and telling club pro Al Nelson how impressed he was with the pro-am and Bies. Nelson, a PGA BC director, thanked Williams and ruefully mentioned that the Open was in serious financial difficulty. "I don't know if we can carry on," Nelson lamented. Williams squashed his freshly lit smoke into the ashtray and blurted out, "How much will it take to keep it going?" Nelson paused, reflectively, and replied, "Oh, about fifteen grand." Williams fumbled in his sports jacket for a pen and made out a cheque to the PGA BC for $20,000.

The generosity of Williams and the business associates he subsequently recruited to support the Open not only saved the tournament from cancellation, but also increased its stature and purse substantially through 1990. "Nelson was pretty crafty that day," Williams recalled with a wink. "He made sure I had a couple of stiff drinks to loosen my pocketbook." In eight years the George Williams BC Open ascended from an uncertain $75,000 tournament to the Canadian Tour's most lucrative event with a $160,000 prize pot.

Williams hadn't been so smitten by anything since he met his wife, Verna. A hard-working man trying to enjoy some of the fruits of his success, he became addicted to a game as foreign to him as caviar. The indulgence was a reward to himself after saving his father's failing moving company from bankruptcy. He had left school after the ninth grade, at 14, to load and drive trucks for his father. With the success of Williams Moving and Storage, Sonny (his father also was George) discovered there were other things in life than work.

When Williams threw his weight and money behind the Open, he enlisted a squad of boosters who followed with cheque books—or else. There was Trev Edwards of Stave Lake Logging, Norm Edgar of Cantins Moving and Storage, Bill Gartside of Commerical Trucking, Shadow Reid of Shadow Lines, Barry Code of Esso, Herb Osen of T.O.S. Insurance Services, Chuck Martin of United Van Lines in Toronto, Gordie Winter and Don Skagan of Mohawk Oil, Joe Delesalle of Lumberland, Jack Mason of Lift Truck Services and Darryl Anderson of Columbia Chrome. Few people dared say no to Sonny Williams.

Almost all the boosters knew Williams through business before they were fellow VGC members. In 1957 Williams took over the company his father had started 30 years earlier by borrowing fifty dollars to put down on a Dodge Touring Car he converted into a truck. When Sonny took over there were 15 vehicles, 40 employees and a mountain of debts. And then he hit a bonanza.

> Ocean Falls turned it completely around for us, put us back into full operation. When CZ closed down the mill up there in '71, we got the contract to move the people out. It took two and a half months and no sooner had we moved out the last family, the NDP was voted in and be damned if they didn't reopen Ocean Falls. We got to move most of the people back up there.

In early 1992 Williams Moving and Storage had expanded as far as Regina, with 400 employees and almost 1,200 pieces of equipment. "When I decided to drop the Open, the other sponsors went too," said Williams, whose departure coincided with health problems. "I left it in good shape, but I didn't leave the same way," he said, referring to his latest diagnosis. "I got the nicest letter from a player after the 1990 Open, the year it rained so damn hard they cancelled the last round. He wrote that it wouldn't stop raining because God was crying so hard when he heard I was leaving."

Soon after, Sonny Williams played his last game of golf. He was struck by Lou Gehrig's disease (amyotrophic lateral sclerosis, or ALS), a muscle debilitating affliction that cruelly crippled his arms. But the man's spirit and his love of life and golf remained strong until his death in 1996.

Individual sponsorship of professional tournaments is largely a thing of the past and even corporate sponsorship has been unreliable over the years. At one time tobacco and beer companies dominated sponsorship but more discerning social guidelines have discouraged that tradition. Xerox and Payless Gas stepped in at different times to finance tournaments and in recent years Victoria's *Times Colonist* newspaper and Island

Savings Credit Union have sponsored the popular Victoria Open, which annually leads off the summer stretch of Canadian tour events that flow across Canada from west to east through the summer months. In Vancouver the two prominent newspapers have long had a role in tournament sponsorship. The event affectionately known as The Province, The Dueck and then The Sun Match Play during its history once rated as the country's second-best tournament. In fact, the PGA BC match play was always the association's bread and butter winner.

Before TV and before some club pros decided to stay in their shops rather than risking defeat to amateurs, the match play attracted more entries and more spectators than the BC Open and BC Amateur combined. Organized in 1946 by pros Leonard, Colk, Wood, Brown, McKinnon and Sutherland, the first purse totalled $1,440. Wood took the first title and $200 over Monty Hill, the "giant-killer" Marine amateur. Some 20 years later the purse was only $1,500, with Dick Munn earning $400 for defeating Bob Cox Jr. before a Point Grey gallery of 3,000. It was rare prize money for the pros and the format gave amateurs the opportunity to go up against stiff competition. The PGA BC got major coverage by persuading Vancouver's two major newspapers, first the *Province* and then the *Vancouver Sun*, to sponsor the tournament. The season-opening event on five successive Sundays of knockout matches and a tradition of major upsets made the format perfect for a newspaper serial. Galleries were huge.

After the final match in 1953, Stan Leonard estimated that 25,000 spectators had watched play from the qualifying round through the 36-hole final. "Only the Canadian Open can compare with that kind of attendance," observed Leonard after taking the F.B. McElroy Trophy for the fourth time.

Crowds of 4,000 weren't uncommon with leading players matched in late rounds, especially on exclusive courses. They were rare opportunities for green-fee players to visit the private clubs. However, interest in regional pro golf tournaments started falling sharply in the early 1970s. Other events and TV conflicted with them and club pros were better off financially attending to their shops. Entry fees of turn-away fields went into PGA BC coffers while sponsors put up the prizes; collections taken among the crowds went to support junior golf.

By 1973, under the banner of the *Sun*, the format changed to team best-ball in an effort to rekindle interest and accommodate larger entries. With additional players the purse increased to $4,300. Pros Gordie Fairbairn and Tom Moryson each collected $600 for their first of two straight victories. Sponsored by Mitsushiba Canada in 1992, when Ward Stouffer and Lanny Sawchuk each pocketed $1,500 as champions, the tournament took place for the last time on the PGA Tour in 2006.

CHARITY

The biggest winner every BC golf season is charity. All other sports combined do not approach the charitable donations generated by golfers. Many local and regional charitable organizations benefit from annual golf functions that are often organized by volunteers and sponsored by golf courses that offer reduced rates and banquet facilities. Local businesses donate prizes and participants contribute large fees for outings. Most events are topped off by auctions of special items that raise additional funds.

There are endless examples. The Alumni Charity Golf Tournament is one of the premier golf tournaments in northern BC and to date has raised over $155,000 to support student athletes at the University of Northern British Columbia. At Morgan Creek, the Children's Wish Foundation has been the recipient of over $350,000 in the past six years, and a Big Sisters annual event at the University Course in Vancouver has averaged over $80,000 per year in the last five years. Since its inception in 1995, the annual Victoria Golf Club Charity Tournament has raised more than $600,000 to support Victoria Women's Transition House Society, which is currently the largest single annual gift for the Shelter. For 18 years the Nanaimo & District Hospital Foundation has sponsored Golf for Life, a September event held in nearby Nanoose at Fairwinds Golf Club. Over $670,000 has been raised to buy golf equipment. New tournaments continue to spring up, often driven by a small group and a good cause. In Cranbrook, what started as realtor Ryan Dayman's local invitational saw his hockey agent friends, Epp and Jarrett Bousquet, recruit three NHL stars to play at the Wildstone Golf Course for a third annual event. They surpassed all goals by raising over $40,000 for local organizations.

VOLUNTEERS

Celebrity-charity golf is greatly enhanced by appearances from noted entertainers and athletes who also lend their names to events; others commemorate special individuals. But the game's most admired participants are those who take on the tasks of running associations and tournaments. Long-serving PGA BC secretary Billy Thompson used to say, "I wouldn't want to have to do this for a living." The pioneers of BC golf administration set a high standard of stewardship.

In 1922, Victoria's Biggerstaff Wilson was elected the BCGA's first president. Hall C. "Sonny" Chiene, a founding member of the revived Jericho course, also presided over the BCGA and served as a BC Racing Commission steward. Chiene, whose father was Scotland's first rugby president, earned international caps while at Edinburgh University. He immigrated to Vancouver in 1905.

Bill Charlton, a charter member at Point Grey, became the first British Columbian elected president of the Royal Canadian Golf Association in 1941. Charlton and Jim Cather founded the BC Seniors Association in 1930; two years later 40 players competed in the first Seniors tournament. Joe Howat won the 1946 Seniors title and for many years handled the BCGA's secretarial duties. Herb Fritz, the Vancouver Club member who developed Nico Wynd in Surrey, has made significant contributions to both the BC and Pacific Northwest associations. Among the greatest junior boosters was Gordon "Pappy" Bowers, who chaired the organizing committee for the 1952 Canadian Amateur at Capilano. His allies included Les Milne, Harry White, Bill MacIntosh and Fred Wellsby.

William "Billy" Thompson, a retired Edmonton school teacher, strolled into Old Quilchena's pro shop one day on a walk from his Pine Crescent residence and asked if there was anything he could do. In 1973, he celebrated his 25th anniversary as PGA BC secretary-treasurer. He was 93. Thompson took over the duties from pro Ernie Brown, receiving an

Billy Thompson served as PGA BC secretary-treasurer for 25 years and scored for countless tournaments. BILL CUNNINGHAM

annual honorarium of fifty dollars. He ran the association's only money-maker, the annual match-play tournament, and quietly assisted pros who over-extended themselves. A non-golfer but a regular visitor to Point Grey, Thompson was former club pro Leroy Goldsworthy's elementary teacher in Edmonton.

Probably BC golf's most efficient organization, the Victoria District Golf Committee was formed in 1932 for clubs within a 30-mile radius of the capital city. If any one committee man stood above the others it was Harry Young. Young, one-time golf columnist and business editor of the *Victoria Colonist*, presided over the district committee for 14 years. He also chaired the 1967 Commonwealth matches at Victoria and the Canadian Amateur at Colwood, and originated Canada's only winter golf event, the Christmas Tree Tournament, every Boxing Day.

Once a Capilano caddie, sportswriter Arv Olson took over the golf beat for the *Vancouver Sun* in 1957 and built relationships in the game over 35 years before penning his original *Backspin* in the early 1990s. BC GOLF HOUSE 007.133.003

Leo "The Hawk" Derman was also a pillar of the committee. He joined Gorge Vale in 1935 after beating Pat Fletcher for the district caddy championship. He became Gorge club captain and champion, and held the position of secretary-manager from 1950 through 1979.

The BCGA's first full-time manager, Ralph Madden, was appointed in 1969. The association's affairs had previously been operated on a part-time basis by BCGA secretary-treasurer Bob Maze, whose workload became so burdensome that in 1967 a permanent secretary, the highly capable Bea Deacon, was hired.

Bill Good Sr. was forever labelled "Breathless Bill" for the live radio broadcasts of the Canadian Open and Amateur championships. Trudging sloped fairways on a hot day while whispering into a microphone tended to take one's breath away.

With a voice to match his stature, Good claimed to be Canada's first full-time freelance sports broadcaster. Good recalled working with Montreal colleague Doug Smith. "We were both tall—Doug was six-four and I'm six-six—so we could see over most spectators. But we still had to deal with crowds and all that short-wave equipment strapped on our backs. We always scrambled to get to the high ground before everyone else.

"Huffing and puffing to keep up with the play and get to the most advantageous viewing places, we had to be saying something. It was between shots but, remember, we were on air, live. The CBC didn't have commercial breaks. And there's nothing worse than dead air."

On the hilliest courses, Good and Smith would each lose up to 15 pounds while broadcasting four to five hours. By day's end their equipment, about 80 pounds, felt like sacks full of boulders.

"I'll never forget one Canadian Amateur in particular," Good said in reference to the 1955 final in which Moe Norman defeated Vancouver's Lyle Crawford after 39 holes at Calgary Golf and Country Club. "That day we really earned our money. We had to face that hill three times."

Calgary's memorable first hole is an arduously steep par-five, and trekking the course that day was more exhausting than usual; both players were noted for playing quickly. After the morning 18, the marshals requested Norman and Crawford to slow down for the gallery's sake. The inimitable, zany Norman walked and talked like a trigger-happy machine gunner and Crawford's back-swing was a blur.

"Many championships seemed to go extra holes," laughed Good, as he reflected on six hours broadcasting the notorious 1952 Canadian Amateur final between Larry Bouchey and Bill Campbell at Capilano. "After the match, I don't remember them shaking hands or a prize presentation."

Bouchey, a husky California car salesman who played with a ubiquitous cigar in his mouth, went on to beat the tall, classy Virginian after being two down with three to play. Bouchey had been awarded the critical 34th hole after Campbell failed to tap in, believing his short putt had been conceded. Throughout the day the two had been giving one another tap-ins.

After consulting with Bouchey, referee Colin Rankin ruled that Campbell had not finished the hole. Bouchey birdied the next and they finished even. The noticeably agitated Campbell then bogeyed Capilano's easy par-five opener, to lose on the first extra hole.

Good and Smith had to be nimble and alert to keep on top of play and often sought volunteers. "We'd ask spectators to find out what was happening behind us or up ahead. Otherwise we couldn't know how anyone out of our range was doing.

"We scouted courses to get the lay of the land . . . we'd have to know location of hazards and approximate distances from certain positions and contours of the greens. Most players understood our difficulties: they'd talk to us on air walking between shots."

Bill Good came west via the CBC from Winnipeg in 1948. When he wasn't on the air waves, he wrote golf and curling for both Vancouver dailies. By 1950 he was doing commercials on behalf of Brown Brother Motors and Macdonald Tobacco, companies with whom he became synonymous; he was earning huge money, almost $50,000 annually.

"That year the *Province* fired me as golf writer," said Good, "not because of incompetence, but because I was making too much money in radio.

"Erwin Swangard. the sports editor, told me he had to cut one person from the department. After I told him I didn't want to quit, he still fired me. Johnny Graham, the shop steward, insisted Swanny had no grounds to let me go. So he farmed me to City Hall, figuring I'd screw up there. He didn't know I'd worked the beat in Winnipeg."

Good, who decided he didn't need the hassle or their paycheques, quit newspapering altogether six months later and went full bore into broadcasting. He came into the Canadian Football League with the BC Lions in 1954 and did a post-game football show for 25 years.

Son Bill Jr. followed in Good's large footsteps. He started broadcasting sports but over four decades has made his biggest impression as a TV news anchor and on CKNW talk radio.

As tall as his father, he emceed prize presentations for the 1968 Molson Canadian Women's Open at Shaughnessy. The winner was six-foot-three Carol Mann. When called to the stage, she grabbed the microphone before Good could utter a word and enquired: "Are you married?"

●　●　●

My 1950 introduction to golf came at Capilano, a veritable local cathedral of the game. I was a naive 14-year-old caddy. Ted Williams had just signed with the Boston Red Sox for a record $125,000; I realized there was big money to be made in sports.

By packing doubles twice around the hilly layout you could make seven dollars a day. Sometimes you got stuck with the deadliest of member combinations: a vicious hooker or a natural slicer. Left, right; right, left. We called it army golf. I marched double-time at Capilano for the money, not because I had any affinity for golf. I never dreamed I'd develop a lifelong lust for the game that would lead to the golf beat at the *Vancouver Sun*.

After a North Vancouver pal, Hugh Harrison, took me to Capilano, where he toted bags when not in school, I concluded earning money there was decidedly better than delivering newspapers or mowing lawns. Hugh quickly informed me the most important person in the pro shop was caddy master Hector Herbert, not pro Jock McKinnon.

McKinnon, Capilano's original pro, was the most intimidating man I would encounter—until I quivered before big gruff Hal Straight, my first boss at *The Sun*. From the caddy quarters, we often heard McKinnon's barking voice. On the first tee, you could almost feel the captious pro's eyes riveted on you in spite of any attempt to follow Herbert's instructions to be as inconspicuous as the bag we were tending.

Herbert was both efficient and fair. When Hugh and I arrived early enough to get around twice, we always hoped to draw at least one double. If both bags were cumbersome, Herbert permitted us to use a pull-cart for one.

I later regretted not taking up golf until after my caddy days, as we were permitted to play Monday mornings when the course was closed for maintenance. It was only upon returning to Capilano as a reporter that I finally played the marvellous course that I had often cursed in my youth. I also discovered that Jock McKinnon was a likeable, warm man. We developed a good working relationship despite his wariness of reporters and the fact that he would never forgive my predecessor at *The Sun*, Pat Slattery, for showing up unannounced with three friends one Saturday afternoon, expecting to play.

McKinnon didn't tolerate slow play and was not subtle in expressing his disdain for dawdling. One spring Sunday he summoned all eight City match play quarter-finalists to the first tee.

"Gentlemen," he announced brusquely, "I've been noticing in the papers it's taking almost five hours to complete matches in this tournament. Let me tell you here and now, there will be none of that nonsense today. You'll not be holding up my members. If any of your matches takes more than four hours, I'll run you off my course and you'll never be back."

All matches were concluded in less than four hours.

I adopted the golf beat in 1957 by default; no one else at the *Sun* wanted it. The primary duties of the dapper Slattery were editing the sports pages and a men's fashion column he fancied. Slats had no time to visit golf courses. Local golf got only minor league coverage and, luckily for me, no avid golfers were on staff.

While golf didn't warrant daily attention, it was a regular beat and the game's popularity was increasing. I knew football, rugby and hockey, which I had played in school, but golf was foreign to me. I thought a stymie was something you got in your eye.

Green as the first grass of spring, my early good fortune was working with exceptionally helpful people. Billy Thompson, the venerable secretary of the PGA BC, played a significant role in my upbringing as a golf reporter. McKinnon, Al Nelson, Alan Campbell, Les Paterson, Duncan MacKenzie, Ron Fitch, Ben Colk, Dick Munn and many others offered helping hands while I groped to find my way around the game.

My tournament debut was the 1957 New Westminster Amateur, a protracted 36-hole Sunday affair conducted by the Gyro Club at Vancouver Golf Club. The event was the season's longest day. One agonizing Sunday, the last foursomes finished with automobiles flood-lighting the 18th green.

The winner was volatile Doug Bajus, whose hunched, deliberate style didn't exactly mirror conformity or conventionality for a cub reporter's eyes. Another top amateur, Bob Kidd, seemed aloof and curt. I later came to realize both players weren't as unfriendly or intimidating as they appeared.

Hal Straight and Stu Keate were among Vancouver's early golf writers dating back to the 1930s. They were both Shaughnessy members and leaned toward news about the private clubs. After serving in the Second World War, Keate became publisher of both the *Victoria Times* and the *Vancouver Sun*. Keate's affection for golf was obvious in his writing and when he was the *Sun* publisher, I couldn't write enough golf. In suggesting story ideas, he was in effect ordering them written. Unlike most superiors, Keate cared for and mixed with his staff.

Tough and testy, Straight made a tremendous managing editor. Curiously, I don't recall that he ever assigned a golf story. As a golf writer, Straight went out of his way to be sardonically cute and stir the game's pacific waters. His column heading was appropriately: "The Straight Goods on Golf."

Those who followed Keate and Straight as regular Vancouver reporters included Bill Forst, an honest observer, the caustic Austin Delany, and Rayner Clark, who played better than he wrote. At the *Province* there was the ever unpredictable Hugh Watson and another friend was Sid Sheard who later became a chiropractor.

Ormie Hall, a freelancer after the war who would later become a lawyer, recalled Hal Straight. "Everyone was frightened to death of [him] even then," said Hall, who played well enough to make UBC's team. "I went to the *Province* after Straight fired me. He'd discovered I made $175 one month getting two-bits an inch and wondered why one of his salaried staff members couldn't do the job."

Eric Whitehead crafted the most copious golf prose and enhanced the game's status on the *Province*'s sports pages by the space he devoted to it. Stan Leonard was his favourite subject.

The venerable Roland Wild was a worldly essayist of uncluttered prose at the *Province* who rarely criticized any individual and relished composing features. Wild, author of *Golf: The Loneliest Game*, was seldom seen without a tweed hat or pipe in hand. He was a slender figure who lost every hair on his head. He died in 1990 at age 86.

Ernie Fedoruk started writing golf for the *Victoria Times* the same year I started and was as reliable as his slice; you always knew where he was coming from and you knew where he was going. In 30 years as a regular on the golf beat, Fedoruk missed only two or three annual meetings of the Victoria and District Golf Committee, which he considered the most efficient organization of its kind anywhere. He was made an honorary life member.

MY MOST MEMORABLE GOLFERS

The most memorable golfers I encountered in 37 years' reporting about the game weren't, as you might suspect, Jack Nicklaus and Gene Sarazen. They were Arthur Thompson of Victoria and Dr. Fahrni of Shaughnessy Heights.

Thompson couldn't break 80 in his lifetime, yet still is regarded as the legend of Uplands in Victoria. Charles Arthur Thompson was 102 years old when he shot 102 at Uplands, the oldest person ever to match or better his age, according to *Golf Digest* magazine's records. He pulled his own clubs 18 holes through most of his 90s, four times a week. One day in August 1968, 10 months shy of turning 100, he carded 92 in the company of Johnny Macmillan.

Arthur Thompson was a remarkable gentleman. He stood tall and straight as a board, a tidy, elegant figure with sparkling blue eyes and a rosy-cheeked complexion. Golf happened to be one of the many things he loved in as full a life as any man ever enjoyed. "I never learned how to play the game," he modestly confessed the week before he reached 100. "But I can't get along without it. Golf is a necessary evil."

Thompson's engaging personality, wit and longevity endeared him to the club he joined in 1932 upon retirement from banking in Montreal. His enthusiasm was infectious. Those who knew him were never surprised by the scope and frequency of his activities, even after his milestone birthday. He fished off his Cadboro Bay waterfront home in a rowboat, baked his own bread, tended his garden and drove a sparkling 1946 Dodge coupe that was meticulous as its owner. The BC Motor Vehicle Branch acknowledged that, at 99, Thompson was the oldest person to hold a driver's licence in the province at that time. "Don't print that for goodness' sake or they'll remember me and take my licence away," he quipped.

The spring before his 100th birthday Thompson had awkwardly slipped off a rubber-matted tee while following through with his drive and he injured his back. "It was beautifully timed . . . the fall, not my swing," he reported. "I don't mind losing the honour but that was a new way to get me off the tee." After three days of treatments, he was at the course getting a lesson from pro John Wren. "It was a refresher course. I wasn't sure if I would still remember how to swing a club."

He liked fresh fish for dinner but said the best part of catching them was rowing the boat. He detested the noise and odour of outboards as much as golfing laggards, arguments and power carts. "I don't care to play with some of my fellow seniors. They play too slowly and usually they go only 12 holes. I'll have nothing to do with those motorized carts."

Thompson had a huge appetite for activity. One morning after rowing for three hours, he landed a nine-pound coho with trout tackle. While cleaning the fish, a neighbour invited him over for a bottle of ale. "Thank you but I have to hurry," he said. "I have a golf game this afternoon."

He quit smoking in 1927, leaving his only weaknesses ale, champagne, ice cream and golf. While impatient on the course, he was a deliberate diner and limited himself to one pint of ale. "My mother once told me to chew my food well 'to never allow my stomach do what my mouth should do.'"

He underwent hyrdotherapy treatments on his back before embarking by train for Toronto to celebrate his 100th birthday with his family of 22. "It'll be easier for me to go there than for all of them coming to Victoria. But this back of mine . . . it's making an old man of me."

The legend of Uplands took up golf in 1903 but never achieved his goal of breaking 80. But he broke his age of 105, passing away peacefully in March 1975.

CHAPTER 21

GOLFING ASSOCIATIONS, SUPPORTERS AND THE HALL OF FAME

The world of golf is bigger than its golf courses. Several organizations support the sport and recognize the accomplishments of the top players—albeit in a rather controversial manner at times.

BC GOLF HOUSE

In 1987 the British Columbia Golf House Society was formed as a non-profit entity intent on preserving and documenting the history of golf in the province and managing a permanent public display of golf memorabilia. Its formation coincided with the fact that a new clubhouse was being constructed and some redesign was being completed as a part of a newly granted operating lease for the University Golf Course. In 1986 the old clubhouse sat abandoned near the new 17th tee. No one person was responsible for the creation of BC Golf House, though Mike Riste, Dick White and Harry White are recognized as the founding members of the society. Certainly, without Mike Riste's dedication, foresight and energy, the University course's old clubhouse would be a hazy memory. The former Capilano caddy not only saved the premises from demolition crews, he also has been the prime mover, donor, labourer and developer of Canada's first provincial golf museum-library. Riste intervened mere days before bulldozers were scheduled to level the building that has stood near the corner of West 10th and Blanca since 1930, making it the oldest surviving clubhouse in British Columbia. The wreckers had been delayed only because the company wanted $10,000 to raze it and there was no money in the budget for that purpose.

Promising to renovate the University Endowment Lands landmark, Riste received government permission through then MLA, and later prime minister, Kim Campbell to sub-lease the building for one dollar a year. Years later Riste reflected back on the undertaking.

> That first step into the building on that cold November evening is forever etched in my mind. There was no power, no heat and the building interior reeked of this pungent odour . . . The mould covered walls and the many rooms strewn with junk seemed endless . . . We would send ten 30-yard containers to the landfill before we even commenced the actual renovation. A sudden cold fear gripped me. Mike, are you actually capable of renovating this building into a Golf Museum or have you undertaken an insurmountable task?

Through the generosity and volunteer labour of the golf community, the British India bungalow–style building was restored to its original appearance and crammed with a showcase of golf treasures—photographs, books, artifacts, trophies and ever-changing displays.

For over a decade BC Golf House has also been home to the BC Golf Hall of Fame. The library includes thousands of books and reference documents and a wide selection of videos. The now retired BC Golf House curator Dorothy Brown estimated that the contents, including historian Riste's donated private collections, are valued at more than $175,000. The building has been appraised at $300,000. On display is an extensive collection of clubs dating back to 1790, bags and antique golf balls.

Twenty years after the museum opened, Harry White recalled,

> Mike [Riste] had the vision and hands-on task of making every detail required to faithfully restore the venerable facility to its 1930 glory . . . So many people and

companies provided materials at cost or by donation that enabled the renovation to proceed and be ready for the driving of the feathery ball for the Golf House opening.

It's a priceless repository that has captured BC golf's rich heritage for the enjoyment and edification of all generations and it welcomes donations toward operational expenses as well as items to augment its vast collection. Golfers in the business community provided the means to preserve and refurbish the premises through contributions of cash, materials and labour. The museum's contents have been built around Riste's personal collection of about 800 books and 4,000 artifacts. He was easily the most tireless volunteer labourer in the project.

More than 30 corporations donated materials and early principal patrons included George Yen, the Peter Bentley family, George Williams and Norm Edgar. The museum was officially opened at a ceremony on May 6, 1989, when touring pro Dave Barr of Kelowna and Richmond struck a feather ball with a 1750 track iron. Since that day, despite enduring bouts of financial hardship, BC Golf House stands as the only independent golf museum and library in any province or state in North America. Executive director Barrie McWha champions The Tradition Golf Classic, a popular series of three one-day golf events played throughout the year on Vancouver Island, in the Okanagan and on May 28, 2012, the 25th annual tournament was played at Vancouver's Shaughnessy Golf & Country Club. It is only fitting that, like many not-for-profits, these tournaments are the major fundraising event for the golf museum and hall of fame.

THE NEW BRITISH COLUMBIA GOLF ASSOCIATION

At a landmark luncheon meeting on October 6, 2003, in downtown Vancouver, golf in British Columbia truly came of age. The men's and women's provincial associations amalgamated as an all-embracing organization to serve and govern 60,000 members representing more than 300 golf facilities in the province. BC Golf, as the merged entity subsequently became known, now includes 40,000 male members, 16,000 female members and more than 4,000 juniors. The separate groups had acted autonomously since 1928: the men as the BC Golf Association and the women as the BC branch of the Canadian Ladies Golf Union. With the two groups under a single roof, the merger instantly reduced operating costs and has been better positioned to deliver services to all members.

Under the banner of BC Golf, the mission statement of the association states: "The British Columbia Golf Association fosters and promotes the sport of golf, preserves the traditions and history of the sport of golf and provides a leadership role for the sport of golf in British Columbia."

"Scheduling our busy tournaments, for example, has been much smoother," says Kris Jonasson, long-time executive director of BC Golf. "The merger has allowed us to better coordinate operations at all levels." The staff includes a permanent provincial coach and director of player development, Debbie Pyne, and three other directors responsible for administration, rules and competitions, and school programs. An emphasis is being placed on introducing the game in schools as well as selecting teams for various international competitions leading to the 2016 Olympics. Every year the staff organizes a full championship schedule for women and men of all ages. They have divided the province into eight active zones with regional representatives serving on the association board and various committees.

Among its duties, BC Golf manages the province-wide Course Rating System to establish course handicap factors and a slope rating system value. These relative rankings are designed to make player handicaps transportable from one facility to another and to establish a means of recognizing and quantifying different skill levels so that individuals may compete on an equitable basis. BritishColumbiagolf.org manages a searchable database of the province's individual course and slope ratings.

BC GOLF HALL OF FAME

The Golf Hall of Fame of BC was founded in 2001 and at time of writing has inducted 30 members. Through a sophisticated points system created to recognize wins, second-place finishes and team appearances in a wide list of events throughout North America and abroad, it recognizes the accomplishments of those qualified by their record while they were BC residents.

Jim Rutherford and Dawn Coe-Jones were inducted into the BC Golf Hall of Fame in a ceremony held at Capilano Golf Course. BC GOLF HOUSE

Cec Ferguson is inducted into the Hall of Fame with a plaque presented by Karen Vanzella representing the Hall and BC Golf House Society. BC GOLF HOUSE

Bert Ticehurst bested Johnny Johnston in the May 1956 Vancouver City Match Play final. Almost 50 years later, they were both inducted into the BC Golf Hall of Fame in 2005.
VANCOUVER PUBLIC LIBRARY 44031

The selection process for induction has not been without some controversy over the years, partly because of the guidelines for making candidates eligible for selection.

The current regulations are remarkably restrictive and severely limit selectors' choices for inductees. At time of writing, nominees must be at least 50 years of age and, significantly, they must have been championship competitors. In other words, the Golf Hall of Fame is open only to top competitors who have become senior golfers. James Lepp, for example, will not be eligible until November 2033, when he reaches 50, while Dawn Coe-Jones finally came of age in 2011. She has been in the BC Sports Hall of Fame since 1995.

Four members of the BC Golf Hall of Fame, (L to R) Bill Mawhinney (2003), Margaret Todd (2001), Johnny Johnston (2005) and Ken Black (2001) share a moment and a scroll of honour. BC GOLF HOUSE 007.85.130

Quite simply, projections indicate a decline of notable candidates available for hand-picking in the coming decades. Perhaps now is the time to review the selection criteria or establish additional inductee categories to sustain both ongoing interest and momentum. Selectors should be encouraged to nominate non-competitors for membership into what is one of the few hall of fame organizations that limits inductees to competitors only. The golf people who administrate and operate the game, along with worthy builders who promote the game, have been left out in the cold since the first nominees were inducted in 2001.

There are those who are happy with, or at least accepting of, the point system established by Mike Riste and the board of directors, but others question the exclusion of invaluable volunteers from eligibility. Volunteers are the heart and soul of such organizations. And several non-competitors have probably amassed more "performance" points than a few players who've already been inducted.

Riste was responsible for saving the museum site at University Golf Course and restoring the original clubhouse. If non-players were eligible for selection, Riste himself would be a prime candidate for induction into the hall as a builder. There is an abundance of worthy choices who have contributed time and effort on behalf of BC golf. They are people who, under the present qualification system, will never qualify to be eligible for selection. The list seems endless: Ernie Brown, Chuck Gage, Les Milne, Lawrie Kerr, Gordon Bowers, Herb Fritz, Jock McKinnon, Russ White, Peter Bentley, Harry White, Alex Duthie, Don Griffiths, Jimmy Huish, Les Furber, Jack McLaughlin, Jim Gibson, Billy Thompson, George Williams. Golf in BC would not be where it is today without them.

Current Members of BC's Golf Hall of Fame

Dave Barr	inducted 2003	Gail Harvey Moore*	inducted 2005
Steve Berry	inducted 2009	Alison Murdoch	inducted 2009
Davey Black*	inducted 2001	Marilyn O'Connor	inducted 2001
Ken Black*	inducted 2001	Doug Roxburgh	inducted 2003
Gayle Hitchens Borthwick	inducted 2003	John Russell	inducted 2005
Dawn Coe-Jones	inducted 2011	Jim Rutledge	inducted 2011
Harvey Combe*	inducted 2007	Violet Sweeny*	inducted 2001
Bob Cox	inducted 2007	Bert Ticehurst*	inducted 2005
Cec Ferguson	inducted 2011	Margaret Todd	inducted 2001
Vera Hutchings Ford*	inducted 2005	Wayne Vollmer	inducted 2007
John Johnston	inducted 2005	Bill Wakeham	inducted 2007
Bob Kidd	inducted 2011	Dorothy Wilks*	inducted 2003
Stan Leonard	inducted 2001	Fred Wood*	inducted 2007
Jackie Little	inducted 2009	Richard Zokol	inducted 2009
Bill Mawhinney*	inducted 2003		
Walter Mawhinney	inducted 2011	*indicates deceased	

CHAPTER 22

THE FUTURE

Much has changed in the century since BC first welcomed golf, and much will continue to change. Politics, economics and the environment will all have an effect on the nature of golf in years to come.

AN UNCERTAIN FUTURE

Hazards abound on the BC golf front. Not only the economy but also changing US border policies and rising gas prices have discouraged the flow of American tourists from exploring BC in recent years. The growth of supply in the form of many new resort courses has outstripped demand, as many Albertans who saw BC as their recreational playground have now turned their attention to the US sunbelt with its excess of cheap real estate. As a result, many courses in BC have been decimated at the cash tills during the past two summers. Hardest hit were courses in the Okanagan and the Kootenays, where revenue had dropped as much as 50 to 60 percent by the fall of 2011.

Several facilities closed down indefinitely for the winter, some posting "for sale" signs. Among those in financial trouble were Tower Ranch in Kelowna, the Thomas McBroom design that opened in 2008 and fell into receivership in September 2011. In Vernon, The Rise, complete with its own winery and a Fred Couples golf course, also got caught in the 2008 downturn. Tobiano in Kamloops, another McBroom course, went into receivership in June 2011 with little expectation of a quick recovery; a local "Save Tobiano" group abandoned its efforts early in 2012.

In Chilliwack, The Falls sought bankruptcy protection in the spring of 2011, closed that fall and currently awaits the business plan of a new purchaser.

The severe economic downturn has also been nightmarish on Vancouver Island. The Nicklaus course proposal for Ucluelet on the remote west coast, Wyndandsea, turned out to be a wait-and-see plan and never advanced beyond a temporary demonstration hole over water. Greg Norman's Cliffs Over Maple Bay in Cowichan didn't overcome water problems and the property is now under new ownership with some possibility that the local First Nation band will get involved. The long-awaited Union Bay Links, south of Courtenay, has cleared several holes for development some day. Silver Spray was the project that didn't happen in East Sooke. And a Robert Trent Jones Jr.–designed course and ambitious resort called Centre Mountain is still on the drawing board.

"The combination of poor early summer weather, the HST and the dollar exchange, which was on par with the American dollar, was tough on tourism," said Doug Fern, BC director of the Canadian Golf Course Owners' Association. "It was particularly noticeable in proximity to the American border." Fern added that related businesses such as "restaurants, hotels and gas stations were equally affected."

In many ways Victoria remains BC's golf capital and even in contemporary times remains the focal point of contrast in BC golf. Scott Kolb, general manager at the Victoria Golf Club, noted at the beginning of the 2012 golf season a definite "oversupply of courses" on southern Vancouver Island. With the shortest waiting list in years, Victoria remained healthy while Royal Colwood was actively advertising attractive incentives for new members.

Meanwhile, local governments in surrounding communities like Metchosin and Saanich are wondering if they should be maintaining money-losing public facilities while some of their tax-paying private enterprises suffer from over-supply.

Despite the economic challenges, Victoria's most intriguing contrast lies in two separate projects that have opened 36 holes of new golf since the downturn. The picturesque Highland Pacific course that sits above

View Royal opened its first nine in 2008 and a second nine two years later, all quietly developed by the pioneer family that owns it. On nearby slopes to the west sits the high-profile, densely built Bear Mountain project, whose story reads like a Shakespeare play—sometimes comedy, sometimes tragedy. At the centre of that story is one name: Len Barrie. A former junior hockey player in both his hometown of Kelowna and Victoria, Barrie was a high school dropout who played about 180 games with four different teams in the NHL and then acted as agent for a number of players after retiring in 2001. Never one to shy away from a faceoff, Barrie's family home abutted the hallowed grounds of Royal Colwood Golf Club, and that very fact would loom large in a story that pretty well starts and ends with lawsuits.

In 2005 Len Barrie took it upon himself to chop down a cluster of trees behind his house, his reasons personal but generally thought to be self-serving at the time. However, more than a dozen of the evergreens were not on his property but on that of the golf course. Royal Colwood sued for damages and banned him from the club for life. Even though he had never built anything beyond his own house, Barrie then set out to build his own course as part of the biggest single mixed-use real estate project in the history of Victoria. His timing was quite perfect and soon Bear Mountain exploded with construction and high-profile media coverage, stoked by the fact that Barrie had rounded up a bunch of his hockey pals and clients to invest in his audacious project. Barrie put up the initial $300,000 non-refundable deposit, then recruited 15 NHLers to put together the full $8 million purchase price.

Barrie fought bureaucracy, First Nations land claims, environmental-ists, financing challenges and eventually his own partners, but as a guy who had spent more than four hours in the penalty box one season he never backed down from a fight. A threat to clear-cut if he didn't get his building permits put the local council at bay. Ignoring Aboriginal claims to a sacred cave on the land, Barrie blew it up and deterred a cluster of cultural protesters from occupying his land.

By 2008, with work on a second golf course well advanced and more than $500 million in real estate sales completed, Barrie was a confident man. "Two years from now, we'll be out of the bank and still have 70 percent of the project left," he bragged. And then he bought a hockey team.

Barrie's demise started the day he committed to becoming part owner of the Tampa Bay Lightning NHL hockey team. His partnership with Hollywood fright-film mogul Oren Koules was rocky from the beginning and after a year-long spat Barrie found his pockets weren't deep enough. He was effectively forced out by the NHL in September 2009. The following March, Barrie was telling the media that his partnership group would not oppose HSBC Bank Canada's placing the development under credit protection.

Barrie put up a brave front over the next 18 months, maintaining residence in the 12,500-square-foot mansion that he had built on Skirt Mountain beside the golf course, looking down on Victoria. Finally, in January 2012, court orders dictated that Barrie hand over the keys to his 10-bathroom castle and move out. Resigned to his fate, Barrie told the *Times Colonist*, "It's been three years of hell and now it's time to move forward." There were still a few hurdles left to clear. The Bellagio Casino in Las Vegas was also in the courts, claiming that Barrie owed over $2.8 million based on a three-day gambling fling back in 2008. In addition, some of his original hockey partners were demanding his head and insisting that criminal fraud charges be added to the list of legal suits Barrie still faced.

The story of Highland Pacific is, quite simply, a very different one. There the family of respected architect and sculptor Herb Plasterer, who bought the property 50 years ago, set out to honour his dream that would ensure the public access to his treasured homestead by building a golf course. Creatively carved into 190 acres and a relatively short 6,600 yards from the back tees, the course quickly won a following because of its appeal to all skill levels and its attractive greens fees. In fact, other local courses had to lower their rates to compete. That in itself won them many points from the golfing consumer.

Herb Plasterer died in 1985 before his dream could be realized but a decade later his widow, Rose Maria, and their six children decided to act. The Highland Pacific HP logo pays tribute to Herb, and the family is very proud of what they have created. With the aid of architect Chris Young and a host of golf pros and other supporters, the first Pacific Nine opened in 2008.

Completing an irrigation system through difficult terrain was one of the biggest challenges during eight years of construction, and a base of six inches of sand was trucked in from Duncan to build up the fairways.

Rose Maria was not only proud of the course but of her family as the Highland Nine was about to open. "[Herb's] dream to turn the land into an affordable golf course has come true," she stated. "Working together as a team was not always easy for the family, but we became more united over the many years it took to produce this unique golf course—and we're all delighted we can now present it to the community."

Eldest child Angela also takes pride in their accomplishment—a course truly sculpted out of a unique setting. At the course opening she quoted her father: "Sculpture is never more radiant than when inspired by love."

GOLF AND THE ENVIRONMENT

One doesn't need to go too far back in time to find that the science of turf management was elementary, to say the least. Water and feed the grass, and then cut it. Water was delivered by dragging hoses to areas that required water and most golf courses had someone employed working nights to get the watering done in time for play the next day. Chemical use was basic and not always the safest. However, the principle behind it hasn't varied much. It was used only as required because of the expense. Sometimes, though, there was no alternative.

Over the past 50 years the role of the golf course superintendent has changed more than any other in golf. The educational and technical demands have grown exponentially; the equipment has become more complex and sophisticated, the irrigation equipment much more precise; and the manpower has increased to meet the demands of the modern golfer. Budgets have grown to be over a million dollars a year at some of the high-end courses. College degrees are now the norm and specialization is the order of the day.

The public has become much more environmentally aware as time has gone by. Not all the information out there is accurate, but there is no question that everyone connected with the game is more sensitive to the pressures on the ecology by what is done on and around the golf course.

The ability to test and measure has affected all parts of the game from playing equipment to turf management. New chemicals, and new methods of storing, handling and applying them, have caused turf managers to re-evaluate what they do.

It is now normal to see signs posted at the first tee advising golfers if something is being applied, what it is for and any issues that may be pertinent to its use. Golf course superintendents are now more conscious than ever about the need to educate golfers about what is being used on the course, why it is being used and how it is handled.

As part of this new and growing awareness, the Audubon Society began a program of accrediting golf courses that embrace the need to be responsible stewards of the environment. Audubon Sanctuary became the highest level of accreditation that a golf course could achieve and thus it became a marketing badge of honour. The program was a six-part process that took considerable time and dedication of manpower and resources, and also engaged the surrounding community. It involved environmental planning, performing an inventory of animal and bird species on the course, chemical use reduction, water conservation management and water quality control, as well as community outreach and education, usually involving schoolchildren.

This program identified the golf facilities that were serious about their commitment to the environment. The challenge for many courses, though, became one of having the resources, both financial and human, to participate. Often the program simply lost out to the economic reality for many golf courses.

More recently, the Golf Environment Organization (GEO), which started in Scotland, has become the poster child for overall responsible management and efficiency. Simply put, GEO operates on the premise that you can't manage what you don't measure. Therefore, everything falls under scrutiny: from electricity consumption to fertilizer and water usage, from recycling programs to purchasing programs that look for local, or as local as possible, suppliers for everything purchased. The aim of the course is to be as environmentally responsible as possible in all departments of the golf course. Minimizing the carbon footprint is a large part of the GEO program. For example, considering the location of suppliers—for everything from clothing sold in the pro shop to food supplies for the restaurant to equipment and supplies for the golf course maintenance department—factors into reducing transportation costs, which equates to less fuel being consumed when transporting products.

While GEO is certainly a marketing tool like the Audubon program, it is really more about a new and better and more efficient way to manage every aspect of the golf business.

Barrie McWha, Executive Director, BC Golf House

THE FINAL ROUND

It was the second Sunday in June; this book was in its final stages of proofing when the ending had to be rewritten. The Canadian Tour opener, the Times Colonist Island Savings Open, was wrapping up and Uplands Golf Club in Victoria was swarming with the largest gallery in years, gradually drawn to the final twosome. Victoria's Cory Renfrew, a Canadian Tour rookie, started the day with a three-stroke lead and would play well under pressure. But at high noon on a perfect, sun-filled day for golf, the next few hours seemed full of unpredictability.

Naturally, most of the cheering would be reserved for the three Canadians still in the hunt for the top prize. But this was Victorian sportsmanship at its best, hospitable to all, applauding birdies and eagles galore, regardless of who made them.

The first player to draw some of the large first-tee gallery out onto the course was Nick Taylor, the highly acclaimed Lower Mainland player still trying to live up to all of the hype that has followed him since he was first declared the best junior player in the world. Taylor played steady enough to have a top-10 finish, but never mounted a charge.

The final six included first-round leader Californian Andrew Roque, who would have been right at the top with Renfrew had he not gone four-over on the back nine on Saturday. After the round, he told the media, "On the back nine, I misjudged the wind with some of my shots and that got me into trouble. Without this wind, I feel that I could shoot 60 on this course."

Roque started slowly but managed a front-nine 33 to stay close. He and his playing partner, Aussie Matt Jager, had little or no gallery. But when they teed off, they made for the comeback story of the week.

Oshawa, Ontario's Derek Gillespie tied for second. Gillespie had gained an international audience back in 2009 when he made a few spectacular shots to win the popular annual Big Break event, sponsored by The Golf Channel. On April 25, 2011 fate turned against him. At first, his golf days seemed numbered, the result of a violent Arizona car accident that had hurled his sleeping body from the back seat and imbedded him in a cactus field. He had a punctured lung, five broken ribs, a broken leg and a body full of cacti needles. Glad to have a second chance at the game he loved, on this Sunday in Victoria he would eagle the seventh hole and gradually pull within one of the lead.

All day, Cory Renfrew had a gallery unlike anything he had ever seen before. He had qualified for the Canadian Tour at a spring event where he had finished third to fellow newcomer Andrew Roque. Renfrew held it together, well maintaining a dwindling lead through the front nine.

Gillespie got close, but the first to tie Renfrew was the long-hitting Brazilian, Lucas Lee, who was playing just ahead with Gillespie. Across the course, leaderboards were constantly changing—with one name inconspicuously moving closer to the front.

In the end, few had seen it. Andrew Roque was actually a stroke behind his playing partner on the seventh tee when he relied on topspin to get his partially sculled drive out onto the fairway. Then, on the 12th hole, something started that has rarely been seen anywhere in golf. Roque commenced a birdie binge that lasted the rest of the day, seven birdies in a row—the final a 14-foot attempt that hung on the lip before falling to the roar of the crowd. From 500 yards away, Cory Renfrew could do little but listen. Roque's final nine, 28, will be remembered for years at Uplands. And for Cory Renfrew, the final rousing cheer as he putted out on the last hole will no doubt spur him on to greater things.

It was a great day for golf in British Columbia.

INDEX

ACKNOWLEDGEMENTS

The release of *Backspin: 120 Years of Golf in British Columbia* has been almost 25 years in the making. I am indebted to many people for their assistance and encouragement in my writing of both the original manuscript and this book.

While I'm hesitant to list names for fear of omitting someone, this book would still be nothing more than a vision without the steadfast support of my wife and best friend, Alice. My original work benefited from the generous support of George Williams, Dick Munn, George Yen, Sid Sheard, Caleb Chan, Herb Fritz and Barry Sharpe. Dorothy Brown and Mike Riste at the BC Golf House museum and the patient staff of the Pacific Press "morgue" were a big help with the first book as were club officials, archivists and museum directors throughout the province.

Mike and Barrie McWha, now the executive director at BC Golf House, were a big help in securing this book's photo content.

I want to express a special thanks to BC Golf's Kris Jonasson as well as old colleagues Bill Cunningham, Ernie Fedoruk, Darren Kloster, Alan Dawe, Peter Watson, Sam Martz and Jack Grundle.

I've had the good fortune to have worked under and alongside newspaper people who've shared my affinity for golf. Thank you, Stuart Keate, Jim Kearney, Don Harrison, Dunc Stewart, Kent Gilchrist, Roland Wild, Hugh Watson, Brad Ziemer and Don Brown.

During my time at the *Vancouver Sun* I've also had the opportunity to interview many of the game's greatest players: Arnold Palmer, Sam Snead, Jack Nicklaus, Gene Sarazen, Lee Trevino, George Knudson, Tom Watson and Roberto de Vicenzo. I'm sorry to say that I came on the scene only after Ken Black and Walt McElroy had retired, after Bill Mawhinney's best days had passed, and after Alex Duthie and Davey Black had departed. I'm grateful that I met Jock McKinnon, Fred Wood, Dick Munn, Bert Ticehurst, Arthur Thompson, Les Milne, Al Nelson, Angus MacKenzie and Dunc Sutherland, and that I saw Stan Leonard in the winter of his great career; Dave Barr and Marilyn Palmer in the beginning of theirs; Rick Gibson, Jim Rutledge, Dick Zokol, Brent Franklin, Dawn Coe-Jones and Lisa Walters striving to reach the top of theirs; and all of Doug Roxburgh's triumphs. I would also like to thank Ward Stouffer for his kind words.

There are too many young men and women professionals still in the midst of their career to pay full tribute here but like golfers of all descriptions and abilities along the way, they have contributed in one way or another to the final content of this book. They have been my inspiration.

At Heritage House, publisher Rodger Touchie became a true champion of this book and aided with some of the recent research while editors Lesley Cameron, Kate Scallion and Vivian Sinclair have all helped make it a book to be proud of.

Thank you, all.
Arv Olson
May 2012

ARV OLSON has been writing about golf and other sports since 1957 and worked for more than 30 years at the *Vancouver Sun*. In his travels, Arv has played on more than 75 golf courses around BC, although he makes no claims about having played any one of them particularly well. A 10-handicap for one fleeting summer, Arv has a trophy to prove that he once won the Vancouver Media Championships. He lives in Fanny Bay, BC.